Thomas Brassey

Foreign Work and English Wages

Considered with Reference to the Depression of Trade

Thomas Brassey

Foreign Work and English Wages
Considered with Reference to the Depression of Trade

ISBN/EAN: 9783744725972

Printed in Europe, USA, Canada, Australia, Japan

Cover: Foto ©ninafisch / pixelio.de

More available books at **www.hansebooks.com**

FOREIGN WORK

AND

ENGLISH WAGES

CONSIDERED WITH REFERENCE TO

THE DEPRESSION OF TRADE

BY

THOMAS BRASSEY, M.P.

LONDON
LONGMANS, GREEN, AND CO.
1879

INTRODUCTION.

THE following papers are the outcome of an engagement, made last winter, to deliver lectures at Edinburgh and Hull on the condition and prospects of trade. The most laborious investigator cannot fully exhaust a subject so difficult and important. Pursuing the inquiry amid many interruptions, but I hope in a spirit of unswerving fairness, I have been led step by step from the main question to various collateral topics, and from one source of information to another. The studies in which I have thus been engaged have been a formidable addition to other more urgent and indeed unavoidable duties. I am obliged to desist from the further prosecution of my task, and I present the result of my inquiry to the considerate examination of the commercial world, with all the imperfections of which I am so deeply conscious.

Not now for the first time I have had under consideration the expediency of retiring from Parliament, with the view of devoting an undivided attention to the elucidation of industrial problems, and the improvement of the relations between capital and labour. The reward of labour, and the profit upon investments, are questions which cannot be settled by legislation. As a member of Parliament, I have felt it my duty to devote myself to the maritime interests of the country; and I find it impossible to follow up simultaneously the twofold and widely divergent specialities of political economy and naval administration. My experience is doubtless shared by the majority of members of the House of Commons. Many subjects are brought under our review, and we are all more or less overtaken and outstripped by the rapid march of events.

While the multitude of idlers is probably greater than in any former generation, those who have any work to do live at a too high pressure in this age of inventions for abridging processes, shortening distances, and economising time. If our literature is condensed into articles in periodicals, the number of topics to which our attention is invited is proportionately multiplied. The overtasked toiler in the nineteenth century may look back with envy to the repose and the contemplative existence of the patriarchal time.

> Man's life was spacious in the early world:
> It paused like some slow ship with sail unfurled,
> Waiting in seas by scarce a wavelet curled:
> Beheld the slow star-paces of the skies,
> And grew from strength to strength through centuries.[1]

As in the domain of politics, and as with investigations in the sphere of the physical sciences, so it is with politico-economic questions; we are encumbered by the rapid accumulation of facts. It becomes more

---

[1] George Eliot, 'The Legend of Jubal.'

and more difficult to evolve and establish general principles, in proportion as we extend our knowledge of details. Mr. Buckle has truly remarked that 'the magnificent generalisations of Newton and Harvey could never have been completed in an age absorbed in one unvarying round of experiments and observations. We are in that predicament that our facts have outstripped our knowledge, and are now encumbering its march. In vain do we demand that they should be generalised and reduced into order. We hear constantly of what nature is doing, but we rarely hear of what man is thinking.'

Readers of the following papers will not fail to discover for themselves my heavy obligations to the press. My task has been mainly one of selection and compilation. I make no pretension to original discovery, and consider it the chief merit of this volume that it is a record and a registry, not a work of fancy, imagination, and theory.

I was originally moved to address the public on the industrial question by the exaggerated charges against the British workman, which were being made when I entered Parliament in 1868. Then, as now, the industrial energies of the country seemed to be enervated and exhausted, and a general disposition was manifested to impute the blame of our financial misfortunes to the working people. My father, after an unequalled personal experience, had discovered that the cost of work, as distinguished from the daily wage of the labourer, was approximately the same in all countries. With his assistance, I was enabled to show that too much significance had been attached to the purchase of a few engines from Creusot for the Great Eastern Railway, and the importation of a few tons of rails from Belgium. I am deeply sensible of the diminished value of the present investigation. Without my father's experience, but, I hope, with an equal desire to be just, I have once more endeavoured to ascertain whether any substantial grounds exist for the allegations so freely made that our trade is suffering from the extravagant cost of labour. After a laborious, careful, and impartial inquiry, I arrive at the conclusion, that our industry has not yet been beaten on a large scale by foreign competition, in any case in which that competition has been carried on under identical conditions both as to natural resources and fiscal legislation. The high prices which have prevailed until recently have not been exclusively or mainly due to the cost of labour. The rise of prices began with a general inflation of trade and the realisation of larger profits. The cycle of events tends to repeat itself in the ebb and flow of commerce. When trade prospers production becomes more active, and a rise of wages ensues. In process of time the augmented supply overtakes the demand for goods. A fall in prices is the inevitable result; and the downward movement is continued until at length the operations of the manufacturer cease to be profitable. A contraction of business and production takes place; the relation between demand and supply is gradually changed in favour of the producer, and a recovery in prices follows.

I retain an implicit faith in the British workman. If he will but do himself justice, he is as capable as he ever was of holding his own against the world. While, however, I am not discouraged by the dread of competition with the ill-paid labour of the Continent, I have no panacea to offer for our misfortunes. Fewer opportunities will be found of realising large profits. Competition will be more severe. The telegraph and the improved facilities of communication have tended to equalise prices. A clear and regular profit of seven or eight per cent. must be accepted as a satisfactory return from commercial enterprise. In these unprosperous times the demand for commodities does not increase in the same ratio as our means of production, and the commercial world is brought face to face with a problem of great difficulty in opening out new markets.

A new demand for our goods must be created, and can only be created by cheapness and excellence of quality. The reputation of the country must be sustained by the diligence, the administrative skill, and the high sense of honour and integrity, with which our commerce is conducted.

CONTENTS.

FOREIGN WORK AND ENGLISH WAGES.

CHAPTER I.

DEPRESSION OF TRADE.

I PROPOSE to examine the present commercial situation of the country as a mediator between employers and employed, and not as a merchant or a practical manufacturer. I owe my position to the harmonious combination of capital and labour, and I desire to see cordial relations maintained between those interdependent yet often conflicting interests. While enjoying the unmerited advantage of comparative immunity from the hazards and fluctuations of trade, I am not an indifferent spectator of the ebb and flow of the tide of commerce. I appreciate the difficulties of our manufacturers in their anxious conflict with the cheap labour, accumulating capital, and protective tariffs of foreign countries; and I sympathise with the legitimate aspirations of our labouring population.

I am fully sensible of the imperfections of the papers which I here present to the public. As we proceed in our investigations in any field of knowledge the horizon enlarges and recedes; we are less

B

and less satisfied as to the completeness of our inquiry, in proportion as we become acquainted with the existence of other sources of information. Whenever I approach the labour question, I regret my inability to devote my whole time to a subject which demands the undivided attention of the most competent and instructive economist. As Miss Byron sententiously remarked to Sir Charles Grandison, the ploughman makes fewer mistakes in the conduct of life than the scholar, because the sphere in which he moves is a more contracted one.

Imparti-
ality.

It is idle to look for strict impartiality from those directly engaged in industry, whether as workmen or as employers. It has been appropriately observed by the late Professor Cairnes that human interests, well understood, are fundamentally one ; but we must not confound the statement that human interests are one, with the statement that class interests are one. Passion, prejudice, custom, *esprit de corps*, combine to draw people aside from knowing their interests, in the sense in which they coincide with the interests of others. A selfish misconception, as to what would really best promote their own interests, induced landlords to oppose the repeal of the Corn Laws, and encouraged manufacturers to raise objections to the merciful provisions of the Short Time Acts. In the same spirit, Trade Unions have laid down rules, restricting the individual energies of their members.

Prevailing
discontent.

The competition between labour and capital, between nation and nation, is intensified at a time like the present, when the commerce of the world is going through a process of contraction, after a cycle of years of over-production. Loss of employment, reductions of wages on the Continent, the pressure of compulsory military service, have provoked an uneasy feeling amongst the working classes, which in one country takes the form of Communism, in another of Socialism, in Russia of Nihilism. In our own country, envy is excited by the unequal distribution of wealth, and by the self-indulgence and luxury of the spoiled favourites of fortune. Here, too, there is ample scope for the invention of schemes for remodelling society. It is by ' detective discussion ' that fallacies will be exposed and the truth established.

The general depression of trade is the first subject with which I propose to deal. The Board of Trade tables have shown to all who take an interest in this subject the fluctuations which have taken place in our exports and imports. The falling away is not observable in every trade, and the depression has of late been far more marked in our home consumption than in our foreign trade.

Fluctuations in export trade.

The following figures exhibit the total declared value of British and Irish produce exported from the United Kingdom.

1870 . . £199,586,822	1874 . . £230,558,121
1871 . . 223,066,162	1875 . . 223,465,963
1872 . . 256,257,347	1876 . . 200,639,204
1873 . . 255,164,603	1877 . . 198,893,065

The imports for 1878 amounted to 363,710,000*l.*, a decrease of 28,860,000*l.* on the total value of 1877. The exports fell, from 198,790,000*l.* in 1877, to 192,814,111*l.* in 1878, a decrease of 5,986,000*l.*

·The change in the course of business exhibits a
decline of values, rather than of quantity. This
opinion was confirmed by Lord Beaconsfield in his
recent speech in the House of Lords, when he stated
that no diminution had taken place in the volume of
production. There had been less profit, but the same
quantity of goods had been manufactured, and there
were no markets from which we had been excluded by
foreign competition. Referring to the figures given
above, the Prime Minister stated that the exports had
fallen from 255,000,000*l.* in 1873 to 198,000,000*l.* in
1877 ; but, if the products of 1877 had been valued at
the same rate as the products of 1873, the difference
between the total amounts would have been reduced to
less than a million.

Comparing the exports of 1878 with those of
1872—a year, be it observed, of inflation and reckless
speculation—the 'Economist' attributes one-fourth of
the loss to a decline in demand, and three-fourths to
reductions in price.

In Cleveland, the largest iron producing centre in
the United Kingdom, we find that the total production
for the year 1878 was about 2,023,000 tons, or scarcely
102,000 tons less than in 1877. Taking into view the
adverse conditions with which the ironmasters have
been contending, such a result exhibits a marvellous
proof of the energy and industrial capacity of the ironmasters and the workmen of Cleveland in competition
with the whole world. The improvements in the
quality are not less remarkable than the sustained
quantity of the product.

The most important items in our export trade are the cotton, woollen, iron, and steel manufactures. The 'Economist' supplies the following table of the principal exports of these articles in 1878. *Exports of British produce in 1878.*

Table of Principal Articles exported from the United Kingdom in 1878. *Quantity and Value, and Excess or Deficiency of same compared with* 1877.

(In Millions to two Decimals.)

Articles	Quantity	Value	More or less than 1877		Value of Increase or Decrease, due	
			Quantity	Value	to Quantity	to Price
(a)	(b)	(c) £	(d)	(e) £	(f) £	(g) £
I.—BRITISH PRODUCE.						
1. Textile manufactures :						
Cotton yarn and thread..lbs	262·72	14·92	23·89	·90	1·38	— ·48
Piece goods........ yards	3,618·18	48·09	—218·34	— 4·30	— 2·98	— 1·82
Jute yarn.............. lbs	12·24	·18	— 2·62	— ·01	— ·04	...
Piece goods........ yards	122·97	1·59	6·42	·04	·08	— ·04
Bags...................... doz.	5·21	1·56	·28	·05	·08	— ·03
Linen yarn .... lbs	18·48	1·21	— ·76	— ·08	— ·05	— ·03
Piece goods........ yards	157·28	4·72	— 16·24	— ·35	·47	·12
Silk piece goods......... —	8·89	·62	·56	·10	·10	...
Woollen yarn .... lbs	31·18	3·91	4·20	·30	·56	— ·26
Piece goods .... yards	251·87	14·77	— 8·74	— ·69	— ·29	— ·40
Carpets .... —	6·68	·84	·17	— ·01	·02	·01
Wool—sheep..............lbs	6·44	·55	— 8·14	— 0·16	— ·28	·07
Hats......................doz.	·90	1·08	·01	— ·03	·01	— ·04
Leather .... cwts	·16	1·18	·02	·01	·17	— ·16
Boots and shoes...... doz.	·43	1·31	— ·01	·03	— ·03	...
Paper, books, and materials for making paper ...cwts	·99	2·12	— ·05	— ·08	— ·06	— ·14
Total textile, &c.........	...	98·65	...	— 4·37	— 1·67	— 2·70
2. Metals and minerals :						
Coals ,...................... tons	15·48	7·32	·12	— ·51	·06	— ·57
Copper.................cwts	·90	3·11	·10	·05	·38	— ·38
Iron ....tons	2·29	18·40	— ·05	— 1·69	— ·57	— 1·12
Lead .... cwts	·69	·65	— ·16	— ·26	·17	— ·09
Tin .... cwts	·12	·41	...	— ·04	...	— ·04
Total mineral............	...	29·89	...	— 2·45	— ·30	— 2·15

In a recent report to the Board of Trade, Mr. Giffen has given a summary of the changes of price in the cotton and iron trades between 1861 and 1877. The price of cotton yarn was 12·54*d.* per lb. in 1861, 28·80*d.* in 1864, 20·04*d.* in 1869, and 12·85*d.* in 1877. *Prices of iron and cotton goods in 1861-77.*

The price of piece goods was 3·02*d*. per yard in 1861, 5·79*d*. in 1864, 3·79*d*. in 1869, and 2·83*d*. in 1877. The price of cotton goods, on the average of the whole trade, has been at one time 100 per cent. higher than in 1861 or 1877, two years of very great depression at the commencement and the close of the period included in Mr. Giffen's analysis. Cotton goods form a third of our exports. Hence a variation of 100 per cent. in values would, other things been equal, amount to a variation of over 30 per cent. in the total trade.

Articles of iron constitute about 10 per cent. of our exportations, and Mr. Giffen records equally remarkable oscillations of price in this important branch of trade. Pig-iron has ranged from 51·77*s*. per ton in 1861 to 124·65*s*. in 1873, while bar, angle, bolt, and rod iron has ranged between 7·29*l*. and 13·09*l*. per ton. Here again we have a variation of 100 per cent., or 10 per cent. in our whole trade.

The average prices of our exports of all classes were lower in 1877 than at any period since 1861, and below the level of 1861 in the proportion of 71·06 to 73·1. In 1878, a further fall of price has taken place.

Commercial features of the past year.

The 'Statist,' in reviewing the general movement of British trade for the year 1878, remarks that 'the distress was confined to a few of the great industries, while elsewhere there was "stationariness," rather than depression. The sweeping away of bankrupt houses, the winding-up of fictitious credit, and an adjustment of the cost of production to present prices, constitute the salient features in the trade of the past year.' We have no evidence of loss of capital. The loss, on the other hand, was serious in the inflation period, when loans were recklessly made to bankrupt states, and money was invested in joint-stock companies as unsoundly constituted as they were unskilfully managed.

The comparatively small increase in pauperism is a proof that, while their earnings may have been contracted, the masses of the population can still secure a livelihood. The continued growth of capital is established by the activity with which building operations have been prosecuted in the large towns, and by the extensive reclamations of land in the rural districts.

The 'Economist' considers that British trade compares favourably with that of our foreign competitors. The last four years have seen scarcely any accumulation of income from profits, either in Europe or in America. In North America, and in a less degree in Central Europe, the previous reserves had been largely diminished. In this country, it is probable that no single year since 1873 has closed with positive loss; but the surpluses have been small and very irregularly distributed. *British compared with foreign trade.*

The Board of Trade Returns for the present year exhibit a falling off in the value of the exports, and a small expansion only as regards quantities. We see, in the returns for March, that the shipments of cotton piece-goods were $4\frac{1}{2}$ per cent. larger than in the corresponding month last year. In previous years we have observed with regret an increased exportation of cotton yarns, and a simultaneous diminution in the exportation of piece-goods. The most recent returns show a decided falling-off in the expor- *Trade of 1879.*

tation of yarns, owing to the contraction of the trade
with India, Japan, and Germany. In iron and steel
the expansion has been general, there being some
increase of exportation even to the United States; but
the fact that the metal exported in the month of
March exhibited an increase in quantity of 25 per
cent., while the increase in value did not exceed
$4\frac{1}{2}$ per cent., affords evidence of a very considerable
reduction in the prices we are enabled to realise.

It is difficult to ascertain with accuracy how far
the fall in price has been compensated by the reduced
cost of raw material and wages. This subject will be
examined in detail in the succeeding chapter.

In this rapid survey of the commercial situation,
we have noticed some encouraging features. The fact,
however, remains that with an increasing population,
the growth of trade has been arrested. Employment
is scarce and business unprofitable. The effects of the
depression extend far beyond the classes directly engaged in productive industry. It is therefore a problem of national importance to discover, and if possible
remove, the causes which have led to the present
melancholy posture of affairs.

International participation in misfortune.

In that interchange of commodities, of which commerce consists, the misfortunes of every country are
shared, more or less, by the other members of the
family of nations. There is an international participation in the happy fortunes of a thriving people; and,
on the other hand, we cannot be indifferent spectators
of the devastation of a neighbouring territory by war.
When a vast population is decimated by famine, or the

resources of other countries shattered by commercial
disaster, we know that the effect of those reverses will
be felt more or less by ourselves; and in seeking for
the causes of the crisis from which we are at present
suffering, our inquiry must be extended beyond our
own borders.

The fall in the value of silver is the first subject
which demands attention. The following particulars
are extracted from an article by Mr. Patterson, contributed to the 'Contemporary Review' in April last.
From 1855 to 1875 the aggregate exports of merchandise from India amounted to 933,813,000*l.* The
value of the imports was 544,207,000*l.* The trade
balance in favour of India amounted to 388,500,000*l.*
sterling; and in the earlier years of the period under
review this enormous deficit in our exports, as compared with our imports, was covered by remittances
of silver. During the latter years, however, of this
period, the financial balance turned heavily against
India ; the bills drawn by the Home Government upon
the Indian Government amounting in the aggregate to
112,000,000*l.* A smaller quantity of silver was required for payments in the East, and the value was
proportionately affected. For upwards of twenty years,
subsequent to 1850, the price of silver stood considerably above its old value—rising from $59\frac{3}{4}d.$ per ounce
to 62*d.*—and then declining to its old value, or a fraction below it, viz., $59\frac{1}{4}d.$ in 1873.

The depreciation of silver is due to another cause,
to the determination of France and Germany, the one
with sixty millions and the other with eighty millions

*The depre-
ciation of
silver.*

*Trade with
India and
China.*

of silver, to establish a gold currency. The trade with India and China has materially suffered from the depreciation of silver, and still more from a pernicious system of long credits, and the reckless competition for business on the part of discounting financial and banking institutions. The recent revelations in connection with the Glasgow Bank have brought to light abuses which have long prevailed, and have been widely extended. An almost incredible amount of over-trading must have been carried on, if, as the representative of a single firm admitted, his losses had exceeded 2,000,000*l.* within the space of some ten years.

State of trade in United States.

Previous to the outbreak of the Civil War, the people of the United States were by far the most extensive consumers of our manufactured products. The vast expenditure caused by the war led to an increase of taxation, and to the imposition of prohibitory tariffs on foreign importations. The sudden exclusion of foreign goods naturally caused an advance in prices at least equal in amount to the duties imposed. The issue of an inconvertible paper currency, as pointed out by the late Professor Cairnes, powerfully accelerated the upward movement. Large manufacturing industries were developed to an inordinate degree by the sudden but ephemeral prosperity, which followed upon a narrow and unwise course of legislation. Railways were extended beyond the requirements of traffic, and the productive capacity of mills, factories, and ironworks was multiplied tenfold. The dearness of labour gave a renewed impulse to the American genius for inventing labour-saving machinery, the effect being

to aggravate that tendency to over-production origi-
nated by other causes. It has been calculated by Mr.
Wells that, while the increase in population in the
United States from 1860 to 1870 was less than 23 per
cent., the gain in the product of the manufacturing industries during the same period, measured in kind, was
52 per cent., or nearly 30 per cent. in excess of the
gain in population.

The American manufacturers, under a rigid system
of protection, cannot produce cheaply. They may
revel in the monopoly of their home market, but they
cannot compete in neutral markets with a country
which has adopted a Free Trade policy. When,
therefore, the home consumption falls away, a collapse
ensues. In the United States the power of production
had been increased to such an extent, that it would
have been impossible for manufacturers to find a market
for their goods, even if the former demand had been
sustained. But consumption was reduced, owing to
the rapid fall in wages, and the diminished incomes
of holders of railway and other securities. The import
trade was prejudicially affected by the same causes. Collapse of the American market.

. In an article contributed to the ' Atlantic Monthly '
in October 1878, Mr. Erastus Bigelow gives a lucid
explanation of the depression of trade in the United
States. All departments of business had been affected
by certain general causes. Mr. Bigelow starts with
the axiom that, whenever the amount of capital employed is proportionate to the amount of business
done, and the credit employed is in proper proportion
to the capital, then business affairs assume their normal Mr. Bige-low's ex-planation.

condition. It is only when the intricate machinery of credit is run at undue speed that over-production and over-trading ensue. The demand created by the Civil War for hundreds upon hundreds of millions of dollars' worth of commodities was superadded to the normal wants of the people, and had the same stimulating effect on the business interests of the country as though that demand had come from abroad. The panic of 1873 disclosed the actual state of affairs. It was then seen that the capital and labour of the country had been largely misapplied; that railroads had been built which were not needed; that the machinery of production had been increased beyond the legitimate demand.

Fall in price of cotton.

Mr. Plunkett supplies some extraordinary instances of the fall in prices in the United States through the excessive production of manufactured goods. A correspondent in the dry-goods trade in New England had informed him that cotton had risen during the war to a dollar per pound, fine bleached cotton to 75 to 85 cents, and printed calicoes to 50 cents per yard. Goods of the latter description had since fallen to 6½ cents per yard, the cost of manufacture remaining the same.

Decrease of British exports.

The Commissioners of Customs give statistics showing the decrease in the value of our exports to the United States. In the year 1864 the value of the British exports to the United States was 16,708,505*l.* In 1872 it reached the highest sum in our records, namely 40,736,597*l.* From that year the value has been on a rapidly descending scale.

1872	. . £40,736,597	1875	. . £21,868,279
1873	. . 33,574,664	1876	. . 16,833,517
1874	. . 28,241,809		

The diminution in the quantities and values of the principal articles is exhibited in detail in the return prepared by the Commissioners :

—	1872	1875	1876	Decrease per cent. on	
				1876 as compared with 1872	1876 as compared with 1875
QUANTITIES.					
Cotton piece goods . . yards	131,617,356	79,897,600	54,869,900	58·3	31·3
Hardware and Cutlery cwts	102,054	53,162	33,356	67·3	37·2
Iron, old . . . . tons	87,293	8,181	5,394	93·8	34·0
„ pig and puddled „	195,151	51,362	41,640	78·6	18·9
„ bar, angle, bolt, and rod . . .	64,583	3,264	2,572	96·0	21·2
„ railroad . . . „	467,304	17,790	374	99·9	97·9
„ hoops, sheets, & galvanised . . „	31,407	11,025	7,014	77·7	36·4
„ cast & wrought . „	13,468	7,816	4,117	69·4	47·3
„ steel unwrought . „	23,821	10,681	7,480	68·6	30·0
Linen piece goods . . yards	118,603,646	95,141,830	73,242,400	38·0	23·0
Woollen cloths . . . „	6,289,876	2,612,519	1,478,190	76·5	43·4
Worsted stuffs . . . „	98,246,141	51,588,280	41,078,620	58·2	20·4
Woollen carpets . . „	6,773,474	2,188,120	1,013,090	85·0	52·6
VALUES.					
	£	£	£		
Apparel	250,455	94,349	74,017	70·4	21·5
Cotton piece goods	3,492,138	1,900,243	1,275,788	63·4	32·8
„ other manufactures .	1,660,599	1,499,255	1,175,963	29·2	21·5
Earthen and china ware .	841,239	620,288	543,221	36·0	11·4
Glass of all kinds . .	290,444	179,904	167,335	42·4	7·0
Haberdashery and millinery	1,384,857	511,663	285,326	79·5	44·7
Hardware and cutlery . .	951,618	552,501	350,809	63·1	36·5
Iron, old	533,461	38,872	23,985	95·5	38·3
„ pig and puddled . . .	1,017,123	195,319	171,331	83·1	12·3
„ bar, angle, bolt, and rod	745,681	55,798	28,236	96·2	49·4
„ railroad	4,812,866	228,904	6,612	99·8	97·2
„ hoops, sheets, and galvanised	427,603	138,603	83,107	80·5	40·0
„ cast or wrought . . .	308,651	143,638	87,846	71·5	38·9
„ steel, unwrought . .	769,658	382,652	247,606	67·8	35·3
Linen piece goods	3,628,143	2,725,873	2,027,978	44·1	25·6
Woollen cloths	1,342,232	767,118	431,918	67·8	43·7
Worsted stuffs	4,282,743	2,276,166	1,547,139	63·9	32·0
Woollen carpets	1,180,725	357,777	175,905	85·1	50·8

As the United States had long been our most important customers, the exclusion of British goods by the combined operation of the prohibitory tariff and the diminished purchasing power of the American people has proved a grave disaster.

State of trade in Germany.

If we turn to Germany, we find our trade suffering from another foreign commercial crisis. The causes, which have brought about the recent financial and commercial misfortunes of Germany, have been ably set forth in a pamphlet by M. Wolowski. The sudden acquisition of an enormous capital by the payment of the War Indemnity exacted from France, produced an effect on the German people which is compared by M. Wolowski to the sudden appearance of a mirage in a thirsty desert. Every description of industrial enterprise was undertaken with rash precipitation, and on a vast scale. The agricultural population gathered into the great cities, causing a portentous rise in rents, and in the cost of living. The working classes were dazzled by the sudden rise of wages; they lost their self-control, and became self-indulgent and extravagant. The landed and the middle classes suffered from the general increase in prices and the cost of living, and they too sought for compensation in wild and disastrous speculations. The effects of the commercial mania, which followed upon the military triumphs in France, have not yet disappeared; and although our trade with Germany has been more satisfactory than in other quarters, it cannot be doubted that its volume would have been greatly increased, if our customers had been more prosperous, and their purchasing power had not been impaired by the losses resulting from wild and unsuccessful enterprise.

The same spirit of speculation was carried from Germany into Austria. In 1870 and the three ensuing years, numerous railway and other undertakings were projected, absorbing all the available capital, involving a heavy load of debt to foreign countries, and, anticipating by a generation the legitimate requirements of the empire. We have felt the consequences of the subsequent reaction in the diminished purchases of our Austro-Hungarian customers. *In Austria.*

It is not, however, by commercial speculation alone, or chiefly, that the commerce of Continental Europe has been reduced to its present state of depression. The rivalries of military despots, the devastating wars which they have waged, and the bloated armaments they maintain, even in time of peace, have brought a larger share of ruin in their train than all the errors of the commercial classes. In the armies of the five chief European Powers more than 2,000,000 men are permanently under arms, and the annual expenditure on the fleets and armies of the so-called civilised world exceeds 150,000,000*l*. Some idea may by formed of the extent to which the power of the tax-payers to purchase commodities has been abridged from this cause, when it is mentioned that since 1860 the National Debts of the world, debts incurred mainly for war purposes, have been increased, according to a computation by Mr. Wells, by a sum exceeding 10,000,000,000 dollars. *Military expenditure.*

The intimate relation between the foreign policy

of France and the commercial movement of the country has been ably illustrated in the columns of the ' Times ' in a review of the 'Bulletin de Statistique' from 1827 to 1876. The mean value of the exports and imports advanced from 5,000,000,000 francs in 1859 to 8,000,000,000 francs in 1869. The amount was reduced to 6,954,000,000 francs in 1870. A slight recovery took place in 1871, and a great stride in advance was made in the following year, when the value rose to 9,258,000,000 francs. The subsequent growth has been slow. · The highest amount reached since 1872 has not exceeded 9,456,000,000 francs. Before the Franco-Prussian war, every two or three years brought an additional thousand millions to the trade of France. During the troublous period after that great disaster, an addition of 200,000,000 francs was slowly made in five years.

The approximate naval and military expenditure of France at the present time is 33,000,000*l.* sterling. In addition to the sums voted by the Chambers we must include the loss to the country and to each individual serving in the army or navy by his compulsory withdrawal from the productive labours in which he might have been engaged. It cannot be an overestimate to put the value of civil labour in France at an average amount of 30*l.* a year. The army permanently embodied numbers 400,000 men. In order, therefore, to arrive at the real cost of the military armaments of France, we must add the sum of 12,000,000*l.* a year to the amounts of the ordinary and extraordinary estimates for the army. We must make a similar calculation in order to arrive at the total cost of the German army. The spectacle of these two great bands of men, each preparing to make war on the other whenever a favourable opportunity arrives, suggests some melancholy reflections on the love of military glory, and the schemes of territorial aggrandisement, which have cast so dark a shadow over the age in which we live.

It would be well if contemporary politicians and statesmen would apply to themselves the admonitions of Montesquieu : ' Une maladie nouvelle s'est répandue en Europe : elle a saisi nos princes, et leur fait entretenir un nombre désordonné de troupes. Elle a ses redoublements, et elle devient nécessairement contagieuse : car, sitôt qu'un Etat augmente ce qu'il appelle ses troupes, les autres soudain augmentent les leurs : de façon qu'on ne gagne rien par là que la ruine commune. Chaque monarque tient sur pied toutes les armées qu'il pourrait avoir si ses peuples étaient en danger d'être exterminés : et on nomme paix cet état d'effort de tous entre tous. Aussi l'Europe est-elle si ruinée, que les particuliers, qui seraient dans la situation où sont les trois puissances de cette partie du monde les plus opulentes, n'auraient pas de quoi vivre. Nous sommes pauvres, avec les richesses et le commerce de tout l'univers ; et bientôt, à force d'avoir des soldats, nous n'aurons plus que des soldats, et nous serons comme des Tartares.'

Montesquieu's admonition.

Lord Beaconsfield's Administration have been too ready to ingratiate themselves with the party which

has been clamorous for war. It has been the most
noisy. It may not long continue the most numerous.

State of trade at home.   Let us pass from foreign countries and review the
situation in the United Kingdom. Here we have suf-
fered from the waste of capital caused by over-production, and from the recklessness with which advances
have been made to bankrupt States. We have been
excluded from foreign markets by an impassable barrier
of tariffs ; at home we have had an almost unprecedented
succession of bad harvests.

Agricultural misfortunes.   It was stated by Lord Beaconsfield, in his recent
speech in the House of Lords, that the loss on a bad
harvest, such as we had in 1875, was no less than
26,000,000*l.* The crops were equally deficient in the
two succeeding years, causing a diminution of wealth
by 80,000,000*l.*; and this succession of bad harvests
was accompanied for the first time by extremely low
prices. The fall in prices in England was caused by
the increased production and abnormal depreciation in
the price of agricultural produce in America. Their
superabundant harvest led to a heavy export movement, and the British farmer is now threatened with a
new and very formidable competition from the United
States. He will be called upon to lead a more laborious life. There must be less supervision and more
manual labour. The occupier of land and his family
must work as the farmers work in the Western States.
It is probable that holdings may tend to diminish
within limits which can be tilled by a single family,
assisted by the best mechanical appliances. Our
farmers possess an incontestable advantage in facility

of access to the home market, but a reduction of rents may be necessary.

Mr. Caird's recent volume, 'The Landed Interest and the Supply of Food,' contains a table showing the comparative quantity and value of home and foreign agricultural produce consumed annually. We learn from this source that while our importations of foreign agricultural produce amount to 110,707,000*l.*, the value of our home agricultural produce is 260,737,000*l.*, or more than double the amount of the imported produce. Agriculture, as the 'Statist' remarks, must be by far the largest industry of the country, and for a series of years our farmers have been contending with adverse seasons. Consumers generally have shared in the mis-fortunes of the agricultural interest. During three years of bad harvests we paid, according to Mr. Caird, 160,000,000*l.* more than in the three preceding years for the purchase of food.

We need not go beyond the returns contained in the 'Statistical Abstract' for evidence to show that our productive industry has been extended with reckless haste. It was quite unreasonable to expect that the increase in the exportation of British produce from 199,586,000*l.* in 1870 to 256,257,000*l.* in 1872 could be permanently maintained.

Over-production.

By their wealth, energy, and enterprise, the British people have often been the first to take advantage of a favourable conjunction of circumstances for the expan-sion of trade. By the same qualities they have as often been betrayed into that exaggeration of production which culminates in a crisis. In the words of Aristotle—

τινὲς ἀπώλοντο διὰ πλοῦτον, ἕτεροι δὲ δι' ἀνδρείαν.[1]

What banker, merchant, or railway contractor has not realised within the sphere of his own experience the full force of the following observations by the late Mr. Bagehot?—'Pascal said that most of the evils of life arose from a man's not being able to sit still in a room. We should have been a far wiser race if we had been readier to sit quiet. In commerce, part of every mania is caused by the impossibility of getting people to confine themselves to the amount of business for which their capital is sufficient. Operations with their own capital will only take four hours in the day, and they wish to be active and to be industrious for the other eight hours, and so they are ruined. If they could only have sat idle the other four hours, they would have been rich men.'

Retirement of experienced merchants.

Changes in the management, which deprive large concerns of the guidance of age and experience, are another fertile cause of commercial disaster. In England, more than in any other country, it is a customary practice for senior partners to retire in the prime of life, and to give the management to younger and less experienced men. This constant change, says the 'Statist,' in the *personnel*, by which a business is carried on, is of obvious importance, and it affords a partial explanation of the recurrence of great failures at intervals of ten or twelve years. The fall of the house of Overend and Gurney was the most striking

[1] 'Ethics,' i. 3.

incident of the crisis of 1866. The loss of its most experienced members was the chief cause of the misfortunes, which subsequently befell that famous establishment.

Mr. Savillé Lumley attributes the commercial depression of Belgium in no inconsiderable degree to inefficient management, arising from the substitution of corporate for individual control, of a manager who has nothing at stake for a proprietor who risks his own capital in the enterprise he is conducting. He states that in former days, when Belgian factories were for the most part conducted under the personal supervision of their proprietors, production was limited, as a matter of prudence, whenever indications appeared of declining consumption. In recent years many large factories have been converted into joint-stock companies, managed by directors who have not the same strong personal motives for prudence. Being paid either by fixed salary, or by commission varying with the output, they are interested in producing as much as possible without regard to consequences.

Inefficient management in Belgium.

The diminished purchasing power of the working classes, which must inevitably follow upon a general reduction of wages, has materially contributed to the depression in trade. We have frequent and periodical returns of the movement in our foreign trade; we have no machinery like that supplied by the Custom House, by which we can gauge the extent and the fluctuations in the consumption of commodities at home. It is on our own people that British manufacturers must chiefly rely, and a small reduction in

Diminished purchasing power of wage-earning classes.

the earnings of the nation must seriously curtail the aggregate amount available for purchases in the home market.

Effects of dear food on general industry.

Mr. Newmarch has shown, in his paper on the progress of the foreign trade of the United Kingdom since 1850, how materially the condition of the agricultural population affects the general industry of the country. After 1873, three bad harvests followed in succession. The cost of some of the principal articles of food consumed by the working classes was proportionately enhanced, and a degree of distress was experienced, such as had not been known for a long period.

During the interval, 1873–77, the price of bread and potatoes had not been less than 12 to 14 per cent. higher than the average prices of the three preceding years. When we take into consideration how large a sum is made up by the extra shillings set free by the lower cost of living, among 25,000,000 persons, and remember that the consumption of the masses constitutes the effective demand for the bulk of manufactured articles, it will be evident that increased price of food involves a corresponding diminution in the demand for manufactured articles. The enhanced cost of living, until a very recent period, among the agricultural population, will go far to explain the slackness of trade.

The woollen trade.

The present situation of the woollen trade is analysed in a recent number of the 'Statist.' In 1878, the net imports of wool were 196,000,000 lbs., against 218,500,000 lbs. in 1877. Our importations of the raw material were 22,000,000 lbs. less ; but our exports of goods were 4,000,000 lbs. in excess of the exports of 1877. There remains, therefore, 26,000,000 lbs. less wool for home consumption in 1878 than in the previous year. This comparison shows that the depression in the woollen industry is due to diminished purchasing power in the United Kingdom rather than to foreign competition.

In considering the falling off in the demand, more particularly for iron and steel, it is to be remembered that the foreign railways, which were furnished with material from England, were constructed mainly by loans obtained on the London Exchange. It is stated by Mr. Wilson in his volumes on the resources of modern countries, that in the interval between 1866–75, 37,000 miles of railway were constructed in the United States, at a nominal cost of several hundred millions sterling. From 70,000,000*l.* to 100,000,000*l.* were raised in Europe by the sale of bonds. In South America, railway extension has been carried on by repeated borrowings in London and Paris. The total amount of foreign loans taken in London has been calculated at 615,000,000*l.* So long as money could be raised in London, the Republics of South America and the effete Governments of Europe enjoyed a brilliant outburst of fictitious prosperity ; but when experience showed how uncertain was the payment of those higher rates of interest, which had allured the credulous public—fifty-four per cent. of the foreign loans issued in London, as it is shown in Mr. Smedley's report, are in default—and when the investigations of the Committee

Cessation of loans to foreign states.

of the House of Commons had revealed the chicanery, by which the public had been duped in numerous instances, all confidence in investments of this character was destroyed. The loans being withheld, the trade with the countries we had hitherto supplied with funds, inevitably decayed. No foreign country, as Mr. Wilson remarks, with the exception of France, Belgium, Holland, and Germany, has had in itself resources to buy and pay for the commodities that we have sold to them so freely.

Benefit from out-flow of capital.

Misrepresentation should be exposed, and the public should be warned against Governments which are persistently in default. It is to be hoped, however, that the revelations of the Foreign Loans Committee will not discourage those sound investments, which, when judiciously made, equally benefit the lender and the borrower. Mr. Mill has truly said that the perpetual outflow of capital into the colonies and foreign countries has been for many years one of the principal causes by which the decline of profits in England has been arrested. It carries off a part of the increase of capital from which a reduction of profits proceeds. On the other hand the emigration of English capital has been the chief means of keeping up a supply of cheap food, and cheap raw materials for industry, to our increasing population.

Ministerial extravagance.

British trade has suffered from the fierce contest lately waged in Eastern Europe. It has suffered from the extravagance of the present Government. They were careless in expenditure on their first accession to office, and before the cloud of impending war was seen. The uncertainties of the future under a government which delights in sensations and surprises, and is swayed by fanciful and imaginative impulses, have been a more serious impediment to the revival of commerce than the increase in the burden of taxation. Security and confidence would have been lightly purchased even at the price of increased taxation. The Government have harassed our commerce by the rash and bellicose spirit in which they have conducted our foreign relations. They have lowered the financial reputation of the country, and demoralised the people, by indulging them in exciting prospects of war and conquest, without attempting to cover the expenditure out of current revenue. Under such a system electors are unconscious that our national resources are being wasted in heedless and unnecessary wars. The conduct of the present Government stands out in striking and unworthy contrast with the more straightforward policy of former Liberal administrators.

A passage relating to the Crimean War in the correspondence of the late Prince Consort is quoted in Mr. Theodore Martin's admirable biography (vol. iii. p. 57). It might be applied with equal force to more recent incidents. Referring to the financial arrangements for the prosecution of the Crimean War, the Prince writes as follows : ' Gladstone wants to pay for the war out of current revenue so long as he does not require more than 10,000,000*l*. sterling above the ordinary expenditure, and to increase the taxes for the purpose. The Opposition are for borrowing. The former course is manly, statesmanlike, and honest; the latter is convenient, cowardly, perhaps popular.'

[marginal note: Provision of war expenditure.]

In the succeeding chapters the various causes to which the depression of trade is attributable, will be further examined and described in more detail than it has been possible to give in a general summary.

Need of political and financial circumspection. It is satisfactory to know that many causes of commercial distress may be removed by greater wisdom on the part of statesmen and financiers. We cannot prevent a recurrence of famines among the populations in the East, who are the most extensive consumers of our textile manufactures ; but public opinion can control the foreign policy of the country. The waste of capital, which we have deplored in recent years, may be avoided by more circumspection in the future. Many incautious and premature investments will soon become more or less productive. The revenue of the vast network of railways in the United States and Austro-Hungary, in which British capital has been largely embarked, will improve; and a general recovery of credit will follow upon the re-establishment of peace.

Misapplication of capital. It will be admitted by every unprejudiced mind that our workmen may have injured trade by their indolence and arbitrary demands. Yet their misconduct is subordinate in importance to other adverse influences. Errors of judgment in the application of capital have been the most potent cause of the suspension of industry and the temporary exhaustion of our resources.

CHAPTER II.

THE FALL IN PRICES.

Much money makes a country poor, for it sets a dearer price on everything.—G. HERBERT, *Jacula Prudentum.*

THE effect of a condition of commercial depression is considerably mitigated in a national point of view by the cheapening of commodities, which is an inevitable consequence of the slackening of demand. When prices are falling and the complaints of the manufacturers continually reach our ears, it is sometimes forgotten that while the general depreciation of values constitutes a loss to the producer, it affords a corresponding relief to the consumer. Mr. Fawcett has given a striking illustration of the loss sustained by consumers from the recent abnormal condition of the coal trade. The sudden increase in the demand led to a rise of 13s. 6d. in the price per ton. The aggregate production of coal in the United Kingdom is 120,000,000 tons, of which not more than 12,000,000 tons are exported. The rise in price represented therefore an additional charge of 81,000,000l. upon the consumers of coal, nine-tenths of which sum was contributed by consumers in this country, and not less than 13,500,000l. by those who use coal for household purposes, and who received no direct advantage from the general prosperity of trade during the period in

Saving to consumers from reduced price of coal.

question.   Thus, by the enhancement in the price of a single article, an extra tax was imposed upon the households of this country not less in amount, as Mr. Fawcett points out, than half the interest on the National Debt.

Reduced cost of living.

When similar changes take place in the price of almost every article in general consumption, the economy in the cost of living goes far to compensate the working classes for reductions in wages.   In his recent speech at Westminster, the First Lord of the Admiralty estimated the alterations in the cost of living as ' making 18s. equivalent in purchasing power to a sovereign, at the prices of two years ago.'   According to a calculation published in the ' Economist ' on the 28th December last : ' Market prices are, taking an average of a great number of commodities in daily use, from 10 to 12 per cent. cheaper than in any of the years of depression which followed the panic of 1866, and from 8 to 10 per cent. below those of 1859—the cheapest year of the series after the crisis of 1857. . . . Tracing further back, to the time of stagnation following upon the railway panic of 1847, we at length obtain a record of prices apparently cheaper than those at present existing, and in 1849, " the cheapest year of the century," the average of marketable commodities was probably 7 per cent. lower than at present.'

Cheapness of wheat.

In another article on the same subject the ' Economist ' remarks that ' while we had received 556,000 cwts. more wheat in October 1878 than in the corresponding month of the previous year, we had actually paid 177,000l. less money ;   for 16,000 cwts. more of cheese we had paid 71,000*l.* less; for 10,000 cwts. more of butter, 8,000*l.* less.' In the first nine months of 1878, we 'had received from the United States Atlantic ports 21,089,000 cwts. of wheat against only 5,892,000 cwts. in the first nine months of 1877; and the price of wheat had fallen to 40*s.* 4*d.*, or 14*s.* 8*d.* per quarter less than at the corresponding date in 1877. The price of wheat is now as low as it was in March 1875, and lower than at any other time during a long period of years. Even when our harvests have been bad, the overflowing supplies from abroad have prevented any burdensome increase in the price of bread, and the better harvest of last year has still further reduced the prices, already very moderate, which we have been paying for imported food. Several other of the commodities, which constitute the principal food of the people, have been considerably reduced in price. Sugar has never been so cheap. The price is from 1*s.* to 3*s.* per cwt. lower than at the corresponding date in 1877. Coffee has fallen in the same interval from 10*s.* to 15*s.* per cwt.'

The compensation afforded by a reduction of prices is not confined to the operatives. The manufacturers derive their share of advantage, not only in the reduction of wages, but in the cheapness of the raw materials of industry. A paper by Mr. Giffen, read at a recent meeting of the Statistical Society, gives some of the principal changes in values which have recently occurred. Mr. Giffen compared the prices of leading wholesale commodities on January 1, 1873, the period of *maximum* inflation, with the prices of the same

Reduced cost of raw materials.

articles on January 1 of the present year.   Thus Scotch
pig-iron fell, per ton, from 127*s.* to 43*s.*; Straits tin,
from 142*l.* to 61*l.*; coals, from 30*s.* to 10*s.*; wheat,
per quarter, from 55*s.* 11*d.* to 39*s.* 7*d.*; cotton, per
pound, from 10*d.* to 5¾*d.*; wool, per pack, from 23*l.*
to 13*l.* 'We should hardly have expected beforehand,'
he remarked, after quoting a series of figures, 'that
prices of wholesale articles not selected with a view to
make out a case, but impartially chosen years ago as
representative of the markets, would exhibit a fall in
the last six years ranging from 66 per cent. in the
most extreme to 10 per cent. in the least extreme case,
and ranging, with three exceptions only, between 26
and 66 per cent.'

Mr. Shaw
Lefevre's
address to
the Statis-
tical So-
ciety.
Mr. Shaw Lefevre gives the following remarkable
illustration of the fall in prices:—' Coal, which in 1870,
before the great rise, was 12*s.* 6*d.* per ton at the pit's
mouth, and in 1873 was 32*s.* 6*d.* per ton, is now reduced to 9*s.* per ton.   The best Staffordshire bar-iron,
which in 1870 was 6*l.* 10*s.* per ton, and in 1873 15*l.*
per ton, is now worth only 5*l.* 10*s.*   Cotton is 25 per
cent. less than in 1869.   American salt beef is 10 per
cent. less, and European salt pork 20 per cent. less
than in 1874.   Sugar is 15 per cent. less than in 1869.
American salt beef is 10 per cent. less, and European
salt pork 20 per cent. less, than in 1869.   Freights are
lower than at any time during the last ten years; and
steamers which were constructed for the emigrant trade
are now mainly employed in bringing over fat cattle
from the United States, to the great benefit of meat
consumers.'

The value of materials for manufactures, imported in 1878, was 122,000,000*l.*, showing a fall of 14,000,000*l.*, or 11½ per cent. on the previous year. Of this fall, 8,210,000*l.* on 122,340,000*l.*, or rather less than 7 per cent., is due, according to the calculations of the 'Economist,' to reductions in prices. Commenting on a mass of valuable statistics, from time to time published in its columns, the 'Statist' remarks : 'In this, as in other cases, the very low prices of the raw material are a sure sign of depression in trade. We have the satisfaction of knowing, however, that such prices are always the beginning of a new start in trade, as soon as the bottom has been touched, which seems to be now the case.' *Reduction of prices in 1878.*

From a similar cause the railways, those vast undertakings in which are accumulated the savings of the middle classes of the United Kingdom, have been enabled in most instances to sustain their former rates of dividend. In 1877 there was a slight decrease in the receipts, the expenditure, and the net earnings per train mile, the final result being a fractional diminution of dividend on the total ordinary capital of from 4·52 to 4·51 per cent. The saving in the expenditure on materials and labour was sufficient to balance the large additions, which are constantly being made to the capital of the most important lines. *Maintenance of railway dividends by diminished expenditure.*

The following remarks occur in a leader in the 'Times' on the railway dividends for the second half of the year 1878. On an ordinary capital of nearly 140,000,000*l.* sterling, the sum payable in dividend amounted to 4,250,000*l.* sterling, and the net reduction in the amount available for dividends, as compared with the corresponding period of 1877, was only 30,000*l.* Many of the companies had been doing a smaller business ; but raw materials had been lower in price, and wages had been reduced. The case of the North-Eastern Railway was quoted, as a striking illustration of the maintenance of dividend by economy in expenditure. 'The dividend was threatened by a decrease of 191,000*l.* in the gross traffic. The reduction of expenditure has not only largely compensated this reduction, but has even exceeded it. The expenditure on permanent way is reduced from 441,000*l.* to 361,000*l.*, or 80,000*l.* ; on locomotive power from 496,000*l.* to 434,000*l.*, or 62,000*l.* ; and traffic expenses from 444,000*l.* to 413,000*l.*, or 31,000*l.*, making, with other reductions, a total saving of 196,000*l.*, or about 11 per cent., the reduction in gross traffic being less than 6 per cent.'

Relief to steamship owners.

The shipping interest, like the railways, has received a sensible relief from the fall in the cost of coal and iron. The result in the case of seventeen leading steam companies was worked out and published in the 'Statist' of June 1878. The capital of the companies enumerated amounted to 10,841,955*l.*, and the aggregate profits distributed as dividend on capital were, in the respective years, as follows :

	Per cent.		Per cent.
1872 . . .	$8\frac{7}{8}$	1875 . . .	$3\frac{3}{8}$
1873 . . .	9	1876 . . .	$4\frac{7}{16}$
1874 . . .	$5\frac{3}{8}$	1877 . . .	$4\frac{7}{16}$

The depression of commerce forbids the idea that this recovery in the rate of dividend can be attributed to an improvement in freights, or to increased commercial activity. It is by a continual reduction in the working expenses that the position of shipowners has been improved. The price of coal is a principal factor in the cost of running steamships, and the fluctuations of recent years are tabulated by the 'Statist' as follows:

Price of Coal.

	s.	d.				s.	d.	
For 1872 .	15	9	per ton	For 1875 .		13	3	per ton
„ 1873 . .	21	0	„	„ 1876 .		11	0	„
„ 1874 .	17	3	„	„ 1877 .		10	3	„

During 1878 the prices for building ships have fallen to the lowest point which they have ever reached.

Reductions in the price of commodities are equally valuable whether as a relief to working people in their hour of necessity, or as a means of restoring to our trade its former prosperity. With cheaper raw materials, a losing may be converted into a profitable trade. By offering goods at lower prices we may increase the demand. Cheap bread and cheap raw materials are the best alleviations of the bad times through which we are now passing, and they present, as Mr. Shaw Lefevre remarks, the best guarantee of ultimate recovery. *Cheapness of commodities the alleviating feature.*

The fall in prices, of which so many illustrations have been given in the preceding pages, has been traced by some of our highest statistical authorities, including Professor Jevons and Mr. Giffen, to the insufficiency in the current supply of gold. With a view to the elucidation of the subject, Mr. Giffen has compiled the following table: *Deficient gold supply.*

D

Estimated Production of Gold in the years 1852-75, in Quinquennial Periods, with the several Averages for each Period.

Period	Total Production	Annual Average
	£	£
1852-56 . . .	149,665,000	29,933,000
1857-61 . . .	123,165,000	24,633,000
1862-66 . . .	113,800,000	22,760,000
1867-71 . . .	108,765,000	21,753,000
1871-75 (4 years) .	76,800,000	19,200,000

While the supply has been dwindling away, the demand for gold has enormously increased. The growth of the population in the gold-using countries cannot be set down at less than 50 per cent.; and the development of mechanical invention has prodigiously increased the supply of goods and the movement in trade. Mr. Giffen infers that, if a supply of six millions sterling was sufficient to maintain the equilibrium of prices before 1848, the natural increment in the population would make the present usual requirements about nine millions. Fifty per cent. must be added for the greater wealth per head, making the total additional requirements not less than thirteen and a half millions. Prices have been more seriously affected by the deficiency in the supply of gold, in consequence of the recent demonetisation of silver in France and Germany.

CHAPTER III.

THE COTTON TRADE.

WE shall now proceed to examine the present condition and recent history of two great branches of the national industry, which have suffered most seriously from the prolonged depression of trade.

The latest returns of the cotton trade, while exhibiting a large reduction in value, do not show a corresponding decrease in quantities. This is clearly proved in a table borrowed from the 'Economist:'

Exports of cotton goods.

Quantity and Value of Yarns and Manufactures exported during each of the past Eleven Years.—(In millions and tenths.)

Years	Yarns		Piece Goods		Hosiery, Small-wares, &c.	Total Value all Kinds
	lbs.	£	yards	£	£	£
1878	250·5	13·0	3606·0	47·7	5·1	65·9
1877	227·6	12·2	3823·0	51·0	4·9	69·7
1876	232·1	12·7	3650·6	49·9	4·9	67·6
1875	215·4	13·1	3547·8	53·1	5·4	71·7
1874	220·5	14·5	3587·1	54·3	5·3	74·2
1873	214·6	15·8	3466·5	55·8	5·5	77·3
1872	212·3	16·6	3517·5	58·2	5·2	80·1
1871	193·0	15·0	3305·1	52·8	4·8	72·8
1870	180·0	14·6	3257·4	53·0	3·7	71·4
1869	169·5	14·1	2860·1	49·9	3·0	67·1
1868	174·2	14·7	2977·1	50·2	2·7	67·6

When, however, the allegations of foreign competition are renewed again and again, the public are naturally disturbed by apprehensions as to the future of British industry.   I propose, therefore, to recount, as briefly as I can, the recent history of the textile industries and the iron trade.

State of the trade,

Not less than 4,000,000 persons, according to the computation of Mr. Bevan, and a capital of 100,000,000*l.* are engaged in these trades.   The wages of the operatives are falling, and the returns upon the capital invested are insufficient.   It is important, therefore, to know to what extent British industry has been affected by foreign competition, and by other causes more immediately within our own control.   The balance-sheets of the joint-stock cotton mills may be accepted as examples of the results obtained in the majority of the private concerns in the trade.

as tested by the Oldham mill dividends,

A circular published in 1878 by Messrs. Ellison & Co. gives a table of the dividends declared in Oldham in the last quarters of 1876 and 1877 respectively. 'It will be observed,' they say, ' that out of forty companies, only four paid a dividend in the third and fourth quarters of 1877.   The average return for the forty mills was $3\frac{3}{4}$ per cent. in 1877 against 11 per cent. in 1876.   Not only are the average dividends reduced for the whole of the mills; in many cases no dividends whatever were declared, and severe losses were sustained during the period in question.   As the Oldham mills are understood, for the most part at least, to possess the latest improvements in machinery, and to be worked upon the most economical principles, the list may be taken as fairly representing the entire cotton industry of the country.'

Another test may be applied in order to ascertain the state of the cotton trade. The variations in the price of cotton may be compared with the price of yarns and cloths. *and by the relative prices of raw and manufac-. tured material.*

The following table, showing the relative prices of raw cotton and cotton goods, was published in the 'Economist:'

An Estimate of the Value of the Production of Cotton Manufactures in Great Britain, with the Cost of Cotton consumed and the Balance remaining for Wages, all other Expenses, Interest of Capital, and Profits for each of the past Twelve Years.

Year	Total Value of Goods produced	Cost of Raw Cotton	Left for Wages, Profit, and other Expenses
	£	£	£
1878	80,700,000	30,300,000	50,300,000
1877	87,300,000	32,500,000	54,700,000
1876	88,700,000	32,800,000	55,900,000
1875	95,400,000	36,500,000	58,900,000
1874	100,500,000	40,200,000	60,300,000
1873	104,600,000	45,400,000	59,100,000
1872	102,200,000	48,000,000	54,200,000
1871	101,900,000	40,800,000	61,100,000
1870	93,100,000	42,100,000	51,000,000
1869	86,100,000	43,700,000	42,400,000
1868	91,700,000	40,900,000	50,700,000
1867	90,400,000	41,200,000	49,100,000

In a later issue, the 'Economist' points out that cotton goods have actually increased in quantity about 10 per cent., though realising some ten millions less. The diminution in the receipts for cotton exports is nearly equally due to the lower value of the cotton itself and the diminished wages and profits accruing from its manufacture.

In October 1878, the 'Statist' gave a series of comparative tables of the quotations for cotton yarn and cloth. From this collection of statistics I select the following:

	Cotton, Mid. Uplands	Yarn, 40 Mule	Cloth, Red End, 39 in.
	d.	*d.*	*d.*
October 1874	8 per lb.	$12\frac{1}{4}$ per lb.	$11\frac{1}{2}$ per lb.
„ 1875	$7\frac{3}{16}$ „	$10\frac{3}{4}$ „	$10\frac{3}{4}$ „
„ 1876	$6\frac{3}{4}$ „	$10\frac{1}{4}$ „	$9\frac{1}{4}$ „
„ 1877	$6\frac{15}{16}$ „	$10\frac{3}{4}$ „	$9\frac{1}{4}$ „
„ 1878	$6\frac{1}{16}$ „	$9\frac{3}{8}$ „	8 „

	Margin, or gross Profit on Yarn	Long Cloth
	d.	*d.*
October 1878	$3\frac{1}{4}$ per lb.	$1\frac{7}{8}$ per lb.
„ 1877	4 „	3 „
„ 1876	$4\frac{1}{8}$ „	$3\frac{1}{4}$ „
„ 1875	$3\frac{3}{4}$ „	$3\frac{1}{4}$ „
„ 1874	$4\frac{1}{4}$ „	$3\frac{1}{4}$ „

Reduced profits of manufacture.

The condition of the cotton trade is summed up by the 'Statist' as follows:—'Thus the position comes out worse now than in the past four years. The spinner obtains only $3\frac{1}{4}d.$ per lb. for yarn in excess of the cost of the raw material, where he used to obtain about $4d.$ The manufacturer of long cloth obtains similarly less than $2d.$ per lb. where he has been accustomed to a margin of more than $3d.$ per lb. above the cost of material. Making all allowance for reduced outlay on wages, machinery, and fuel during the past year or two, the reduction of margin runs from 25 to 45 per cent., as compared with 1874. In other words, consumers of raw cotton find the gross profit, on working it up, only two-thirds of what they then obtained; they have to pay wages, buy coal and machinery, make repairs, and live themselves, upon that fraction of the sums left for such purposes in 1874. More than that, the prices of cotton and cotton goods have been for years on the decline, and falling prices are always fruitful of loss in a trade.'

The gradual and considerable fall in the price of cotton is the one consolatory feature amid the prevailing gloom. It has fallen in the last ten years from $11\frac{1}{16}d.$ to $5\frac{3}{8}d.$ per lb., and the supply has never been more abundant than it is at the present time. The crop of 1878 was estimated by the Agricultural Bureau at Washington at 5,500,000 bales, by far the largest ever known, the nearest approach being the crop of 1877, with 4,811,000 bales. Cheapness of the raw material.

The history of the woollen trade for 1878 was also reviewed in the 'Economist.' This branch of industry has not received the same compensation for the fall in prices through the reduced cost of the raw materials, which has been obtained in the cotton trade. 'Of woollen fabrics, a total of 32,000,000*l.* in 1872 has shrunk to 17,000,000*l.* in 1877, at least two-thirds being in the quantity of goods exported, and of the six or seven millions loss in value there is no saving whatever in the price of the raw wool, which the import tables show to have been as costly as before, though probably the cotton mixed with a large number of the articles coming under this denomination may have cost from one to two millions less.' The woollen trade.

The causes of recent fluctuations in the cotton trade have been traced back by the 'Statist' to the American Civil War, which, 'by cutting off for four consecutive Fluctuations due to the American Civil War.

years the supply of raw cotton from the Southern States, had not only given time for clearing off the surplus stock of goods previously accumulated, but had created an actual scarcity. Prices accordingly rose to an unprecedented height, and fortunes were rapidly made. Capital eagerly rushed into a business so exceptionally fortunate, and during the ten following years there was a rivalry among nations in the building of mills and the multiplication of spindles. . . . But gradually consumption began to lag behind production. The void that had been occasioned by the American Civil War was filled up, and the restriction of the purchasing power of the nations of the world, to which we have already referred as manifesting itself in 1873, began to tell seriously.'

Depression mainly due to over-production. It cannot be doubted that over-production is a main cause of the depression in the cotton trade. An important admission in this sense was made by the President of the Chamber of Commerce at Manchester. His words have been quoted by Mr. Morley. 'It is well known,' he said, 'that during the last ten years the building of spinning factories by private firms, and more especially by joint-stock companies, has been *in the nature of a mania.*' The enormous outlay of 10,000,000*l.* sterling represents the extension from 1865 to 1875. During this interval, 'the exports followed the increased production, until within the last three or four years the over-production of both yarn and cloth has filled every available market.'

Increased number of spindles. The growth in the productive capacity of our cotton mills can be most accurately gauged by a comparison of the number of spindles at successive dates. A table published in the 'Statist' gives the following figures :

	1860	1877
United Kingdom .	29,000,000	30,500,000
United States . .	5,235,727	10,000,000
European Continent .	13,250,000	10,603,000
India	338,000	1,231,000
Total	47,823,727	70,334,000

At the annual meeting of the Manchester Chamber of Commerce in 1878, an important discussion took place on the growth of our cotton industry, a condensed report of which was published in the 'Economist.' Mr. W. Hoyle declared that 'in the three years ended in 1851, the number of spindles in the United Kingdom was 20,937,000; in the three years ended 1861 it had risen to 30,387,000; in the three years which closed in 1871 it had further advanced to 34,600,000, while for the three years which expired in 1877 the number was 39,000,000. Taking the exports of cotton yarns for the same period, it was found that in the three years ended 1851 there were 424,000 lbs. of yarn exported; in the three years ended 1861 the export was 567,000,000 lbs.; in the three years which terminated in 1871 the quantity exported had fallen to 538,000,000 lbs., but in the triennial period ended 1877 it had increased to 675,000,000 lbs. Turning to the number of looms in the country, he found that in 1851 there were 249,627; in 1861 the number had risen to 399,900; in 1871 to 440,676; and in 1877 to 470,000. Still more rapid had been the growth in the export of cotton goods. In the three years ended 1851 the export amounted to 423,900,000 yards; in the three years ended 1861 there were exported 7,902,000,000 yards; in the three years terminated in 1871, 9,553,000,000 yards; and in the three years ended 1877 the export had increased to 11,068,000,000.'

The cotton manufacture has been developed with a rapidity which has exceeded the consuming power of the world. Hence a large proportion—probably from twenty to thirty per cent.—of our machinery is standing idle. The British manufacturers have gone far beyond their rivals abroad in the rashness with which factories have been multiplied. The proportionate increase may not be so great in the United Kingdom as in some other countries which were in a singularly backward condition as compared with ourselves ; but if we take the actual, as distinguished from the proportionate increase, we find that we have added ten and a half millions, while Europe and the United States together have added not more than twelve millions, to the number of spindles in operation in 1860. Our new spindles, in the seventeen years from 1860 to 1877, are more numerous than all the spindles, both new and old, existing at this moment in the United States, and show an augmentation in what the 'Statist' calls 'the potential producing power' of over 50 per cent.

Tempo-
rary limi-
tation of
produc-
tion,

As the depression has been mainly caused by excessive production, a combination of circumstances must sometimes occur in which a temporary limitation of production will be the most effectual means of restoring a trade to a healthy condition. Thus far I entirely agree with the operatives, and disagree with those who contend that mere cheapness, if only we go low enough, will be sufficient to raise the consumption to a level with the productive capacity of our mills.

It is argued by Mr. Greg, the able author of 'Rectifications,' that it is the duty of operatives engaged in the textile manufactures to reduce to the utmost possible degree the cost of the commodities they produce, and that they are wrong in seeking to diminish the amount of commodities created by their labours. I cannot admit that the consumers of cotton goods—those at least who are in a position to pay a reasonable price for manufactured articles—however great their numbers, could take our goods in indefinite quantities. It will be admitted that cheapness stimulates consumption, especially among the poor but multitudinous populations within the tropics, who are supplied from the looms of Yorkshire and Lancashire. It is difficult, and indeed impossible, to set a limit to the quantity of goods which may ultimately be absorbed. But the growth in the demand must be gradual. When, therefore, by our excessive production, we overtake their wants, the markets are glutted, and the condition of the operatives, even though they work their hardest for mere subsistence wages, becomes once more as precarious as ever. It has been truly said by Mr. Mill that productive labour may render the nation poorer, if the wealth it produces—that is to say the increase it makes in the stock of useful or agreeable things—is of a

[marginal note:] compared with production at reduced cost.

kind not immediately wanted. I contend, therefore, that some curtailment of production is inevitable, whenever it is found that reductions of price afford no sufficient relief to an over-stocked market.

The short time question. In the prolonged altercations which arose in connection with the cotton trade last year, it was urged, on the part of the operatives, that if they submitted to a reduction of wage as a necessary sacrifice in an unprosperous state of trade, the manufacturers on their part should consent to work short time, the limitation of production being the only means of re-establishing remunerative prices for goods. To this suggestion it was replied by the manufacturers ·that production could not be curtailed without an augmentation of cost; that whether the mills were run full time or short time, in either case the fixed expenditure remained the same. The proposition of the operatives was accordingly rejected. The resumption, however, of full time, and the return of the operatives to their employment, soon led to an accumulation of stocks and a further depression in prices. Some mills ceased running. Other firms decided to run short time. Others went into liquidation. In an economical point of view, it may have been more advantageous that weak firms and ill-constructed mills should be stopped, and that stronger and more perfectly equipped establishments should be employed to the full extent of their capacity; but if such a proposal had been advanced by the operatives, it would have been denounced in un-measured terms by the masters' association. Since the termination of the strike at Blackburn and Burnley further reductions in wages have been insisted upon.

I cannot dismiss the subject of strikes without a reference to the argument, on which Mr. Greg very fairly insists, that the sacrifices required from the operatives are, after all, very small as compared with the losses sustained by their employers. The workpeople were asked to forego six shillings out of an aggregate receipt of 3*l.*, the ordinary earnings of a family employed in cotton spinning in Lancashire. Their employers, on the other hand, had been losing from 50*l.* to 100*l.* a week for many months. *The refusal to work at reduced wages.*

The recommendations urged by the operatives in favour of a policy of restricted production were doubtless supported by very powerful arguments; but I hold that it is inexpedient and inconsistent on their part to concern themselves directly in questions relating to the financial administration, and the commercial situation, of the trades in which they are employed. As the 'Saturday Review' truly said, it may be a question whether prices can be reduced sufficiently to stimulate consumption and yet leave the operatives enough to live upon. But this is certain, that the only way in which employers and workpeople can themselves contribute to the resuscitation of trade is by cutting down the cost of production rigorously and in every item. The workman must fix his own standard of living. He is justified in refusing to accept wages which will not furnish him with the means of supporting himself and his family in that condition of comfort in which he desires that they should be maintained. *The workmen's demand for restricted production.*

Let him, if he is in a sufficiently independent position, contend against a reduction in his standard of living, and change his employment; but when he proceeds to dictate a commercial policy to his employers, he goes beyond his proper sphere, and pronounces judgment upon a case which he has not fully heard. The course of trade must be watched in the counting-house and on the exchange, and it belongs rather to the merchant, the manufacturer, and the broker, than to the operative spinner and weaver, to bargain for the sale of goods, and form a judgment as to the prospects of the market.

The sound rule for the conduct of the workman must be to make as large earnings as he can in the actual condition of trade. In the case under considera-tion it would have been far more advantageous for the operatives to work full time at the reduced wages than to work short time at their full wages.

Messrs. Ellison on foreign competi-tion.

In their latest circular Messrs. Ellison attribute the present crisis in great measure to foreign competition. Let us examine the facts upon which their opinion rests. Messrs. Ellison and other authorities have often referred to the increased consumption of raw cotton on the Continent, and in the United States and India, as evidence of a retrogression in the cotton manufacture in this country. The following is one of several tables which they have from time to time prepared and published in their valuable circulars:

	Great Britain		Continent	
	Deliveries	Consumption	Deliveries	Consumption
	lbs.	lbs	lbs.	lbs.
1870-71	1,203,024,000	1,195,272,000	898,700,000	784,700,000
1871-72	1,127,520,000	1,105,272,000	693,350,000	788,350,000
1872-73	1,280,640,000	1,227,453,000	802,638,000	821,638,000
1873-74	1,240,706,000	1,259,836,000	893,113,000	872,000,000
1874-75	1,198,838,000	1,224,377,000	894,262,000	915,375,000
1875-76	1,270,287,000	1,270,287,000	1,026,374,000	961,143,000
1876-77	1,278,538,000	1,273,256,000	920,032,000	979,895,000
1877-78	1,193,158,000	1,193,158,000	1,014,597,000	989,415,000
Total	9,852,711,000	9,838,911,000	7,143,060,000	7,112,516,000

The subjoined table has also been compiled by Messrs.
Ellison. It shows the consumption of cotton in
1860, 1870-1, and 1877-8, in thousands of bales, of
the uniform weight of 400 lbs. each.

	1860		1870-1		1877-8	
	Bales	Per cent.	Bales	Per cent.	Bales	Per cent.
Great Britain	2,817	40·4	2,088	47·9	2,983	40·6
Continent	1,794	31·5	1,962	31·4	2,473	33·7
United States	1,088	19·1	1,209	19·3	1,657	22·6
India	—	—	87	1·4	230	3·1
Total	5,699	100·0	6,246	100·	7,343	100·0

Having admitted that Great Britain held her ground
pretty well between 1860 and 1871, they point to the
subsequent increase of the consumption of cotton on
the Continent and in the United States as a ground of
apprehension for the future.

The 'Economist,' reviewing the Transactions of the
Manchester Statistical Society for the year 1876-7,
directs especial attention to the reasons urged by
Mr. Joseph Spencer why statistics of the mere
weight of cotton consumed in the various producing

Consumption no gauge of progress.

districts of the world ought not to be regarded as a gauge of their relative progress. He draws attention also to the increased number of spindles at work in different countries. The result of this double investigation is to show that while Great Britain consumed a smaller proportion of the total cotton supply of the world during the five years ended with 1875, than at any previous period of five years since 1830, yet ' our spinners have set to work 243 per cent. more spindles than the Americans, and 72 per cent. more than the continental spinners,' during the past fifty years.

Protective tariffs.

It is doubtless true that the accumulations of capital abroad have been applied to the purchase of our most improved machinery, and that, as regards mechanical resources, foreign manufacturers are now on a level with ourselves. It is equally certain that, under the protection of a heavy tariff, foreign countries are able for the most part fully to supply their own requirements. However admirable the quality, however moderate the cost, of our goods, they will be excluded absolutely from the protected market, if only the .tariff be sufficiently exorbitant. Even the silk manufacturers of Lyons can no longer find a market in the United States for their unrivalled productions, the only classes of French silks, which can now be sold in that country, being those of the very finest quality—articles, in short, of luxury, for which there is a limited demand among the opulent classes. Protected industries, on the other hand, are not likely to succeed as foreign exporters. They cannot meet the manufacturers of free-trade countries in a neutral market. The higher the tariff they impose, the more jealously they protect themselves at home, the more difficult they will find it to compete with manufacturers, who have not been enervated by the relaxing atmosphere of protection.

A correspondent of the ' Times,' in a recent letter, gives a striking illustration of the fatal effect of protection in destroying a flourishing export trade. Thirty years ago, as he tells us, the Americans exported large quantities of goods to India and China. The trade was destroyed through the enhancement of cost resulting from the Morrill Tariff. With the return of peace the Americans resumed their efforts to gain a foreign outlet for cotton goods; but the artificial conditions, with which protection surrounded them, interposed such grave hindrances that for some years their annual export did not exceed from 20,000 to 30,000 packages.

Their destructive effect on an export trade.

The 'Saturday Review,' in criticising Messrs. Ellison's latest circular, remarks that, while the increased demand for cotton goods, from the natural growth of the population in France, Germany, Austria, Holland, Belgium, and Italy, has been supplied from native looms, our exports having fallen since 1860 from 1·1 lb. per head to 1 lb. per head, on the other hand those countries are not themselves exporters to any considerable extent.

The following extract from the 'Statist' gives the most recent figures relating to the export trade of Germany.

Export trade of Germany.

E

	1878	1877
	lbs.	lbs.
Cotton yarn . .	27,072,810	22,884,020
Woollen ,, . .	12,787,300	10,354,300
Linen ,, . .	4,720,050	5,242,380
Silk, dyed . .	1,075,030	560,780
Cotton stuff . .	31,116,580	27,069,150
Woollen ,, . .	31,491,350	29,982,810
Linen ,, . .	13,072,400	13,700,830
Silk ,, . .	5,244,910	4,651,130

The expansion of the export trade is ascribed, not to improved demand from outside for German goods, but *first* to the necessity of finding foreign markets because of depression in Germany, and *second* to the overwhelming quantities of cheap yarn poured into the country from England. According to the Berlin ' Börsen Zeitung,' German spinners are in several cases compelled to suspend their operations because of English competition. Plainly, then, German producers derived little benefit from their increased exports last year.

French and Italian exports to India.

An able advocate of the alarmist school, Mr. R. Raynsford Jackson, in an address delivered at Blackburn, in November 1878, on ' Our Chances of Foreign Competition,' spoke as follows :—' We are told that continental manufacturers have no chance against us. Well, but I find that before 1873 neither France nor Italy sent any goods to India. In 1873, France sent 185,000 yards, and last year she quadrupled it. Italy sent about 500,000 yards in 1873, which increased to 2,000,000 the next year; then it was reduced to 1,000,000, then it increased to 3,000,000, and last year it was 1,750,000; so that we find that the continental manufacturers are beginning a rivalry with us in India itself. Now in giving you these figures I do not want you to dwell upon the quantities. or upon their magnitude. There is nothing in those figures alarming to us ; but what is alarming is to see that the various nations of the world on all sides are at all events commencing an invasion of those markets, the possession of which is essential to our prosperity. If you review how our goods have been dispersed, where they have gone to, you will find that in 1870 our goods were exported to certain States in somewhere about the following proportions:—To India, China, and other Eastern markets we sent about 1,435,000,000 yards; to the continental States that manufacture and that protect their manufactures by heavy duties we sent 200,000,000 yards; to the United States we sent, if I recollect rightly, 106,000,000 yards ; and to the rest of the world—to the neutral markets—we sent 1,526,000 yards. If you come to 1877, you find that we have sent to the Eastern market 2,055,000,000 yards, or an increase of somewhere about 40 per cent.'

It seems scarcely reasonable to refer in terms of apprehension to the exportation to India of 740,000 yards from France, and 1,750,000 yards from Italy, at a time when we are ourselves exporting 2,055,000,000 yards to the East, and 342,000,000 yards to the Continent.

The establishment of cotton factories in India has been viewed with alarm, as threatening the British manufacturer with a new and formidable competition. The result, however, of the operations in India does not appear to have been of a very satisfactory character

The cotton factories in India.

to those directly concerned.   The following extract
from the 'Bombay Price Current' was published in the
'Statist' in March last:—'Our local spinning and
weaving companies are in a disastrous position; it is
currently reported that about one-third of those now
in existence are about to be wound up; two of them
during the week have been handed over to the tender
mercies of the Insolvent Court, and others must follow.
No doubt many of the mills now in a state of bankruptcy will be resuscitated. . . . But the lesson seems
plain that a " bankrupt " competition from the side of
Manchester soon kills off bankrupt competition in India.'

Exclusion of English goods from the United States.

The falling-off in the consumption in non-manufacturing countries is easily explained by the commercial depression in those countries, the result of
the damaged credit of their respective governments
and the cessation of foreign loans; but the most important market, from which we have been excluded, is
that of the United States, our exports to that country
having fallen off from 229,800,000 yards in 1860, to
47,400,000 in 1866–7.   We have been driven out of
the United States, not by the increased cost of our
productions, but by a tariff designedly prohibitory.

Reduced cost of production there.

The cost of production in the United States has, however, been materially reduced since the panic of 1873.
Wages have fallen.   It is stated in the 'Economist' of
July 1878, that 'for the first time in the history of
the United States, skilled labour only commands the
English scale of wages, and in some cases has fallen
even lower.'   Machinery has been improved; at every
stage of the manufacture economy has been carefully

studied. The following valuable details, showing the reductions in the cost of labour, were given by the 'Times' correspondent, from whom I have already quoted :—'In 1875 the average annual earning of females engaged in the cotton trade of Massachusetts was $199 currency (or about 37*l.*) gained by the labour of 238 days. The earning of males was $443 (or about 82*l.*) gained by the labour of 252 days. Two years later—in 1877—wages had fallen 9 per cent., and the working time had increased by 5 days. The working time in 1877 was therefore 243 days for females and 257 for males, and the wages earned were about 33*l.* and 75*l.* respectively, yielding an average, for the numbers actually employed, of 50*l.* 10*s.* for 249 days. The Massachusetts working day in all industries (we have no separate return for cotton) averages 10·21 hours for males and 10·49 for females. The English working day is 9½ hours. In Blackburn, where the operatives are reputedly of a superior class, the average weekly earning for male and female together, and counting two half-timers as one, is 19*s.*, which would yield 42*l.* 14*s.* for 249 working days of the American length. These *data* form a very imperfect basis of comparison, but they favour the conclusion that factory labour when calculated by a fixed period, as an hour, and not by a period of varying duration, as a day or week, will be found to cost about 20 per cent. more in America than in England.'

With reference to the advance in the productive capability of the American operative the same authority Productive capability of the gives the following details:—' In 1853 the average English production per weaver of 8¼ lb. shirting was 825 yards per week of 60 hours. In 1878 the working hours had fallen to 57, and the production had risen to 975 yards. An increased production of 23 per cent. is thus due to improvement in the processes of manufacture.

'In 1865 there were 24,151 persons employed in Massachusetts in the production of cotton goods, and they produced 175,000,000 yards. In 1875 the operatives numbered 60,176, and their product was 874,000,000 yards. The operatives had increased 150 per cent., and their products had increased 500 per cent.

'The increase of production due to improved methods was thus in England 23 per cent., and in Massachusetts 100 per cent. I do not, of course, suppose that the American manufacturer is in advance of his English rival to the extent of this difference, for I presume that he started upon the career of improvement from a lower platform. But a progress so greatly more rapid than ours will be admitted to cast much light on the change which has occurred in our relative positions.'

In England the work-people have succumbed to the pressure of hard times. The last two ill-advised strikes in Oldham have been followed by a reduction of 15 per cent. in wages, while in North-East Lancashire the reduction has amounted to 10 per cent.

An impetus has been given to the export trade of the United States through the reduced cost of production.

The shipments, which had been 12,000,000 yards in the United States. 1872, were 106,000,000 in 1877, and they still increase. The 'Economist' has given the values of cotton manufactures exported from the States in the year of the panic, and for the last two seasons :

1873	1876	1877
£	£	£
610,000	1,540,000	2,040,000

The following table is taken from the ' Statist : '

Exports from New York of Domestic Cotton Piece Goods.

Year	Yards
1878	86,856,191
1877	81,270,527
1876	62,329,914
1875	26,801,442
1874	13,283,827
1873	8,603,554

' From an aggregate value of 250,000*l.* in 1873, these exports advanced to 1,400,000*l.* in 1878. But the rate of increase in the export trade from New York was last year small, and with the profitless manufactures of Lancashire now to contend against, it will hardly continue.'

My own experience of the quality of the textiles Inferior quality of American textile fabrics. exported from the United States is unfavourable. When the 'Sunbeam' was at Valparaiso, a bale of dungaree was purchased, and the seamen were fitted out with new suits of working clothes. On the first occasion after we put to sea, when the hands were ordered aloft, the inferior quality of our American purchase was detected. The men descended to the deck in rags. English dungaree would have lasted for weeks, even months.

Taking a general view of the American export trade, it will be admitted that, while the percentage of increase is very considerable, yet the aggregate export is small, when compared with the trade of the United Kingdom. We exported in 1877 of cotton piece goods 3,837,821,000 yards, and in 1878 3,618,126,000 yards.

Insignificance of American compared with British exports. The comparative insignificance of the export trade from the United States is proved by the figures quoted by Professor Fawcett in his lecture on the present commercial depression. He gives the value of the manufacture of cotton exported from England at 67,640,000*l.* as against 1,540,000*l.* exported from the United States. The 'Statist' has published a table giving the export of piece goods and yarns to France, Germany, Holland, Belgium, Italy, and Austria. The quantities are given in millions of yards and pounds, for 1861 and for the last ten seasons, ending with September 30 in each year.

	Piece Goods	Goods	Yarn	Total	Equal in Cotton to	
	yards	lbs.	lbs.	lbs.	lbs.	bales
1861	284·1	56·8	113·6	170·4	191·7	470,250
1868–69	319·6	63·9	98·4	162·3	182·6	456,500
1869–70	260·2	52·0	85·6	137·6	154·8	387,000
1870–71	312·8	62·5	104·3	166·8	187·6	400,000
1871–72	379·2	75·8	101·9	177·7	199·9	499,750
1872–73	409·6	81·9	116·5	198·4	223·2	558,000
1873–74	387·7	77·5	106·6	184·1	207·1	517,750
1874–75	383·1	76·6	104·3	180·9	203·5	508,750
1875–76	367·8	73·5	108·7	182·2	205·0	512,500
1876–77	357·3	71·5	102·1	173·6	195·3	488,250
1877–78	332·7	66·5	89·2	155·7	175·1	437,750

These figures give our exportations to those countries only where we have to contend with heavy protectionist tariffs ; yet even to these comparatively limited markets for our goods the aggregate quantity of our exportation is forty-three and a half times as large as the entire exportation from the United States.

Indications are not wanting that the export trade of the United States has been to some extent inflated by the same fictitious system of credits and advances, which has been suffered to grow up with such mischievous consequences in many branches of the export trade of the United Kingdom, especially in our trade with the East. *Artificial stimulation.*

In a paper lately published in the 'Contemporary Review,' Mr. Henderson describes the system, pursued by the manufacturers of the United States, of disposing of goods, for which no market could be found at home, in Canada, at prices considerably below the current quotations in Boston and New York. This reckless sacrifice of manufactured goods at any price is called 'slaughtering,' and necessarily culminates in the bankruptcy of the vendors.

The 'Economist' sums up an exhaustive comparison of the condition and prospects of the cotton manufactures in the United States and Great Britain as follows: 'It seems not unlikely that American competition will be especially felt in our two leading industries—cotton and iron. In the first, the American manufacturer starts with a slight advantage in the cost of the raw material, the freight from the Southern plantations to the mills in New England being somewhat less than to Liverpool. This, however, is balanced by the superior fitness of our climate for spinning, owing to its humidity. The cost of working the machinery is *Conditions of competition.*

probably a far more important item. In New England
the mills are principally run by water power against
steam in Lancashire, and the relative price at which
this power is obtained will go far to decide which
country can manufacture cotton the cheapest. If the
decision is in favour of steam, the American factories
will have to be built in closer proximity to the coal
fields than at present.'

The de-
cline of
British
trade with
the East,

The falling off in the aggregate exports of British
cotton manufactures in the last two years is confined
to the trade with the East, and is mainly attributable,
as it has already been said, to the collapse of a certain number of commercial houses, which have been
engaged for years in carrying on an illegitimate trade.
Goods were purchased, not to meet a demand from
abroad, but in order to obtain temporary advances
from the Glasgow Bank and elsewhere. The most
extensive purchases were made from manufacturers,
with reckless disregard of the prices which consumers
might be willing to pay. The following table was
published in the 'Statist' in February last :

Exports of Cotton Piece Goods to the East.
[000's omitted.]

	1878		1877		Decrease in 1878	
	Quantities	Values	Quantities	Values	Quantities	Values
	yards	£	yards	£	yards	£
India, Ceylon, and Straits Settle-ments . .	1,295,400	14,082	1,446,500	15,973	151,100	1,891
China and Japan .	382,420	4,634	394,490	4,832	12,070	198
Java . . .	58,800	876	81,270	1,300	22,470	424
Total .	1,736,620	19,592	1,922,260	22,105	185,640	2,513

M. Leroy Beaulieu, in an article lately published in
the 'Economiste Français,' is at no pains to disguise

the feeling of satisfaction with which he views the failure of a number of commercial houses, which have been enabled, by means of a fictitious system of credit, to transact business on an enormous scale. He sees in the cessation of this unfair competition the surest means of restoring the trade with the East to a sound and wholesome condition.

From the point of view, from which the present writer has examined these questions, it is important to remark that the collapse of our Eastern trade has been caused not so much by the indolence and incapacity of the workmen as by the unprincipled and reckless administration of reckless merchants and pseudo-capitalists. I was at Edinburgh during the trial of the City of Glasgow Bank directors, and I shall not easily forget the melancholy spectacle presented by that row of hoary heads, awaiting their sentence of condemnation. I came away with the impression that the prisoners gave no external indication of the mental and moral qualities which should be sought for in men entrusted with many millions of deposits. Are the shareholders to blame for laxity in the appointment of directors? Are the salaries of the directors proportionate to their responsibilities? To employ both profitably and safely resources, computed by tens of millions sterling, is a task that should be entrusted only to men of the highest character and ability. It demands, in a high degree, both commercial experience and prescience. The market value of the services of competent men is considerably higher than the salaries generally awarded by narrow-minded shareholders to their most responsible officers.

[margin note: attributable to commercial and financial recklessness.]

Our pro-
ductive
power.

While the textile manufactures have grown in a more rapid ratio in foreign countries, in which they have been but recently established, we retain an undisputed ascendency in the aggregate extent of our industry. We possess thirty-nine and three-quarter million spindles, against a little more than thirty and three-quarter millions possessed by the United States, India, and the Continent of Europe. In other words, our potential producing power exceeds by one-fourth that of all our competitors combined.

Quality of
our textile
fabrics.

That we have lost nothing of our former excellence of workmanship was abundantly proved at the recent Exhibition in Paris. The 'Economist' concludes an able paper on the textile products exhibited with the re-assuring assertion that ' there can be no doubt about the sterling character of all the goods exhibited, and we may look in vain for any serious rivalry, as regards these productions, either in quality, colour, or finish.'

French
rivalry in
woollens.

The ' Economist' speaks in a less confident tone of the comparative excellence of our woollens. Here we are threatened with a serious competition by the French manufacturers. In the class of merinos, 'the technical power, which the French designer and weaver has obtained over these materials, and the perfection to which the dye and finish has, for years past, been brought, is a lesson, which the English manufacturer of mixed fabrics appears only now to have taken to heart ; whilst the French have for nearly three genera-tions systematically and continuously educated their fore-men weavers and dyers in the application of mechanical and chemical science to their special industries.'

I see no present indication that our textile indus- tries will be overcome by foreign competition. Our manufacturers have at their disposal an ample supply of cheap capital. Their industrial and administrative faculties are an inherited gift. They are not deficient in ingenuity, and they are enterprising to the point of rashness. During their past and present trials, the operatives have exhibited many admirable qualities. It is but natural that they should be found less docile and tractable in good times than in bad times, when labour is scarce than when it is superabundant. But they have been good workers, and on equal terms can still defy the world.

Mr. Raynsford Jackson, whose name has been so prominent in the recent trade disputes in Lancashire, in his speech at Blackburn, expressed a highly favourable opinion of the powers of the workmen. 'I take this opportunity of saying that, notwithstanding all that has passed, I still have confidence in our Lancashire operatives. I believe that they are right at heart. I believe they are hard-working, tractable, and intelligent. I believe that their confidence is easily won, and we have evidence that it can be easily abused. We have been placed in an extremely difficult position. You must recollect that we are face to face with a generation which has not seen much depression excepting during the American War, and that was regarded as an exceptional state of things which was borne with wonderful fortitude in these districts. We have not seen much of adversity in this generation, and our young people have grown up seeing improved machinery, increased occupation, growing prosperity, and a larger share of comfort in each succeeding period of years ; and when it was proposed that a change should be made which they looked upon as retrograding in those respects, and as calculated to take them backwards in what they no doubt regarded as the march of civilisation, they very readily believed those who told them that the proposal was gratuitous and unnecessary, and was rather intended as a blow at their trade organisations than as a result of the necessities of their employers. I am not surprised at all that the trade-union leaders should have thought it expedient to make the proposal they did.'

Importance of technical improvements.

Relying on the impartial opinion of Mr. Redgrave, and on the assertion so often repeated of foreign employers, that the labour at their command is inferior to our own, I do not accept it as proved that the English operatives have executed less work in proportion to their wages, than their Continental rivals. I see more ground for apprehension lest our master manufacturers should confine their attention too exclusively to the commercial aspects of their business. Quality, taste and design must not be regarded as matters of subordinate importance in comparison with mere cheapness. In mechanical ingenuity American manufacturers are our serious rivals. In taste and design we are hard pressed, perhaps not unfrequently surpassed, on the Continent.

Adulteration.

It has been said that we are losing our reputation as manufacturers by adulterating our cotton goods with a dressing of china clay. The practice has been resorted to by our rivals abroad; but we may wisely give heed to the warning of Sir Brooke Robertson and other consuls, and abandon the attempt to make trashy goods at impossible prices.

In the preceding pages it has been shown how our trade has fallen away from a state of expansion and inflation which it was impossible to maintain. We cannot claim a monopoly, but we ought to retain our share of the textile industry of the world. We have not escaped the almost universal depression of trade; but we must not despair of a return of prosperity.

CHAPTER IV.

THE IRON TRADE.

Losses in the iron trade.

THE depression in the iron trade may be tested, as in the case of the cotton trade, by the value of the shares in ironworks conducted on the joint-stock principle. Thirty-five companies were enumerated in the 'Statist,' which have suffered an average depreciation in the price of their shares of 46·5 per cent. as compared with the high quotations of 1873. The market value of their capital fell from 20,500,000*l.* in January 1874, to 11,085,000*l.* in May 1878. We must add to the loss from the depreciation of capital the loss sustained on almost every manufacturing operation, in order to obtain a full view of the injury the iron trade has sustained.

Scotch pig-iron.

The fall in the prices of Scotch pig-iron may be appreciated from the following figures, published by Messrs. Fallows of Liverpool :

Scotch Pig-Iron.

Year	Range of Prices			
	s.		*s.*	*d.*
1851	38	to	43	0 per ton
1802	40	,,	56	0 ,,
1868	51	,,	54	0 ,,
1873	101	,,	145	0 ,,
1877	51	,,	57	0 ,,
Present time			47	3 ,,

The fluctuations in the prices of pig-iron during 1878 were given in detail in an article which appeared in 'Engineering' in February last : 'Influenced occasionally by speculative buying, and by political events at home, on the Continent, and in India, the price fluctuated now and then during the spring and summer, but always with a more or less declining tendency till the beginning of October, when the banking crisis burst out, bringing with it a sudden decline to 43*s.* 6*d.*, from which there was subsequently an improvement to 45*s.* 4½*d.*, which was paid on the 8th of October. That advance, however, was not maintained, and by the 26th of November 42*s.* 3*d.* was accepted, which was the lowest price touched during the past twenty-six years. From that point there was a little rallying, and the year closed with the price standing at 43*s.* 6*d.*, the average over the year being 48*s.* 5*d.* as compared with 54*s.* 4*d.* for the previous year, to which it had declined from the year 1873, when the average price was 117*s.* 3*d.*, or almost double what it was only two years previously. And here we may mention that over the nine years, 1862 to 1871, the yearly average never rose higher than 60*s.* 6*d.* per ton (1866), nor fell lower than 52*s.* 9*d.* (1868).'

The average price of rails, plates, bars, and angle iron, fell from 11*l.* 18*s.* 11*d.* per ton in 1874, to 6*l.* 15*s.* per ton in 1877. The scale of prices is now lower than in any year since 1851.

Let us endeavour to ascertain the cause of these remarkable fluctuations. In 1871, at the close of the Franco-German War, an extensive and sudden demand

Recent fluctuations of prices.

Their causes.

arose for machinery and railway material both on the Continent and in America. The result was shown by Mr. Lowthian Bell in his report on the Exhibition at Philadelphia. 'In pig-iron,' he says, 'an increased production of about 664,000 tons in 1871 enabled this country to keep pace with the additional demand on its resources, and prices remained stationary. The following year, however, with a still further rise in the make of about 110,000 tons, the supply was in deficit; and small as this shortcoming may have been, it sufficed to cause a rapid rise in value, prices having reached 122s. 6d. in August. In 1873 the quotations for four months averaged 127s. 6d., the average for the whole year being 115s. It is needless to point out the immense inducement to manufacturers to strain every effort to keep up their output; nevertheless the quantity made fell off to the extent of 175,000 tons. This diminution was chiefly due to the difficulty of obtaining raw materials. Coke, which in 1870 could be had for 12s. or 13s. per ton, commanded as high a price as 40s. to 42s. in 1873.'

Supply and demand.

The course of prices in the iron trade affords an illustration of the disproportionate enhancement in the price which invariably results from a deficiency in the supply of an article of primary necessity. When the demand for an article exceeds the supply, competition takes place on the side of buyers, and the value rises, not, however, in the ratio of the deficiency, but in a ratio which varies according as the article in question is in a greater or lesser degree an article of necessity. 'If there be a deficiency,' says Mr. Mill, 'in a necessity of life, which, rather than resign, people are willing to pay for at any price, a deficiency of one-third may raise the price to double, triple, or quadruple its former amount. The price of corn, in the era preceding the repeal of the corn laws, has risen, according to Tooke, from 100 to 200 per cent., when the utmost computed deficiency of the crops has not been more than one-fourth or one-third below the average. The rise in price ceases when the competition of buyers ceases—in other words, at the point which equalises the demand and the supply.'

As in the case of cotton, so in the coal and iron trades, high prices have led to excessive production. The continued increase in the output of coal is a most remarkable phenomenon in our recent commercial history. The following details are taken from an article published in the ' Times ' of January 3, 1879. In 1873 the production of coal was 3,519,000 tons more than that of 1872. This was a much smaller increase than that of 1872 over 1871, which amounted to 6,145,000 tons. In 1874 the total production of coal showed a decrease of 1,948,000 tons. It was generally regarded as the inevitable reaction from the inflation of the two previous years. Hence, when the returns of 1875 exhibited an increase, concurrently with intensified weakness in other industries, of 6,799,000 tons in the output of coal, it was deemed a result altogether outside the regular sequence of events. The output of 1876 exhibited a yet further increase of 1,477,000 tons on the output of 1875. The latter year, as everybody knows, was disastrous.

Output of coal.

'It was obvious that an industry which in the face of such adverse conditions could so greatly extend its productiveness must be possessed of an uncommon vigour. Probably, however, even the greatest optimist was unprepared to find that in 1877, which repeated, with compound interest, the direful disasters of 1876, the coal trade would be more productive than in the latter year. And yet such has been the case. The output of coal in 1877 was actually 1,266,000 tons more than in 1876. and this, too, in the face of a diminished export trade to the extent of 1,059,000 tons!'

The transition from iron to steel.

In the same able paper, attention is very properly directed to the diminished demand for coal, through the general substitution of steel for iron.

'This transition from iron to steel involves issues that are not yet adequately understood. Steel rails are produced with one-fourth the fuel and one-third the labour required in the production of iron. At some works, indeed, where the pig metal is run direct from the blast furnaces into the Bessemer converters—as at the Cleveland, Barrow, and Dowlais Works in England, and at the St. Chamond and Seraing Works abroad—

Its effect on the coal trade.

there is practically no fuel used at all. When we add that from three to four tons of coal are required to produce a ton of iron rails, it will at once be observed that the transition from iron to steel has been concurrent with an enormous economy of fuel, and consequently accompanied by a very considerable decline in the quantity of coal used for metallurgical purposes. The exact volume of this decline is not easily determined, because we have not access to statistics of the

quantities of malleable iron produced in the United
Kingdom from year to year. If, however, we calculate,
as did the Commissioners appointed to inquire into the
coal famine, that 20,170,000 tons of coal were used in
the conversion of pig into rolled iron in 1873, we shall
be safe in assuming that since that year the quantity
has declined by nearly one-half, and is now on the eve
of a much greater decline. Within the next two or
three years iron rails, by universal consent, will be
known only as things of the past. It is very probable
that iron plates for boiler and ship-building purposes
will share the same fate. In that event the quantity of
coal used for the manufacture of rolled iron will be
a mere fraction of what it has been, and this is a
contingency which coalowners—particularly in the
North of England, where nearly one-half the whole of
the coal hitherto raised has been applied to metallurgic
uses—can hardly contemplate without serious apprehension.'

'The increase in the production of fuel, simulta- Idle fur-
neously with a diminution in the requirements of the naces.
industry in which the chief consumption takes place,
is a remarkable circumstance. The wide interval, by
which the productive capacity of the blast and puddling
furnaces of the United Kingdom exceeds the demand
for iron, may be measured by the following statistics,
extracted from the columns of the 'Engineer.' In
1877 only 489 furnaces were in blast out of 974 then
in existence in the United Kingdom. If we take the
cost of a blast furnace at 10,000*l.*, we have a capital
of 4,850,000*l.* lying unproductive. The number of

puddling furnaces at the same date was 7,159, and, if each furnace were assumed capable of producing 600 tons a week, their aggregate capacity would be 4,295,000 tons. The total product of the mills and forges of the country in 1877 did not exceed 1,500,000 tons. The difference between the consumption of iron and the unused capacity of production shows with what imprudent haste the iron industry had been developed.

Reduced cost of manufacture.

Under the stimulus of a keen competition both at home and abroad, manufacturers have continually striven to improve their machinery and to cheapen production. They have succeeded so well that a ton of iron can now be puddled for half the fuel formerly required, while steel rails are now produced at one-third the price of 1873—prices now ranging from 6*l*. 1*s*. to 6*l*. 5*s*., whereas four years ago 18*l*. 10*s*. was the ruling quotation. North-country pig-iron in the same period has fallen from 7*l*. 5*s*. to 2*l*. 1*s*. While the consumer has been benefited by the fall in prices, thousands of men have been thrown out of employment. It is obvious that the demand for iron is not capable of being increased indefinitely, however low the price may fall. On the contrary, the more general use of steel must tend to limit the demand. Mr. T. E. Harrison believes that good steel rails will last three times as long as the ordinary rails of iron. Many authorities estimate their endurance as six times, and some even nine times, longer than that of iron rails. The trade may be compensated for the diminished demand, consequent on the superior durability of the

Demand limited by greater durability.

article, by its more extended use. The Admiralty have already used the admirable quality of steel prepared by the Siemens process for the large and swift vessels of the 'Iris' class. The makers of iron may find their consolation in the increasing consumption of that metal as a substitute for timber. For railway sleepers, it appears highly probable that iron will be largely employed.

It is satisfactory to know that, as producers of steel at moderate prices, our own manufacturers have nothing to fear from foreign competition. The fact that our ironmasters are fellow-sufferers with the makers of iron in every iron-making country is a poor consolation ; but it supplies an argument in answer to those, who contend that our trade has been ruined by the high price of British as compared with continental labour. If we had passed through a crisis in the United Kingdom, from which other countries had escaped, we might with reason indulge in grave misgivings. It is certain, however, that the pecuniary embarrassments of foreign countries have been at least as extensive as our own. *Alleged foreign rivalry.*

The writer of an able article in 'Iron' remarks : 'It must be confessed that the general " shrinkage " of English trade since 1875 would inspire misgivings as to the future of this country were it not obvious that every other nation is in an equally bad position. France, the most favourably situated of all—thanks to her wine production, which alone more than pays her enormous budget, and her wealth of corn and oil—is yet suffering from a falling off in her manufactures. *The depression shared abroad.*

Neither the iron nor coal trade of France is in a healthy condition, and the manufacturers of textile fabrics are complaining sadly of the hardness of the times. Belgium is almost as badly off as France, and industrial Germany is in an evil case indeed, while the depression of trade in the United States has brought about a revulsion of feeling in favour of free trade. It is a poor consolation in affliction to reflect that we are no whit worse off than other people, but it at any rate helps to the conviction that we have no special and peculiar crime to lay to our charge.'

Statistics of the chief producing countries.   The following figures, showing the relative progress and retrogression of the iron trade in the chief iron-making countries, are taken from a circular recently issued by Messrs. Fallows :

Production of Pig Iron.

	1867	1873	Increase over 1867	1877
	Tons	Tons	Per cent.	Tons
Great Britain .	4,761,023	6,566,451	38	6,608,664 [1]
United States .	1,461,626	2,868,278	96½	2,314,585 [2]
Germany . .	987,163	2,174,058	120	1,566,600 [2]
France . .	1,229,044	1,366,971	11½	1,250,394 [2]
Belgium . .	423,069	607,373	43½	425,200 [2]
Total	8,861,925	13,583,131		12,165,443
	Total increase, 53¼ per cent.			

While the production of other countries has fallen off considerably between 1873 and 1877, the production of the United Kingdom has been well sustained.

[1] Increase since 1873 in Great Britain, ¾ per cent.

[2] Decrease since 1873: United States, 10 per cent.; Germany, 28 per cent.; France, 8½ per cent.; Belgium, 30 per cent.

The maximum production was 6,741,929 tons in 1872, and the total production in 1878 may be estimated at about 6,300,000 tons. Even in the face of unexampled depression, stocks have not increased to any great extent.

In comparing our exports for 1878 with those of 1868, we find that the falling away is confined to the trade with the United States, from which we have been shut out by a prohibitory tariff. Comparison with the year 1872 shows an immense loss in the American trade. There is also a reduction in the exports to Germany, which had been unduly expanded at the earlier date by the inflation which followed on the Franco-Prussian war. The dullness in the trade with other countries was caused by the cessation of the foreign loans. In no instance was the decay of trade attributable to the excessive price of British labour, apart from other and more potent causes of collapse. The following table, prepared by Messrs. Fallows, gives the principal changes in the last decade :

Diminution of our export trade.

Total Exports from United Kingdom of Iron, Steel, and Tin Plates to the following Countries, in 1868, 1872, and 1878.

	1868	1872	1878
	Tons	Tons	Tons
United States . . .	502,000	888,000	157,000
Germany and Holland .	146,000	816,000	551,000
India	185,000	69,000	210,000
Russia . . .	126,000	137,000	85,000
British North America .	64,000	165,000	101,000
Australia . . .	54,000	94,000	205,000
France . . .	107,000	108,000	112,000
Other countries . .	854,000	1,102,000	874,000
Total	2,041,000	3,382,000	2,299,000

Reduced production of France;   In France, the profit realised in the great establishment of Creusot has fallen below the average maintained for several years. The value of the work turned out in 1874–5 was 3,256,000*l.*; it was reduced to 2,185,000*l.* in 1876–7. Nearly every undertaking of a similar character, formed since 1870, has proved a failure.

of Austria;   The activity, exhibited in railway construction in Austria between 1870 and 1873, has completely subsided.

of Germany.   In North Germany, between 1875 and 1876, the great works of Herr Krupp were reduced from 12,000 to 9,000 hands. The general condition of the trade may be gathered from a statement republished in 'Iron,' and prepared by the German Iron and Steel Trades Association. It shows the condition of the principal limited liability works in the years 1874, 1875, and 1876. The balance-sheets of forty-five iron works and fifty iron foundries were analysed. The profits of the iron works which paid a dividend amounted to 176,296*l.*, while the losses of those which paid no dividend amounted to 1,013,305*l.* In the foundries the profits amounted to 229,487*l.*, and the total losses to 454,998*l.* The capital invested in these works was 21,999,985*l.*, and the total profit on this large amount was only 405,783*l.*, against losses amounting to 1,468,283*l.* In April 1873, 95,035 workmen were in employment; in April 1877 only 60,624; and whereas, in April 1873, 371,171*l.* was distributed in wages, the amount distributed in April 1877 was 192,793*l.*

In Berlin in 1877 the number of persons employed in the engine factories was reduced by 2,362 men, a reduction of 14·6 per cent. on the numbers employed in the previous year.

The ' Times ' stated that between April 1873, and April 1877, the number of workmen employed by twenty-two of the principal companies engaged in the iron trade, excluding Krupp, fell from 27,700 to 14,600. Within the same period, the value of the stock of the Phœnix Company fell from 16,200,000 marks to 4,860,000 marks; of the Hörde Company from 15,000,000 marks to 3,210,000 marks; of the Bochum Company from 15,000,000 marks to 3,375,000 marks; of the Dortmund Union Company from 41,400,000 marks to 2,070,000 marks; and of the Donnersmarkhütte Company from 18,000,000 marks to 3,906,000 marks. Of thirty-two companies, whose united capital amounted to 15,600,000*l.*, only six showed any dividend whatever for the year 1876, and the aggregate accounts published for that period showed a balance of loss on the year's operations of 359,000*l.* as compared with a loss of 195,000*l.* for the previous year. *Losses of German manufacturers.*

The arguments urged by the British Iron Trade Association against the proposed protective duties in Germany tend to show that the trade of that country has suffered as much from over-production as our own. The increased price of iron and coal, in many cases as much as, or more than, 100 per cent., led to an immense increase in the number of iron and steel works, and, besides this, all the works then in operation were largely *Over-production in Germany.*

extended, causing expenses that could only be covered in the event of prices remaining high and steady. The report of the Cologne Chamber of Commerce for 1876 points out that old firms with good names, that had paid the highest dividends to their shareholders for years previously, found themselves placed in a false position by increasing their capital to three times its original amount.

Exportation from Germany.   The increased exportation of iron from Germany was stated by the Berlin ' Börsen Zeitung ' to be not really a sign of the approach of better times, but of the utter prostration of the German iron industries. German ironmasters were selling their products abroad for what they would fetch, because there was absolutely no demand at home. So soon as prices improved, the German trade would again be swamped by an enormous influx of British iron.

Our exports thither.   The following is a table showing the fluctuations in the British exportations of iron to Germany :

Exports to Germany.

Year	Pig-Iron	Bar, Angle, Rod, and Bolt Iron	Railroad Iron	Hoops, Sheets, and Plates	Other Iron
	Tons	Tons	Tons	Tons	Tons
1870	126,178	11,511	52,660	9,837	17,035
1871	203,353	15,093	50,288	14,446	23,204
1872	310,597	17,799	50,105	16,034	28,007
1873	260,703	26,842	40,060	26,010	28,090
1874	177,037	7,078	7,177	10,714	13,929
1875	255,370	7,199	4,147	12,173	20,009
1876	245,042	5,127	14,171	12,232	21,844
1877	234,261	5,540	23,306	9,498	12,405

Quality of French   In France the iron and hardware trades are in the hands of a few wealthy monopolists, who have won

deserved honour by their strenuous efforts to improve
the quality of their productions. The Creusot works
employ 8,000 men. They are renowned for the excellence of their workmanship. In certain articles
they are at least equal to our best efforts, and they
have not suffered their energy to be relaxed by the
protective duty of 30 per cent., which the revised
Tariff still gives them. In November last I saw the
huge ironclad, the ' Italia,' in construction at Castella-
mare. All the armour plating and the steel frames,
which were being worked up into the ship, had been
supplied from Creusot. The marine engine exhibited
by the same establishment in Paris, and several specimens of their forgings and castings, excited the un-
reserved admiration of the most competent critics.

In order to make a fair comparison of the relative French
progress of the mechanical trades in England and ture thirty
France, the backward state of those industries on the years ago.
Continent thirty years ago must be taken into consideration. When railways were introduced into France in
1842, the resources of that country were so limited
that it became necessary for the English capitalists,
who had undertaken the construction of the railway
from Paris to Rouen, to establish works at Sotteville, in
the vicinity of Rouen, for the construction of the
locomotives and other rolling stock required. English
materials were used, and English workmen were almost
exclusively employed. The French labourers, employed by the contractors for the Paris and Rouen
Railway, used wooden spades and huge barrows of
antiquated shape. The iron shovel and pick-axe, and

an improved form of barrow, were introduced by the English navvies.

This state of things was not likely to continue. The brilliant genius of the French nation, and their superior theoretical instruction, ensured success to their mechanical industry so soon as the introduction of the iron roads created a continuous and growing demand for railway material. The low point from which mechanical industry took its rise makes the relative progress appear more considerable than with us, although, in point of fact, the actual increase in the trade of the United Kingdom is incomparably greater than that of any European country.

Export trade from France and England. The following comparative figures, relating to the export trade from France and England, are taken from the 'Statistical Abstract:'

Value of Metal Wares exported from France.

								Francs
1871	.	.	.	.	.	.	.	42,000,000
1872	.	.	.	.	.	.	.	91,200,000
1873	.	.	.	.	.	.	.	99,300,000
1874	.	.	.	.	.	.	.	98,600,000
1875	.	.	.	.	.	.	.	70,600,000
1876	.	.	.	.	.	.	.	72,000,000
1877	.	.	.	.	.	.	.	58,300,000

The declared values of the exports of the United Kingdom are given in pounds sterling.

	1871 £	1872 £	1873 £	1874 £	1875 £	1876 £	1877 £
Machinery:							
Steam engines	2,064,004	2,594,996	2,927,617	3,255,685	2,031,333	1,930,117	2,018,804
Of other sorts	3,902,037	5,006,110	7,002,312	6,535,229	6,427,314	5,271,309	4,704,004
Metals:							
Iron, old, for re-manufacture	672,096	656,262	390,522	245,381	102,837	95,977	100,788
„ pig and puddled	3,229,408	6,712,579	7,118,037	3,673,734	3,449,916	2,842,434	2,528,655
„ bar, angle, bolt, and rod	2,921,777	3,632,818	3,755,980	3,054,547	2,725,907	1,045,445	1,928,103
„ railroad, of all sorts	8,084,019	10,225,492	10,418,852	9,638,236	5,453,836	3,700,105	3,868,106
Iron wire	446,150	672,914	632,470	760,927	780,037	731,148	752,278
„ hoops, sheet and boiler plates	2,309,203	3,414,906	3,722,880	2,975,409	3,304,148	2,853,621	2,732,313
„ tinned plates	2,900,625	3,806,973	3,953,042	3,714,810	3,686,607	2,801,693	3,033,126
„ cast or wrought, and all other manufactures	3,538,364	4,772,304	5,478,750	5,122,588	4,342,492	4,041,418	3,045,061
„ steel, unwrought	1,198,428	1,478,737	1,462,867	1,203,719	1,073,733	878,412	807,850
„ manufactures of steel, or of steel and iron combined	682,855	623,122	728,831	791,905	827,758	757,167	717,035
Total of iron and steel	26,124,134	35,996,167	37,731,239	31,190,256	25,747,271	20,737,410	20,113,915

The crisis in Belgium.

Belgium has passed through a crisis in the iron and coal trade, not less serious than that experienced in Germany. According to Professor Neumann-Spellart, 55 per cent. of the furnaces in the United Kingdom were in blast, as against 33 per cent. in Belgium. The shares of Cockerill & Company, the largest and most successful establishment in the country, were quoted at 1,550 francs in 1873 and 700 francs in 1876. Comparing 1875-6 and 1877, we find a great reduction in the export of iron, and the business actually transacted has been done at unremunerative prices.

Belgian competition:

Our recent experiences prove that, for the cheaper descriptions of manufactured iron, Belgian is more formidable than French competition. According to Mr. Saville Lumley : 'Of the total amount of manufactured iron exported, 25,889 tons were imported by Great Britain, an increase of 9,579 tons on 1876. The exports to Great Britain consisted, as before, of merchant iron-girders and beams, accounting for 18,000 tons, while 1,495 tons were sent in the shape of plates and sheets, and 1,900 tons were iron rails.'

In 1877 Belgium imported 81,300 tons of pig-iron from Great Britain, and sent back in return 52,061 tons of merchant iron. English firms, who are themselves iron manufacturers, have used Belgian girders in the erection of new fitting shops, paying 10s. per ton less than for English iron. This was actually done, according to a statement in the 'Engineer,' by the 'Bowling' Company.

its extent.

A comparison, however, of the exports of the two countries would be sufficient to show that the success

achieved by the Belgian manufacturers in certain
special branches can have produced no sensible effect
on the industry of the United Kingdom as a whole.
The total value of the exports of iron and steel from
Belgium in 1874 was 60,353,000 francs; the value of
British exports of iron and steel for the same year was
31,190,000*l*. In 1876 the Belgian exports had fallen
to 45,789,000 francs; those of the United Kingdom to
20,737,000*l*. The following figures are from Messrs.
Fallows' circular:

	1873	1875	1876	1877
	Tons	Tons	Tons	Tons
Total exports of pig, rail, bars, plates, and sheets, hardware castings, &c. . . .	230,718	222,095	204,263	213,716
(Of which to United Kingdom)	—	33,792	36,752	52,622

Belgian industry has suffered severely from the
general depression, the falling off having been quite as
conspicuous in the trade carried on with our own
country as in other branches. The Belgian exportations
of iron, as officially reported, were as follows :—

Exports from Belgium, 1872-7.

	Tons	Value
		£
1872	210,000	2,087,000
1873	182,000	2,266,280
1874	227,000	2,414,120
1875	183,000	1,074,060
1876	106,000	1,811,560
1877	174,000	1,903,480

The following remarks on the iron trade are taken
from Mr. Saville Lumley's report: 'During the Franco-
German war, the iron trade in Belgium was excessively
brisk; but when that war ceased, and those countries

Progress of the depression there.

began to make for themselves, the stocks accumulated, and from that time to the present over-production has made itself felt. By the end of 1876, only 31 furnaces were in blast, 11 fresh ones having been blown out during the year. The value of pig-iron produced has fallen from 2,809,929*l.* in 1873, to 1,325,724*l.* in 1876. Nearly all the native iron ore is obtained from the province of Namur; and the output fell from 628,151 tons in 1865 to 175,799 in 1876. The production of manufactured iron in 1876 was 369,560 tons, a decrease of 66,680 tons from that of the previous year, and the value of this iron was 2,677,192*l.*, or 1,000,000*l.* less. In Liége, the principal place for iron rails, the rail trade has decreased from 25 per cent. of the total production to 8 per cent. ; but of course the displacement of iron rails by steel has much to do with this. Of wrought iron, 17,576 tons were produced in 1876, of the value of 229,520*l.*, being a decrease of 2,864 tons and 79,473*l.* as compared with 1875.'

Trade of 1876 compared with 1873.

Further information on the same subject is contained in the subjoined extract from the 'Glasgow Herald : '—' The iron industry of Belgium, bad in 1875, became worse in 1876. The numbers of blast furnaces, foundries, and ironworks were further reduced, while both the quantity and value of pig-iron, castings, rod, bar, and railway iron, and general hardware, declined in still larger proportion. But the altered position of the trade in 1876 will be better understood by a comparision between the results of that year and those of 1873. In the latter the production of pig-iron was 607,373 tons, and the value 2,809,929*l.*; whereas in 1876 the

figures were 490,508 tons and 1,325,724*l.* respectively,
a reduction in quantity of 19 per cent., and in value of
52¾ per cent.—indicating not only a most serious
decline in the volume of trade, but a much more
serious decline in profit. In regard to manufactured
iron—sheets, plates, bars, rods, and rails—the figures
are quite as remarkable, the production of 1873 being
480,374 tons, valued at 5,573,002*l.*, while that of 1876
was 369,560 tons, valued at 2,677,192*l.*, a reduction in
quantity equal to 23 per cent., and in value to ·52 per
cent. In articles of more elaborate workmanship, such
as ordnance, small arms, and general hardware, the
figures tell the same story of falling trade and vanishing
profits. In 1873 the aggregate production amounted
to 23,058 tons, and in 1876 to 17,576 tons, a reduction of 23¾ per cent., the value in the respective years
being 428,020*l.* and 229,520*l.*, or a reduction of 46¼
per cent.'

While the prospects in Belgium are discouraging,
the 'Economist,' in the review of the trade of 1878,
gives a brighter picture of the posture of affairs, especially in Durham. The substitution of mechanical
power for manual labour in the steel rail manufacture,
and for the old process of puddling, gives reason to
hope that the British iron industry will hold its own
against foreign competition.

In a French trade journal, the 'Bulletin of the
Ironmasters' Committee,' we find the following statement of the exports of iron and steel from France,
Belgium, and England during 1877 and 1876. This
statement showed the respective exports to have been:

Exports of
iron and
steel from
France,
Belgium,
and Eng-
land.

France (January to August).

	1877 Tons	1876 Tons
Iron and steel, all kinds .	112,861	139,604 − 26,743 = 19 per cent.

Belgium (January to July)

	1877 Tons	1876 Tons
Pig iron	6,459	6,386
Wrought iron . .	59,528	56,154
Sheet iron . . .	9,655	11,624
Rails	25,400	31,757
Total . . .	101,132	105,921 − 4,789 = 4½ per cent.

England (January to August).

	1877 Tons	1876 Tons
Pig iron	582,962	575,406
Bars, &c. . . .	169,118	141,614
Cast or wrought . .	171,776	169,588
Rails	323,628	274,233
Other kinds . . .	303,391	277,063
Total . . .	1,550,875	1,437,904 + 112,971 = 7 per cent.

It is evident that the iron-makers in foreign countries, from which we were threatened with the most
serious competition, had not been gaining ground on
the manufacturers of this country.

American rivalry in tools and machinery.   While Belgium has proved its ability to compete
with the United Kingdom in the cheap descriptions of
iron employed for building purposes, the United States
have shown themselves formidable competitors in the
production of edged tools and some kinds of machinery.
They exhibited admirable cutlery at Philadelphia.
They have sent large quantities of hardware to
Australia, and the Baldwin Company is said to have
made an offer to supply a locomotive for 1,000*l.* less
than the cost of an English engine.   I cannot believe

that our manufacturers will suffer themselves to be beaten in the production of tools or locomotives. The competition they at present experience must be ascribed to the superior ingenuity of the American manufacturers, in producing light and well-shaped tools at a cheap rate by machinery, rather than to any advantage which they enjoy in the cost of labour. The comparative insignificance of the export trade in iron from the United States is conclusively established by the figures lately published by Mr. Fallows : Exports of iron from the United States.

Exports from the United States.

	1873	1874	1876	1877
	Tons	Tons	Tons	Tons
Pig iron . . .	10,013	16,039	3,397	6,864
Bar iron . . .	367	4,717	3,020	2,642
Railroad iron . .	375	1,257	3,130	6,507

We have an important contribution, to what may be described as the pessimist literature on foreign competition, in the exhaustive report by Mr. Harris Gastrell on the iron trade of the United States. It was prepared by that gentleman when holding the appointment of Secretary of Legation at Washington. He gives a general comparison of the iron manufacture in Great Britain and the United States in the following passage : Mr. Gastrell's comparative view of American and British manufacture.

' If one takes a general view of the States as producers of iron and steel, there are to be discovered several disadvantages as compared with a more compact and an older country like England. The higher price of labour, the higher rates of interest, the smaller accumulation of capital, the lesser period of manufacturing activity, are the chief of these, and need only to be

mentioned.   The iron and steel industries are, out of
Pennsylvania, at their beginning, except in a few large
districts ; and nascent industries are always at a disadvantage.   Moreover, the manufacturing population is,
under such circumstances, so to speak, sporadic, and
the evils of shifting labour are doubly felt ; whereas in
Pennsylvania and the large centres of manufacture
there is a trained and experienced manufacturing population.   Against such disadvantages, however, the
United States have an important advantage over an
older country like England.   America has no " past "
in manufacturing.   There are no honoured ruts to up-
set the honest inventor.   If a man makes a suggestion,
it is readily tried ; and, if the theory fail in practice,
his superiors think no worse of him.   He does not lose
his place ; but he tries again, and generally does better
the next time.   In England it used not to be uncommon to treat a man of suggestions as unpractical, and
failure in one suggestion would have lost him his place
and lost to him any future employment.   It is true
that there is a danger of having the manufacturing
prospects spoiled by trusting too much to what are
expressively called the " high-heeled " men of ideas ;
but " high-heelism " occurs more in costly construction
than in suggestive invention.   The general outcome of
the readiness to try suggestions, and the respect for
men of ideas, is, however, a decided advantage in
favour of the United States.   Hence the Americans
are repeatedly getting a good start in saving labour and
improving processes and machinery.   A new suggestion is immediately inquired into, and, if it looks prac-

tical, is forthwith tried, and, in case of success, forthwith applied. The utilisation of the waste heat of the blast and other furnaces, the Burden Rotary Squeezer, the three high rolls, the nail, screw, and horse-shoe machines, the improvements on the Bessemer plant, and many other equally important and less important improvements, testify to the practical manner in which the United States have successfully striven to overcome disadvantages by intelligently avoiding the ruts of the past. Indeed, it is often affirmed on this side of the Atlantic that " England uses to-day in many of her manufactures tools and machinery inferior to American inventions which meet similar requirements." '

It seemed to me very important to ascertain how far Mr. Harris Gastrell's criticisms were confirmed by men practically acquainted not only with the manufacture of iron, but with the ironworks in both countries. I accordingly consulted Mr. Lowthian Bell on this subject, and received from him the following interesting communication in answer to my inquiries :

Mr. Lowthian Bell's report.

' In 1874, the date of Mr. Gastrell's report, the wages paid to all classes of men at the converters in America were much higher than those now prevalent there. In fact, at the same works, between my first and last visits to the United States, the difference is exactly 33 per cent. I have compared the cost for labour on this branch with that recently given me from a work in Great Britain, and there is a trifling difference on the ton of ingots in favour of this country at the present time.

' Mr. Gastrell mentions the quantity of steel made at

one blow as 5·3 tons. This week I saw in an English steel work a heat of 7·6 tons. I have, I think, in some of my reports, admitted that up to 1876 the American steel-makers, having laid down their Bessemer works with the light of our experience, were perhaps in advance of the older works in Great Britain.

‘ I challenge any steel-maker, British or foreign, to show a plant superior, or even equal, to that recently erected by Mr. Richards for Bolckow & Vaughan, near Middlesborough.

‘ I do not remember a single work in the United States where the pig-iron, direct from the blast furnace, is taken to the converter in the fluid state. In Great Britain this is now considered indispensable to proper economy.

‘ At the present moment Bessemer pig-iron is worth 60*s.* to 65*s.* per ton, and rails have been sold at less than 5*l.* 10*s.* at works.

‘ *Iron Rails.*

‘ In an iron rail mill, the cost of labour could bear no comparison with ours in point of economy, owing to the extravagant rates paid to puddlers. The other branches were also highly paid, but not to the same extent. In 1874 I estimated the difference to be one half higher than our own.

‘ Since that time puddlers’ wages have been greatly reduced in the United States. The average in 1874 was about 22*s.* In 1876, at Reading, U.S., it was only 12*s.*, and is probably lower now.

'Very dear-wages usually mean that the regular men engaged in the operation demand more help than when more moderate rates are paid.

'The high cost of wages on a ton of rails, viz. $23·05 per ton, confirms me in an opinion formerly expressed that on the iron rail mills of the United States there is not the slightest proof of any superiority. Indeed I should say, in point of general efficiency and economy, we were far in advance. Iron rails with pig-iron at 40s. would scarcely bring more than 5l. 10s. here at present leaving only 3l. 10s. for manufacturing. This includes coal, stoves, &c., whereas Mr. Gastrell mentions nearly 4l. 10s. for labour alone.

' Blast Furnaces.

'I have looked over various memoranda, and I consider in point of arrangement no nation in the world can excel the best constructed works at Middlesborough.

'I would invite you to go and inspect ours at Port Clarence. The railway company's locomotives travel over our works on elevated railways 40 or 50 feet high. You may assume five tons of raw material are consumed for every ton of iron made, and when we are at full work our daily make is equal to about 750 tons, equal to 3,750 tons of coke, to be received every day, Sundays included.

'The whole of this is received into bunkers, or into kilns for calcining, of such a construction that not one ounce is lifted by a shovel, the whole sliding or dropping into the charging wagons by gravitation.

'I much question whether, looking at the weight of material we have to deal with, there is any work in the world where the labour is more economised.

'The same facilities for working are to be found in other works in our neighbourhood.'

Stimulating effect of foreign competition.

.The occasional pressure of foreign competition is not to be regretted. The writer in 'Engineering' on the Scotch iron trade, from whom I have already quoted, rests his hopes of a future improvement in the trade on the stimulus derived from the pressure of competition in that country. 'It is interesting,' he says, 'to know that the weekly make per furnace rose during the year 1878 to an average of 192 tons, whereas in the year immediately preceding it. was 183 tons per furnace, thus showing an increase of 9 tons per furnace per week, which was doubtless the result of larger furnaces being brought into use in some instances, and of improved methods of working the furnaces generally.

Prospects of the Scotch trade.

'It cannot be said that the prospects of the Scotch pig-iron trade are at the present in any way encouraging; still there are facts from which encouragement may be taken. Prices are lower now than they have been any time during the last twenty-six years; the most rigorous economy has been enforced upon the ironmasters by the dulness of times; the latest scientific improvements have been applied in the construction and remodelling of the furnaces; the railway companies have agreed to make concessions in the carriage rates on the.raw materials for making pig-iron; and labour, which was so arbitrary in its demands, has been brought to feel the necessity of being more reasonable. Combined, these elements have greatly reduced the cost of production, which will enable the Scotch ironmasters more successfully to compete with other iron-producing districts at home and abroad. The financial tempest which has passed over the country has swept away much that was unsatisfactory and hollow, thereby preparing the way for the legitimate trader doing business at a profit in the future.'

British manufacturers of the articles, in the production of which American competition has been felt, have directed their attention too exclusively to mere economy, to reducing the price of labour and to administrative details; their ingenuity has not been sufficiently exercised in the technical branch of their business, in the improvement of the pattern and the quality of their goods. _{Errors of our manufacturers.}

The success of the Baldwin Company, as exporters of locomotives to Russia and South America, is not quite so easily explained. They exported 44 engines in 1872, and 99 in 1873, the average value of each locomotive being 2,650*l.* We do not know the terms of payment; we do not know whether shares and bonds were accepted as the equivalent of gold by one manufacturer while payment in paper was refused by another. _{Export of locomotives from America.}

The 'Economist' of July 27, 1878, referring to the export trade in locomotives from the United States, remarks:

'The United States possess no special advantages in the production of iron, and, notwithstanding the fall in labour and capital, it is doubtful if they can yet compete with us in cheapness of production. When we hear of Americans taking contracts for locomotives at prices which English makers are compelled to decline, it is manifestly not a question of the cost of the raw material, or they would be underselling us in pig-iron and rails rather than in manufactures of the highest quality. The truth seems to be that the article supplied is better adapted to the wants of the buyer. Englishmen are too apt to conclude that what suits this country is adapted for all others. But it would be absurd to build and equip a line running through a thinly settled country like the Western States, or Russia or Brazil, in the same manner as a first-class English railway. In America a line is built cheaply, with steep gradients, and sharp curves. Their locomotives are less costly, because of lighter construction. The diminished weight lessens the wear and tear of both road and engine, while the strength of the latter is sufficient for the low rate of speed required. Moreover, the 'bogie' truck on which they are built greatly lessens the friction in rounding sharp curves, and their engineers contend that there is more "give" in the general construction than in a stiffly built English engine.' American locomotive builders have reduced the cost by adhering to uniform patterns to a far greater extent than our own builders.

English locomotive building. Locomotive building in the United Kingdom, as an export trade, has doubtless suffered to some extent from the practice, now almost universal among the larger railway companies, of building their own locomotives. If those locomotives had been built by private establishments, an economy would have been attained by the construction of numbers of engines from the same patterns. In the works at Crewe, where engines of identical type are turned out in large numbers, the price has been brought down to a level, which I am confident has never been reached, with all their advantages of a low nominal rate of wages, in the most skilfully administered establishments on the Continent.

An artisan reporter at the Paris Exhibition, in a letter addressed to the 'Engineer,' observes : ' If there was one thing that surprised me more than another, it was the character of the locomotive engines on the French railways. The proverbial good taste of the French people did not seem to manifest itself here, for even those engines which worked the local passenger traffic up to the very gates of the Exhibition itself, were black ungainly-looking objects. The only things to which they can be compared in this country are the tank engines, which may sometimes be seen working the mineral traffic on colliery sidings, or doing shunting duty at some of our large coal shipping ports.'

With reference to prices, the same writer says : 'The facts do not bear out your opinion that steam engines can be purchased cheaper in France than in this country. In some instances it is impossible to make a comparison between makers' prices, as they still adhere to that ambiguous phrase, " horse-power," but in one or two

[marginal notes:] French locomotives : their unsightliness and costliness.

cases I am able to give some of the dimensions, so that the disparity in regard to prices becomes evident at once. As a first example, I will take a small vertical steam engine with boiler and feed pump. The French engine has a cylinder 11 in. diameter and 18 in. stroke, and the English engine has a cylinder 11¼ in. diameter and 16 in. stroke, so that there is a slight advantage on the side of the French engine. The price of that French engine is 400*l.*, and the English one is only 200*l.*, a difference in price which cannot be accounted for in increased dimensions. Let me take one or two horizontal engines, and although I am unable to give the length of the stroke in the case of the French engines, yet, after every allowance has been made, it will be seen that the French engines are considerably dearer than English :—

Maker	Diameter of cylinder	Length of stroke	Price
	in.	in.	£
French . . .	13¾	—	300
English . . .	14½	26	150
English . . .	14	28	190
French . . .	16½	—	400
English . . .	16	32	230

From these figures, it is evident that steam machinery cannot be purchased as cheaply in France as in this country.'

Our rivals in Cuba :   The subjoined extract from the report by Consul-General Cowper, on competition in the trade with Cuba, deserves attention, as an example of reports of a similar character, received from time to time from the British consuls in all parts of the world :

' The English,' says Mr. Cowper, ' are becoming less and less interested in the commerce of Cuba each year, and the United States more and more so. Machinery and hardware, in which we were once unapproachable, are falling into the hands of our rivals, the only remnants being a limited import of cutlery and large pieces of machinery, such as steam ploughs, sugar engines, &c. ; but even these, from various causes, are now coming from other countries, notably the beautiful machinery from France, such as centrifugal machines, vacuum pans, and those connected with distilling. One of the largest imports from England was the large cane knife, or machete ; some of these are still imported from England, but the fact cannot be, and is not, disguised from the buyers, that these knives are inferior to those made in the United States and in Germany at equal prices. The only advantage possessed by the English article is superiority of polish ; hence the decrease of the import from England. Take the English plough ; it has no chance against the American, for not only is the latter one-third cheaper, but the American manufacturer makes a study of the island of Cuba, and his plough is consequently perfectly adapted to its requirements. So with heavy machinery on sugar estates ; the planters find that, as a matter of course, an article whose prime cost is less, which has less freight to pay, and which is made expressly to suit the island, is preferable to the English one, which does not possess these advantages. In railway plant also the Americans are beating us, for the same objection is raised to the English manufacturers ; rails for instance, of the section required here, have to be rolled expressly in England, so that the purchaser has to give his orders four months in advance, whereas in the United States he finds his rails ready for immediate shipment, and cheaper into the bargain.'

Cause of their success.
It is to be observed in this case that the French and Americans are said to have gained ground upon the British manufacturer, at least as much by superiority of contrivance and pattern as by mere cheapness. It may reasonably be inferred, therefore, that orders for certain descriptions of machinery have been diverted to foreign countries, because our manufacturers have not given their attention to the apparatus required in the process of sugar-making, and the particular form of plough, which is best suited for Cuba. These matters have probably been made a speciality by certain foreign makers.

American trade with Australia.
The Americans have made a determined effort to open up a trade with our Australian colonies. The following statement is from Mr. Drummond's report of last year:

'Mr. Weston W. Evans, the distinguished American civil engineer of New York, who is largely engaged in the purchase of railroad equipment and material for foreign countries, in a recent letter to Mr. Joseph Nimmo, jun., Chief of the Division of Internal Commerce, presents the following interesting facts:

'The New Zealanders have taken to admiring American things and American ways of doing business pretty strongly. I have sent them some American locomotives and some bogies, and am now getting made for them some more locomotives and machine tools for their railway repair shops. I have sent them also windmills, stationary engines, pumps, wheels, &c. ; and now they say that they expect to send here for many more things which they require on their railways. I have sent locomotives and cars to Victoria, Australia, and am now getting some machines made for that country. I have just shipped bolts, nuts, rivets, &c., to New South Wales. They have already had a trial locomotive and cars, and now ask for more locomotives. Cars have also been sent from here to Queensland, Australia. A large trade is growing up for America in these colonies. It looks strange indeed to see people of distant English colonies coming to this country to order things made of iron and steel. A ship lying at New York is now loading street railroad cars for Wellington, New Zealand.'

The succeeding pages are so far reassuring, that they show an immense predominance at present of the British over the American trade with Australia : , *Its amount,*

'Prior to 1852 commerce between the United States and Australia scarcely existed. In that year it amounted to but 208,000 dollars. The following year it suddenly increased to 4,287,000 dollars, and from that time forward has been maintained at a rate that gives an average for the twenty-five years ended June 30, 1876, of 4,551,408 dollars per annum. For the last ten years of that period the average was 5,402,439 dollars, and for the last five years it was, as we have already stated, 6,479,988 dollars per annum.

H

compared with that of England.

'While these figures show a steady increase they are utterly unsatisfactory when compared with the magnitude of the lucrative commerce England has with Australia, and which is now largely transacted by means of correspondence carried across our territory as the shortest route to reach her distant Pacific colonies. During the five years ending with 1876 her commerce with Australia has averaged 98 dol. 36 c. *per capita* per annum of the population of those colonies, while our commerce with them for the same period has amounted to an average of but 2 dol. 84 c. *per capita* per annum. England's exports thither have been 42 dol. 26 c. *per capita*, while ours have been but 1 dol. 61 c. *per capita*, and her imports 56 dol. 10 c. *per capita*, while ours have been but 1 dol. 23 c. *per capita*.'

British predominance.

The aggregate trade of England in machinery is incomparably greater than that of France or the United States. The value of the total exportation of machinery from the United Kingdom in 1877 was 6,700,000*l*. The exportation of machinery from the United States in the same period was under 700,000*l*. Our exportation reached a total of 9,000,000*l*. in 1875. The American exportation had fallen from a maximum of 1,020,000*l*. The total exportation of metal wares from France in 1877 was under 2,000,000*l*. The exportation from the United Kingdom was over 26,700,000*l*. The inference to be drawn from these comparisons is clear. We may have lost ground in certain special competitions ; but we are still doing an immensely larger trade than any other country.

In their last report on the engineering trade, Messrs. Matheson & Grant, of 32 Walbrook, remark : 'There is no doubt that individual trades will be closely pressed by foreign competition, and if with a fair field the English makers allow themselves to be beaten, it is for the general good of the country at large that it should be so, and that prices unnecessarily high should not be paid. But though American tools, German hardware, or Belgian joist-iron of doubtful quality may be sold at low prices in England and in the colonies, such isolated instances afford no real criterion for estimating the staple manufactures of the country, and though England will not again enjoy a monopoly of the engineering trades, the resources and ability available are far too great to justify any anxiety that the extension of trade will cease. Nowhere is capital so abundant and powerful, coal and iron so plentiful or so well placed, and facilities for shipment so great as in England; and if the cost of labour be measured by the value of products, and not by the mere rates of' wages, the English workman still distances all competitors. The low prices of goods sold by German and American manufacturers, which are from time to time quoted as proofs of British degeneracy, do not alone afford much clue, for English manufacturers are in the present time stronger to withstand the stress of enforced idleness than their rivals ; and both in Germany and in the United States the immediate needs of joint-stock manufacturing companies render the prices and terms at which contracts have been made utterly fallacious as a measure of trade.'

(margin note: Position of the British manufacturer.)

German
contracts
executed
from Eng-
land.
The following observations are taken from 'Iron :' 'It is no secret that one of the greatest, if not the greatest iron house in Germany, fills its orders by supplies from England. It is well known that the maker of an engine, or a sword, or a watch, is not always the person whose name is on the plate, and that a great German house imports from this country many of the goods it contracts to deliver.'

Our suc-
cess in
neutral
markets.
If we examine the general condition of the iron manufacture in foreign countries, we find that every country is becoming more capable of satisfying the demands of its own market. We experience an increasing difficulty in contending against the heavy import duties behind which our rivals have taken shelter; but we are rarely beaten in the neutral markets.

Excep-
tional
nature of
competi-
tion.
Messrs. Fallows sum up their views of the situation in the iron trade in the following terms : 'The depression in England has been aggravated to some extent by foreign competition, other countries having been stimulated to find outlets for their surplus production, but much of this competition is understood to be of an exceptional character, and not likely to be permanently maintained. The following figures show the total import of foreign iron into the United Kingdom during the years :

	1868	1873	1875	1877	1878
	Tons	Tons	Tons	Tons	Tons
Iron in bars . .	64,689	74,666	89,822	91,817	100,574
Iron and steel, wrought and manufactured .	16,063	30,718	57,988	84,146	108,325

The figures of iron in bars include a large quantity

of Swedish iron (probably not less than 60,000 tons)
imported for the use of Sheffield steel manufacturers
and for re-export, which cannot be said to compete
with English makers. There is, however, a large increase under the head of " Iron and Steel, Wrought
and Manufactured," which seems to indicate that the
more labour is expended on any article the less able
we appear to meet the competition of foreigners.'

An elaborate paper was prepared for the recent
meeting of the Iron and Steel Institute in Paris by Professor Akerman, of the School of Mines at Stockholm.
The paper gave a general review of the exhibits of
iron and steel at Paris. The author directs attention
to all the most important inventions of the present day
in connection with the industry of which he treats.
The names of the English manufacturers, including
foreigners who have made England the land of their
adoption, hold a place of honour in that record of
metallurgical discoveries and improvements. The
author alludes in befitting terms of commendation to
Mr. Bessemer's process, by which steel rails have supplanted rails of puddled iron ; to the Siemens-Martin
process, which has led to still further substitutions of a
lighter, stronger, and more durable metal for ordinary
iron; to the success achieved by Messrs. Hopkins and
Gilkes in freeing the Cleveland iron from phosphorus by
adding rich iron ore or other materials rich in oxidised
iron during the puddling ; to the efforts of Mr. Lowthian
Bell in the same direction; and to the process adopted
by Sir Joseph Whitworth for preventing the formation
of blow holes in steel by hydraulic pressure. We may

British
metal-
lurgical
and me-
chanical
progress.

venture to set the labours of those men side by side
with the armour-plates of M. Marrel, which exhibited
such fine quality at Spezzia, and the admirable productions of Creusot and Herr Krupp, in the firm conviction that the United Kingdom has done her part in
the progressive development of metallurgy. If we
pass from iron making to machinery, the names of
Armstrong, Whitworth, and Rendel, of Penn and
Platt, and a long roll of illustrious mechanics should
suffice to remove all misgivings as to our capability of
sustaining foreign competition.

Mr. Lowthian Bell's report on foreign manufacturing processes. During the former exhibition, held in Paris in
1867, Mr. Lowthian Bell undertook a journey for the
express object of ascertaining what grounds existed for
the alarming assertions, so frequently urged at that
time, as to the rapid gain which foreign manufacturers
were making on our old-established industry. The
result was published in a pamphlet entitled ' Our
Foreign Competitors in the Iron Trade,' from which the
following passages have been extracted. Mr. Lowthian
Bell, in company with Mr. Lancaster, having visited the
largest collieries in France, Belgium, and Westphalia,
reported that 'these investigations failed entirely to
convince either my companion or myself, that there
was to be found the smallest reason for the sweeping
conclusions arrived at by those who assigned to us a
lower place than that accorded to our foreign competitors.

'It might have been fairly put to us, " How is it that
you, with as fine coal fields and as rich beds of ore as
are to be found in the world, permit yourselves to be

outstripped by less favoured nations; you, who are the descendants or fellow-countrymen of those men who first applied pit coal in the blast furnace, who first suggested the puddling furnace, invented the rolling mill, and discovered the immense value of heated air to the smelting of iron—four, indeed it may be said *the* four 'steps in advance' which have given you ships of iron instead of wood, and roads of metal instead of stone—rendering the present age truly one of iron?"

'Against these services rendered to the manufacture of iron by English ironmasters, what have we to enumerate as the contribution of foreign nations? In number they are two—viz., the washing of coal otherwise unfit for the coking process, and the use of the waste gases from the blast furnaces—both inventions of undoubtedly great value, but taking no rank in point of importance with those previously referred to.

'Where, we may ask, is there any evidence of our indifference to improvement, or want of intelligence in the management of our furnaces? Within fifteen years we have learnt to utilise the gases formerly wasted, and we have succeeded in reducing the consumption of coke per ton of iron to something like one-half what it was previous to the period spoken of. We have our blast heated to a point never dreamt of abroad, and we have furnaces, the dimensions of which have excited the astonishment of Continental ironmasters, whose opinions are in strict confirmation of the superiority now maintained, and which opinions I have upon a previous occasion made public.

'M. de Wendel writes: "I hear that a Mr. Plimsoll has recently drawn public attention to the defective state of the pig-iron manufacture in your country compared with that of France and Belgium. The two visits I paid to your works enable me to state that, so far as Cleveland is concerned, the assertion is without any foundation whatever. The high temperature of the blast you use, and the dimensions of your furnaces, hitherto unknown in France, have secured for your neighbourhood a superiority which I shall at once set about imitating."

'M. Judey states: "We and others in France have still a margin for economy in the manufacture of pig-iron, by avoiding the present heavy charges for transport in bringing coal and ore to our works. We must try to improve our method of working, and thus seek to consume more of the minerals found nearer home. Cleveland, on the other hand, by the excellent results obtained in furnaces of recent construction, and by the great care taken to avoid unnecessary labour, appears to have reached almost the minimum cost of production."—*Vide* "Pall Mall Gazette," Feb. 20, 1868. Reply to Mr. Samuel Plimsoll's letter to the editor of the "Times."

'So far as the possession of the ordinary education taught in schools is concerned, I do not apprehend there is the slightest reason for supposing that French workmen enjoy any superiority over our fellow-countrymen in a similar position; and to imagine that there exists any knowledge whatever among them of those higher branches of science, as has been pretended by some of our advocates for what they term technical education, is a pure and simple fallacy, without any ground whatever whereupon to rest the assertion. I do believe, however, that among the higher officers engaged in French mines and ironworks, you will find more frequently than is the case with ourselves gentlemen of considerable attainments in the physical sciences.'

Mr. Lowthian Bell has pointed out, in his more recent notes on the progress of the iron trade of Cleveland, the valuable improvements in the manufacture of iron, which have been made in that district : 'Nothing had been ascertained prior to 1850, which indicated that any advantage was to be derived by materially departing from the shape or dimensions of blast furnaces, in common use in other localities.' *Improvements in blast furnaces.*

To Middlesborough belongs the credit not only of demonstrating the great advantage arising from the use of furnaces of large dimensions, driven with highly heated air, but of proving the extreme limit to which, in the matter of fuel consumption, these two changes can be carried.

I believe the general condition of the iron trade to be fairly and faithfully summed up in the language of the 'Statist:' 'Foreign competition, though it has sharpened the struggle, has not gained largely upon us.' We have unrivalled resources in respect of capital, undeniable superiority in machine-making, an expensive but highly skilled body of workmen, endued with matchless powers for sustained effort. In our coal and iron trades great and sudden profits have invariably *Summary of the general condition of the trade.*

led to over-production. This is an inevitable consequence in a country so remarkable for enterprise as our own. A trade carried on under such conditions is of necessity subject to wide fluctuations, and commands an average rate of profit considerably lower than one of a more stable character.

Labour is not responsible for the frequent perturbations in the trade; although the workmen are compelled to bear their share of the losses sustained by their employers, and to submit to a proportionate reduction of wages.

CHAPTER V.

THE AGRICULTURAL INTEREST.

THE depressed condition of agriculture has been a prominent cause of the falling off in the demand for goods for the home market. The agricultural interest has suffered from two causes, which had never before been combined. The bad harvests of 1875-76-77 were followed by an exceptionally low price of wheat in 1878-79. In his paper on the Fall in Prices, Mr. Giffen quotes the estimate of Mr. Caird, according to which, taking the average yield of the last thirty years to be 100, the yield of 1875, 1876, and 1877 was respectively 78, 76, and 74. Our wheat harvest was deficient by one-fourth as compared with the average, and much more of course as compared with a good year. In March last the 'Gazette' average for wheat was 39s. 7d. against 49s. 6d. at the corresponding date in 1878, and 51s. 3d. in the previous year. The fall in the price of wheat in England is the result of the heavy importations from America. Our annual consumption is estimated at twenty-two to twenty-three millions of quarters, while the importation for 1877 was 12,310,957 quarters, and for 1876 10,069,050 quarters. The increased growth of wheat in the United States was caused partly by the panic of 1873, which

Conjunction of bad harvests and low prices.

American importations of wheat.

led to an extensive migration from the industrial centres to the fertile lands in the Western prairies, and partly by the unprecedented abundance of the last two harvests in America. The importation of wheat has apparently been checked by the fall in prices. The Illinois farmer has found, says the 'Economist,' that the cost of conveying his grain to London absorbs nearly the whole of the price obtained here. Hence the import of wheat and flour has diminished about $22\frac{1}{2}$ per cent., while the price, which we are paying for that smaller quantity, is reduced by $37\frac{1}{2}$ per cent. The recent collapse in the corn trade confirms the statement of Mr. Caird that the cost of transport from the grain-growing countries to England is equal to the rent ordinarily paid by the British farmer. In average years he will have nothing to fear from foreign competition.

Failures in other kinds of farm produce.

The difficulties of our agriculturists have not been confined to the bad harvests and the unprecedented fall in the price of wheat. The grain and root crops had partially failed, and a considerable diminution in the number of cattle and sheep had ensued. In Great Britain between 1874 and 1877, there was a total reduction of 427,000 on a stock of 6,125,000 cattle, or about seven per cent. The number of sheep was reduced by 2,153,000 on a stock of 30,314,000, or seven per cent. in three years.

Foreign competition in meat.

Not only have their flocks and herds decreased, but the British farmers, for the first time in our experience, have been brought face to face with competition in the production of meat. The quantity of meat imported in 1876 was 788,973 cwts., showing an increase of 257,065 cwts. over 1875. In 1877 the quantity was 1,277,686 cwts., being 488,713 cwts. in excess of the imports in 1876.

A permanent failure in this new field of competition would undoubtedly be fraught with the gravest consequences to the British farmer. The importance of the cattle trade is shown in the subjoined extract from the ' Statist : '—' Since the repeal of the Corn Laws the farmers have been more and more giving up the cultivation of wheat and concentrating their efforts upon the breeding and fattening of cattle. In Ireland and Scotland wheat has almost gone out of cultivation, and in the western half of England also it is less and less grown. In Great Britain alone the land in tillage has decreased 400,000 acres in the last nine years, while the permanent pastures have increased 1,800,000 acres. Much more than the addition to the cultivated area has thus been laid down in grass, and the energies of British agriculturists are being devoted to the rearing and feeding of stock. So long as they had only Continental competition to contend with, they felt no apprehensions. But here also the American panic has had unexpected consequences. The vast Atlantic trade had called into existence great railways, built at immense expense, to connect the principal Atlantic ports with the West, and also splendid fleets of steamers to ply regularly between this country and the United States. When the regular traffic failed, enterprising speculators were tempted by the low fares to send American cattle and American dead meat across the

[margin note:] Stock-raising in England.

ocean.   The venture proved profitable, was repeated,
and rapidly developed into an important trade.'

Here again we find a reassuring opinion as to the
future prospects expressed by Mr. Caird.   He estimates
the cost of transportation for cattle from America at 4*l.*
per head, an ample sum, in his judgment, to enable our
agriculturists to compete against the foreign produce.
In the case of wheat, however, the charge for freight
is a less adequate equivalent for the rent and the higher
cost of cultivation which the British farmer has to
bear.

Cost of transporting cattle from America.

In connection with this subject it is interesting to
compare the cost of growing wheat in England and in
the United States.   Ample materials for such comparison are supplied in a recent article in the ' Economist,' where the writer points out that ' the cheapest
growers of wheat, under the present conditions of agriculture in the West, are men little, if at all, above the
position of artisans.   In the last two years they have
been largely recruited from the ranks of the unemployed
operatives of the Eastern States, and, until a wonderful.
change comes over manufacturing industry in America,
no other field of labour has greater inducements to offer.
The main advantage of the American farmer seems
to lie in the cheapness with which he obtains his crop.
It is somewhat surprising to find that wheat grown in
the Far West still pays as much freight, before it can
be placed in the English market, as the rent charge
amounts to at home.   The average yield of an acre
of land in England is 30 bushels, against 13 in the
Western States.   The American farmer must therefore

Wheat-growing in America.

cultivate 2½ acres before he can sell as much produce as is grown on a single acre in England. This, however, he does at an incredibly small outlay. The difference in tillage is most striking. An English farmer accustomed to drive three or four horses painfully over a stiff clay, can scarcely imagine the ease with which a light plough runs through the rich loam of a Western State.'

But the cheapness with which land is cultivated in the United States is due not alone or chiefly to the quality of the soil; it is because the ownership of land and the labour of cultivation are generally associated together that such a remarkable economy has been secured. The influence of this favourable economic condition of agriculture is equally felt in every quarter of the globe. Reason of its cheapness.

In his essay on the Position of the British Labourer, Mr. Fawcett observes: 'In Switzerland, France, Flanders, and the Rhineland, the small proprietors who cultivate their own land economise their time with the most scrupulous care; they earnestly strive to turn every half-hour to the utmost possible advantage; they work early and late, and their labour exhibits a watchfulness, and a fostering attention, which is never acquired by hired labourers. Magical is the influence which the feeling of property exerts. And truly indeed has it been said by Arthur Young, that it is potent enough to turn sand into gold, and convert a desert into a garden.' Personal management of small farms.

The American farmer, as we learn from the correspondent of the 'Economist,' 'as a rule does his own Practice of the American farmer.

work, or the greater part of it. The amount of wages paid in actual money is comparatively small. If he cultivates 50 acres of wheat, and has growing sons, he may manage without any help, except at harvest time, when he hires an extra hand for a month. If he has no family to assist him, he will probably hire a hand for the year at $12 or $15 a month. In all cases board and wages are included; the hired men sitting down to meals with the farmer and his family. We may fairly estimate, then, the capital of 12*l.* required by an English farmer to cultivate properly a single acre of land will not more than suffice to purchase and cultivate the 2½ acres which will yield the same amount of wheat in America. Up to this point neither competitor has a decided advantage, and, if anything, the difference is, in our opinion, on the side of the home agriculturist. But the heavy yield in England is only obtained by the application of costly manures, and this outlay is spared the American grower. At present only the richest lands are cultivated, and the earth yields her increase without any assistance at his hands. Of course this will not last for ever. . . . But until this stage of exhaustion is reached in the Western States, the English farmer will require something more than the set-off of freight against rent-charge. . . . It lies entirely at the option of the landlords whether this shall be wholly given in abatement of rent, or partly take the form of security of tenure and protection to the occupier's capital.'

Conces-sions to the English farmer.

Prospects of British agriculture. While security of tenure would undoubtedly be the most satisfactory mode of meeting the just claims of the farmer to consideration, it is not easy to determine the rent of land for a long period in advance. Are the conditions in which the British agriculturist finds himself at this moment temporary or likely to endure? What expectation can we form as to the future cost of freights? How soon will the wonderful capabilities of the virgin soil of the United States be impaired, and render it necessary to use artificial stimulants to maintain the produce of the land? There seems no reason for apprehension as to the ultimate prospects of British agriculture; but nothing must be neglected to insure the utmost economy in the tillage of the soil. It is probable that we may see a gradual reduction in the acreage of farms in the United Kingdom. Land is generally held in the United States in parcels or properties of moderate extent. We are assured by Professor Baldwin that much of the land in Ireland produces more under the spade than when cultivated on a larger scale. I speak from personal experience in recommending holdings of about sixty acres in the neighbourhood of large towns, where poultry and dairy produce find a ready sale at high prices. *Reduced area of holdings.*

The British farmer and his family must work as their American and colonial competitors work. Farm labour must be more energetic, more efficient, more economical. In order to attain this result wages need not be reduced; indeed it is quite possible that they might be increased while yet the cost of labour was diminished. *Farm work of the future.*

More attention should be devoted to the secondary produce of agriculture, such as milk, eggs, and poultry. *Secondary produce.*

I

The proportion which this description of produce bears
to the total realised value of agricultural products in
France is far more considerable than in this country.
In this department of their business, the wives and
daughters of our farmers might do well to emulate the
example afforded them in France. I should be sorry to
see the novel closed and the piano silenced for ever;
but the whole of life should not be consumed in easy
enjoyment, nor will the social position of the occupiers
of the soil be improved, in the estimation of those
whose good opinion it is worth while to gain, by an
affectation of indifference and contempt for the unro-
mantic details of the farmyard.

Temporary
reduction
of rents.

It is possible that a temporary reduction of rents
may be required. The ' Statist,' in advocating this
opinion, relies upon the statistics collected by Mr. Caird.
' Between 1870 and 1878 rent rose on an average from
13*s.* to 30*s.* an acre, or almost 131 per cent., and of this
increase a very large part was due to the growth of
population and of the general prosperity of the country,
not to landlords' outlay upon the land. While prices
continued to go up, the increase of rents was natural;
their decrease is equally inevitable now that prices are
falling.'

However this may be, landlords may rest assured
that their property will never be depreciated below its
legitimate value. Agriculture has always been an
attractive and a congenial pursuit. The competition
for farms will revive with the general recovery of commercial prosperity. In process of time, as the lands in
the more favourably situated and fertile districts in the

United States are settled, their value will increase.
Rent will then be paid for advantages in point of accessi-
bility, and the conditions of agriculture in the New
World will be assimilated to those which exist in our
own country. Such changes, however, must be gradual.
Liberal and intelligent landlords, like the Speaker of the
House of Commons, will not refuse concessions when
they are shown to be necessary, nor will they be
induced to take a too desponding view of the future
prospects of landowners.

It is no answer to the demand of the farmer for
concessions in respect of rent to point to the already
inadequate return upon the capital value of the land.
The present value of land is due to the superior
attractiveness of a property which can be seen, and is
adjacent to the residence of the proprietor, over one
which is remote and invisible. A farmstead in
' merrie Englande' will always have a charm for its
possessor that cannot attach to the bonds and shares of
a foreign railway. Few proprietors obtain a net return of more than two per cent. upon the capital value
of their land, even under skilful administration. It
requires very little skill to secure a return of four per
cent. upon the most approved foreign securities. *Profits of land-owners.*

Looking back from the present depression over the
preceding decade, we have irrefragable proof of a solid
accumulation of wealth. We learn from Mr. Caird
that between 1853 and 1878 the capital value of the
live stock of the United Kingdom had risen from
146,000,000*l.* to 260,000,000*l.* ; while in the interval of
twenty years, 1858–1878, the increase in the land rent *Accumula-tion of wealth.*

of the United Kingdom, when capitalised at thirty years'
purchase, shows an increased value of 31,000,000*l*.

Improved
condition
of the
labourer.
Another most important fact has been brought out
by Mr. Caird. He has set out, in a tabular form,
statistics which establish a conspicuous improvement
in the condition of the agricultural labourer.

Table showing the Rent of Cultivated Land, the Price of Provisions, the
Wages of the Agricultural Labourer, the Rent of Cottages, and the
average Produce of Wheat, in three periods during the last hundred
years in England.

	1770		1850		1878	
	s.	*d.*	*s.*	*d.*	*s.*	*d.*
Rent of cultivated land per acre . .	13	0	27	0	30	0
Price of bread per lb.	0	1¼	0	1¼	0	1½
„ meat „	0	3¾	0	5	0	9
„ butter „ . . .	0	6	1	0	1	8
Agricultural labourer's wages per week .	7	3	9	7	14	0
Rent of labourer's cottage . . .	0	8	1	5	2	0
	Bushels		Bushels		Bushels	
Produce of wheat, per acre, in bushels .	23		26½		28	

We see in the advance in the prices of meat, as
shown in the table, an explanation of the rise in rents.
Wages having risen, while the price of bread has remained stationary, the condition of the labourer has
materially improved. He is enabled to maintain himself and his family on his earnings. He is now independent, while formerly he was dependent on the
parish for a portion of his maintenance. The cost of
labour is not increased under the new conditions, but
it is paid in a more satisfactory form. Gratifying as
the progress already realised has been, the rate of
wages might be further raised, and the cost of labour
reduced, provided the labourer would attack his work
with greater vigour. In order to be enabled to accom-

plish a larger task he must raise his standard of living. He must not idle away his time, nor waste his substance in beer.

Great as is the difference in agricultural wages between our Northern and Southern counties, the work is more cheaply done in the north than in the south, where the traditions of low wages and exhausting poor-rates are not altogether forgotten. In the south the evils of the old and most objectionable system of poor relief are perpetuated in the feeble frames and languid movements of the peasantry.

CHAPTER VI.

FOREIGN COMPETITION—COMPARATIVE EFFICIENCY OF ENGLISH AND FOREIGN LABOUR.

Excess of imports over exports:

BEFORE entering upon other subjects, some observations may not be superfluous with reference to the excess of our imports over our exports. It has been assumed that we have paid for our importations by calling in capital from abroad, and that the debts due to us from foreign nations have been rapidly diminishing in amount. A clear and satisfactory explanation of the disproportion in question has, however, been given by Mr. Shaw Lefevre in his address to the Statistical Society.

Mr. Shaw Lefevre's explanation.

'The excess in the value of our imports over that of our exports has increased from the average of 58,000,000*l.* in 1867–69, to 118,000,000*l.* in 1875-77, and reached the enormous sum of 142,000,000*l.* in 1877. Making, however, an addition of 10 per cent. to the value of our exports, in respect of freight, insurance, and profit, and a deduction of 5 per cent. from the value of our imports in respect of freight and other charges, as Mr. Newmarch has explained is necessary, the difference is considerably reduced; for the years 1863 to 1870, this difference averaged 25,000,000*l.* ; in

1871 it fell to 4,000,000*l.* ; in 1872 there was an excess value of exports of 8,000,000*l.* ; in 1873 the excess of imports was 12,000,000*l.* ; in 1874, 26,000,000*l.* ; in 1875, 47,000,000*l.* ; in 1876, 77,000,000*l.* ; and 1877, 97,000,000*l.* ; and for ten months of the current year it is 74,000,000*l.* Comparing the three years of great commercial activity, 1871-73, with the three last years, the total difference in value for the first period was 5,000,000*l.*, or nearly 2,000,000*l.* a year, and for the last period 217,000,000*l.*, or 72,000,000*l.* a year.'

In this connection, the remittances of dividends and interest on capital invested abroad must also be taken into view. Mr. Giffen has estimated the annual income from the capital so invested at 65,000,000*l.* In the ten years, 1867-77, nearly six hundred millions sterling must have been invested in foreign securities. *Payments on capital invested abroad,*

According to Mr. Seyd, the indebtedness of foreign countries to the United Kingdom is not less than from 1,000,000,000*l.* to 1,100,000,000*l.*, bearing an annual interest of from 40,000,000*l.* to 50,000,000*l.* Making allowance for defaulters, the sum to be remitted annually to this country cannot be less than 30,000,000*l.* In addition to these large remittances on private account, the Government draws some 15,000,000*l.* a year on India. It is by the excess in the value of the imports that the vast sums annually due to England for interest on our foreign investments are paid, and the means provided for meeting the various charges, and for paying to us the profits we realise on our exported goods. *supplied by excess in value of imports.*

The large expenditure in England imposes a most

serious burden on the finances of India. The revenue is singularly deficient in elasticity, and the mass of the people live from hand to mouth on mere subsistence wages. The interest on foreign loans, and the drawings on India, should be nearly sufficient to restore the balance between the value of the imports and the exports. But we must also bring into account the sums payable to this country, in ˙ respect of the profits of trading on the goods exported and imported, and the earnings of the ships, chiefly sailing under the British flag, in which those goods are carried. The value, at which imported goods are calculated, includes every element of cost, freight, profit, commissions, and insurance. ˙ The value of the exports, on the other hand, is incomplete : it is the mere cost of the manufacture, exclusive ˙ of freights, insurance, commissions, and profits. Again, as M. Leroy Beaulieu points out, there is a natural tendency to undervalue goods exported to countries where heavy duties are levied *ad valorem*. Hence we find in the trade of every commercial, or rather manufacturing nation, in a greater or less degree, a similar excess in the value of the imports over the exports.

The total importations of the commercial nations exceed their exportations by not less than 15 per cent. The table published in a statistical work by Dr. Neumann-Spellart gives the total importations and exportations for the five quarters of the globe.

	Importations	Exportations
	Francs	Francs
Europe . . .	28,202,000,000	21,681,000,000
America . . .	4,864,000,000	5,636,000,000
Asia	2,445,000,000	3,208,000,000
Australia . . .	1,189,000,000	1,122,000,000
Africa . . .	672,000,000	783,000,000
Total . .	37,372,000,000	32,430,000,000

The causes of the disparity between the total values of the exports and imports have been explained in the preceding remarks, and it will be evident, on a full consideration of the circumstances, that the apprehension that we are living as a nation beyond our means rests on no solid foundation. Indeed, as M. Leroy Beaulieu remarks, the magnitude of our import trade, so far from its affording a just ground for anxiety, must be regarded as a proof of the greatness of our resources and the stability of our power. The large balance against this country which formerly existed can be fully and satisfactorily explained, and a marked reduction in the excess value of our imports has recently taken place.

The nation not living beyond its means.

The crisis, through which we are passing, has been attributed by many to foreign competition. I differ from this view. After a careful and impartial investigation I can arrive at no other conclusion than that expressed by the Earl of Beaconsfield in the House of Lords. Our foreign competitors may have succeeded for a time in producing a limited number of articles at a lower cost, or of a more convenient pattern; but we have not been beaten in any important branch of trade

Alleged production of the crisis by foreign competition.

in a fair and open competition. Some have gone so far as to allege that our textile industry has been injured by the invasion of American manufactures into Manchester, and our manufacture of iron and steel by the importation of Belgian goods into the midland counties. The latest report of the Commissioners of Customs contains a tabular statement, designed to show in what respects and to what extent foreign manufacturers are employed in the production of articles for use in this country. The value of the goods imported in 1877 exceeded by 19,000,000*l.* the importations of the previous year. The totals were :

Increased imports from abroad.

	1876 £	1877 £	Increase per cent.
Foreign countries .	290,822,127	304,865,684	4·8
British possessions .	84,332,576	89,558,998	6·1

Here the advantage is on the side of the trade with our own possessions, which has increased 1·3 per cent. more than that with foreign countries.

Nature of articles so imported.

In commenting on these figures, the Commissioners point out that the articles imported in increased quantities are chiefly food and raw materials. For example, the goods sent to us by Russia, valued at 22,000,000*l.*, or 4,500,000*l.* in excess of our importations in 1876, consisted mainly of corn, flax, linseed, sugar, and tallow. The increased importations from Germany consisted of corn, potatoes, and sugar. A certain increase was observable in the silk and woollen goods imported through Holland, but neither Belgium, France, nor Portugal showed any appreciable change in the value of the import trade from those countries. The import trade from the United States, amounting to the vast sum of 78,000,000*l.*, is composed almost exclusively of food and raw materials.

The main augmentation in the American exports in the interval from 1868 to 1878 consists of food and the raw materials of industry. The exportation of the principal manufactured articles is still on an insignificant scale.

The following table gives the comparative value of the exportations of manufactured articles from Great Britain and the United States for 1876.

British and American exports of manufactured articles for 1876.

	England	America
	£	£
Manufactures of cotton . .	67,644,000	1,540,000
Iron and iron manufactures .	19,100,000	1,000,000
Machinery	7,620,000	1,480,000
Linen and jute yarn . . .	1,670,000	—
Linen manufactures . . .	7,170,000	—
Silk yarn and manufactures .	2,870,000	—
Woollen and worsted yarn and manufactures . . .	23,000,000	—
Giving a total of . . .	129,070,000	4,020,000

Mr. Plunket states, in his commercial report, that, speaking in round numbers, it may be said that more than one-half of the exports from the United States are made up of breadstuffs, mineral oils, provisions, and tobacco leaf; and if we add to them the value of the export of raw cotton (187,662,425 dollars), we find that the five together represent about four-fifths of the total amount exported in 1876. Of the total domestic exports in 1877, less than 11 per cent. consisted of manufactured articles, and they showed an increase of only 377,856 dollars (75,571*l.*) over the previous year.

The following table of the values of the principal commodities of domestic production, the exportation of which from America greatly increased from June 30, 1868, to June 30, 1878, is taken from the ' Economist : '

Commodities	Year ending June 30 1868	1878	Increase since 1868
	£	£	£
Agricultural implements .	140,288	536,499	396,211
Live animals . . .	152,791	1,217,636	1,064,845
Bread and breadstuffs .	14,371,041	37,869,689	23,498,648
Coal	315,879	491,556	175,676
Copper, brass, and manufactures of . . .	195,677	641,323	445,646
Cotton, manufactures of .	1,014,803	2,382,422	1,367,619
Fruit	84,690	286,869	202,179
Iron, steel, and manufactures of	1,331,131	2,517,510	1,186,379
Leather, and manufactures of	294,661	1,682,845	1,388,184
Oilcake	606,968	1,061,493	454,525
Coal, oil, and petroleum .	4,543,891	9,703,119	5,159,228
Provisions . . .	6,307,970	25,739,580	19,431,610
Total . . .	29,359,790	84,130,541	54,770,750

Commenting on the figures relating to manufactured articles, M. Leroy Beaulieu observes that they are comparatively trifling in amount, affording no indication, as the ' pessimist ' writers would have us believe, that the United States are on the point of inundating Europe with their manufactured goods.

Mr. Drummond states in his recent report that the United States cannot compete with us in heavy machinery, that the increased exportation is confined to the smaller articles. The increase in the cotton manufactured goods exported in 1878, compared with 1877, was only a quarter of a million sterling.

Since 1851, the value and percentage of agricultural products has always been more than 50 per cent. of the total domestic and foreign exports from the United States. In 1878 the percentage amounted to 81·98.

The Commissioners of Customs give a tabular state- Imports of manufactured goods in 1873 and 1877. ment of the manufactured goods imported into the United Kingdom in the years 1873 and 1877. The most important items are cotton, silk, and woollen goods, glass, iron, and leather manufactures. The results are set forth in the following table :

	1873	1877
	£	£
Cotton goods . . .	1,666,000	2,144,000
Silk „ . . .	10,260,000	12,969,000
Woollen „ . . .	5,458,000	7,090,000
Glass	1,463,000	1,908,000
Iron	1,008,000	1,537,000

The increase of our imports is considerable, but we can show a still larger increase in our own exportations of the same commodities.

Mr. Newmarch has shown, in a clear and compre- Our predominance in the export trade. hensive tabular statement, the conspicuous superiority of the United Kingdom over every other manufacturing country in respect to the exportation of articles of native production and manufacture. The subjoined table, with Mr. Newmarch's commentary on the figures, has been extracted from his able paper, recently read before the Statistical Society, on the progress of the Foreign Trade of the United Kingdom, 1856–77.

Foreign Work and English Wages.

Imports (General) and Exports (Special or of Native Production and Manufacture), Four Periods, 1860-75. Totals per Head of Population. Five Leading Protectionist Countries. (From 'Stat. Ab. For. Cts.,' iv. p. 31.)

Imports

Year	France (General).	Germany	Austria	Russia	United States	United Kingdom
	£	£	£	£	£	£
1860 .	125,000,000	—	32,000,000	25,000,000	74,000,000	210,000,000
1865 .	163,000,000	—	37,000,000	24,000,000	50,000,000	271,000,000
1869 .	160,000,000	—	60,000,000	54,000,000	87,000,000	295,000,000
1875 .	178,000,000	237,000,000	84,000,000	85,000,000	115,000,000	374,000,000
Increase	53,000,000	—	52,000,000	60,000,000	41,000,000	104,000,000

Imports per head

Year	France	Germany	Austria	Russia	United States	United Kingdom
	l.	l.	l.	l.	l.	l.
1860 .	68	—	20	7	48	140
1865 .	88	—	22	7	30	186
1869 .	88	—	34	14	40	198
1875 .	100	105	46	22	58	240
Increase	32	—	26	15	10	100

Exports

Year	France (General).	Germany	Austria	Russia	United States	United Kingdom
	£	£	£	£	£	£
1860 .	91,000,000	—	26,000,000	27,000,000	66,000,000	135,000,000
1865 .	123,000,000	—	34,000,000	32,000,000	28,000,000	165,000,000
1869 .	123,000,000	—	44,000,000	42,000,000	57,000,000	190,000,000
1875 .	155,000,000	176,000,000	50,000,000	60,000,000	104,000,000	225,000,000
Increase	64,000,000	—	24,000,000	33,000,000	38,000,000	90,000,000

Exports per head

Year	France	Germany	Austria	Russia	United States	United Kingdom
	l.	l.	l.	l.	l.	l.
1860 .	50	—	16	7	43	92
1865 .	63	—	20	8	18	115
1869 .	63	—	24	10	30	121
1875 .	84	80	28	16	54	142
Increase	34	—	12	9	11	52

Note.—As regards Germany, I find, on inquiry of Mr. Giffen, that there are as yet no official figures for 1860-65-69.

'It will scarcely be said that on the face of these figures the United Kingdom suffers in any particular when compared with any one of the four countries for which the imports and exports are given at each of the four dates during the sixteen years; or indeed with all the four countries (France, Austria, Russia, and United States) in combination; in other words, the 30,000,000 people in the United Kingdom, aided by Free Trade, bear most advantageous comparison with the 150,000,000 relying upon protection. Thus:

Increase in Imports, 1860–75.

Four foreign countries, France, Austria, } 206,000,000*l.* = 26*s.* per head
  Russia, and United States. . . }
United Kingdom . . . . . 164,000,000*l.* = 100*s.* „

Increase in Exports, 1860–75.

Four foreign countries . . . . 160,000,000*l.* = 22*s.* per head
United Kingdom . . . . . 90,000,000*l.* = 52*s.* „

If the several countries be compared *singly* with the United Kingdom, as in fairness they should be, seeing that the population is about equal (Russia excepted), and the climate better, and the natural resources greater than the United Kingdom, not one of them exhibits progress in any degree approaching that of the United Kingdom.'

Mr. Newmarch proceeds to examine the statistics of the supplementary imports and exports—that is to say, the large number of new and miscellaneous articles which grow up year by year, and, for the sake of conciseness and uniformity, have to be entered in the official tables under the title of '*Un*enumerated Articles.' Unenumerated articles.

It will be found that these two classes present the
following highly satisfactory results :

Progress of Supplemental Imports and Exports.   United Kingdom,
1856–1877.   Declared Values.

	1877	1870	1865	1860	1856
IMPORTS (a) Remainder of enumerated.	£	£	£	£	£
enumerated.	45,000,000	17,000,000	6,000,000	4,000,000	3,000,000
(b) Unenumerated .	39,000,000	64,000,000	55,000,000	42,000,000	35,000,000
	84,000,000	81,000,000	61,000,000	46,000,000	38,000,000
	Per cent.	Per cent.	Per cent.	Per cent.	Per cent.
Percentage of total Imports . .	21	25	22	21	22
EXPORTS (a) Remainder of enumerated.	£	£	£	£	£
enumerated.	21,000,000	16,000,000	10,000,000	4,000,000	5,000,000
(b) Unenumerated .	17,000,000	11,000,000	8,000,000	9,000,000	8,000,000
	37,000,000	27,000,000	18,000,000	13,000,000	13,000,000
	Per cent.	Per cent.	Per cent.	Per cent.	Per cent.
Percentage of total Exports . .	19	13	11	10	11

'We have here a doubling of the supplemental
imports in the twenty-one years 1856–77, or from
38,000,000*l.* to 84,000,000*l.*, the proportion of the total
imports remaining at 21 per cent.

'The supplemental *exports* increase nearly threefold,
as from 13,000,000*l.* to 37,000,000*l.*, and the proportion
to the total exports rises from 11 to 19 per cent.

' In both cases the progression of the figures is rapid
and large, and strongly suggestive of a vigorous and
inventive trade in which the rapid appearance of new
commodities is perpetually pressing open and enlarging
the previous classifications and vocabularies.'

Wages on the Continent have always been lower than in the United Kingdom. Low wages, however, have not prevented a decline in the export trade of our continental competitors, both greater in the aggregate amount and far greater in proportion than that which has taken place in the export trade of the United Kingdom. The most recent figures on this subject are contained in the subjoined table published by the ' Economist ' in January of the present year :

(margin note: Decline of foreign exports notwithstanding low wages.)

Exports from	1877	1876	1877, less	
	£	£	£	Per cent.
France . . .	175,000,000	181,000,000	6,000,000	3
Belgium . . .	80,000,000	83,000,000	3,000,000	3
Italy . . .	40,000,000	52,000,000	12,000,000	23
Hamburg (transit) .	58,000,000	85,000,000	27,000,000	32
	353,000,000	401,000,000	48,000,000	12
United Kingdom .	252,000,000	256,000,000	4,000,000	—
Total . .	605,000,000	657,000,000	52,000,000	12

In the general trade between England and Belgium, there are no indications of a failure on the part of the British manufacturers to retain their due proportion. of the productive industry of the two countries. The value of the Belgian exports to England fell from 222,337,000 francs in 1874 to 141,662,000 francs in 1876. A recovery took place the following year, when the total value of the exports of merchandise from Belgium to Great Britain amounted to 220,000,000 francs. The total value of the exports of Belgian produce in 1876 was 42,550,787*l.*, a decrease of three per cent. on the preceding year ; and while a very

(margin note: Position of British trade in regard to Belgium.)

K

slight decrease took place in the imports from England, the exports to England had fallen eight per cent. The value of British produce imported into Belgium during the year amounted to 9,755,920*l.* ; the value of Belgian merchandise exported to England was 7,668,000*l.*, showing an excess of importation over exportation of 23 per cent. The following figures, taken from Mr. Saville Lumley, show the amount by which the articles exported have principally increased :

			£	£
Cattle	. . . . .	from	376,000 to	646,040
Eggs	. . . . .	„	41,680 „	156,200
Machinery	. . . .	„	136,840 „	216,800
Glass	. . . . .	„	594,920 „	653,160

The exports of potatoes, lead and zinc unwrought, oils and raw sugar, are also larger than in 1875.

The principal diminutions in the exports are :

			£	£
Vegetable fibres	. .	from	1,503,920 to	1,092,480
Woollen yarns	. .	„	880,360 „	584,040
Hops	. . . .	„	234,440 „	83,560
Sugar, refined	. .	„	179,760 „	107,420

It is evident, from these statistics, that the productions of the United Kingdom are not being supplanted to any considerable extent by those of Belgium. The movement is rather in the opposite direction.

The two essentials of manufacture.

Our manufacturers and operatives must, however, be on the alert ; they must be progressive both in quality and cheapness. As to quality, our progress in ceramic industry and the decorative arts, as applied to furniture and upholstery, shows the capabilities of our people in those art manufactures which are a new phase of industry in the United Kingdom. They are an ingathering of the harvest sown from South Kensington. It is a national duty to see that the scientific training of those engaged in the metallurgical industries shall be on a level with the admirable training in art which is now provided. Cheapness depends on ingenuity, a quality in which we have never been deficient. It also depends on the skill and energy and the wages of our operatives. The pressure of foreign competition demands their best efforts to enable them to hold their own in competition with the world.

The wise statesmanship which has generally distinguished the government of this country has placed our trade and commerce in the most favourable position for international competition. The 'Westminster Review,' in an article published on January 1, 1876, points out that in no other country but our own have wealth and population kept pace with debt. The figures are compared in a most instructive table (see next page). *[margin: Our political advantages as a trading nation.]*

In our case the burden has been lessened more than half, but in the other countries mentioned a twofold or threefold increase is seen. The result must in fairness be ascribed to the tenure of office by Liberal administrations during the greater portion of the interval under review. We enjoy advantages here which are not shared by any country in the New or Old World. The beneficial results of the wise fiscal policy adopted in the United Kingdom were summed up by the First Lord of the Admiralty in his recent speech at Westminster. He showed that while our *[margin: Relative diminution of debt.]*

Countries	Population	National Income	Annual Charge	Charge per Head of Pop.	Percentage on Income
Great Britain, 1843 .	27,000,000	£ 500,000,000 @ £18 10s.	£ 27,550,000	s. d. 20 5	5·51
,, 1875 .	32,700,000	915,000,000 @ £28	23,000,000	14 0	2·51
France, . 1848 .	35,700,000	535,000,000 @ £15	7,070,000	4 0	1·32
,, . 1875 .	36,500,000	840,000,000 @ £22	40,000,000	21 10	4·76
Austria, . 1848 .	37,000,000	440,000,000 @ £12	5,500,000	3 0	·1·25
,, . 1875 .	38,000,000	680,000,000 @ £18	15,169,000	8 0	2·23
Russia in Europe, 1853	60,000,000	360,000,000 @ £6	6,000,000	2 0	1·66
,, 1875	72,000,000 (?)	540,000,000 @ £7 10s.	14,000,000	3 10	2·60
Italy, . 1861 .	22,000,000	260,000,000 @ £12	4,500,000	4 1	1·73
,, . 1875 .	27,800,000	415,000,000 @ £15	19,500,000	14 0	4·70
United States, 1848 .	22,000,000	440,000,000 @ £20	2,710,000	2 6	0·61
,, 1875 .	44,000,000	1,100,000,000 @ £25	24,500,000	11 0	2·23

Moderate rate of taxation. total taxation is about 100,000,000*l.*, or approximately the same as that of the United States, the public charge in France amounts to 121,000,000*l.* Again, in London, which is probably the largest manufacturing city in the world, and has probably the largest trading interest in the world, having a population of about 3,600,000, the gross amount of the local and imperial taxation is at the rate of 3*l.* 8*s.* 11*d.* per head ; while in New York the figure is 6*l.* 14*s.* 7*d.* ; and in Paris 5*l.* 14*s.* 1*d.* The comparative lightness of the taxation is an obvious advantage in our favour. We possess advantages of climate to which Mr. Smith very properly adverted. Our climate may be fickle, and our skies obscured by clouds, but there is no season of year in which manual labour cannot be efficiently performed. Our working classes are free from the conscription, which imposes such an oppressive burden on the populations of France and Germany. In the universal liability to military service the industry of those powers is burdened with a tax which more than neutralises any advantage they may possess in the comparative cheapness of labour. Mr. Smith summed up his able statement with a cheering and well-founded assertion, that our working classes can, if they choose, beat all their foreign rivals, both in the excellence and in the thorough honesty and cheapness of their work, and may thus maintain their long-established supremacy in the markets of the world.

Exemption from conscription.

The increase in the exports of cotton and woollen yarn and pig-iron, *pari passu* with the falling away in the exports of more finished manufactures, constitutes one of the most discouraging features of the present commercial situation. The textile manufactures show a decrease in 1878, as compared with the previous year, of 4·37 millions sterling on a total of 98·65 millions. The 'Economist' assigns 1·67 millions of the diminution to quantity, and 2·70 to price. But whilst a serious loss is observable on the total exportation, and especially on the exportation of piece goods, the exports of yarn have increased no less than nine per cent.

Decreased exports of finished goods,

The total value of the exportation of metals and

minerals for 1878 was 29·89 millions sterling, being 2·45 millions or eight per cent. below the exports of the previous year.   One-eighth of the loss is due to the diminished quantity, and seven-eighths to the fall in price.   Here again we find a decrease in the total value of our exports, but an increase in pig-iron from 882,000 to 925,000 tons.

as affected by foreign fiscal policy.   If the competition with foreign countries were conducted on fair and equitable terms, the inference from these figures would doubtless be unfavourable to British labour, in point of economy, if not efficiency. It will be found, however, that the import duties levied by the protectionist countries are systematically graduated, and that they increase in proportion to the labour required for the production of the more finished articles.

The following items are selected from Sir Charles Adderley's 'Return of Foreign Import Duties on British Goods,' Parliamentary Paper 205, Session 1876.

Cotton, per Cwt.

	France	Germany
Yarn, unbleached . .	6s. 1d.	6s. 1d.
„ bleached . . .	15 per cent. additional	12s. 2d.
Cotton Tissues . . .	1l. 12s. 6d.	1l. 10s. 6d.
Woollen Yarn undyed .	9s. 6d.	1s. 6¼d.
Woollen Tissues . .	10 per cent. *ad valorem*	

Iron, per Cwt.

Belgium :

	s.	d.
Iron, rough cast	0	2½
„ manufactured cast . . .	0	9¾
„ „ wrought . . .	1	7½

Iron, per Cwt.—continued.

France:

									s.	*d.*
Bars, rails	.	:	.	.	.	.	.	.	2	5¼
Hoops						.	.	.	4	0¾
Sheet, rolled or hammered }										
Engines	.	.	.	.	.	.	.	4	10½
Tubes	.	.	.	.	.	from 4*s.* 5¾*d.* to 8	2		

United States:

Chains,	35 per cent. *ad valorem.*
Sheet,	30 „ „
Bar,	35 „ „
Other kinds	45 „ „

The tariff question has assumed a new importance from the recent declaration of Prince Bismarck in favour of the reimposition of duties on all articles imported into the German Empire. Germany had quite recently removed all restrictions on the importation of iron. It is now to be feared that she may shortly follow the usual course of impecunious governments, and endeavour to supply the demands of a needy exchequer by levying high import duties.

Prince Bismarck proposes to re-establish a general taxation of all foreign produce imported into Germany. He would make exceptions only in favour of certain raw materials, such as cotton, and other articles which are not produced in Germany in sufficient quantity. This general tariff would be at the rate of 5 per cent. *ad valorem.* If a protectionist policy be adopted in Germany, it is possible that our exportation of yarns and pig-iron to that country may be diminished. On the other hand, we may dismiss henceforward all apprehension of German competition in foreign markets. The fatal consequences which must immediately ensue

The proposed German tariff.

Dr. Bamberger's remonstrance.

to German trade were set forth by Dr. Bamberger in his recent speech in the Reichstag on the Customs Tariff. 'He mentioned,' says the 'Economist,' 'as a curious instance of the keen instincts of trade, " that the scanty band of tin manufacturers, six in all, felt so safe behind the walls of the protective duty (Zollmauer) that they have already again made a coalition among themselves. They have resolved to raise their prices, and already are settling the districts among themselves in which they will vend their goods." Dr. Bamberger pointed out, also, the effect on the plate makers, the raw materials used in their trade being enhanced in price 11 to $12\frac{1}{2}$ per cent., and commented on the position of the seaport cities, which will have to raise prices against the whole of Germany to make up for the disadvantages inflicted on them. Though the fate of the Bill is hardly doubtful, it is satisfactory to see how strong a protest has been made against it.'

Twofold nature of tariffs:

It is not so much the particular scale of duties which may from time to time be enforced, as the general policy of exclusion it implies, that constitutes the most discouraging feature of the fiscal policy of the protectionist Governments. A tariff may be imposed

1. For revenue purposes;

for two reasons. It may be imposed, as it is by the South American Republics and by our own colonies, for revenue purposes. In such a case it may be presumed that it will be levied impartially on the productions of the manufacturers of all countries. Or,

2. Protective.

again, a tariff may be imposed, as it is in the United States and France, for the purpose of protecting the home trade against foreign competition. When the object is to give protection rather than to collect revenue, the barrier becomes insurmountable; for if, by improvements in the system of manufacture or by reductions of wages, we should succeed in producing an article at such a price as to enable us to sell it, after payment of duty, at a lower price than that at which it can be produced by the protected industry, against which we are competing, that industry will appeal to its Government to raise the duty to such a point as will render foreign competition impossible. It is by a tariff designedly prohibitory that we now find ourselves shut out from the United States, and the revival of our former interchange of trade depends on the abandonment of the present policy of rigid protection. I do not despair of a change in the fiscal policy of the United States, but a considerable interval may elapse before our trade can be revived in its former proportions. In process of time, however, the country will be fully occupied. The expanding numbers will then be driven to remoter districts and compelled to resort to modes of cultivation like those of old countries, and less productive in proportion to the labour and expense. As an illustration of the extravagant charge imposed upon the consumer in the United States for the benefit of the manufacturers of iron, it may be sufficient to give the figures relating to railway metal. It is stated in ' Iron ' that Bessemer steel rails can be bought in Sheffield at 4*l.* 10*s.* per ton. For 1*l.* per ton they can be carried to New York, and the *ad valorem* duty of 35 per cent. amounts to 1*l.* 15*s.*, making a total of 7*l.* 5*s.*, or 36·37 dollars. But the last quotation for Bessemer rails at the works in the United States is from 42 dollars to 43 dollars. Prices are kept up in America

[marginal note: Prohibitory tariff of United States.]

[marginal note: Example of its working.]

by an organised combination among the iron manufacturers in concert with the great railway interest. It
is obvious, from this comparison, that, under the
artificially restricted conditions imposed in America,
very handsome profits are realised both by importers
and manufacturers, at the expense of the consumers.

Its pressure on the agricultural interest.

It is incredible that such a condition of affairs can
long continue to be tamely endured. As agriculture becomes less profitable the farmers will grow
less tolerant of a protective system, maintained at
their expense for the benefit of a comparatively
limited number of wealthy manufacturers, ironmasters,
and railway proprietors. Already the pioneers of
civilisation in the West are far less prosperous than is
generally imagined. Their position has been described
by a well-informed contributor to the ' Economist : '
' The great majority of them are poor. They have
abundance of food and fairly good shelter, but they
have very little margin for spending, and they want a
margin very much. They have taxes to pay, and
education to buy, and children to start in life, and law-
yers and doctors to fee, and repairs to make, and they
want manure, and they wish to save, and they know
that as soon as they die their property will be divided ;
and altogether the plenty of food does not make them
feel rich. Great numbers of them are compelled from
time to time to raise loans on mortgage which they are
hardly ever able to pay off. The prices they get for
stock are not large—not approaching English prices—
and the prices for cereals are distinctly low. The
English market rules these, and to grow corn at such a

price that it can be 'railed' for 1,000 miles, then shipped to Mark Lane, and then sold for 45s. a quarter, is very difficult indeed. It is true they pay no rent and few rates, but if they farm much land they have to pay high for labour, and if they farm little land the margin becomes very small.'

It is not probable that a potato famine will occur to lend to the arguments for free trade the irresistible force which they acquired in England in 1843–45 ; but as the pressure upon the agricultural interest increases, the burden of the present tariff will at last become intolerable. The result of remission of duties would be a more extensive interchange of commerce between the two countries. We should be able to employ the resources of our accumulated capital and our manufacturing capabilities, while the New World would supply us from its boundless stores with the raw materials of industry. It is lamentable that both nations should have been deprived of these reciprocal advantages by selfish legislation. True it is that the two chief members of the Anglo-Saxon family are bound together by bonds more enduring than any which the most prosperous commerce can supply. A common literature, as Professor Hoppin has truly said, is the main source of the most genuine sympathy felt in America for England; ' because we read the same English Bible and sing the same sweet English hymns ; because we comprehend the words of William Shakespeare, John Milton, and John Bunyan ; because we laugh and weep over the same pages of Hawthorne, Whittier, Thackeray, and Dickens. This is a spiritual

An argument for a free-trade policy.

bond more profound than commercial ties and international treaties, and more present and vital than past historic associations.' The arguments of the economist for a closer commercial union seem feeble beside this eloquent appeal to a nobler order of ideas. Material interests, however, are substantial things, and it should be the aim of the statesmen of both countries to remove every artificial obstacle which prevents the one country from contributing to the welfare of the other.

Flickerings of free trade on the Continent.

On the Continent the lamp of free trade is kept alight by a few gifted economists, but it burns with an unsteady flame. Russia, with its vast population, is enshrouded in a Cimmerian darkness of protection. In Germany, where there had been some progress towards the truth, we are threatened with a retrograde movement. In France we have little reason to look for a renunciation of her protective policy. The effect of this protection has hitherto been to limit the French trade, at least in those branches which alone derive any benefit from protection to the home market. The present duty of 2*l.* 8*s.* per ton on iron rails is quite as prohibitory as a duty of 9*l.* in 1851. The fact that my father found it cheaper to import the rails for the Rouen and Havre Railway, though subject to a duty of 9*l.* per ton, rather than to buy them in France, only shows how limited were the resources of France at that date for the manufacture of iron. Taking into view their increased capacity for production, the ironmasters of the present day are as effectually protected as were

their predecessors a generation ago by the higher duties
then imposed.

In his paper on the Progress of the Foreign Trade
with the United Kingdom, from which we have already
quoted, Mr. Newmarch has given an exhaustive
enumeration of the beneficial results of the bold and
enlightened fiscal policy adopted in our own country.
He appropriately refers to the inauguration of free
trade by Sir Robert Peel in 1846, and to the advice
tendered by that great statesman, that the best way to
compete with hostile tariffs was to encourage free
imports. At the end of a generation, as Mr.
Newmarch points out, having faithfully followed Sir
Robert Peel's advice, we have seen our imports rise
from 70,000,000*l.* to 380,000,000*l.*, and a fabulous
accumulation of wealth has been formed in the country.
By our free-trade system the United Kingdom has
become the great mart of the world for the exchange
of merchandise, and for settling international claims.
It has given rise to what Mr. Newmarch designates as
a triangular system of trade which goes very far to
neutralise the evils of protective tariffs.

'The United States cannot help taking tea and silk
from China, and cannot help China refusing to take
tobacco and raw cotton in exchange. Hence the
United States cannot help sending the tobacco and raw
cotton to England, and using the proceeds in the
purchase of English credits available to discharge the
China debt. In like manner it is every day more true
that England pays for a large part of its imports not
directly to the country A from whence they come, but

Beneficial results of free trade in England.

indirectly to other countries to which A happens to be in debt.

'The true nature of foreign trade is, that the nations of the world should resemble not merely a single country, but a large town within that country, throughout the streets, lanes, and alleys of which there shall be kept up as constant, rapid, and easy a current of dealings as prevails among the natives of the town itself.'

Mr. Newmarch steadfastly maintains that, tried by every statistical test, the extraordinary growth of our foreign trade and the accumulation of capital in the United Kingdom have been the result of steady adherence to the free-trade maxims of

(1) Cultivating the imports, and leaving the exports to cultivate themselves;

(2) Regarding the benefit of the consumer as the paramount object to be attained.

While experience has shown that free trade has conferred immense benefits on Great Britain, it cannot be doubted that it would have been a still better thing if the same enlightened principles had been more universally adopted.

Future commercial supremacy of America.

It is not from the cheap labour of Belgium, as the writers of the manifestoes from time to time issued by the associations of employers would have us believe, but from the dear, but skilful and energetic labour of the United States, that the most formidable competition will hereafter arise. Mr. Gladstone, in his contribution to the 'North American Review,' entitled 'Kin beyond

Sea,' has rightly said that the commercial supremacy of the world must ultimately pass from the United Kingdom to the United States. The territory at their command is, in comparison with the narrow area of the United Kingdom, unlimited, and it possesses every natural advantage. The soil is fertile; the mineral wealth is inexhaustible; and the increase in the population has been so rapid that Professor Huxley has predicted that, when the second centenary of the republic is celebrated, the American people will have increased from 40,000,000 to 200,000,000.

The marvellous energy of this vast population, in utilising the great resources of their country, called forth the approving testimony of Sir John Hawkshaw in his report on the Exhibition at Philadelphia: 'The 70,000 miles of railway already constructed, the ramifications of the electric telegraph, and its application to uses more extended and varied even than in our own country, the crowd of steamboats wherever navigation is possible and public convenience can be promoted, the building of cities like Chicago, which, after the great fire, in four or five years has arisen out of its ashes a more beautiful city than before—all these tell of the increase of wealth, and speak still more strongly of the public and patriotic spirit of the people.

'To me who visited the United States on a former occasion, but so long ago that Chicago was then but a village, and Philadelphia had not more than one half its present population, when its railways were only beginning to be made, with wooden bridges and tem-

Sir J. Hawkshaw's testimony to the progress of her people.

porary works, when its vast mineral wealth was nearly
untouched, and wood was burned where coal is now
consumed, the astonishing changes, and the vast progress since made, appear greater than perhaps to others
whose visits have been more frequent.'

That the United States must hereafter command a
dominant position is certain, but there is no immediate
prospect of a competition which can be injurious to
our own manufacturers. The American export trade
is continually increasing, both in bulk and value ; but
hitherto the growth in the export of manufactured
goods has been unimportant. Agricultural products
constitute the great bulk of their export trade. The
success of the American manufacturers, in so far
as it depends on the effective application of labour, is
certainly not due to the low scale of wages. On the
contrary it is the high price of labour, which has been
the main incentive to the application of the national
genius to the invention of labour-saving machinery.

American
labour-
saving
machinery.
The surprising economical results, which followed
the outbreak of the Civil War, are thus described by
Mr. Wells:—' The outbreak of Civil War in 1861, and
its vigorous prosecution until 1865, acted as an immense
stimulus to invention and discovery in the Northern
States, and led to an application of labour-saving
machinery and methods to the work of production
which, taking time into consideration, has probably no
parallel in the world's experience. . . . With certainly
not more than five millions of male adults engaged in
agriculture, mechanic arts, manufactures, and transportation in the Northern States in 1860, the close of

the war, in 1865, found more than a million of adults
enrolled in the service of the Northern armies. But
the industrial products of these same States, especially
the products of agriculture, did not in general
decrease during the war period by reason of the
diversion of labour noted, but, on the contrary, and
mainly through the invention and use of labour-saving
machinery, they largely increased. Thus, for example,
the amount of wheat raised in Indiana in 1859 was
15,219,000 bushels, but in 1863, notwithstanding that
this State, out of a population in 1860 of 1,350,000,
had furnished to the army more than 124,000 fighting
men, its product of wheat exceeded 20,000,000 bushels;
and what was true of Indiana was also true of Iowa,
Illinois, and other agricultural States, and in respect to
productions other than wheat.'

By ingenious mechanical labour the Americans
are now competing successfully against the cheap
manual labour of Switzerland; and we learn from
the report of Mr. Beauclerk, the Secretary of the
Legation at Berne, for the year 1878, that the
diminished exportation of watches to the United States
has inflicted severe losses on the hand-workers in
Switzerland.

Industry and ingenuity have enabled the Americans
to conquer in a remarkable degree the many difficulties
which obstruct their industrial development; but while
a wide extent of soil remains untilled, the most profitable and congenial occupation of the people must be
pastoral and agricultural rather than manufacturing.

The natural expansion of the population over the

Farming
in the
Western
States.

plains of the West was for a time arrested by the high
protective duties, which secured excessive profits to
manufacturers, and led to a development of production
beyond the requirements of the country. A reaction
has naturally followed from the excessive development
of manufacturing industry. Of 716 furnaces in existence in 1877, 446 are out of blast, and the workmen
are rapidly leaving the factories and ironworks and
resorting to the unsettled lands in the Western States.

Growth of Kansas. The rapid growth of Kansas may be taken as an
example of the impetus given to an agricultural State
by the extensive migration from the manufacturing
districts. The population has increased since 1875
from 531,000 to 700,000. In 1872 the entire number
of acres under cultivation in the State was 2,476,862,
and the value of the product thereof 25,265,109
dollars. In 1877 the acres under cultivation reached
5,595,304, and the value of the product therefrom
45,597,051 dollars. In 1878 the acres under cultivation exceeded 6,500,000, the increase being nearly a
million acres in a single year. A similar movement,
though of course on a smaller scale, is taking place in
our own country, where agricultural labour is gradually .
returning from the furnaces to the farms.

Migration of artisans: The migration from the industrial centres to the
agricultural States of the West is prominently noticed in
the annual report of the American mercantile agency of
Messrs. Dun & Co., quoted by the ' Economist ' in the
annual review of the trade of 1878. The sales of land
by the national government increased from 3,338,000
acres in the year ending the 30th of June, 1877, to

7,562,000 acres in the succeeding year. An equal increase has taken place in the sale of lands by the State land agencies and railroad land offices. It is estimated that no less than 20,000,000 acres were newly settled in 1878, and that not less than a hundred thousand families, representing a population of half a million, have changed their abodes and their pursuits in the same period.

Wages can never long remain at a low level in the United States, while the working man can transport himself and his family from the irksome employment of the factory to the free life of the Western plains. The profits realised upon agriculture in the Mississippi Valley, as the 'Economist' observes, exercise a paramount influence in determining the average rate of wages in the manufacturing industries of the United States. The prospects of agriculture in the West were never more favourable than at the present time, and we have, therefore, reason to believe that the cost of industrial labour will be sustained for some time to come on the existing scale. As an evidence of the attractions of an agricultural life to populations engaged in factories and ironworks, I may refer to the fact mentioned by Mr. Henderson in his recent paper in the 'Contemporary Review,' that, on the average, the working staff of the American factories is changed once in three years. *its influence on wages.*

Having given an extract from the 'Economist' which describes in somewhat gloomy terms the condition of the agriculturists of the United States, it may not be uninteresting to show that a more cheerful view *An American's view of agricultural life.*

of the situation is taken by other equally well-informed observers. The following passages are extracted from a recent letter from a correspondent in Boston. They present a characteristic specimen of the broad-minded go-ahead ideas of an American man of business.

'If men wish to migrate, let them go into Nebraska, or Kansas, or possibly Texas. The population is for the most part active and industrious, constantly striving for something more. The land is fresh and strong, and easily tilled. The crops can be marketed at some price usually, and the railroads are constantly pushing in here and there. The life is rough and hard to the last degree, and calls for health, strength, skill, and patience, but it is morally healthy. I have been expecting an exodus from England and the Continent, and can only say that the really first-rate lands are going fast. A man with a family of half-grown children to help him, and with a wife who is good and steady in her efforts, should do well in these new lands; for he can get a living, raise his children well, and see the value of his property increase yearly. He can also lay by a little each year, if he has fair luck. But he had better have a little money to carry him over the first year or so.

'I have always thought money well placed in these new States, in buying lands along the lines of the good railroads, and in the really promising new cities. I have had some there for years, and have seen large sums made in such ventures. But it is necessary to buy land adjoining railroad land, for the railroads always try to sell to real settlers. . . .

'I have always thought that the labourers by hand

did not have half a chance, and that we, the luckier class, can only help and control them by giving them every opportunity of enjoying comfort and education and happiness—i.e. by really civilising them. Heaven knows that we have all we can handle in the way of troubles and fermentation in the nineteenth century, and we cannot stop or recede.

' I hope that you are not to have long wars in India or in Africa, and that peace and prosperity are to rule for a while for you. But the present government must pass out before you can really move on—at least so we think.'

In a paper contributed to the ' Fortnightly Review ' by Mr. Atkinson, of Boston, we are informed that during the last thirty years the factory population of New England has passed through three phases. First came the sons and daughters of the New England farmer ; but they have now betaken themselves to easier and better paid employments. The native operatives of New England were succeeded by the Irish ; but the Irish, in their turn, saved money, and bought the farms deserted by the New England yeomen who had emigrated to the richer lands in the west. French Canadians now supply the labour formerly furnished by the Irish emigration, and, it is said, exhibit in manufacturing industry a vigour and energy of which they gave no indications while dwelling on their little strips of land on the banks of the River St. Lawrence. It will be admitted that American industrial enterprise has made great progress, and that an abundant supply of labour will at all times be furnished by emigration ;

Mutations of the factory population.

but, for the reasons which have been enumerated, commodities, in the production of which labour is a principal factor, must at the present time be cheaper in England than in the United States, although our goods may be excluded from the American market by a prohibitory tariff.

CHAPTER VII.

THE MERCANTILE MARINE.

SUCCESS in maritime enterprise is a sure indication of industrial power, and of those personal qualities in the people which make a nation great. The ascendency of British maritime enterprise should allay the anxiety and misgivings of those who take a desponding view of our power to compete with foreign industry and enterprise. *Maritime enterprise a test of industrial power.*

The 'Statist' gives the following summary of the latest figures published by the Board of Trade: 'The aggregate tonnage of merchant vessels bearing the British flag approximately equals the combined tonnage of all the other merchant navies of the world. And when we come to steam tonnage, which is the more efficient and costly part of a merchant navy, the preponderance of English over foreign mercantile marines stands out in a still more marked manner.' Our superiority is conclusively established in the subjoined statistics. *Statistics of British and foreign tonnage.*

According to the latest Board of Trade returns, the proportion of national tonnage to the total tonnage of steam shipping, entered and cleared in some of the principal maritime countries of Europe, and in the United States, was as follows :

Proportion of National Ships to total Steam Tonnage.

In the United Kingdom	83·3
In Russia	8·5
In Norway and Sweden	40·7
In Germany	31·4
In France	34·9
In the United States	21·5

Total Tonnage of the Merchant Navies of the principal Countries of Europe and of the United States.

	Tons
British Empire (including United Kingdom) .	8,320,421
Total German Empire	1,117,935
France	980,128
Italy	1,068,449
United States (registered for oversea) . .	1,629,047

Steam Tonnage of principal Maritime Countries.

	Tons
British Empire	2,492,327
Total German Empire	183,379
France	230,804
Italy	58,319
United States	170,838

Tonnage added to Register of principal Foreign Countries.

		Tons
1878	United Kingdom	464,511
1877	Germany	82,520
1877	France	54,900

Tonnage of Vessels built in the United Kingdom.

Years	For Home and the Colonies .	For Foreigners
1874 . . . . . . :	521,203	82,604 .
1877	433,694	17,260
1878	428,301	42,474

Tonnage of Vessels built in France, bought abroad, and sold to Foreigners.

Years	Tonnage of Vessels built	Tonnage of Vessels bought abroad	Tonnage of Vessels sold to Foreigners
1874	34,917	17,404	27,092
1876 . . .	32,707	15,581	16,148
1877 . . .	26,884	12,864	14,751

Mr. Drummond quotes the following table, showing the number and tonnage of iron steamships built in England and the United States since 1868:

BUILT IN GREAT BRITAIN.		
Iron Sailing Ships	Steamers	Total Tonnage
162	188	200,840
157	238	256,824
63	382	271,760
30	416	311,822
18	446	350,897
48	335	327,205
116	393	471,322
404	2,398	2,196,670

where the years 1868, 1869, 1870, 1871, 1872, 1873, 1874 correspond to the rows above.

BUILT IN THE UNITED STATES.		
Iron Sailing Ships	Steamers	Total Tonnage
—	6	2,801
2	8	4,584
1	14	8,281
—	20	15,480
—	20	12,767
—	26	26,548
—	23	33,097
—	20	21,632
—	25	21,347
3	102	146,537

where the years 1868, 1869, 1870, 1871, 1872, 1873, 1874, 1875, 1876 correspond to the rows above.

In his judgment there are no present indications of competition to our carrying trade from the United States; for although it is possible that steam-ships may be built as cheaply as in England, iron, and wood, and labour being cheap, England, Italy, and Sweden have an immense surplus tonnage which comes to American ports for employment.

In the annual commercial review, the 'Economist' supplies the subjoined particulars relating to the employment of the shipping of the United Kingdom during the past year:

	Vessels			Tons		
	1878	1877	Increase	1878	1877	Increase
Entered .	346,768	340,318	6,450	63,186,548	62,510,702	675,846
Cleared .	310,651	303,223	7,428	59,121,151	57,864,853	1,256,298

It is British shipping exclusively that has increased, both the number and tonnage of foreign vessels entered and cleared being slightly less than in the previous year. The entries of British ships in 1878 were 316,887 vessels, with an aggregate tonnage of 54,218,769 tons, being an increase of 8,222 vessels and 1,081,393 tons as compared with 1877. The clearances were 280,976 vessels of 50,092,885 tons, being an increase of 8,542 vessels and 1,431,211 tons.

The 'Bureau Veritas' of Paris has published the following statistics, showing the aggregate tonnage of the merchant navies of the principal maritime countries for the year 1877–78. From this document I extract the following figures :

Sailing Vessels	Number	Tonnage
England . . .	18,394	5,696,000
United States . .	6,050	2,076,000
Norway . .	4,157	1,375,000
Italy . . .	3,135	963,625
Germany . . .	3,201	815,000
France . . .	2,972	596,000
Russia . . .	1,814	414,000
Total . . .	49,524	14,317,430
Steamships	**Number**	**Tonnage**
England . . .	3,216	3,465,000
United States . .	516	609,000
France . . .	275	335,000
Germany . . .	220	254,000
Russia . . .	148	105,000
Italy . . .	92	84,000
Total . . .	5,462	5,595,000

If the figures published by the 'Bureau Veritas' be examined in detail, it will be seen that the diminution in the tonnage of sailing ships has not extended to all countries. In a single year we see a diminution of 71,000 tons in the tonnage of American sailing ships, a reduction of 533,000 tons in Italian sailing ships, of 71,000 tons under the French, and 221,518 tons under the Spanish flags. No change took place in the mercantile marine of Norway, Russia, Sweden, Austria, Greece, Portugal, Denmark, and Turkey, while, on the other hand, under the British flag we find an increase of 170,000 tons, and under the German flag an increase of 39,000 tons.

In the number of steam vessels an unimportant reduction will be observed in the total, but the tonnage of the British steamships, so far from diminishing, shows an increase of 83 vessels and 181,277 tons. In the other merchant navies of Europe we trace a slender increase, while under the flag of the United States we notice a reduction of 65,000 tons, and in Sweden of 9,000 tons. All the recent changes in the tonnage of the mercantile marine of the world have tended to make the ascendency of British maritime enterprise even more conspicuous than before.

Ascendency of British maritime enterprise.

As a further illustration of its growth, I may refer to Professor Neumann-Spellart's analysis of the traffic on the Suez Canal since the commencement. 'In 1876 the total tonnage of ships passing through the canal was 3,072,000, or nearly double the average tonnage of the preceding seven years. Of the 3,072,000 tons, 2,344,000, or 76 per cent., were British, the next

Our share of the Suez Canal traffic.

largest amount, 237,000 tons, being contributed by France. In 1877 the total was 3,419,000, an increase of 347,000 tons. The British tonnage was 2,699,000, or nearly 79 per cent. of the whole. The average pro- portion of British ships during the seven years 1869–75 was only 57 per cent.' And we are gaining ground year by year in an accelerated ratio.

Before the opening of the canal it was predicted that our sailing ships would be displaced by steamers from every port in the Mediterranean. Those mis- givings are now dispelled by the astonishing success which we have achieved. At present, absolutely no foreign competition is attempted in the steam trade to the East without the aid of a Government subsidy.

British invention.

Can any single production of human ingenuity and labour be compared for concentrated difficulty and perplexity with a powerful ironclad? Can such vessels be produced in any country of superior quality and at a lower price than in the United Kingdom? Has any invention of modern times surpassed in prac- tical utility the railway, the steamship, the electric telegraph, or the submarine cable? Has not our country been the pioneer in originating these valuable inventions and in extending their use?

157

CHAPTER VIII.

COMPARATIVE EFFICIENCY OF ENGLISH AND FOREIGN LABOUR.

I now proceed to discuss the character and conduct of the British workman, always so severely criticised in a time of commercial depression. When trade expands and every available man finds employment, wages inevitably rise, and the workman is disliked because he is in a position to enforce compliance with his ever-growing demands. When trade collapses it is always said, and often most unjustly, that the inflation of wages has been the main cause of our disasters ; as if those who control the application of the capital, which constitutes the wage fund of the country, were not responsible for the over-production of textile goods and iron, and for the multiplication of furnaces, factories, and ships. It is owing to this constant and unnecessary augmentation of our manufacturing resources that the market has been overstocked, and that a general depreciation of prices has been brought about.

If we test the comparative efficiency of British labour by the amount of our exports, we shall see that we have lost ground chiefly in our trade with the great manufacturing countries, where the s pply of

[margin: Wages not answerable for collapses of trade.]

[margin: Our loss of trade apparent with protected countries,]

capital and labour has been abundant, and where we have to encounter a serious protective tariff. It is a curious circumstance that it is in those very countries in which the growth of manufactures has been most rapid, and against which we have been told to be on our guard as formidable rivals, that the apprehension of British competition is most keenly felt. The progress of our trade with non-manufacturing countries and in neutral markets is not unsatisfactory.

not in neutral markets.
The following figures are taken from the Board of Trade tables. The comparison is made between 1873, when our exports were at the highest point they have ever attained, and 1877.

Countries	Exports	
	1873	1877
	£	£
Java and other possessions in the Indian Seas . .	774,673	2,088,775
Algeria	65,565	276,000
The Philippines . .	439,177	1,314,169
Morocco	365,364	465,258
Venezuela	541,620	633,740
Ecuador	109,383	255,618
Japan	1,884,145	2,460,275
British possessions . .	71,147,707	75,752,150

It is difficult to obtain an impartial opinion on the subject of our investigation from persons practically familiar with the capabilities of the working man. In pursuing my inquiry I have keenly felt the loss of the valuable counsels of my late father. He had enjoyed unequalled opportunities of comparing the industrial powers of many nations. He felt generously towards the working man, and he was ever ready to pay liberally for vigorous and efficient labour.

In seeking for opinions on this difficult question of the relative efficiency of English and foreign labour, it is before all things necessary that the witnesses should be free from bias. I would rather take the opinion of a literary man, or of an economist, than that of a manufacturer, on such a subject; although I am sensible that in the former case I am leaning on the judgment of a theorist rather than a practical man.

Mr. Lecky, in his 'History of the Eighteenth Century,' quotes a passage from Defoe's pamphlet entitled 'Giving Alms no Charity,' which gives a vivid picture of the labouring men of England in the beginning of the last century. A bad system of poor relief had already wrought a pernicious influence on the peasantry. 'I affirm,' says Defoe, in the passage quoted by Mr. Lecky, 'of my own knowledge, that when I wanted a man for labouring work, and offered 9s. per week to strolling fellows at my door, they have frequently told me to my face that they could get more a begging. Good husbandry is no English virtue. . . . It neither loves nor is beloved by an Englishman. The English get fortunes, and the Dutch save them; and this observation I have made between Dutchmen and Englishmen, that where an Englishman earns his 20s. a week, and but just lives, as we call it, a Dutchman with the same earnings grows rich, and leaves his children in a very good condition. Where an English labouring man with his 9s. a week lives wretchedly, a Dutchman with the same money will live tolerably.'

By the kindness of Mr. Watson, who has had ex-

Marginal notes:
English compared with foreign labour.

Defoe's comparison of English and Dutch labourers.

tensive experience in the construction of public works
in Holland, I am enabled to give some facts, which
show how the Englishman compares with the Dutchman in our own day, nearly two centuries after Defoe's
pamphlet was written.

In summer the Dutch mechanic begins his day's
labour at 5 a.m. and ends at 7 p.m., with two and
a half hours' interval.   In winter he commences work
at 7 a.m. and ends at 5.30 p.m., with pauses of an hour
and a half.   The workman's food costs from 1s. 3d. to
1s. 6d. a day.   The English labourer, who consumes
more meat and beer, would probably spend from 2s.
to 2s. 6d.

Education amongst Dutch mechanics is more advanced than with us.   Carpenters and bricklayers can
generally understand and work to a drawing, and write
and read fluently.

With the view of comparing the cost of work in
Holland and in England, Mr. Watson analysed the cost
of some sea locks executed in Holland in 1870, 1871,
and 1872.   The brickwork cost 1l. 1s. 2d. per cubic
yard.   On a railway contract near London executed
in 1878 the price of ordinary brickwork was found to
be 1l. 4s. 4d. per yard.   The quality of the Dutch
work is better than the English.   The bricks are
excellent, and the workmanship cannot be surpassed.
In Holland the wages of a good bricklayer average
3s 10d. per day of ten hours.   The Englishman will
do about the same amount of work, but his wages for
ten hours of labour in or near London, until a recent
date, were about 8s. a day.

Extending the comparison to earth-work, the cubic yard costs by Dutch labour 3·02*d.* ; by English labour 3·63*d.* The transport of earth to long distances is of rare occurrence in Holland. In this particular the men are not expert, and the work is quite as costly as in England.

Carpenters for rough work are paid in Holland from 4*d.* to 4¾*d.* per hour. They are good workmen, but not so active as Englishmen. It may be assumed that the labour of four Englishmen would be equal to that of five Dutchmen ; but the four Englishmen, at the London price of 6*s.* 6*d.* per day, would cost 1*l.* 6*s.* as compared with the sum of 18*s.* 9*d.* which would be paid for the five Dutchmen—thus making the English work about 46 per cent. dearer than the Dutch. The quality of the carpenters' work is excellent, but joiners cannot compete in quality or finish with London workmen.

In a report made by the director of a large engineering establishment at Amsterdam to the proprietors, comparing the Thames and the Clyde prices and results with those obtained on his own works, it is assumed that three Englishmen would accomplish as much as four Dutchmen, but the wages of the former averaged 8*d.* per hour, and the wages of the latter were 5*d.* As regards quality, though not equal in finish to London work, excellent steam-engines and machinery are now turned out of the Dutch establishments.

The cost of labour of all descriptions in Holland has risen at least 30 per cent. during the last ten years, with a corresponding rise in the cost of living.

It will be observed that Mr. Watson sets the cost of labour in the rural districts of Holland in comparison with its cost in the vicinity of London, during a period of exceptional activity in the building trades. I cannot, therefore, accept his statement as a final judgment. We ought to take the prices paid for piece-work in the provinces, and the rates of wages paid throughout a period of at least ten years, in order to arrive at a fair average.

The English navvy. Gangs of navvies are to be·seen at work at the present day in the vicinity of London, composed of men whose physical power and energy have never been exceeded in any former generation. They are worthy successors of the stalwart delvers of the earth who excavated the canals and constructed our vast network of railways. Having witnessed with the highest admiration the performances of the Lincolnshire labourers recently employed upon the extension of the Victoria Docks, I addressed some inquiries to Messrs. Lucas & Aird as to the amount of work executed and the remuneration paid to the navvies. It should be explained that the depth of the excavation is about thirty feet below the level upon which the excavated earth is deposited. The earth to be removed consisted mostly of heavy clay and peat. It is cut up with a grafting tool into cubes twelve inches deep by ten inches by nine inches, and carefully packed on the barrows, which will hold about ten pieces. Each barrow-load weighs from three and a half to four hundredweight. Four navvies are employed in filling the barrows and running them to the foot of an incline. The runner runs his barrow with the assistance of a horse up the incline, making an ascent of thirty feet in perpendicular height, at an angle of perhaps sixty degrees. Having arrived at the summit of the incline, he wheels the barrow a distance of eighteen yards to the tip. The average quantity these men fill in one day is about eighteen cubic yards of clay and twenty-two cubic yards of peat. Their average earnings are seven shillings, and they work about eight hours per day.

The quantity of victuals they consume may be estimated at 2 lbs. of meat, 2 lbs. of bread, but not so much vegetables in proportion. Ale is their principal drink, of which they consume about five quarts during the working hours. On Monday morning these men are remarkable for a great display of clean white clothes in which they begin their week's work. As a rule they are quiet, and, with a few exceptions, are civil to those in charge of the work, and, so long as they are fairly treated, give very little trouble.

The average stature of the Lincolnshire navvies is not inferior to the standard of the Household Cavalry, and the development of physical strength in their sinewy frames is greater in proportion as their labours are more arduous than those of a mounted trooper in the piping times of peace.

It would have been interesting to examine the cost of engineering works in all parts of Europe, and materials are not wanting; time and space, however, do not admit of such an investigation on the present occasion. We will therefore proceed to examine the comparative cost of labour in the mines and iron works. Mr. Lowthian Bell is a high authority on this subject.

Cost of labour at ironworks and collieries in France;

With reference to the cost of labour in the iron-works and collieries in France, the inquiries instituted by Mr. Lowthian Bell in 1867 furnish most ample information. No reason exists for the belief that the French have made greater progress than the English manufacturers, in regard to economy of labour, in the interval which has since elapsed. Mr. Lowthian Bell extended his inquiry to all the conditions which affect the price of labour. He showed that the price of meat had increased in France in the preceding quarter of a century by 25 per cent. ; and that the ordinary price at the period of his visit was from 7*d.* to 8½*d.* per pound, there being no difference in this respect between the prices in France and England. The cost of bread was 2*d.* per pound, while house-rent was about 2*s.* 4*d.* per week for two good rooms. Firing was provided by the work-man himself, the price of coal being 12*s.* 6*d.* per ton. No material difference was found in the cost of clothing in England and France. Workmen engaged in French mines had no advantage over the miners in our own country in the cost of schooling and medical attendance. The price of labour in France had grown with the augmented cost of living. The wages of ordinary labourers had risen in twenty years from 1*s.* 6*d.* a day to from 2*s.* 2*d.* to 2*s.* 4*d.* The effect of the former low wages was clearly apparent in the absence of labour-saving appliances.

Comparing the wages paid in France with the British standard, Mr. Lowthian Bell reported that blast furnace keepers in France were satisfied with four shillings for a day's wages, a low rate no doubt as compared with English wages, but every French furnace had a second keeper. Mr. Lowthian Bell took infinite pains to obtain correct data as to the quality of the work and the quantity of iron made at each furnace. He found that, at the furnaces on the Tees, twenty-five individuals performed an amount of work identical with that executed by forty-two men at a French furnace. In spite, therefore, of the wages being, as nearly as he could estimate, twenty per cent. cheaper, the cost of the labour employed in smelting a ton of pig-iron was sensibly greater at the French works than at Middlesborough.

The enhanced value of provisions had produced the same influence on the price of labour in Belgium as in France. Colliers worked in six-hour shifts, and went down the pit twice in the twenty-four hours; they worked, therefore, twelve hours a day, and earned from 2s. to 2s. 4¾d. per shift. A blast furnace keeper only earned 2s. 4¾d. to 2s. 9½d. per day; but then he had such help as brought up the cost of this description of labour to 6½d. to 7d. a ton for foundry iron, and for forge iron to a trifle above 4d. There were two chargers to each furnace, who, however, only received 2s. a day. The women were chiefly employed in coke burn-

in Belgium;

ing, and their wages were 1s. a day. In Belgium, the
same want of appliances for the saving of labour at the
furnaces was observed as in France ; the result being
that, notwithstanding the low rate of wages, the sum
paid on a ton of iron in Belgium was about the same
as in England.

in the
United
States.

The following comparative data are taken from a
paper written on the occasion of Mr. Lowthian Bell's
visit to the Exhibition at Philadelphia :

Coal-hewers	Hours of actual Work	Tons of Coal daily	Daily Net Earnings
			s. *d.*
Durham . . .	5·39	3·90	5 0
Northumberland . .	5·52	3·15	4 9
United States (bituminous coal)	10·0	5·00	8 6

The average earnings throughout Great Britain
were about 5s. 2d. per day, or 11¼d. per hour of actual
work.   In 1874 the rates were 1s. 2d. per hour, for
which the quantity worked was about 11 cwt. per
man.   In Northumberland and Durham the miners are
supplied with firing and live rent free, which makes
their wages worth an additional 1½d. per hour, as
compared with the earnings of colliers in the United
States.

In America in 1874 the hewers got 13 cwt. of coal
and were paid about 1s. 1d. per hour.   It thus appears
that at that date the advantage was rather on the side
of the pitmen of this country.

In November 1874 the price paid for puddling
iron on the Tees was 10s. 9d. per ton ; the average
price in the United States at the same date was 1l. 0s. 7d.

Since 1874 the price at Middlesborough has been reduced from 10s. 9d. to 8s. 3d., or 2s. 6d. per ton. During the same period the amount of reduction in the United States varied from 2s. to 4s. 6d. per ton; but these concessions had been obtained at the expense of considerable interruptions to work and some serious disturbances.

Mr. Lowthian Bell could detect no difference between the Old and the New country in the skill of manipulation exhibited by the workmen employed in the rolling-mills, but the cost for labour per ton was fully 25 per cent. higher in America than in our own country.

Mr. Lowthian Bell gives the following as the earnings of workmen employed in ironworks on the continent of Europe for the year 1873, the period of the highest wages in this country and in America :

	Coal-hewers.	Ironstone Miners	Puddlers (12 hours)	
			s. d. s. d.	
Belgium .	4s. to 7s. 2d. in 8 hours	2s. 6d. to 3s. 7d. per day	1st hand 5 6 2nd „ 2 10 to 3 2	
Silesia .	3s. 6d. in 10 hours	1s. 10d. in 8 hours	1st „ 4 9 2nd „ 3 2	

It is satisfactory to know that, after his wide and searching inquiry both in the United Kingdom and in America, Mr. Lowthian Bell arrives at the conclusion that, in regard to cheapness and efficiency of the labour, the workmen engaged in the ironworks of Great Britain have nothing to fear from foreign competition, even where the hours are longer and the

The comparison in favour of England.

168   *Foreign Work and English Wages.*

scale of wages, measured by the day, is much lower than in our own country.

We shall now proceed to give some information bearing on the comparative efficiency of workmen employed in mining.

Output of the coal-miners of Belgium :

Mr. Lumley, in his report on the Belgian coal trade for 1876, gives details as to the average output of coal per man in the province of Hainault.

Years	1st Division	2nd Division	3rd Division	Average for whole Province
	Tons	Tons	Tons	Tons
1867	157	193	198	180
1868	151	209	204	183
1869	156	215	217	190
1870	162	211	215	191
1871	158	212	206	188
1872	178	224	229	206
1873	169	202	210	191
1874	152	184	193	174
1875	157	191	195	178
1876	155	·192	184	174
Average .	159	203	205	185

From this table it appears that the productive power of the workman has not increased, the fact being, that it does not depend solely on the progress of the industry, but also on the will and the calculations of the workman, who regulates his production according to his impressions of the position of the trade and the future course of prices.

their wages;

The average wages in the Hainault collieries in 1876 were 41*l.* 8*s.* per man, a reduction of 5*l.* 15*s.* on the previous year. When business is brisk, the Belgian miner is not afraid to work his best, ' knowing that his wages will not be questioned; when demand wanes, and he sees no chance of a revival, he diminishes his production, for fear of having his wages reduced. This accounts for the increase of 1866, and the subsequent fall, and for the improvement which took place during the revival towards the end of 1869 and the beginning of 1870, but which was succeeded by a decrease during 1870 and 1871.'

It is somewhat curious to observe how diametrically different is the conduct of the Belgian and the English miner under the same conditions. Let us compare the Belgian figures with some English statistics, extracted from the columns of the 'Times.'

Superior productive capacity of the British miner.

In 1861 the industrial census discovered that 385,000 miners were employed to get 86,000,000 tons of coal, showing an average of 223·3 tons of coal raised per man. Last year, however, 494,000 miners raised 134,610,000 tons of coal, being an average of 272·4 tons per man.

I have also taken from the last reports of the Inspectors of Mines, the output of mineral in the collieries of the United Kingdom. Mr. Dickenson gives the average in the districts of North and East Lancashire at 301 tons per person employed, being an increase of 23 tons per head. He attributes the increase to the efforts of the miner to make up for lower wages. From the mining districts of Scotland Mr. Alexander gives the output per workman for 1873 at 256 tons, increasing in 1877 to 318 tons. Mr. Evans reports as follows from the Midland district: 'The quantity of minerals raised during the year was 13,000,000 tons, giving employment to 50,285 persons. In the year immediately preceding this the production was about 12,500,000 tons, persons employed 52,448.   This shows that a decrease of 2,163 persons worked half a million more tons of coal than the year before.'

The relative capacity of the miners in Belgium and England may be measured by the difference between the output in the province of Hainault and the general average for the United Kingdom.   In the one case it is 272 tons per man, in the other 185 tons.   I believe the average relative industrial capability of the work-men of the two countries approximates very closely to the proportion, which the output from the English mines bears to the output from the Belgian.

Energy of the British operative.

The Manchester correspondent of the 'Times' gives the following illustration of the endurance of our operatives and of their energy and capacity for making a rational use of adversity.

'In a large mill where the wages paid before the late reduction were 500*l.* a week, and where the simple reduction of 10 per cent. would leave the amount 450*l.*, it turned out, that, after the reduction had been submitted to, the employers had 510*l.* to pay instead of any smaller sum.   The explanation is that the work-people had been more diligent at their looms, and by this effort of self-discipline some of them, if not all, earned more money at the reduced rate than they had earned before the strike.   They also did more work, and produced a larger quantity of cloth at the cheaper rate, so that their employers could afford to sell it more cheaply in proportion ; and they contributed, in their degree, towards swelling the production which their leaders are so anxious to limit. They were not to be blamed, but commended, for making the best of their own situation.'

The industrial capabilities of Germany are seriously impaired by the disaffection of the workmen to the Government and the established order of things, both social and commercial. A well-informed contributor to the 'Edinburgh Review' of July 1878 states that German workmen abhor all forms of religion as antago- nistic to Socialism. The great commercial centres afford a congenial soil for the new doctrines. *German labour and Socialism.*

In the debates in 1876 on the German Criminal Supplementary Law, Prince Bismarck declared that the Socialist Press ' contributed to cause the stagnation of trade, and to make a German working day less pro- ductive than a French or English working day. The Prince referred the members of the Reichstag, in proof of this, to their own observation of Frenchmen working by the side of Germans in Berlin ; and he declared any one could see that a French builder executed in a day more and better work than a German : the result is that German work cannot compete in the world's markets with French. Prince Bismarck traced the decline to Socialist agitation for undefined and unreal- isable objects ; and he was not sanguine of any cure for the disease except poverty.' Commenting on Prince Bismarck's observations, the 'Edinburgh Reviewer' very truly observes that poverty is the most certain cure for the onslaught which labour designs against capital. If the Socialist schemes were carried into effect, the workmen would speedily find that capital does something more than feed on their earnings. The practical consequences of social disaffection in Germany were brought out at a conference of the several ship-owning associations of Germany recently held at Berlin. It was stated that German shipowners had been com-pelled to have recourse to foreign ship-building yards, their own workmen being unsteady and unreliable, and entirely under the pernicious influence of Trades Unions and Socialistic associations.

Inferiority of German to British workmen.

An interesting comparison of the relative capabilities of English and German workmen was lately given in the 'Leeds Mercury.' It was supplied from an occasional correspondent, and was the result of in-quiries made in Prussia, in Saxony, in Bohemia, in Austria, in Hungary, and in Roumania.

'" We find our Englishmen," said one gentleman who employs about a score of English mechanics along with three or four score North Germans, " by far the best men we can possibly get. I have no doubt, indeed, that a single Englishman is worth two Germans."

'" In what way ? " I asked.

'" In the power of using his head as well as his hands. Your German mechanic can do his routine work very well, and he will do it at wages of only half the amount paid to an Englishman ; but let him get into any difficulty—such as the break-down of part of the machinery—and you see at once his inferiority to his English colleague. He doesn't know what to do, but his first idea is that he must make a great noise, and let everybody know that a terrible misfortune has happened. Then, if by any accident he is able to put the thing right again, he gets all the more credit from his master for his wonderful achievement; whilst if, on the other hand, he cannot do anything, he has the satisfaction of knowing that nobody has expected him to succeed in repairing the mischief. The Englishman, however, in such a case, says nothing to anybody; but he looks about him, finds out for himself where the injuries are, uses his wits, and gets the thing put right again before anybody is aware that an accident has happened."

' "Yes," interrupted one of my companions, who happened to have a special knowledge of the subject; " but remember that you are speaking of picked Englishmen, carefully selected for you out of one of the largest manufacturing shops in Great Britain. You will not find that the average English workman has anything like the superiority to the average German that you claim for him."

' "I am not so sure of that," pursued my original informant. " It is true that mine are picked men, but I have the pick of the Germans also, and my conclusion is that whilst the German may be trusted to do a routine piece of work, in which he has been thoroughly trained, nearly, if not quite, as well as the Englishman, in all labour in which you use your head, or, as Opie said, ' mix your colours with brains,' the Englishman ranks far before all foreigners." '

Very recently it has been determined to man the engine-rooms and stoke-holes of the French mail steamers, running between Dover and Calais, with

Frenchmen. It is a significant circumstance that one Englishman is still to be retained as second engineer. In case a bad break-down should occur, it is needless to say that the entire responsibility would devolve on our fellow-countryman.

The textile industries: Mr. Mundella's comparison of British and foreign labour. Turning to the textile industries we have in Mr. Mundella a most competent authority, from personal experience both in Nottingham and on the Continent. He tells us that the Englishman, though much less sober, less instructed, and less refined, is yet more inventive, and can give more good suggestions to his master, than the artisan of any other country.

Mr. Mundella has published a valuable collection of evidence in a paper on the 'Conditions on which the Commercial and Manufacturing Supremacy of Great Britain depends,' which was read before the Statistical Society in March 1878. He says that 'no question has been so fully discussed as that of the present efficiency of English labour. According to some, both its quality and productiveness have declined in proportion as its costliness has increased. While expressing my belief that much that has been said has been unnecessarily severe and, in some instances, grossly unjust, it is impossible to deny that the high wages earned in the coal and iron trades during the late period of inflation, have added little to the material or moral well-being of many of the workers in these branches of industry. But if this is true, as I fear it is of too many, it is not true of all.[1]   A sudden and ex-

---

[1] Mr. J. W. Pease, M.P., in giving evidence before the Coal Committee of 1873, said : 'I found from the secretary of one of the building

ceptional rise of the rate of profits or of wages in any branch of business is seldom more than temporary, and rarely brings with it lasting benefit to either employer or employed. This part of our inquiry has such an important bearing upon the question under consideration, that I propose to consider it more fully than any other. . . .

'While fully and painfully conscious of the defects of my countrymen, and regretful as any man of that recklessness, intemperance, and thriftlessness which are the characteristics of too many, and which have led them to waste the opportunities afforded them by a time of exceptional prosperity, I am of opinion that their energy, efficiency, and skill have suffered no diminution, and that they are to-day, as they have been in the past, superior in these qualities to the workmen of any other nation. There is a strenuousness of effort, a rapidity and deftness in their movements, which I have never seen equalled except in the United States. The American, being of the same race, I rank as the equal of the Englishman. I do not believe he is superior, only so far as he excels in temperance and intelligence. This opinion is founded upon long experience, personal observation, and the evidence afforded by competent and impartial witnesses. I have often, in my own experience, compared the production of French, German, and American workmen with that of the English, from machinery in

societies, that he had on his books 268 pitmen from the district in which our collieries are worked. . . . Those men had deposited in the year 1872, 3,900*l.* Another secretary said, that from looking over his books he found that the men in the group of collieries just named had deposited, on an average, 300*l.* a month in his building society.'

every case made in England, and I have never known the Frenchman or German to produce the same quantity of work as the Englishman, although their working hours were longer. Generally the production fell short from 20 to 25 per cent. The American, under equal conditions, will produce nearly, though not quite, as much. Wherever I have found him producing more, it was due to his having been furnished with better machinery and appliances to work with. Where considerable physical strength is required in connection with technical skill, I have invariably found the continental workman much slower than the Englishman, and the production in this case not more than two-thirds of our own. It is quite true that even more than a corresponding reduction is made from the wages, but this does not compensate for the diminished productiveness of the capital, machinery, and plant employed, and for the consequent increase in the working expenses.

'In a lecture delivered by Mr. Alexander Redgrave, in November 1871, before the Philosophic Institute of Bradford, he gives the following statistics as to the proportion of spindles to persons employed in the cotton factories of the various continental States :

In France	.	.	. 14	In Belgium	.	. .	. 50
„ Russia	.	.	. 28	„ Saxony	.	. .	. 50
„ Prussia	.	.	. 37	„ Switzerland	.	.	. 55
„ Bavaria	.	.	. 46	„ Smaller States of Germany			55
„ Austria	.	.	. 40	„ United Kingdom	.	.	74

'"Incidentally," he adds, "the following statements have been made me by managers of cotton factories, showing the relative capacity of work of the Englishman and foreigner.

' " In Germany the working hours were (at that time) from 5.30 a.m. to 8.30 p.m. every day, including. Saturday. In a cotton factory there, a manager calculated that the same weight was produced when superintended by English overlookers as in sixty hours in England; but if the work was superintended by German overlookers, the weight produced would be much less.

' " As another instance : in Russia the factories work night and day one hundred and fifty hours per week, there being two sets each, working seventy-five hours per week. Taking the year round, the manager of a .cotton factory there considered that, in England, as much would be produced in sixty hours per week. He also said that no weaver ever had more than two looms, and that the speed of the machinery was about one-third less than in this country.

' " Some few years since I had opportunities of inquiring into this subject, both in France and in Germany, and from every quarter, and especially from English overlookers, I received the strongest assurances that the English workman was unapproachable in the amount of good work turned out, and in steadiness ; that the relative cheapness of wages did not counter-balance the steadiness and quickness of the Englishman at his work."

' I have reason to know that the proportion of spindles to operatives employed on the Continent, quoted by Mr. Redgrave in 1871, has in the interim considerably augmented; but improved machinery has in the same period been largely introduced in our own cotton-mills, while the hours of continental labour have considerably diminished, and the wages increased. The restrictions on the employment of children and young persons are now more severe in France, Germany, and Switzerland than with us.

' From M. Taine's well-known " Notes of England," we draw the following comparison between the English and French workman.

' After referring to the more salient types of British workmen, to their strongly nourished, hardy, and active frames, their phlegmatic, cool, and persevering natures, he thus continues :

' " French manufacturers tell me that with them the workman labours perfectly during the first hour, less efficiently during the second, still less during the third, and so goes on diminishing in efficiency, until, in the last hour, he does little good at all. His muscular force flags, and, above all, his attention becomes relaxed. Here " (in England), " on the contrary, the workman labours as well during the last as the first hour; but, on the other hand, his work-day is one of ten hours, and not of twelve, as with us. By reason, however, of this better sustained attention, the Englishman gets through more work. At Messrs. Shaw's, of Manchester, to manage 2,400 spindles, one man and two children are found sufficient ; in France, it needs two men, and three, four, and sometimes more children, for the same purpose. . . . But in certain qualities " (says M. Taine), " as in the matter of taste, artistic finish, and the like, the Frenchman has the advantage. He is more *imaginative*, less mechanical; and, by consequence, that power of concentration, of stubborn, persevering, and sustained application where the labour is monotonous, which so distinguishes the English workman and gives him his pre-eminence, is lacking in the French."

'In 1873 a circular was addressed to Her Majesty's representatives abroad, at the instance of the National Association of Factory Occupiers, requesting them to furnish information as to the spinning and weaving of textile fabrics in the countries to which they were accredited. This was in anticipation of the factory legislation which took place in the following year. In Belgium, where there are no legislative restrictions, and where labour is cheap and abundant, Mr. Kennedy, our representative, reported " that the flax and cotton industries have remained stationary during the past ten years. The two or three factory occupiers whom I met " (he further observes) " asserted that they could not pretend to compete with England. Manchester manufacturers, they said, could select their cotton on its arrival at Liverpool, close to their mills. Coal was cheaper and handier at Manchester than at Ghent. England, again, was the only producer of good machinery, and likewise possessed ready markets for her products in her vast colonial possessions. And lastly, English operatives were far superior to Flemish. On this latter point all were agreed that the Englishman, being better fed, possesses greater physical power, and produces as much work in ten as the

Fleming in twelve hours; and, having greater intelligence and mechanical knowledge, comprehends the machinery he works, and can point out to the foreman, in case of obstruction, the cause of the accident, whereas in Ghent half an hour is constantly lost in seeking for the cause of a stoppage in the machinery.

'"With the exception" (continues Mr. Kennedy) " of the long-established export trade of Belgian woollen yarn to Scotland, I may state, as the result of my inquiries, that there is little, if any, regular exportation of Belgian textile fabrics to Great Britain for consumption there. Occupiers of factories at Verviers assured me that they never exported a piece of cloth directly to England; and the same story was repeated to me by mill-owners at Ghent in regard to yarns and tissues both of flax and cotton. . . . The reasons for the possible successful competition of Belgian with British textile fabrics must be sought for in the lower rate of wages, the longer hours of labour, and the cheaper railway transport in Belgium as compared with Great Britain. But, notwithstanding these apparent advantages, it does not appear that British manufacturers have anything to fear from their rivals in Belgium."

' Our minister in Switzerland thus expresses himself, in his report, as to the workman in that country :

' " The Swiss workman is in most respects inferior to the British workman. He has neither the physical strength nor the energy and activity of the latter.

He is stolid in appearance, apathetic in temperament, slow and awkward in his movements, yet by no means wanting in intelligence. He is steady, methodical, industrious, and painstaking. Though of a saving disposition, no inducement in the shape of higher wages will stimulate him to extra exertion."

' Mr. Harris, our representative in the Netherlands, reports thus :

' "There is a general opinion, not unfrequently shared by the workmen themselves, that the Dutch labourer is not equal in point of skill to the foreign workman—that he is slower at his work, and turns it out in a less finished state."

' The single exception in which equality is claimed, is that of the United States, where it is urged that, although the wages are higher than with us, the additional labour performed nearly compensates. As I have already intimated, I believe this statement to be erroneous where all the conditions are equal.

' In 1873, Mr. Alexander Redgrave, Chief Inspector of Factories, accompanied by Mr. Jasper Redgrave, sub-inspector, visited France and Belgium, for the purpose of investigating the " hours of labour, wages, produc-tion, and like details," in the textile industries of those countries. They were armed with letters from the Right Honourable H. A. Bruce, the Home Secretary, which secured for them " the official recognition of the French and Belgian Governments." They instituted the most searching investigation into the questions which formed the subject of their inquiry, and the result was given in a most interesting pamphlet of fifty pages. I give the following extract from their concluding remarks :

' " The value of the English workman still remains preëminent, though the interval between him and his competitors is not so great as it was. He has not retrograded, but they have advanced, and that advance has been chiefly caused by manufacturers importing and copying from England that machinery which supplies the place of strength, steadiness, and perseverance. The Belgians are an industrious and painstaking race, but, with the French, they lack that intentness of purpose which is the characteristic of the Englishman. They are given to gossiping, their attention is not as close, they are moved and excited by more trifling causes than an Englishman. Then, again, whatever may be the proneness of the Englishman to indulgence in habits of intemperance, there is no question for a moment of the vast superiority of the cotton, woollen, and flax factory operative in England over the French and Belgian workman of the same class.

' " In every town the complaint against the operative was ' drunkenness.' It was difficult to make manufacturers understand that the English textile factory operatives went to their work as punctually on the Monday as on any other morning. Those who knew England were of course aware of the different manner in which Sunday is kept ; but they nevertheless thought that quiet drinking would go on to such an extent on the Sunday as to make its mark on the Monday morning's work.

' " Although the foreign factory operative is not, as

has been said, nearly so far behind an Englishman as he was a few years since, yet in all those occupations in which a call is made upon physical endurance and perseverance, the Englishman certainly maintains his pristine eminence. The Yorkshire foreman of founders who has been mentioned was certainly not backward in speaking well of his Belgian workmen, but he said they could not do the work like an Englishman ; they could neither keep to their work nor do the same amount in the same time. This was a fact acknowledged by all, and accounted for partially by the difference in the nature of the sustenance of the operatives in England."

'There is a striking family likeness in the allegations made by the employers of all countries against the efficiency of their workmen. In a series of valuable and exhaustive papers on the "Wage Statistics of Germany," by Dr. Leo de Leeuw, he shows that in various branches of the iron trade, wages advanced from 60 to 100 per cent., and in some instances reached as high as 500 per cent. "Yet," he says, "according to the unvarying testimony of the employers, the actual wages earned in 1872 and subsequent years were scarcely in excess of the wages earned before 1867. The workmen took the difference in idleness and dissipation ; in most establishments it became the rule to close from Saturday night to Tuesday morning, and it was only on Wednesdays that work was fairly resumed."

'I have seen extracts from the German newspapers respecting the dissipated habits and general deterioration of the German workman, that corresponded so closely with what has been said about English workmen, that one might have been the translation of the other. Even the champagne story has been current, but the consumption has been attributed, in Germany, to the working builders, whereas, in England, it was accredited to the miner.

'Dr. Leeuw adduces statistics to show how large a diminution of work accompanied the increase of wages in the building trade of Berlin. The following is a literal translation of his statement :

' " It has lately been shown in the Berlin building trade that the rise in wages went hand in hand with the decrease of labour in the following proportions :

' " From 1862 to 1873 the time of work was reduced from eleven to ten hours per day ; the day-labourer's wages rose in the same period from 1 reichsthaler to 1 reichsthaler 14·5 silbergroschen, i.e. 50 per cent. Out of fifty buildings constructed in each year, the numbers are found as follows :

Year	Number of Days worked	Number of Stones laid	Number per Man per Day
1862	30,217	18,795,000	623
1863	31,419	21,114,000	672
1864	36,504	24,349,000	667
1865	41,305	27,020,000	654
1866	28,428	19,260,000	681
1867	26,608	17,084,000	642
1868	27,204	16,814,000	618
1869	47,599	20,230,000	446
1871	33,364	13,379,000	401
1872	36,666	12,052,300	326
1873	38,888	11,683,000	304

And now let us turn to our most eminent statisticians

—men who survey the oscillations of trade from an absolutely neutral standpoint, and who have spent their lives, not in battling with more or less numerous bodies of workmen for small reductions of wages, or in minimising concessions, when they are compelled to make them, but in measuring the broad results of international competition. Testimonies to the superiority of British labour:

I take, first, the following passage from Porter's 'Progress of the Nation : ' 'The amount of skilled labour performed in a given time by any given number of our countrymen is commonly greater than that accomplished by the like number of any other people in Europe. To this circumstance it is in great part owing that, with a higher rate of daily wages paid for fewer hours of toil than are required in other countries, our manufacturers have been able, under otherwise adverse circumstances, to maintain the superiority over their rivals.' Mr. Porter;

The work of Mr. Porter has been carried down to the present day by Professor Leone Levi. Confirming the favourable opinion of Mr. Porter, he describes Britain as a perfect beehive of human labour. Taking space and population into account, possibly there is no other country in the world where there is a larger proportion of labourers, where harder work is gone through all the year round, and where the reward of labour is more liberal, than in the United Kingdom. Professor Leone Levi;

Mr. Mill summed up what he conceived to be the main features in the character of the British workman in the following passage : Mr. Mill;

'Individuals or nations do not differ so much in the efforts they are able and willing to make under strong immediate incentives, as in their capacity of present exertion for a distant object, and in the thoroughness of their application to work on ordinary occasions. This last quality is the principal industrial excellence of the English people. This efficiency of labour is connected with their whole character; with their defects as much as with their good qualities.'

A generation has passed away since Mr. Mill placed on record the opinion I have quoted, and I find his views confirmed in the pages of Mr. Wilson, who in his valuable volume, entitled 'The Resources of Modern Countries Compared,' has given us the latest collection of evidence on this subject. The following passage embodies the final result of Mr. Wilson's elaborate inquiry : 'I have generally come to the conclusion that as yet our supremacy has not been substantially interfered with. The backward wave, which has swept the trade of the whole world downwards, has been due to causes too universal to lead us to suppose that any special decrease in the producing and monopolising capacity of England has occurred. Let the conditions be the same as they are now, when business enterprise again revives, and we shall on the whole be able to retain the position we now hold. We shall be the largest carriers in the world, the largest manufacturers, and the most extensive employers of both labour and money. The resources and advantages of the country in ships, in machinery, in mines, in skilled labour, in teeming population, in unopened stores of coal and iron, and in geographical position, are such as no other country can at present lay claim to, and with these we have nothing to fear. Not only so, but year by year the growth of our own colonies in wealth and certain kinds of producing capacities must tend to strengthen our hands and to make the trade supremacy of England more assured. No other country that the world has ever seen has had so extended an influence, and as yet there are almost no signs of the decay of this vast empire.'

The advantages acquired by Great Britain in international commerce during the last twenty years are shown with admirable force and clearness by Mr. Newmarch, in his recent essay on ' Reciprocity.' He there shows us, to use his own words, ' why it is that, since 1856, the foreign merchandise imported has risen in amount or value by 117 per cent., while the British merchandise exported has risen in value only 74 per cent., or, put in a more simple form, why it is that in 1877–75 we got 20*s.* worth of foreign goods for 11*s.*, while in 1859–56 we had to pay 14*s.* In the twenty years we have acquired such an enlarged power over the foreigner by means of accumulation of capital and improved production, that he now has to send us 14*s.* worth of his merchandise in all the cases in which twenty years ago he had to send us only 11*s.* worth.' Mr. Newmarch;

Again, when it is attempted to raise an alarm as to the incursions of the manufacturers of the United States into the Manchester markets, we may point to some examples of successful competition by British with American manufacturers. I quote the following from Mr. Wells;

an essay by Mr. Wells, entitled, ' How shall the Nation regain Prosperity ? '   ' In 1874 Chili imported from Great Britain more than 55,000,000 yards, and from the United States only 5,000,000 yards, of cotton cloth.   This little State, one of the smallest among the nations, with a population of about 2,000,000, imported more cotton cloth, to supply her wants, from Great Britain in 1874, than the United States exported that same year in the aggregate to all foreign countries combined.'

In 1874 the export of cotton goods to the Argentine Republic was in excess of 40,000,000 yards, while for the year 1875-6 the export from the United States of the same fabrics was officially reported at 155,000 yards.

Mr. Morley ; Mr. Morley may not be accepted as an impartial witness, but his testimony will be accepted on matters of fact. ' They are turning out,' he said in a recent paper, ' a greater quantity of work in Lancashire for each spindle and loom per week than at any previous period in the history of the trade, and more than they are doing in any other country in Europe, however many hours they may work.' He reminds us that it was admitted by the Manchester Chamber of Commerce in 1876, when trade was still profitable to employers, that the price of calico was lower than in any year save one in the history of the cotton trade. Again, as he most fairly argues, ' if it were true that it is the action of the workmen that disables us in foreign competition, then we should expect that the more labour entered into the cost of production, the greater would be our disadvantage in the competition. But in the cotton trade, at all events, exactly the contrary of this is true. The articles in the production of which labour is the most expensive element, are just those in which competition is least formidable. A common shirting, sold, say, at 7s., and which has cost only 2s. in wages, is exposed to competition. But a piece of fine cambric, sold, say, at 9s. 3d., has cost 4s. 6d. in wages, and yet in this description of goods, in which labour is the main element of cost, we have complete command of the markets.'

The 'Economist,' in reviewing Mr. Courtney's papers in the 'Fortnightly Review,' gives a more sanguine, and, as I believe, a truer view of the capabilities of the British workman than we have been accustomed to hear expressed by those, who find an easy explanation of the present condition of trade in the increased wages and diminished energy of our workmen. 'At this moment industries cleave to particular places in spite of equally favourable or more favourable conditions existing in other spots. No reason, for example, in the way of " cheap power " retains the alpaca trade of Bradford in that town. There is quite as much " power " in Creusot, as is shown in the iron industry of that place ; wool and cotton are as easily procurable, and the market, Paris, is, if anything, more accessible. Yet the mixed wool and cotton manufacture does not go there, but remains in Bradford. There are ports in the United States which are better fitted in all respects for the shipbuilding trade than any ports in England, and yet shipbuilding flourishes here and does not flourish across the Atlantic. We do not know of

The Economist.'

any sound reason in economics why Nottingham should beat Genoa in the manufacture of its special fabrics. Genoa can obtain cotton as easily as Nottingham, and silk more easily ; its artisans are probably the more adaptable of the two ; and the difference in the cost of the fuel used must, if we consider the minute cost of coal-carrying, and the small amount required, be nearly imperceptible. Nothing in the cheapness of coal can enable English manufacturers to import silk from Japan, manufacture it, and then sell dresses in Yeddo of a fabric with which no Japanese can hope to compete. There must be something in the English character, in its strenuousness, its love of order, and its fidelity to work, which gives it a superiority ; and we see no reason why this character should in any degree deteriorate. Certainly it will not deteriorate because we are nearly at the end of our resources in easily obtained coal. We incline to believe that our countrymen have been injured, if at all, by a superiority too easily acquired, and that continued adversity would develope in them an energy, industry, and power of combination, with which no nation can compete, not even America, where a stimulus is lacking which is always present in England. This stimulus is want of choice. Mr. Courtney forgets that the option of working on the land, which is present to the American and the French handicraftsman, is wanting to the English. He cannot take a farm, or grow grapes, or do anything else but manufacture. He is shut up in an island so small, and cultivated on so peculiar a system, that he must manufacture or go away, and acquires of necessity

the hereditary skill which in India appertains to the
man, who is forced by caste or opinion to continue an
hereditary trade. Even if he has to import coal—and
the transit of coal across the Atlantic would not greatly
increase its price—he would find in his own energy
the means of compensating for that outlay, as he already
has done for his outlay upon food. His great competitor, the American, though quite as full of energy,
has not the same inducement to expend it upon work,
and, as a matter of fact, does not expend it. He has,
for example, as Mr. Hussey Vivian says, coal and iron
as ready to his hand as the Englishman. He has quite
as much knowledge, and perhaps, on the whole, rather
greater inventiveness. He is no further from Asia for
commercial purposes, and ought, therefore, to obtain a
monopoly of the Asiatic trade in small steel goods.
Yet he does not, his only preference being in the axe,
which, residing in a half-cleared country, he has been
compelled by immediate necessity to make decidedly
better than his English rival. The Englishman may of
course, like the Cornish miner, be induced to emigrate,
but if he does not he will retain, we conceive, a manufacturing faculty akin to his political faculty, which will
still give him a fair chance in the markets of the world.'

The opinion has gained wide acceptance that a large Drinking
proportion of the earnings during the period of pro- habits of
our opera-
sperity, which preceded the present crisis, was wasted tives.
in intemperance. We learn from Dr. Farr's report to
the Registrar-General that, during the three years of
high wages in 1871–73, the consumption of spirits in
the United Kingdom was 36,000,000 gallons a year.

During the three subsequent years of idleness the average consumption was 42,000,000 gallons. Dr. Farr conjectures that the hours formerly spent in the workshop were passed idly in the public house, and that this is the reason why a larger consumption took place in a period, during which a very considerable reduction of wages had taken place.

Prodi-
gality of
American
miners.

Complaints of the misconduct of their workmen are at least as frequent in America as in this country. Describing the cost of mining in the Lake Champlain district, Mr. Harris Gastrell states: 'The labourers are largely foreign, Irish and others. The miners do not, as a rule, save. One of their chief modes of spending is to keep a horse and "buggy" and drive about. The vehicles in a miners' village were certainly astonishingly numerous. A library, provided for the men at a cost to each of 1s. a month, has been given up on account of the men objecting to the payment, and a former condition of work, that their children should be sent to the free school provided, has been abandoned.

In 1860 the standard of wages was 87½ cents a day. It then rose to 2 dollars in 1872, and was, in 1873, 2 dollars 25 cents for common labour. It was believed that the men saved more when paid at the rate of 87½ cents a day, than they did when the great rise in their wages had taken place.

Drunken-
ness in
France,

M. Favre admits in his report to the Duc d'Audiffret-Pasquier's Commission that drunkenness, though still rare in the south, had become a threatening scourge in the north, the east, the west, and the centre of France.

I might have added largely to the opinions which have been quoted, but I question whether I could have had recourse to more impartial authorities than those which I have laid under contribution. It was my father's conclusion, after a long and wide experience, that in fully peopled countries the cost of railways and other public works was nearly the same all over the world, and that for every country the native labour, when obtainable, was, with rare exceptions, the cheapest and the best. *Indigenous labour.*

For a task of exceptional difficulty, one requiring all that dogged courage and determination to which Mr. Mill refers, the British miner and navvy are unsurpassed. After a long residence abroad the Englishman adopts the diet and habits of the population around him. He lives as they live, and works as they work. Climate counts for much in the physical condition of the human frame. *The English labourer abroad.*

The preceding observations as to the uniformity observable in the cost of works do not apply to newly settled countries. Amid the sparse populations of the colonies labour is necessarily dearer than elsewhere.

I have referred to the invigorating effects of a cold climate. In my judgment the influence both of climate and race is abundantly displayed in the many admirable qualities of the British people. *Advantages of climate and race.*

In ancient times the English commanders again and again attacked an enemy superior in numbers, trusting for victory to the ancestral prowess of their nation. It is to tradition and example that Shakespeare makes

King Henry V. appeal in his stirring speech to the army which he had mustered at Barfleur.

> On, on, you nobless English,
> Whose blood is fet from fathers of war proof!
> :   .   . And you, good yeomen,
> Whose limbs were made in England, show us here
> The mettle of your pasture; let us swear
> That you are worth your breeding; which I doubt not;
> For there is none of you so mean and base,
> That hath not noble lustre in your eyes.
> I see you stand like greyhounds in the slips,
> Straining upon the start. The game's afoot:
> Follow your spirit, and upon this charge
> Cry, 'God for Harry, England, and Saint George!'

We live in happier times, when men have other opportunities of showing courage and spirit; when greater victories may be won, and more valuable annexations may be made, by the arts of peace than in the field of battle. It does not follow that the British nation has for ever lost the sterling qualities displayed by our stalwart soldiery in the middle ages.

British enterprise in Cyprus. The enterprise of our colonists and our merchants is irrepressible. During my visit to Cyprus I rode side by side with a man who had been driven only a few weeks before by the Kaffirs from his farm on the borders of Natal. He was then making a gallant effort to retrieve his fortunes in Cyprus by carrying parcels on horseback between Kyrenia and Larnaka, riding a distance of forty miles every day under a burning sun. On the following morning I purchased some Australian preserved meat from a merchant at Larnaka, who had just arrived from Vancouver's Island, where trade had been flagging ever since the island ceased to be a free port, and who had come to try his fortune in another outpost of the British Empire.

If we turn from the merchant to the manufacturer, we recognise less brilliancy, perhaps, and less of that wise caution which distinguish the Frenchman, but we perceive an inexhaustible energy and admirable skill in administration.

For the workman I contend that, with all his admitted faults, and notwithstanding his incessant clamour for higher wages in prosperous seasons, and his hopeless resistance to reductions in adverse times, he stands before all his rivals in many essential qualities. The faults of the British workmen seem inseparable from their characteristic national virtues. As M. Renan truly says, 'On a toujours les défauts de ses qualités.' Beaten we may be at last by the exhaustion of our natural resources, but I do not believe that we shall ever be beaten through the inferiority of the iron-workers, the spinners, and the weavers of the United Kingdom. Their habits of industry are derived by inheritance from their forefathers, confirmed by the example of their fellow-workmen, and stimulated by emulation. Their labours are wrought in the most favourable climate in the world for the development of the bodily and mental energy of man.

Faults and excellences of the British workman.

My knowledge of the working qualities of our labouring population has been chiefly acquired afloat, and my confidence in the British workman is strengthened by intimacy with our seafaring people. I find my own experience confirmed in a recent report from our Consul at Nantes, who gives a practical illustration of the

Character of the British seaman.

distinguishing characteristics of the English and French seamen. An English vessel, manned by an English crew, will generally, he says, beat a French competitor out of the field, though in many ways the latter navigates his vessel more cheaply; and why? Because there is on board the French vessel a laxity of discipline unknown to us. Captain and crew *naviguent en famille*; both law and custom require the captain to consult his men in an emergency.

It has often been said that the British seaman submits less readily to discipline than the Swede or the Dane, and that in the ordinary routine of a sea life he cannot always be relied upon to use his utmost energies; but when the trial comes of nerve, and strength, and skill, he is rarely found wanting.

The character of the English mariner was admirably depicted by Shakespeare in 'The Tempest.' The boatswain, with his 'Heigh, my hearts; cheerly, cheerly, my hearts! Yare, yare! Take in the topsail; tend to the master's whistle. Down with the topmast! yare: lower, lower. Bring her to by the main course!' and his dauntless remonstrances with his craven passengers, 'Shall we give o'er and drown? Have you a mind to sink?' was a portrait drawn from nature by a master hand.

CHAPTER IX.

TRADES UNIONS.

TRADES UNIONS are equally dreaded and detested by a large number of those who are engaged on the side of capital in its perpetual contests with labour. But they are the natural outcome of the growth and development of industry, which leads to the assembling and the dispersion of large multitudes of workmen, recruited over the whole country and never brought into personal contact with their employers. Similar causes led to the formation of the guilds of the Middle Ages. It is stated by Mr. Green, in his 'Short History of the English People,' that 'the burghers of the merchant-guild gradually concentrated themselves on trades which required a larger capital, while the meaner employments were abandoned to their poorer neighbours. . . . From the eleventh century the control of trade passed from the merchant-guilds to the new craft-guilds.' *Cause of formation of Trades Unions.*

The relations between these associations were far from friendly, and a long and severe struggle took place of the 'greater folk' against the 'lesser folk,' or of the 'commune,' the general mass of the inhabitants, against the 'prudhommes.'

Mighty changes, not always tending to the improvement of our social condition, have taken place since the age of the Stuarts, so graphically described by Lord Macaulay.   The merchant and his clerks, the millowner and the operative, cared more for one another when they lived in the same parish and shared in the same local attachments.   'To their dwelling-place they were bound by the strongest ties of interest and affection.   There they had passed their youth, had made their friendships, had courted their wives, had seen their children grow up, had laid the remains of their parents in the earth, and expected that their own remains would be laid.   That intense patriotism which is peculiar to the members of societies congregated within a narrow space was, in such circumstances, strongly developed.   London was, to the Londoner, what Athens was to the Athenian of the age of Pericles, what Florence was to the Florentine of the fifteenth century.   The citizen was proud of the grandeur of his city, punctilious about her claims to respect, ambitious of her offices, and zealous for her franchises.'

The absence of personal attachment in the present day, and the fluctuating character of the employment, are necessarily attended with regrettable consequences. Mr. Carlyle has well said that 'permanence, persistence, is the first condition of all fruitfulness in the ways of men. The tendency to persevere, it is this that in all things distinguishes the strong soul from the weak, the civilised burgher from the nomadic savage. Month-long contracts do not answer well even with

Marginal notes:

Absence of personal attachment between employer and employed.

Lord Macaulay on local ties.

Carlyle on permanency as a stimulus to exertion.

your house servants. The principle of permanence once secured, the basis of all good results is laid. Once permanent, you do not quarrel with the first difficulty in your path, and quit it in weak disgust: you reflect that it cannot be quitted, that it must be conquered, and wise arrangements fallen on with regard to it.

'The very horse that is permanent, how much kindlier do his rider and he work than the temporary one hired on any hack principle yet known. I am for permanence in all things at the earliest possible moment and to the latest possible.'

I have said that the absence of that personal attachment, which binds together the small master and the few hands in his employment, men in much the same condition of life as his own, is a dark feature of the industrial combinations of modern times. The examples are not few where an effective competition is maintained under an almost patriarchal system with the colossal factories of the great cities. The manufacture of hardware is carried on in Germany, and the watchmaking in the Jura, with much success in small workshops, each limiting itself to a speciality, which reaches the hands of the consumer through the medium of travellers and commission agents.

The tendency, however, of modern industry is in another direction—towards those large combinations which are favourable to the formation of Trades Unions. We have, therefore, to deal with Trades Unionism as an accomplished fact. The registered Trades Unions in 1877 had an income of 254,565*l*.

Strength of Trades Unions.

accumulated funds of the value of 374,989*l.*, and 260,222 members. In his book on the ' Manufacturing Industries,' Mr. Bevan gives a list of Trades Unions, established in almost every branch of trade. It is clear, from an examination of the statistics he has collected, that the members of the Trades Unions are a limited minority of the whole body of our working people. They are nevertheless a power, and, in the interests of the workmen themselves, it is most important that such a power should be prudently exercised.

Limits to their control of wages.

Mere organisation and combination will not enable Trades Unions arbitrarily to fix the rate of wages. The consent of the employers must be obtained ; and an employer will speedily withdraw from a business in which the ordinary interest upon capital cannot be obtained, together with such additional sum as may be necessary to insure against any exceptional risk incurred, and to remunerate him for the skill and the labour bestowed in the management of the undertaking. Trades Unions may secure an earlier advance of wages in prosperous times, and delay a reduction in adverse times ; but if they try to exact such terms as render it impossible that the trade in which they are employed can be carried on at a profit, its speedy cessation is inevitable.

Higher wages gained by non-unionists.

It is established by the recent inquiries of Professor Levi that a greater advance has taken place in the last decade in the wages of workmen who have no trades unions, than in the wages of men who have organised the most powerful trade societies.

The average wage represented by the total amount of earnings, divided among the respective number of earners, compared with 1866, is as follows :

Years	Men		Women	
	Under 20	20 and upwds	Under 20	20 and upwds
	Per Week	Per Week	Per Week	Per Week
1866 . . .	7 6	19 6	8 0	11 0
1878 . . .	8 0	21 9	9 0 .	13 8
Increase per cent. .	6½	6¾	12	24

Women's wages have advanced more in proportion than men's wages. This is especially the case among domestic servants and dressmakers.

If it be admitted that a profitable condition of trade is an essential preliminary to an advance of wages, and that a fall of wages cannot be prevented when trade is languishing and unprofitable, the value of Trades Unions to the workmen, considered as an instrumentality for raising wages, becomes extremely questionable. The eagerness of employers to extend their business with every favourable opportunity causes a competition for labour, aud insures to the workman an advance of wages, which he wrongly believes to have been gained only by the pressure exercised through the Trades Union to which he contributes. *Wages regulated by demand for labour.*

The building trades have succeeded in enforcing many obnoxious rules, because they have not been exposed to foreign competition in neutral markets, and because the lavish expenditure of the public in buildings, and the facility with which money can be borrowed by speculative builders, have, until a recent *The building trades.*

period, kept up the demand for the labour of mechanics engaged in this branch of industry. Mechanics in the building trades command exceptionally high wages in all newly settled countries; indeed, they are always the first to profit by a local scarcity of labour. Houses must be built, *in situ*. Textiles, iron, and many descriptions of food can be bought in the cheapest market, and can be imported by the railway and the steamship from remote districts. The wages of the manufacturing operative, on the other hand, are fixed by competition with the whole world. In the building trades the competition is limited to the workmen on the spot. Mr. Lowthian Bell gives the following wages as the average earnings of tradesmen in America: 'Blacksmiths, 7*s*. 6*d*. to 8*s*. 6*d*. per day; masons and bricklayers, 11*s*. 3*d*. to 15*s*., and the latter had received in 1873 as much as 18*s*. 10*d*.' In 1874 Mr. Bell found the bricklayers at Ireton, in the United States, earning an average wage of 18*s*. 10½*d*. per day.

Dictation successful only when labour is scarce.

It is only when labour is scarce that the working men are enabled to dictate terms to their employers. The effect of the scarcity of labour, during the Civil War in America, in raising wages, may be appreciated from a few striking examples. At Pittsburg ordinary labourers were paid, before the war, 3*s*. 4½*d*. per day; while during the war wages rose to 7*s*. 6*d*. a day. They had fallen, at the date of Mr. Lowthian Bell's paper, to 5*s*. 7¾*d*. In the Lehigh Valley, the furnace labour on a ton of pig-iron rose from 5*s*. 9*d*. to 12*s*. 3*d*. during the war; it had subsequently fallen to about 8*s*. 6*d*. As a rule, all over the States we find a steady increase in the price of wages for the last twenty years. It reached its culminating point during the rebellion, since which time it has receded to from 50 to 75 per cent. higher than it was a quarter of a century ago.

The latest reports of the most powerful Trades Unions clearly show how little can be effected by their instrumentality to arrest the downward movement in wages when trade is depressed. As a striking illustration I may point to the following observations in the recent Report of the Durham Miners' Association: For the year 1874 our income was 47,004*l.*, and expenditure 23,613*l.*, or an income above the expenditure for this year alone of 23,390*l.* But now a rapid change has set in, so that during the years 1875, 1876, and 1877 there was a gradual but constant decrease in the income, with an ever and rapidly increasing expenditure, until in the latter year matters stood as follows: Income for 1877, 33,290*l.*; expenditure for 1877, 60,513*l.*, or an expenditure above the income of no less than 27,223*l.* Everyone must see that this state of things must soon come to an end. We must either curtail our benefits or expect the entire breaking up and destruction of our association.' These remarks indicate an early close of the present extensive strike in Durham. The more general it is, the more certain its speedy termination must be.

The same inability to withstand the downward movement in wages in a time of depressed trade is frankly acknowledged in the report presented in 1878 by the Parliamentary Committee to the Conference of Trades Unions at Bristol. Reviewing the incidents of

Marginal note: Inability of unions to arrest reduction in times of depression.

the previous year, they refer to the two great disputes which had recently taken place in the building trade, the strike of the masons in London, and the strike of the joiners at Manchester. They regret that in both cases the men failed to establish their demands; and they give two explanations of this failure. 'Firstly, under the powers of the Strike Clauses now inserted in all contracts, the employers are enabled to postpone the completion of the works till an indefinite period. Secondly, the employers in nearly all branches of industry are united in powerful organisations, whose almost unlimited wealth, severe discipline, and concentrated authority give them a power of offence and resistance hardly equalled by the best Unions.' The President of the Congress, to which their report was addressed, acknowledged in his opening speech that the rate of wages was determined not by the artificial and limited influence of the Trades Unions, but by the competition of the unemployed for employment. He was of opinion that the result of the contests alluded to affords the most convincing proof that the price of labour, like that of commodities, is governed by the proportion between supply and demand. Reviewing the general features of the strike in London, with special reference to the foreign labour which had been imported, he said that that was not the cause of the men having failed in their purpose. It was not till the London market became flooded with labour from Liverpool and Scotland, that the men saw but little chance of success before them. Wages depended on the greater or less competition for employment. It was not the employed but the unemployed workman who fixed the price of labour.

The reduction of the hours of labour in the engineering trades has often been quoted as a crowning instance of the power exercised by Trades Unions. I approve of the action of the working men in taking advantage of a period of prosperity to secure to themselves some share of that leisure, which is an indispensable condition of their physical strength and vigour and their social and intellectual improvement. Reduction of hours gained by the engineers.

The just claims of the working man to leisure and recreation were advocated by Lord Macaulay in a noble passage in his speech on the Factory Acts: 'Man, man is the great instrument that produces wealth. The natural difference between Campania and Spitzbergen is trifling, when compared with the difference between a country inhabited by men full of bodily and mental vigour, and a country inhabited by men sunk in bodily and mental decrepitude. Therefore it is that we are not poorer, but richer, because we have through many ages rested from our labours one day in seven. That day is not lost. While industry is suspended, while the plough lies in the furrow, while the exchange is silent, while no smoke ascends from the factory, a process is going on, quite as important to the wealth of nations as any process that is performed on more busy days. Man, the machine of machines, the machine compared with which all the contrivances of the Watts and the Arkwrights are worthless, is repairing and winding up, so that he returns to his labours on the Monday Lord Macaulay on the working man's rest.

with clearer intellect, with livelier spirits, with renewed corporal vigour. Never will I believe that what makes a population stronger, and healthier, and wiser, and better, can ultimately make it poorer.'

For the reasons so powerfully stated by Lord Macaulay, I should rejoice to see the working classes obtain as large a share of leisure as they can. It is good for them to enjoy rest and recreation. It is necessary that their labour should be at least as cheap and more efficient than that of the foreigner, whose competition they must encounter both at home and abroad.

Mutual obligations of capital and labour.

It is the duty and the interest of the capitalist to encourage the labourer with an ample reward for his industry and skill. It is no less the duty and the interest of the English workman that the capital by which his employment is created, and by which he is furnished with the means of subsistence, should command an adequate profit. Capital is a highly sensitive and volatile element in production. It is inevitably attracted from a country in which it commands a low rate, to one in which it commands a high rate, of interest. It is in the new countries, and not in the old, that our surplus capital finds employment. The old-fashioned securities of Europe are gradually being changed for more remunerative investments in America and Australasia. The process is natural and inevitable; but the welfare of the workmen will not be promoted by accelerating the movement, by making arbitrary and unjustifiable demands, whether in relation to the hours of work or the rates of wages.   .

Having guarded myself with these explanations, I fully recognise the power wielded by Mr. Burnett, and the organisation he directed during the great strike at Newcastle; but the concession demanded from the employers would not have been obtained if trade had been languishing and thousands of men had been out of employment. Although the mechanical trades have been less affected by the prevailing depression than any other branch of industry, it now appears by no means improbable that a return to longer hours may be temporarily resorted to, as a means of cheapening production and stimulating the demand for the products of our engineering works.

Why the engineers' strike succeeded.

For the reasons already stated, I question whether the services rendered to the working men in securing from employers advances of wages are such as to make it worth their while to establish and maintain Trades Unions. There are, however, other valuable functions which the committee of a Union may appropriately undertake on behalf of its clients. We shall return to this subject in the following chapters.

Proper work of Trades Unions:

Trades Unions may do excellent service to workmen by collecting information on the condition and prospects of trade. It is by a knowledge of these facts that the workman must be guided in his negotiations with his employers on the question of wages. The aim of a trades union should be to acquire, according to the formula of M. Comte, ' science, d'où prévoyance; prévoyance, d'où action.' Trades Unions may do good service by watching legislation on behalf of the working class. It is eminently desirable that the people should

collection of information on trade matters.

be accustomed to look to Parliament for the redress of their grievances. The report of the Parliamentary Committee to the Congress in Bristol shows that the workmen have been encouraged by the sympathy evinced for their class in Parliament, and are content to seek relief by legislation rather than revolution.

Parlia-
mentary
pro-
gramme of
Associa-
ted Trades
Unions,
1879.

The programme of the Parliamentary Committee of the Associated Trades Unions for 1879 stands out in striking and gratifying contrast to the wild theories promulgated at Ghent and Lyons for the amelioration of the masses by the sacrifice of individual freedom, and by other equally arbitrary measures.

'*Parliamentary Programme for the Session* 1879.

'1. To amend the law of compensation in cases of accidents, so that workmen or their families may recover from an employer in the event of injury or death from accidents due to negligence.

'2. Reform of the administration of justice.

'(*a*) Summary jurisdiction of magistrates, especially in securing the right of appeal and trial by jury, and rendering less frequent unnecessary imprisonment.

'(*b*) The mode of appointing unpaid and unqualified magistrates.

'3. The codification of the criminal laws.

'4. Reform of the jury law, by lowering the qualification for jurymen, so as to admit a large number of workmen to the discharge of the important duties of jurymen, and thereby prevent the necessity of men serving as jurors so frequently, and provide reasonable payment for loss of time.

' 5. The extension of the Employer and Workman Act, 1875, to English seamen whilst in British waters.

' 6. The desirability of increasing the number of factory and workshop inspectors.

' 7. Reform of Patent Laws.

' 8. Abolition of imprisonment for debt.

' 9. Certificates of competency for men in charge of steam-engines and boilers.'

The question of boiler management has lately been brought before the House of Commons by Mr. Burt, in a speech marked by his habitual excellent taste and clearness of thought and diction. Mr. Burt's suggestions were received most favourably by the House, and the Government will probably be induced, at his instance, to move in the direction which he has indicated. Boiler management.

The President of the Trades Unions Congress at Bristol gave no encouragement to the lawlessness which had marked the recent struggle between the operatives and the millowners in Lancashire. 'It is with the deepest regret,' he said, 'that I revert to the overt acts of violence and lawlessness which a short time ago were rampant in North and North-east Lancashire. It would have been to me a far greater pleasure to record the fortitude and law-abiding character exhibited by our kinsmen in the Principality under the most trying circumstances, as applicable to each and every district. I say that we have not the slightest sympathy with the perpetrators of the dia-bolical outrages that were committed either on person or property under any circumstances whatever. Per- Trade outrages.

fect freedom of action we have already contended for. The policy of menace simply destroys the chance of reasonable concessions—the very fact of disregarding the law under such circumstances simply means disaster for the workman.'

Mis-
chievous
action
of the
masters'
associa-
tions.

The officials employed by the associations of masters exercise quite as mischievous an influence as the officers of the Trades Unions, in estranging from one another employers and employed. The reports prepared by the masters' associations are not unfrequently highly irritating documents. The report of the Iron-founders' Society for July 1878 speaks of the sixth annual report of the Iron-trade Employers' Association, which had just been issued, as urging ' a unanimous system of operations, to be carried on by the society and its members during the ensuing twelve months; counselling them especially to take advantage of the present condition of trade to reduce wages in all departments, enforce piecework, lengthen hours of employ, and, where possible, put down Trades Unionism by dismissing all foremen Unionists.' The report concludes with the following exhortation: ' Brother members, read, learn, and inwardly digest this specimen of man's love to his fellow-man !'

The influence cannot but be evil, which is exercised by men employed as a standing army to carry on an unceasing conflict between masters and workmen. They cannot indeed be peacemakers, whose livelihood is derived from the mutual irritation and hostility of labourers and capitalists. Much vaporous nonsense is written by mercenary speakers and writers on both

sides. Their speeches and circulars may be described
in the satirical verses of Dryden:

> A numerous host of dreaming saints succeed,
> Of the true old enthusiastic creed:
> 'Gainst form and order they their power employ,
> Nothing to build, and all things to destroy.
> But far too numerous was the herd of such,
> Who think too little, and who talk too much.

The organisation of large masses of operatives may
sometimes tend to facilitate a negotiation. It may be
the means, on the other hand, of creating an *esprit de
corps*, and arousing a spirit of animosity on the part
of the workmen against their employers. It may
foster a 'pride ashamed to yield, an obstinacy delight-
ing to contend.' Admitting that Trades Unions are an
inevitable result of the modern development of industry, and may be employed beneficially for the
working classes, it must certainly be conceded that
the utmost self-restraint and sagacity are required to
prevent them from becoming mischievous. *Tendencies of trade organisations.*

In their opposition to the system of piece-work,
and their desire to restrain the wholesome influence of
emulation, Trades Unions are wholly in the wrong.
The objection to piece-work is sometimes disavowed;
but the system has been uncompromisingly opposed by
the leading Trades Union Society of Engineers. It was
in resistance to the introduction of this system that the
engineers went out on a prolonged strike at Messrs.
Easton's works at Erith. *The objection to piece-work. .*

To establish among the labourers a feeling of interest in the work they perform is an essential condition
of efficient and economical organisation. 'What makes *Labourers' Wages Committee of 1824.*

life dreary,' says George Eliot, 'is the want of motive.'
Under the form of piece-work, or payment by results,
this principle has been introduced by every successful
employer of labour.

The Committee on Labourers' Wages, over which
Earl Russell presided in 1824, were deeply impressed
by the evidence they had heard of the flagging spirit
and impaired strength and energy resulting from a
system of payments at fixed rates, and on a scale
carefully devised, so as to leave but a bare subsistence
to the labourer. The following passage occurs in their
report :

'There are but two motives by which men are
induced to work : the one, the hope of improving the
condition of themselves and their families; the other,
the fear of punishment. The one is the principle of
free labour, the other the principle of slave labour.
The one produces industry, frugality, sobriety, family
affection, and puts the labouring class in a friendly
relation with the rest of the community ; the other
causes, as certainly, idleness, imprudence, vice, dissen-
sion, and places the master and the labourer in a
perpetual state of jealousy and mistrust.'

Mr. Her-
bert
Spencer on
the cost of
slave la-
bour.

The Committee refer to the inferior economic
results of slave labour. Mr. Herbert Spencer, dis-
cussing the same subject in his volume on 'Social
Statics,' writes as follows :

'The enslavement of the negroes serves for a good
example. Could but a sufficiency of labourers be
imported, maintained at a cheap rate, made to work
hard, and to keep long at it, what a surplus would

they not create! Here was a mine of wealth! . . .
Slave countries are comparatively poverty-stricken all
over the world. . . . Though worked in some cases
sixteen hours out of the twenty-four ; though supported
on "a pint of flour and one salt herring per day;"
though kept to his work by whips, yet did not the
slave bring to his owner the large profit calculated
upon. Indeed it has turned out that, under like circumstances, free labour is much cheaper.'

The cost of executing any given amount of labour
cannot be estimated by the daily wages of the workmen. Work may be dear when wages are low,
and cheap when wages are high. The principle of
piece-work was adopted in all cases by my father.
Step by step, from the contractor, who was responsible
for the undertaking in its entirety, down to the individual navvy, the principle of payment by results was
enforced as the only effective stimulus to exertion.
The original contract was split up into a number of
small sections and let to sub-contractors, men whose
resources were not sufficient to enable them to assume
a large pecuniary liability. The contract taken for the
entire work was redistributed in sub-contracts, bridges,
cuttings, and stations constituting finally so many separate undertakings, the workmen in all cases being paid
by the piece and not by the day. On no other system
would it have been practicable for an individual sitting
in an office in London to undertake large contracts in
every quarter of the globe. If it had been attempted
to make men diligent by mere supervision, an immense
expenditure would have been incurred, while the most

Piece-work
principle
as enforced
by the
late Mr.
Brassey.

vigilant watchfulness would have failed to give the same incentives to exertion, which were supplied by the consciousness of every man that the amount of his earnings depended on the quantity and quality of the work executed.

Mr. Siemens on the mutual interest of employers and workmen.

In his recent presidential address to the Iron and Steel Institute Mr. Siemens quoted my father's opinion, that the cost of labour (or, in other words, the coefficient resulting from the division of the work done per day by the day's wage) was approximately the same in all countries. He went on to recommend the more general adoption of the principle by which that remarkable result was attained. 'One of the most available methods,' he said, 'would be by establishing the relations between employers and employed upon the basis of mutual interest. Capital has its duties to perform as well as its rights to maintain, and whilst the minimum of wages is that which enables the workman to live with reasonable comfort, both parties would be materially benefited by so arranging wages as to make them depend in great measure upon the quality and quantity of work produced. By the establishment of mechanics' institutes, reading-rooms, and mutual benefit associations in connection with individual works, the feeling of community of interest would be further strengthened, and a recurrence of antagonistic action, so destructive to commercial results, would be avoided.'

Coleridge on the furtherance of labour as an end of government.

Philosophers will concur with employers of labour as to the principles upon which wages should be paid. In this connection, some suggestive remarks by Coleridge will be found in the ninth essay in 'The Friend:'

' What are the ends of government? They are of two kinds, negative and positive. The negative ends of government are the protection of life, of personal freedom, of property, of reputation, and of religion. The positive ends are :

' First. To make the means of subsistence more easy to each individual.

' Second. That in addition to the necessaries of life he should derive from the union and division of labour a share of the comforts and conveniences, which humanise and ennoble his nature. . . .

' Third. The hope of bettering his own condition and that of his children. The civilised man gives up those stimulants of hope and fear which constitute the chief charm of the savage life; and yet his Maker has distinguished him from the brute that perishes, by making hope an instinct of his nature and an indispensable condition of his moral and intellectual progression. But a natural instinct constitutes a natural right, as far as its gratification is compatible with the equal rights of others.

' The prizes are indeed few and rare, but still they are possible; and the hope is universal, and perhaps occasions more happiness than even its fulfilment.' [1]

We shall proceed to give a few practical illustrations of the increasing effectiveness of labour when paid by results.

Advantages of payment by results illustrated.

Mr. Brittain, who has recently published in ' Iron' a description of the principal iron-making establishments in France, gives the full details of the plan adopted for the payment of wages upon the piece-work

The Terrenoire ironworks in France.

[1] Coleridge, 'The Friend,' Essay ix. p. 100.

system at Terrenoire, one of the principal ironworks in France. A schedule is affixed to the door of each workshop every morning, giving the details of all the work done therein on the previous day. Each schedule contains the names of the puddlers, and of their first and second under-hands, and states the number of heats worked off, the quantity of coal and pig given out, the maximum and minimum of iron required from the men, the actual production realised, and the wages earned by each man. If the weight of iron produced exceeds the minimum required, the men are paid at a higher than the normal rate for the surplus; but if it does not reach the minimum the deficiency is deducted from their wages. M. Euverte introduced this system into Terrenoire in 1858, after having seen its excellent results at the great ironworks at Creusot, of which he was the director from 1851 to 1858. He affirms that its effect at Creusot was to raise wages fifty or sixty per cent., without prolonging the day's work, and to increase production prodigiously, without rendering necessary any augmentation of capital. The result of his second experiment was equally satisfactory. Among the men at Terrenoire drunkenness is rare, and the application to work is intense. The men toil twelve hours a day, and earn wages varying from 2*s*. 6*d*. for labourers to 7*s*., 8*s*., or as much as 12*s*. a day for puddlers.

The efficiency of piece-work has been proved in every department of industry. We have a strong opinion as to its value from Mr. Denny in his able paper on 'The Worth of Wages.' He tells us 'that

Mr. Denny's opinion of the system.

a workman under piece-work generally increases his output in the long run, partly by working hard, but principally by exercising more intelligence, and arranging his work better, by about 75 per cent., while the total amount of his wages is increased by about 50 per cent.' Thus a direct saving is effected, on the wages portion of the cost of a given article, of about 14 per cent. The benefit derived from this economy, as he appropriately observes, is generally shared in very liberal proportions with the buyer or consumer. It is scarcely necessary to remark that this appropriation of the advantages secured by their administrative skill and scientific knowledge takes place much against the masters' will. But the influence of keen competition is irresistible.

To the workman, Mr. Denny points out that the increase of from 25 to 30 per cent. in his wages—and this increase his experience confirms as the rule—secures at once a more comfortable and easy style of living. Mr. Denny rightly says that the system of piece-work on a larger scale, where a more or less numerous body of men unite to undertake such an operation as the plating and framing of a ship, is the foundation of a more extended system of co-operation.

Having shown how important are the advantages which have been gained in a private shipbuilding yard on the Clyde from the introduction of piece-work, I turn to the speech of M. Eugène Farcy, in the Chamber of Deputies, on the French naval estimates for the year 1879–80. After commenting on some other administrative questions, he says : ' J'arrive au nombre

Cost of ship-building in French public and private yards.

des journées employées pour la construction. Il y a un fait qui a dû vous frapper dans le rapport de l'honorable rapporteur : c'est que le nombre des journées employées aux constructions est tout-à-fait excessif. Ainsi, pour ne vous citer qu'un exemple—et celui-là très-frappant—le plus grand navire de la marine française, l'Amiral Duperré, construit par l'industrie, comporte 411,000 journées de travail, et il a 10,487 tonneaux de déplacement ; si on lui compare un navire construit dans les ports, n'ayant que 8,000 et tant de tonneaux, on voit que le nombre de journées accusé dans les états de la marine est tout d'abord de 800,000 journées : 800,000 au lieu de 411,000 ! Mais ce qu'il y a de singulier, c'est que, en prévoyant presque le double, on s'était encore trompé. Ce chiffre de 800,000 journées n'est pas encore exact, car lorsque M. le rapporteur a demandé lui-même le nombre de journées, on lui a dit : c'est 900,000. Et quand on a su que j'avais demandé l'état justificatif, on a dit au rapporteur que le chiffre dépassait 1,000,000 de journées ; de sorte que, pour un type qui est de 2,000 tonnes inférieur à celui de l'Amiral Duperré, on dépense plus d'un million de journées de travail, alors que pour l'Amiral Duperré on n'en compte que 411,000.

'L'industrie privée, quand on s'adresse à elle, est obligée, sous peine de pertes énormes, de s'en tenir au nombre des journées de travail qu'elle a calculé, et au prix qu'elle a estimé le navire ; tandis que dans les arsenaux de la marine on se trompe continuellement, et nous voyons de cette manière augmenter d'une façon énorme le prix des navires.

'Il y a une raison capitale : c'est le peu de travail produit par les ouvriers des arsenaux. Cette raison, je la trouve dans le rapport de l'enquête de 1850, présidée par M. Dufaure, dont on vous parlait tout à l'heure. ·

'Voici ce que je trouve dans la déposition de M. l'amiral Baudin, qui était préfet maritime.

'L'amiral s'exprime ainsi : "J'ai dit au ministre : 'Permettez-moi de renvoyer un tiers ou un quart des ouvriers, en augmentant la solde du restant ; je vous promets plus de besogne avec ce personnel réduit.'"

'Voici maintenant la déposition du ministre lui-même à cette commission : "M. l'amiral Verninac déclare qu'il s'est arrêté à l'idée d'une réduction d'ouvriers, parce qu'il avait acquis la preuve que dans le port de Lorient—où il avait commandé—un travail, pour lequel on gardait cent cinquante ouvriers, pouvait être fait par dix ouvriers appartenant à l'industrie."'

I break off from the speech of M. Farcy in order to interpolate an extract from the report of the Committee on Labourers' Wages, which, after quoting a case very similar to that referred to by the French Admiral, gives the true explanation of the apparent anomaly : 'He, whose subsistence is secure without work, and who cannot obtain more than a mere sufficiency by the hardest work, will naturally be an idle and careless labourer. Frequently the work done by four or five such labourers does not amount to what might easily be performed by a single labourer working at task-work.'

To return to M. Farcy. 'Ce qui prouve encore la grande différence du prix de revient par navire fait dans les arsenaux avec ceux faits par l'industrie, c'est

que si l'on divise le chiffre de revient par le nombre de
tonnes du navire, on constate que pour les plus gros
navires de la marine, comme pour l'Amiral Duperré,
par exemple, le prix du navire revient à 562 fr. par
tonne, tandis que pour le Redoutable il revient à 662 fr.
C'est-à-dire que par tonne la différence est de 100 francs
au préjudice du travail des ports.'

M. Lebelin de Dionne, an eminent member of the
constructors' staff at the French Admiralty, was sent
down to the Chamber to defend the estimates of his
department. He did not attempt to dispute M. Farcy's
figures. He pointed out, however, that the average
wages of the workmen in the dockyards were less than
three francs a day, while the earnings in the private
yards often exceeded six francs. With this immense
difference in their wages, he did not claim for the
dockyards any advantages in point of economy. On
the contrary, he conceded a certain superiority to the
private establishments. In all my investigations I have
never found a more striking illustration of the failure
of industrial energy where men are working without
the stimulus, which the prospect of participation in the
results attained by their labour alone supplies.

Greater
efficiency
of English dockyards.

The amount of the work performed in the dockyards of England and France may be accepted as a
test of the capabilities of the workmen of the two
countries. It is needless to point out that a far larger
amount of tonnage is annually built in the British
dockyards, and that a still greater difference presents
itself in the number of ships in commission, and in the
demand on the dockyards for repairs ; and yet we find

that while the ship-building and repairing of the British
Navy is carried out by 16,000 men, no less than
25,000 men are employed in the French dockyards.
The average pay of the French workman is 2*s.* 6*d.* per
day, some thousands of men being paid at the lower
rate of 2*s.* 1*d.* per day.

In his Report on the Industrial Classes in France, Rates of
wages in
Lord Brabazon gives the following average rates of the French
dockyards.
wages in the Government dockyards. The hours of
labour, according to the season, are from eight to
thirteen hours, with from an hour and a half to two
hours interval for meals. Carpenters, first class, earn
from 2*s.* 6*d.* to 4*s.* 2*d.* a day; journeymen carpenters,
1*s.* 8*d.* to 3*s.* 9*d.*; labourers, 1*s.* 4½*d.* to 2*s.* 1*d.* per
day. The inferior results obtained from the ill-paid
labour in the French dockyards are a striking illustration of the short-sighted policy of paying workmen by
the day. The mistake is common, however, to both
countries, and in France the rates are insufficient to
stimulate the energy of the workmen, and to supply
them with the means of maintaining a high condition
of physical strength.

The objection often taken by Trades Unions, that The objec-
tion to
piece-work leads to competition between workmen, is a competi-
tion be-
singular anachronism in an era, in which competitive tween
workmen.
examinations have become the condition of admission,
and the test of fitness for promotion, in every branch
of the public service. What claim, as the 'British'
Reviewer truly says, has a working man to be protected whilst everybody else is, for his benefit, un-
protected?

Suggested neutralisation of the benefits of machinery.

In the last report of the Society of Ironfounders it is said that 'machinery has supplanted, and is supplanting, manual labour; and the only cure for the disease, in our opinion, is to produce less and work shorter hours.' If, unhappily for themselves, the working-men of England should be led astray by such doctrines as these, they will soon be deprived by their more vigorous competitors in the United States of the opportunity of carrying out the policy of restriction in this country.

The warmest friends of the working classes unite in condemning the mischievous influence of Trades Unionism in this regard. I quote from 'Le Travail,' by M. Jules Simon: 'C'est aux sectaires à promettre une émancipation immédiate, sans efforts et sans sacrifices. Pour nous, au contraire, c'est l'effort que nous prêchons; c'est la volonté persévérante que nous demandons.'

Impolicy of restraining the workman's energy.

The old craft-guilds, to which reference has already been made, exercised an equally pernicious influence in restraining the natural energy of the workmen in the Middle Ages. 'A seven years' apprenticeship,' says Mr. Green, 'formed the necessary prelude to full membership of any trade-guild. Their regulations were of the minutest character, the quality and value of work was rigidly prescribed, the hours of toil fixed "from daybreak to curfew," and strict provision made against competition in labour.'

Emulation in daily life.

The stimulating influence of emulation is felt in Parliament, in commerce, in the press, by individuals, and in the wider sphere of competition between nations.

The magical effect of the piece-work system may be traced in the most varied spheres of human labour. 'Dr. Johnson,' says Boswell, 'dining at an excellent inn at Chapel House, remarked: "There is no private house where people can enjoy themselves so well as at a capital tavern; and no servants will attend you with the alacrity that waiters do, who are incited by the prospect of an immediate reward, in proportion as they please." '

When our fleets are detained for a lengthened period in remote foreign harbours, the energy and spirit of officers and men would gradually be impaired by the monotony of the service but for the emulation between the different ships in the squadron, which a skilful commander knows both how to excite and how to control. We see the effects of emulation every day, in accelerating the speed of rival hansoms conveying honourable members to St. Stephen's, and in the tournaments at which the latter afterwards assist on the floor of the Houses of Parliament.

The Trades Unions do wrong not only in objecting to piece-work, but in giving no positive and direct encouragement to diligence and superior intelligence amongst their members. The 'British Quarterly' Reviewer quotes the opinion of Mr. Markham, the manager of the Staveley Works, to the effect that the tendency of Trades Unions for many years past has been to minimise the work of each individual. *Mistaken policy of Trades Unions.*

A letter was lately addressed by Mr. John Burns, of the Cunard Steamship Company, to the Lord Provost of Glasgow, which contains several things well worthy *Inlets for foreign competition.*

of consideration at the present time. Mr. Burns says:
' The new Cunard steamship " Gallia " is being supplied
with parquetry, made in Belgium, for the cabin floor
of the main deck. It is being laid by Belgian workmen, who on Saturday were faithfully and diligently
doing their work, when at one o'clock, the hour at
which our home workmen leave the ship, these Belgians
specially asked that they might be allowed to continue
at their work until dark. I inquired if these men
were paid overtime, but was unhesitatingly told that
they were not, but only received reasonable wages for
their labour, and that their sole object in spontaneously
desiring to be allowed to work beyond the usual early
hour ruling on the Clyde was to get the job finished
without delay. Here now is a fact for the serious
consideration of our working men. It is but a speck
in what is now going on, to the great detriment of
this country and to the increasing distress of our
artisans; for I might cite the fact that the entire pa-
nelling of the " Gallia's " cabin has been executed by
Japanese carpenters, and that the ironwork of the
office in which I now sit was made in Belgium; and
instance after instance could be given of how all nations
are competing with us, not only as regards the manufacture of articles used in their respective countries—
hitherto to a great extent supplied by Britain—but the
artificers of foreign countries are, in spite of us, advancing into our own country, and compelling us to
employ them, simply because they can do our work as
well and much cheaper than it can be done by our
own workmen. What does this bring us to but that

the arbitrary curtailment of the hours of labour is a snare and delusion to our working-classes, and the sooner they cast to the winds the doctrine of those who are imposing upon them, the better for themselves? The demands of our workmen are fast becoming so unreasonable as to put it beyond the power of employers to accede to them, and unless, by the aid of foreign workmen unfettered by Trades-Unionism, or otherwise, there can be obtained a fair day's work for a fair day's pay, British capitalists will simply have to abandon the development of commercial industries for sheer lack of ability to conduct them profitably. Here we are in a time of languishing trade, and spring coming on, with our working men throwing down their tools at five o'clock in the afternoon and one o'clock on Saturdays, when I and hundreds of men are in the thick of our work, and could never pretend to compete with the world if we were to be circumvented by mechanically limited hours of labour. I hold strongly that every working man, in the ordinary sense of the word, may, by his own merits, rise to any position ; but never will he do so if he enslaves himself to hard and fast rules which, on the face of them, are irrational and contrary to every principle of free trade and free action. I have no hesitation in saying that, in my belief, the future prosperity or adversity of this country depends, in a great degree, upon the action of the working classes. I have not a word to say against increase of wages. Let every man get as much as he can. Labour will be paid for according to its worth ; but if the British working man does not wish to live in a fool's paradise, let him realise to himself that people of other nations will work when he is sitting still, and that, therefore, it behoves him to rouse himself to the contemplation of stern necessity, and hold his own and his country's own before the time comes when he may be forced to emigrate for lack of profitable work in the mother country.'

Future of British industry dependent upon the workman's freedom from restraint. As an advocate of liberal wages for an equivalent in work well accomplished, I cannot too strongly express my conviction that the future of British industry depends upon our workmen being allowed to give full scope to the natural energies with which they are endowed. If their native vigour be repressed by a baneful influence from without, the star of British commerce must decline behind that great continent in the West peopled by our own descendants, and where we see already so many striking evidences of German and Anglo-Saxon energy and enterprise.

> Vixi, et, quem dederat cursum fortuna, peregi;
> Et nunc magna mei sub terras ibit imago.
> Urbem præclaram statui; mea mœnia vidi;
> Ulta virum.[1]

Among the working classes in the United States an almost universal determination is found to gain their independence, and to better their condition by strenuous exertion. It has been remarked by Mr. Bagehot that the civilisation of India, Japan, and China, every oriental civilisation, has been arrested because the development of individual capabilities was prevented by the thraldom of fixed customs. The deliverance of

[1] Virgil, ' Æneid,' iv. 653.

man from the yoke of inherited usage has been called
by Goethe the liberation of humanity. In so far as
Trades Unions discourage individual exertion and
originality in the artisan, they tend to sap the very
foundations of industrial success.

Dante has put into the mouth of Virgil these
words of solemn warning:

> Non per far, ma per non fare, ho perduto
> Di veder l'alto sol, che tu disiri.[1]

The subjugation of the individual to the arbitrary
authority of a guild or a corporate body is a cherished
fallacy of the workmen of all countries. The French
delegates sent by public subscription to the Exhibition
at Vienna drew up a report, in which the general
organisation of productive industry was fully discussed.
The delegates displayed the most complete ignorance
of economic science. Their general view seemed to
be that the workman ought to be wholly deprived of
his personal liberty. His education was to be directed
by a representative committee, to whom it was proposed
to confide the interests of the whole body of their
fellow-workmen. The report is inspired with a blind
faith in the superiority of corporate over individual
discretion and vigilance, which is certainly not supported by any experience acquired in our country of
the administrative capacity of Boards of Directors.
The right of every man to liberty of action, to be
sovereign over himself, is an absolute and indefeasible
privilege. In the famous declaration, framed by Turgot and published in 1776, forming the preamble to

The fallacy underlying trade orga- nisations.

---

[1] Dante, 'Purgatorio,' vii. 25.

the edict by which Louis XVI. suppressed the guilds and monopolies established by Colbert, the freedom of labour was asserted in these memorable words : ' Dieu, en donnant à l'homme des besoins, en lui rendant nécessaire la ressource du travail, a fait, du droit de travailler, la propriété de tout homme ; et cette propriété est la première, la plus sacrée et la plus imprescriptible de toutes.

' Nous regardons comme un des premiers devoirs de notre justice d'affranchir nos sujets de toutes les atteintes portées à ce droit inaliénable de l'humanité . . . qui éloignent l'émulation et l'industrie, et rendent inutiles les talents.'

After the lapse of a century, the elaborate report of the latest French Commission on the Condition of the Working Classes concludes with a similar declaration. The unrestricted right to labour is proclaimed as the ground-work of industrial prosperity. No corporate body, under whatsoever plea, or by whatever name it may be designated, is entitled to deprive the individual workman of his freedom.

CHAPTER X.

LABOUR STATISTICS.

Of the necessity for more perfect labour statistics I can speak from experience, acquired in ten years of close study of that much-debated question, the relative efficiency and economy of English and foreign labour. Whenever the trade of this country passes through a phase of depression, a disposition is evinced to impute the entire blame and responsibility for our commercial misfortunes to the British workman. It is said that he is deficient in technical knowledge, that he is ill-disciplined, an idler, and a drunkard. These grave charges cannot be disposed of by mere assertion on either side. *Denunciation of the workman in times of depression.*

The impartial public will be reluctant to believe in the degeneracy of masses of the population. On the other hand, we do not wish our working-men to live in a fool's paradise, and to find themselves beaten in the international competition, in which they have so long been victorious, because they have not been made acquainted in due time with the industrial progress of foreign countries. In•so far as it lies in the power of a private individual, I have endeavoured to bring together the best information on the subject, and to place it fairly before employers and employed. I have been a *Compilation of labour statistics left to private individuals in England,* humble labourer in the same field in which Mr. Mundella, Mr. Lowthian Bell, Mr. Newmarch, and others have shown the way. But the task is too extensive to be carried out by a private individual, and it is scarcely satisfactory that the greatest industrial nation in the world should rely on the desultory labours of a few independent inquirers, and on the facts and details— admirably collected and digested though they be—set forth in the 'Economist' and 'Statist.' Information on the relative efficiency of labour is of vital importance to the nation at large, and especially to that vast body of operatives whose livelihood depends on successful

but undertaken in foreign countries by Government.

competition with foreigners. In France, and still more in the United States, the greatest pains are taken by the Governments in the preparation of labour statistics. Mr. William Holms has directed public attention to the minute statistics, relating to wages in the various industries, prepared from time to time by the French authorities. I would support his suggestions by pointing to the still more comprehensive information collected and published by the Government of the United States. In 1876, Mr. Young, the chief of the Bureau of Statistics, produced an invaluable volume, of nearly 900 pages, on Labour in Europe and America. The book contained, according to the declaration on its title-page, a special report on the rates of wages, cost of subsistence, and condition of the working-classes in Great Britain and all the manufacturing countries of Europe. The relative position of the working-classes in America was minutely and impartially compared with that occupied by persons in the same sphere of employment abroad. The industrial capacity was investigated, as well as the material and moral condition of the people. It is impossible to exaggerate the importance of such a publication, issuing from a Government department having at its command resources, which cannot be within the reach of a private individual. If the United States Government find it worth their while to issue such a publication, it must be obvious that the subject is worth an effort on the part of this country, where a policy of free trade has been adopted, and where the industrial population has to contend against the industry of all nations—not, as in the United States, behind a high rampart of protection, but in the open field. Not only has the collection of labour statistics been undertaken by the American Government, but the several States of the Union have organised a bureau of statistics of labour, from which very valuable publications are annually issued. Massachusetts has led the way in this important work. The census of 1875 was most complete, not only in relation to population, but to all matters pertaining to wages, cost of material, value of products, running time of manufacture, classification of labour, hours employed, day and piece work. In the introduction to the volume of labour statistics, issued for 1877, Mr. Wright very truly says that the bureau under his superintendence cannot solve the labour question, for it is not solvable; but the State can provide materials for more satisfactory adjustments of the relations between labour and capital.

Having shown what important improvements had been effected in these matters in Massachusetts by the

Completeness of the inquiry in America.

instrumentality of his department, Mr. Wright makes some observations, which I strongly commend to the appreciation of Her Majesty's Government: 'These desirable results are attained, not by unhappy and unfortunate agitations, not by strikes and their consequent demoralising influences, but by all the contributions to the sum of the intelligence of the labourer and the capitalist; and any means which the legislature can adopt, which will add to the information of the people on subjects concerning their daily lives, are of untold value, and surely return to the Government a hundredfold.   To popularise statistics, to put them before the masses in a way which shall attract, and yet not deceive, is a work every government, which cares for its future stability, should encourage and enlarge.'

Labour Statistic Department proposed for England.

I urge this subject on the attention of the Government the more confidently, because I feel convinced that all that is necessary can be done with very little additional trouble to the various departments, whose co-operation would be necessary.   Mr. Hunt would be responsible for the department of mining, Mr. Redgrave for the textile industries, the Commissioners of Customs for the foreign trade.   These departments are already in possession of most of the information required; and it only remains to have that information collated, compared, digested, and presented in a compendious form, under the supervision of Mr. Giffen, in a few additional pages to the 'Statistical Abstract.'   If the information already collected is incomplete, any questions which it may be thought necessary to address, either to foreign governments or to manufacturers at home or abroad, will be more readily answered, if they emanate from a department of the State, than if they were proposed by a private individual. In this connection, I desire to pay a hearty tribute of acknowledgment to Mr. Redgrave, Mr. Giffen, and our Secretaries of Legation for the labour and ability they have already brought to bear on these questions. What we now need is, as I have already said, to bring into a focus the information they collect, and to have that information reported periodically, and in a compendious form, to the country.

I will venture to give a few illustrations, to show how inconveniently the particulars at present available are scattered through a number of volumes, and also to indicate the form in which they might be put together for the instruction of the public. *Present sources of information.*

The 'Statistical Abstract' gives a return (Table 13 of the last number issued) showing the fluctuations in the value of imports and exports per head of the population of the United Kingdom from year to year. Nothing can be more valuable as an indication of the industrial activity of the country. We can trace the growth of the export trade from the low level of 5*l.* 17*s.* 4*d.*, to which it had fallen in 1868, to the maximum of 8*l.* 1*s.* which it reached in 1872. We can follow the gradual falling away down to 1877, when the value of the exports had been reduced to 5*l.* 18*s.* 1*d.* per head. We have also volumes of statistics, of great value, for the principal foreign countries and for the colonies. These volumes contain the materials for the

compilation of the same useful table which is given
for the United Kingdom ; but the calculations have
not been published—at least, they were not given in
the last number, the fifth, of the abstracts relating to
foreign countries.   We have therefore to turn to the
valuable publications of Mr. Newmarch for the information in question.   On a half-page of the ' Journal
of the Statistical Society ' inserted in an earlier chapter
of this work, Mr. Newmarch has contrived to bring
together a summary of the exports and imports of all
the leading manufacturing countries, showing both the
total amounts and the amounts per head of the population.   We can trace at a glance the fluctuations, and
we can see abundant cause for congratulation as to the
position held by the United Kingdom, within the
period, from 1860 to 1875, included in the table.   The
total value of the exports per head of the population
in 1875 was, for France, 84*s.*; for Germany, 80*s.*; for
the United States, 54*s.*; and for the United Kingdom,
142*s.*   The increase since 1860 was, for France, 34*s.* ;
for the United States, 11*s.* ; and for the United Kingdom, 52*s.*   For the period from 1869 to 1875, the
increase was, for France, 18*s.* ; for the United States,
24*s.* ; and for the United Kingdom, 21*s.*

Kind of
compend
required.
We want a compendious statement, similar to that
prepared by Mr. Newmarch, which should be included
in the ' Statistical Abstract,' and be put into the hands
of employers and workmen every year.   Considerable pains have been taken in the preparation of the
large volumes entitled ' Miscellaneous Statistics.'   But
they are only published triennially, and their value

would be immensely increased, as a means of information to the working classes of this country, if the amount of the wages paid in the same trades on the Continent or in the United States were published side by side with the scale of wages in our own country. The information would be rendered still more complete by the addition of particulars, such as Mr. Redgrave has from time to time collected and published in his report, showing the rate at which machinery was being run on the Continent, the hours of labour, the number of spindles attended to by each operative, and other details, tending to throw light on the relative efficiency of English and foreign labour.

I turn from the statistics showing the total exports and imports of the country to the statistics of particular trades.

At the present moment we are all watching with deep anxiety the strike of the miners in Durham. I offer no opinion on the merits of the case. I confine myself to the indisputable assertion that the miners can never succeed, by any violence of conduct or combination of numbers, in extorting from their employers a scale of wages which would leave capital entirely unremunerated. Such a condition of affairs may exist for a time, but it cannot continue. It has been frequently stated that the output of coal in the collieries of the United Kingdom was very seriously diminished during the period of inflated prices; that men took advantage of their high wages to work less vigorously and for shorter hours; and that the Englishman is being beaten by the cheap labour of Belgium. These asser-

The want illustrated by the Durham miners' strike.

tions naturally alarm the public, and the Government ought to furnish us with the means of verifying assertions of such a nature. But the sources of information are scattered, and beyond the reach of any individual who does not happen to make such things a speciality. I believe that I have ascertained the facts by collating and comparing the report of Mr. Saville Lumley, our Secretary of Legation in Brussels, with the remarks on this subject made by the Inspectors of Mines in the United Kingdom. The results were set forth in detail in a former chapter. Mr. Lumley gives the output of coal for the Province of Hainault at 188 tons per man for 1871, 206 tons for 1872, and 174 tons for 1876, the average over a period of ten years being 185 tons. Turning to the reports of the Inspectors of Mines, Mr. Dickenson gives the average output of coal in Lancashire at 301 tons per person employed, being an increase on the previous year of 23 tons per head. The output in Scotland increased from 256 tons in 1873 to 318 tons in 1877. The output in the mines of the United Kingdom was increased from 223 tons in 1861 to 272 tons in 1877. As compared with Belgium, the superior efficiency of the miners of the United Kingdom is clearly indicated by a comparison of the figures I have given, showing an output of 185 tons per man for Belgium, and 272 tons per man for the United Kingdom.

Utility of information to the working man.

I conclude as I began by saying that we do not want to flatter the working man, but to furnish him with facts. Socially, it is important to disabuse the public mind of prejudices. For myself, I place confidence in the industrial capacity of our people. Show them that it is necessary, and their efforts will be found equal to the occasion. I have never failed to impress on leading members of Trades Unions, with whom I have been brought in contact, the grave consequences which must follow, if artificial restrictions are placed on the native energy of the British workman. Neither have I ever admitted that the Trades Unions were capable of rendering any essential service to the workmen by raising their wages. Recognising, however, that Trades Unions arc an inevitable outcome of modern industry, I have urged them to direct their attention to the collection of information rather than the organisation of strikes. I have sometimes felt that there was a certain irony in such advice. How can the poor and comparatively uneducated men at the head of the Trades Unions conduct an international inquiry into the state of trade? The task properly belongs to the Government; a public department can alone obtain complete information, and digest it in an impartial spirit for the edification of the public.

CHAPTER XI.

CO-OPERATION.

Labour and capital in antago- nism.
WE have already traced out some of the consequences which must follow when labour and capital are employed as two separate interests in industry. It is inevitable that each will seek to make as advantageous a bargain as possible with the other, and that the easy affluence of the employer, who is always seen in the attitude of an antagonistic rather than a head partner in the common undertaking, will excite the jealousy of the workmen. If I may turn for a moment from the great operations of industry to household affairs, how few there are who could not confirm from their personal experience the remark of Mr. Mill that 'the relation between master and servant is nearly as unsatisfactory to the payer of wages as to the receiver. The rich regard the poor as by a kind of natural law their servants and dependants; the rich in their turn are regarded as a mere prey and pasture for the poor, the subject of demands and expectations wholly indefinite, increasing in extent with every concession made to them, while the return given in the shape of service is sought to be reduced to the lowest minimum.'

Remedy for this condi- tion.
To remedy the state of things to which Mr. Mill refers is one of the most practical and perplexing

problems of social life. The magnitude of the evil
increases in proportion as houses are enlarged, and the
number of retainers is multiplied. One of the most
effectual remedies, therefore, must be to live simply
and unostentatiously.

> E le Romane antiche per lor bere
> Contente furon d'acqua; e Daniello
> Dispregiò cibo, ed acquistò savere.
> Lo secol primo quant' oro fu bello;
> Fe savorose per fame le ghiande,
> E nèttare per sete ogni ruscello.[1]

Such a remedy would be impossible for the great
nobles of the land; but those who bear hereditary
honours have usually inherited with their rank and
wealth an effective system of control and a faithful
body of retainers. The great mass, however, of the
people—of those, I mean, who are in easy circumstances—are not called upon to bear the same social
responsibilities. Their happiness would be greatly
increased, if they would mutually consent to lay aside
the fulsome pomp and circumstance, which burden their
existence.

Further, let us ask ourselves whether it be altogether impracticable to introduce a system of payment
by the piece for many domestic services. The difficulties must be acknowledged, but the employer would
be served with greater diligence, and the servant

Piece-work in domestic service.

---

[1] The passage is thus translated by Longfellow:

> 'And for their drink the ancient Roman women
>   With water were content; and Daniel
>   Disparaged food, and understanding won.
> The primal age was beautiful as gold;
>   Acorns it made with hunger savorous,
>   And nectar every rivulet with thirst.'

DANTE, *Purgatorio*, xxii. 145.

encouraged by seeing a more direct connection between the work done and the payment received.

Industrial organisation on the co-operative principle.   In an abstract, or social and moral, as distinguished from a commercial, point of view, the co-operative principle offers the most satisfactory type of industrial organisation. Co-operation, according to Mr. Holyoake, is a scheme by which profit can be obtained by concert and divided by consent. If co-operation could be carried out in conformity with its definition, as stated by its most eminent advocate, it would supply the final solution of all the social, and most of the economic, difficulties of productive industry.

> Heaven forming each on other to depend,
> A master, or a servant, or a friend,
> Bids each on other for assistance call,
> Till one man's weakness grows the strength of all.[1]

Sound in theory, co-operation is difficult of application in practice. The representative form of government is better adapted to political than to commercial affairs, and a republic does not always present a model of good government. It is not easy for an officer promoted from the ranks to command the unquestioning obedience of his men ; and in the factory, as in the regiment, there must be discipline.

> Therefore doth Heaven divide
> The state of man in divers functions,
> Setting endeavour in continual motion ;
> To which is fixed, as an aim or butt,
> Obedience : for so work the honey-bees ;
> Creatures that, by a rule in nature, teach
> The act of order to a peopled kingdom.
> They have a king, and officers of sorts.[2]

---

[1] Dryden, 'Absalom and Achitophel.'
[2] Shakespeare, 'Henry V.' i. 2.

'Order,' says Mr. Bagehot, 'tacit obedience, pre-
scription, and governability are the foundation of
modern society.' Without their aid, industry cannot
be organised on a large scale. In a former paper on
co-operation, I insisted at considerable length on the
short-sighted jealousy of co-operators in denying to
their managers, when entrusted with heavy pecuniary
responsibilities, that adequate remuneration, which the
frailty of human nature requires as a defence against
temptations to peculation and dishonesty.

The President of the Trades Unions Congress in Difficulties in the way of co-oper-ation.
1878 made some valuable observations on the diffi-
culties of co-operation. 'The confident belief,' he
said, 'that the difficulties between capital and labour
would find their solution in the growth of the system
of co-operation, has been but indifferently fulfilled. It
is evident that the extension of a system, which would
demand from our working men the unswerving attention and intelligent devotion to business required by
the fierceness of sudden industrial competition; such
economy and self-reliance as would accumulate the
necessary capital, and secure a provision for seasons of
depressed trade; and such a regard for economic laws,
and such an unselfish interest in the welfare of their
fellows, as would prevent mutual encroachments, sup-
poses a higher standard of social and intellectual refinement than at present exists among them. Towards
the creation of such a standard much has, however,
been done, and is still being done, by Trades Unions.'

' These remarks may be compared with Dean Swift's
discourse on the 'contests and dissensions in Athens

and Rome :' 'The most powerful commonwealth of Greece was utterly destroyed by the rash, jealous, and inconstant humour of the people, which was never satisfied to see a general either victorious or unfortunate : such ill judges, as well as rewarders, have popular assemblies been of those who best deserved from them.'

Instances of success.

Co-operative distribution is an undoubted success, but co-operative production is, as Mr. Denny observes in his essay on 'The Worth of Wages,' to co-operative distribution, as dynamics to statics, and therefore much more difficult. Instances, however, are not wanting of successful co-operative organisation. The co-operative stores are themselves manufacturers on a considerable scale. But co-operation has worked hitherto most satisfactorily when only the industrial or practical part of the business has been handed over to the workman, the capitalist retaining the general control in his own hands. Professor Cairnes has given an interesting

The slate quarries of North Wales.

description of such an application of the co-operative principle in the slate quarries of North Wales. The whole quarrying population in North Wales is employed under a system of co operation with their employers. Three or four men form a co-partnery, and contract to produce slates from the section of rock assigned to them, at so much per thousand. The men who take part directly in these contracts form about one-third of the whole number. The remainder are employed by them as labourers. The more expensive plant for the quarry is furnished by the proprietors, the contractor supplying the smaller tools and blasting powder. Wages are paid monthly.

This system of working is well worthy of imitation. It tends both to stimulate the energies of the workman and to elevate him socially. The *status* of contractor in a slate quarry forms an easy stepping-stone for the elevation of the masses from the precarious position of dependence upon the general labour market. The wages earned by contractors vary from 3*l.* to 10*l.* per month, those of the labourers from 12*s.* to 20*s.* per week. The industrial organisation of the Welsh slate quarries has encouraged a disposition to frugality, and led the workmen to make an intelligent application of the money they have saved. Several considerable towns in North Wales, among them Llandudno, Rhyl, and Upper Bangor, have been almost entirely built by the capital supplied through the workmen's building societies.

The operatives of the United Kingdom have lately manifested a disposition to invest their savings in joint-stock undertakings in the trade with which they are themselves connected. In Lancashire, more particularly, they are the principal proprietors in a considerable number of mills established on the joint-stock principle. These undertakings have passed under the dark cloud which at present overshadows the textile industry of the country. *The joint-stock mills of Lancashire.*

The failure of the Lancashire cotton mills may be mainly attributable to temporary causes; but shareholders not trained to business are seldom happy in their selection of directors, and corporate can seldom be as successful as individual management, where close attention to details is required. The great art of administration consists in the judicious choice of agents. It has been truly said by Mr. Emerson : 'The circumstance of circumstances is timing and placing.' To make a happy choice of men, and to do the right thing at the right time, demands a knowledge of individuals and of details, an uninterrupted attention to the course of events, which can rarely be obtained in a board, and for which we must look, as a rule, to individual management.

Mr. Bigelow, in an article already alluded to, has some interesting observations on co-operation : 'In France several years ago, M. Reybaud, a member of the Institute, on behalf of the Academy of Moral Science, made inquiries in regard to the condition of workmen in the woollen industry. In his report he gives an account of the formation and temporary success of several co-operative societies for .spinning worsted in Fourmies in the north of France ; and after narrating the steps by which these societies passed from the co-operative to the competitive system in the conduct of their affairs, he makes the following philosophical remarks : " In these ephemeral communities, that which emerges insensibly is a return towards the demand and respect for individual faculties. Among these workmen some absorb, others are absorbed. The rights after trial become fixed according to merits and proportions of interest. The control follows the same progress, so that, after a circuit more or less long, there is a return to society in its collective name, and to the *régime* of wages. A work of industry can never be anything else than an affair of speculation ; disin-

Mr. Bigelow on co-operation as tried in France.

terestedness slips in only on occasions, and by calculation. Sooner or later the nature of things takes its
revenge, and shakes or overturns whatever does not
conform to it." '

It should not be inferred from the foregoing obser-
tions that 1 despair of the future of co-operative productive industry. But the system is best adapted to
small undertakings and establishments. Education is
an indispensable condition of success; and the rising
generation will enjoy advantages in this respect which
were denied to their forefathers. In the meanwhile,
by the payment of labour by the piece, and by gathering together the capital of the co-operatives into joint-
stock undertakings, we are making progress towards
that equitable association of capital and labour which
is the aim of co-operation.

In view of the difficulties inseparable from the
joint-stock system in its application to manufacturing
enterprise, it is desirable that other opportunities should
be afforded for the investment of the periodical savings
of the working class. M. Turgot, in his memoran-
dum on ' Loans of Money,' complained that small
savings were an embarrassment to the artisan, that they
remained in his hands absolutely unproductive until a
considerable sum had been accumulated, and that it
was hard for men to hoard up money, when they were
constantly exposed to the temptations of the public-
house.

The inquiry of the House of Lords Committee on
Intemperance elicited some valuable evidence from Mr.
J W. Pease, M.P. for South Durham, with regard to

[margin:] Future of co-opera-tion.

[margin:] Invest-ments for the work-ing man's savings.

[margin:] Mr. Pease's sugges-tions as to payment of wages.

the habits of colliers, and some practical suggestions for diminishing the temptations with which the workmen are usually beset after leaving the pay-table. Mr. Pease remarked that if he had works which were concentrated he believed he should adopt the plan of crediting every man his wages on the day following that on which they were earned, allowing him to draw it when he liked, and giving him interest on the balance. He had heard of that plan being carried out with great success; it had promoted better habits of thrift and economy and less drinking than almost any other style of paying wages. Another thing which they had endeavoured to do was to give the men the greatest possible amount of small change, so that they might not have to go to the public-houses to change their money.

French and English investors in the funds.

The opportunities which M. Turgot wished to create for the working classes of France have been supplied only too freely in recent years by the rapid augmentation of the public debt. The French people responded with unabated confidence to the repeated demands of the Second Empire; and it was by the financial assistance, thus readily afforded, that the late Emperor was enabled to carry out his costly and disastrous schemes of military aggression.

The great difference in the number of persons interested respectively in the English and French funds has formed the subject of a recent article in the 'Economist.' Comparing the years 1857 and 1874, while the total amount of the debt of the United Kingdom was approximately the same—being 780,000,000*l.* in the

former and 779,000,000*l.* in the latter year—we find
that the number of persons entitled to dividends had
fallen in the interval from 269,712 to 228,696. The
gradual diminution in the number of the smaller holders
is shown in the following table :

*British Public Funds—Number of Persons entitled to Dividends in the
Public Funds.*

	1857. Persons	Proportion per cent.	1874. Persons	Proportion per cent.
Dividends not exceeding—				
5*l.*	92,281	34	76,130	33
10*l.*	43,412	16	35,327	16
50*l.*	89,741	33	77,890	34
100*l.*	23,296	9	20,606	9
200*l.*	13,050	5	11,453	5
300*l.*	3,791	1	3,317	1
500*l.*	2,428	1	2,170	0·9
1,000*l.*	1,136	0·5	1,142	0·4
2,000*l.*	349	0·1	410	0·2
Exceeding 2,000*l.*	228	0·1	251	0·1
Total number of persons.	269,712		228,696	

The number of bondholders in France is estimated
at from 1,000,000 to 1,500,000.

The diffusion of the holding of the national debt
is of public advantage. A larger number of persons
are interested in the stability of the Government and in
economy in the public expenditure, and the area from
which loans may be raised is extended. In France,
the facilities for making investments in the public
funds are far greater than in this country. Depositors
are not allowed to keep a balance exceeding 40*l.* in
the savings banks. If the surplus is not withdrawn
after a certain date, it is invested in the public funds.
Under the provisions of another regulation in force in

Facilities for public investment in France.

France, a still more considerable sum is invested by small capitalists. All depositors in the savings banks may instruct the authorities to invest their deposits in the funds free of charge. The amounts invested under the above regulations are shown in the subjoined statement :

French Savings Banks.

Year	Purchases *ex officio* by the Savings Banks for Depositors	Purchases at the demand of Depositors in Savings Banks
	Francs	Francs
1868	663,720	8,008,230
1869	854,862	9,722,876
1870	} 1,277	{ 9,764,742
1871		72,702,110
1872	571,351	18,454,491
1873	505,982	19,067,407
1874	477,737	17,571,446
1875	549,044	13,586,055
1876	783,363	15,725,500

The savings banks collect the dividends for the depositors. The amounts so collected in Paris yielded, according to the latest return, an average annual income of 1*l*. 1*s*. a year to each investor.

In France, orders for the purchase and sale of *rente* are received by the Government treasury agents in the provinces, and their subordinates the local tax-collectors ; and the limit of capital allowed to be purchased has been gradually reduced from an amount sufficient to bring in an annual dividend of 2*l*. per annum to an investment producing only 2*s*. 6*d*. per annum.

How similar facilities might be provided by The French regulations for encouraging investments by the masses of the population in the public funds merit the attention of our own Government.

The facilities provided in France could readily be our own
Govern-
ment. created in the United Kingdom, through the instrumentality of the Post Office or the Inland Revenue Department.

Attention has been directed, in a recent article in Public
invest-
ments in
the United
States. the 'Saturday Review,' to the efforts made by Mr. Sherman to give to the people of the United States the same facilities for investing in the Government funds which have been provided in France. The smallest bond issued by the United States Government is for 50 dollars, or 10*l.* sterling. Mr. Sherman desires to create facilities for the investment of a still smaller sum. He has accordingly determined to offer a part of the four per cent. loan in such a shape as would suit the humblest person who had money to put by. He does not issue a smaller class of bonds than those already known to American investors; but instead he offers interest-bearing certificates of the value of 10 dollars or 2*l.* When five of these certificates are obtained, they may be exchanged for a fifty-dollar bond ; but this exchange is not obligatory.

Mr. Gladstone's scheme for the creation of small Mr. Glad-
stone's
small
annuity
scheme. annuities was a most beneficial measure. It has enabled a workman, by depositing a small sum weekly, to secure a certain income to commence at an age when he will probably be incapacitated from severe physical toil. Railway companies would do well to create a certain proportion of 1*l.* shares, to be reserved for distribution among the numerous body of servants in their employment.

The rate of interest on deposits in the Post Office

Savings Banks should be increased. It could be done without loss to the public exchequer. It is pointed out, in an article in the 'Industrial Review,' published in December 1878, that while the Post Office banks are greatly in favour in England and Wales, and are not neglected in Ireland, they find but moderate custom in Scotland. In that country for 1*l.* in the new banks there are 12*l.* in the older ones. The latter afford exactly 9*s.* 5*d.* per cent. more interest than the former, which probably attracts the very thrifty among the poor ; while local predilections may tend to the same result.'

This question has recently been discussed, and a simple and effective method of dealing with it has been propounded, in the columns of the 'Pall Mall Gazette.' ' The question of securing profitable investments for the poorer classes is once more suggested by a correspondent of the " Daily News," who wishes to add 1½ per cent. to the 2½ per cent. allowed by the Post Office on the savings in his own village, so as to bring the rate of interest up to that obtainable on mortgage. It is certainly to be regretted that sound investments bearing a higher rate of interest than 2½ per cent. are not, as in France and in the United States, brought within the reach of every class. Yet the working classes may congratulate themselves that some of the loans bearing high interest, which have found favour with their richer countrymen, were not offered to them in small lots. There seems to be no reason, however, why Consols, or the Indian, colonial, and municipal loans, should not be offered to the poorer classes in small sums. Either the Post Office Savings Bank might take up portions of such loans for this purpose, and divide them for the convenience of those who are only able to make small savings, or a special agency might be formed to the like end. By charging a small percentage above the rate at which the securities were bought, and working through an old-established life assurance agency (presuming the Post Office not to be available), the whole machinery would soon be self-sustaining. In this country a whole stratum of small investors remains at present untapped; and the plan here suggested would not only tend to promote thrift, but in the case of Indian and colonial loans would enlarge the interest of the community in the concerns of the Empire.'

CHAPTER XII.

SOCIALISM.

Excuse for the existence of Socialism.   FAR be it from me to extenuate the invariable folly and the occasional crime of the Socialistic machinations on the Continent. But it is idle to denounce the conduct of men whose fault consists in the concoction of schemes for the reconstitution of a society in which they find their own lot very hopeless and unenviable, merely because they exhibit an absurd ignorance of political economy. Mr. Herbert Spencer has well said that ' men leading laborious lives, relieved by little in the shape of enjoyment, give willing ear to the doctrine that the State should provide them with various positive advantages and gratifications. The much-enduring poor cannot be expected to deal very critically with those who promise them, gratis, pleasures. We must not, therefore, blame the working classes for being ready converts to Socialistic schemes.'

Freedom of England from Socialist errors.   It is not the least among the numerous claims of the English workmen as a body to the favourable appreciation of the public that they have never been led astray by those theoretical denunciations of property which culminated at Paris in the Commune, which were exhibited in the railway riots in the United States,

and have given occasion for the repressive legislation
recently carried through the German Parliament. In
England the influence of the International has been
magnified, in order to raise a prejudice against the
working class. Its real influence here may be appreciated from the limited pecuniary support which it has
received. The entire income is stated in a table published by Mr. Howell:

1864–5	.	.	.	23*l.* 0*s.*	1868	.	.		14*l.* 4*s.*
1866	.	.	.	9*l.* 13*s.*	1869	.	.	.	30*l.* 12*s.*
1867	.	.	.	5*l.* 17*s.*	1870	.	.	.	28*l.* 1*s.*

In justice to the British workmen, the debates and
proceedings of our Trades Union Congresses should be
read in parallel columns with the mad declamation at
the Congress of Socialists at Ghent, or at the Congress
of French workmen, so graphically described by Mr.
Frederic Harrison, whose name I cannot mention
without expressing that gratitude, which all persons
interested in maintaining amicable relations between
workman and employer ought to feel towards one,
who has done such excellent service in the capacity of
mediator. The number of men must always be small
who can maintain friendly relations both with capital
and labour, and who are able to appreciate the claims
which each interest has upon the other. ‘We habitually
live in our ordinary selves,’ says Mr. Matthew Arnold,
‘which do not carry us beyond the ideas and wishes of
the class to which we happen to belong.’ Mr. Cromp-
ton, Mr. Morley, and others have laboured in the same
field. By their sympathy with the masses, and by the
pains they have taken to appreciate and interpret their

ideas to the world, these gentlemen have shown to the workmen that a high culture teaches no narrow or selfish lessons, and that wealth, where it is ill gotten and ill spent, is as contemptible a thing in the estimation of the leaders of thought in the so-called upper classes, as it is in the jealous eyes of the Trades Unionists themselves.

Socialism in France.

Socialistic schemes have been more or less in favour on the Continent since the period preceding the outbreak of the French Revolution. Marat was the chosen prophet of the working men, whose confidence he gained by his adhesion to a programme not dissimilar to the scheme adopted by the Revolutionary Government of 1848. The fervid imagination of the French nation has been prolific of novel plans for the regeneration of society by fundamental changes in the distribution of property and the relations of capital to labour.

The characteristic tenets of the authors of the most remarkable social and industrial theories promulgated in France are concisely summed up in the report of the recent Parliamentary Committee on the condition of the labourers in that country. The keynote of St. Simon was, ' To every man according to his capacity; to every capacity according to his work.' The Fourierists insisted that every man should have full scope for the free and congenial employment of his powers. Proudhon asked for gratuitous credits and loans without interest. St. Simon proposed to entrust the partition of the products of labour to an authority, whom he designated as the high-priest of his ideal society. Fourier proposed to regulate the earnings of each individual according to the harmonious verdict of individual opinions. Another school framed regulations for the distribution of property according to the necessities of each individual. The principle of the Luxembourg school was equality for all. The inevitable outcome of all these systems was anarchy.

In Germany, the general spread of education has prepared the soil for Socialistic doctrines, under conditions most favourable for their growth. Where the many are poor and the few are rich, where there is a national taste for speculation, and where compulsory military service is enforced with the utmost stringency, in the very throes of a commercial crisis, and when the people are engaged in a hard struggle for bare existence, there is obviously much to foment a spirit of rebellion among the masses against the social order, under which they find their lot so hard. *Conditions favouring its growth in Germany.*

The short-lived outburst of prosperity which followed the conclusion of the Franco-German war served but to aggravate the sufferings of a population, who have been driven back into a still lower depth of poverty than that from which they had lately emerged. Prices had risen with the general inflation of wages, and, when the reaction came, it was not easy to curtail the cost of living, in proportion to the diminution of earnings.

For the dreamy German people, in their distressed condition, Socialistic doctrines possessed a peculiar attraction; and the authorities were already becoming uneasy at the progress of the revolutionary spirit, when the cowardly attempt to assassinate the Emperor of *Attempted assassination of the German Emperor.*

Germany took place, and gave an impetus to repressive legislation. In the course of the debates in the German Parliament, Prince Bismarck declared that they had to contend with a dangerous foe in social democracy, a foe who threatened both the State and society. If they were to live on under the tyranny of such a company of bandits, all existence must come to an end. It was possible that some more victims might fall on the side of order ; but each who met such a fate might remember that he fell on the field of honour for the good of his country.

Repressive legislation evoked by it.

A recent letter from the ' Times ' correspondent at Berlin gives particulars of the proceedings taken under the new legislation. During the first two months after the Socialist law came into force, 375 repressive injunctions were addressed to 174 clubs and societies, 44 newspapers, and 157 non-periodical publications. The Socialists have fixed their head-quarters at Leipsic, where they sit at the feet of MM. Liebknecht and Bebel. The Government will be aided in its efforts by the jealousy of rival prophets of Socialism. Continental governments have always been prone to coercive measures. The principles, which have guided our legislation, have been more just and more wise. We have allowed a large latitude to discussion, but have been prompt and severe in the punishment of crime.

The railway riots in America.

In the United States, the Irish and German immigrants have imported communistic theories into the country ; and the shameless combinations of certain railway companies and coal proprietors to maintain prices, by an artificial restriction of supplies to the public, made it natural that some resistance should be offered to the reduction of wages. The accumulation of colossal fortunes in the hands of a knot of speculators had naturally excited a feeling of irritation.

The policy pursued by the companies in question is described by Mr. Lowthian Bell. Referring to the increase in the cost of coal and in the manufacture of pig-iron, he says that, ' of the 46,000,000 tons of coal worked in the United States, about 21,000,000 are anthracite, and yet the market of this large quantity of mineral is practically in the hands of six large companies, who represent 80 to 85 per cent. of the entire output. It was no secret that under such a system the profits of coal property had been very great.'

When the railway servants united with the lawless mobs, which had already begun to establish themselves in American cities, and proceeded from orderly remonstrance to incendiarism, they forfeited all claim to sympathy. The previous conduct of those responsible for the administration of the railway companies was, nevertheless, deserving of censure.

CHAPTER XIII.

COLONISATION.

Patriotism is a necessary link in the golden chain of our affections and virtues. It is a false philosophy to believe that cosmopolitism is nobler than nationality, and the human race a sublimer object of love than a people. The powers of men are most fitly exercised in a circle defined by human affections, whence they spread without confusion through a common sphere, like the vibrations propagated in the air by a single voice, distinct, yet coherent, and all uniting to express one thought and the same feeling.—COLERIDGE, *The Friend.*

New markets.   EXCLUDED from the principal manufacturing countries by a protectionist policy, it is to the colonies, and to the half-civilised countries, that we must look for new openings for the expansion of our trade. The development of our commerce in this direction will afford us additional satisfaction, in that the results arising from our success must be mutually beneficial.

Africa.   We cannot create a trade with Africa or New Guinea without first raising those countries in the scale of nations. We must co-operate with the native populations in the development of their resources, we must help them to accumulate wealth, or they cannot purchase our goods.

Statesmen and merchants, in their efforts to procure new outlets for commerce, may wisely direct their attention to Africa—that vast untravelled continent, with a population of from 350 to 400 millions of people, and where 500,000 human beings, according to Mr. Bradshaw's computation, are annually destroyed in the wars that are carried on for the capture of slaves. The first condition to be fulfilled is the establishment of peace and order among these savage races.

China, again, has been well described by the China. 'Quarterly' Reviewer as a storehouse of men and means. Its outer door has scarcely yet been opened. The future of the commerce with China is dimly shadowed forth in Professor Levi's calculation. 'Assuming,' he says, 'the population of the world to be considerably over a thousand million human beings, that at the very minimum they will require food and clothing to the value of 10*l.* per annum each, and that not more than half that amount is produced in the same countries in which the consumption takes place, the aggregate exports will be increased from the present total of a thousand millions to more than three thousand millions. If the productive power of the world is great, the consuming power is still greater. The field of international commerce, present and future, is vast, and what we see of its progress gives but an imperfect idea of its probable expansion.'

The recent fluctuations in trade afford abundant Colonial evidence of the importance of the colonies to the trade. mother country from a commercial, no less than a political, point of view. While our commerce with the continent of Europe, and with the United States, has been contracted, our exportations to our colonies have steadily increased. This valuable source of employment to our population has been developed, partly because national sympathies exert an influence in trade as in higher things, but mainly because no tariff, exceptionally unfavourable to the mother country, has been imposed. If an import duty is levied, it is levied impartially on the products of all countries. In her commercial relations with her colonies, England may rest assured that she will always be placed on the footing of 'the most favoured nation.'

The Commissioners of Customs in their last Report direct particular attention to the elasticity exhibited in our colonial trade. 'Taking for the points of comparison the years 1872 and 1877, we find that the value of the exports to foreign countries diminished from 195,701,350*l.* to 128,969,715*l.*, a difference of 66,731,635*l.*, or 34·1 per cent., and that the value of the exports to the British possessions increased from 60,555,997*l.* to 69,923,350*l.*, or 15·5 per cent.

' This is so far satisfactory as showing that, notwithstanding the decline in our exports generally, we have as yet encountered no serious competition in the supply of manufactured articles, such as apparel, cotton, yarn and piece goods, haberdashery, hardware, and cutlery, leather, wrought (especially boots and shoes), machinery and millwork, iron and steel, paper of all sorts, and woollen and worsted goods, to our own colonies.'

In the year 1877, there was a decrease of 6,811,000*l.* in the value of British exports to foreign countries ; while the export trade to the colonies increased by 5,000,064*l.*

Value of British Goods Exported.

Year	Foreign Countries	British Possessions	Total
	£	£	£
1872	195,701,350	60,555,007	256,257,347
1873	188,836,132	66,328,471	255,164,603
1874	167,278,029	72,280,092	239,558,121
1875	152,373,800	71,092,163	223,465,963
1876	135,779,980	64,859,224	200,639,204
1877	128,969,715	69,923,350	198,893,065

These figures afford a convincing testimony of the value of our colonial connection to our trade and commerce; and it is not alone by their demand for the produce of her looms and ironworks that the colonies lend their valuable support to the mother country. Large remittances are sent home to their less fortunate relatives by successful emigrants. Between 1848 and 1876 the emigrants to the colonies and the United States are estimated to have remitted no less than 19,800,000*l.* In many instances large fortunes are brought home, or at least the proceeds of colonial enterprise and investments are spent in the mother country.

Remittances from emigrants.

Emigration confers reciprocal advantages on the colonies. Mr. Graham has made an interesting calculation of the wealth which the United Kingdom has bestowed on the colonies by emigration. The United Kingdom sent forth in the thirty-nine years, 1837–1876, eight million emigrants, chiefly to the English-speaking nations in America and Australia. Mr. Graham estimates the value of the emigrants at 175*l.* per head.

Money value of emigration.

Commenting on this extensive emigration, he remarks that the average money value of the emigration from the United Kingdom since 1837 may be estimated at 35,000,000*l.* a year.

Growth
of the co-
lonies.
Austral-

The Australian Governments did wisely in seizing the opportunity, afforded by the recent Exhibition in Paris, of setting before the world some striking evidences of the results achieved by this extensive emigration into countries possessed of great national resources, and wanting only the hand of man to convert a wilderness into a garden.

A still more accurate and complete knowledge may be gained in the volumes of Mr. Wilson, from which I have derived so much assistance in the preparation of these papers. The Colonial Abstract published by our Statistical Department contains a mass of well-arranged statistics.

The total yield of gold in Australia and New Zealand, since the first discovery in Victoria, was estimated by Mr. Wells at 247,000,000*l.*; but the value of gold is small compared with the accumulation of agricultural wealth. According to the tables appended to the Agricultural Returns of Great Britain for 1876, the Australian colonies own altogether about 52,000,000 sheep; New Zealand has nearly 12,000,000. The number of sheep in Russia is estimated at 48,000,000; in France, 26,000,000; in Germany, about 22,000,000; and in the United States, 34,000,000. New South Wales has more than 3,000,000 head of horses and cattle.

Mr. Read's essay on New South Wales contains a striking summary of the growth of the population, and of the trade of the Antipodes. The population of Australia increased in thirty years from 214,000 to 2,000,000, or 834 per cent. The population of the

United States increased in the same period by 660 per cent. The trade rose in the same period from less than 6,000,000*l.* to more than 63,000,000*l.*, or 950 per cent. Two thousand two hundred miles of railway had been opened, and the annual revenue of the Australian governments was 14,000,000*l.*

It was believed, until a recent period, that the fertile lands formed a comparatively narrow fringe round the coasts of Australia. Later experiences have shown that the interior of the continent contains vast tracts of fertile land, well adapted for settlement.

The following statistics and observations are from an article by Sir Julius Vogel, lately published in the ' Princeton Review : '

' There is probably no country in the world at the present time in which prosperity more uniformly reigns, or in which the inhabitants are more completely contented, than New Zealand. The following figures for the year ending 1870, and for the year ending 1877, tell their own tale.

	1870	1877
Revenue . . .	£1,287,000	£4,000,000
Exports . . .	£4,544,000	£6,327,000
Imports . . .	£4,630,000	£6,973,000
Population . . .	*248,000	*408,000

* Exclusive of Maoris in each case.

' The mineral wealth of New Zealand is very large. As yet it has scarcely been tapped. It was not until 1861 that its goldfields were worked to any extent. Since then they have yielded, to the end of 1877, 8,600,000 ounces valued at 33,593,000*l.* The islands abound in iron.

	New South Wales	Victoria
Estimated Mean Population of 1877 .	645,994	849,870
Revenue of 1877	5,748,245*l.*	ª4,723,877*l.*
Proportion of Revenue of 1877, raised by Taxation . .	1,235,021*l.*	ª1,770,685*l.*
Rate of Taxation per head of Population	1*l.* 18*s.* 2¾*d.*	ª2*l.* 2*s.* 2¼*d.*
Value of Imports for 1877 . .	14,606,594*l.*	16,362,304*l.*
Value of Imports per head of the Population	22*l.* 12*s.* 2½*d.*	19*l.* 5*s.* 0¾*d.*
Value of Exports for 1877 . . .	13,125,819*l.*	15,157,687*l.*
Value of Exports per head of the Population	20*l.* 6*s.* 4½*d.*	17*l.* 16*s.* 8¼*d.*
Total Value of Trade, Imports, and Exports	27,732,413*l.*	31,519,991*l.*
Value of Trade per head of the Population	42*l.* 18*s.* 7*d.*	37*l.* 1*s.* 9¼*d.*
	Miles	Miles
Miles of Railway Open, Dec. 31, 1877	ª643	931
Miles of Railway in course of Construction, Dec. 31, 1877 .	217¾	193
Miles of Telegraph Lines Open, Dec. 31, 1877 . . .	6,000	2,885
Miles of Telegraph Wire Open, Dec. 31, 1877 . . .	9,761	,5,200
Miles of Telegraph in course of Construction, Dec. 31, 1877 :—		
Length of Lines . . .	ᵇ—	44
Length of Wire . . .	1,758	45
No. of Acres under Crop in 1877 .	546,556	1,420,502
No. of Horses in 1877 . . .	328,150	203,150
No. of Cattle in 1877 . . .	2,746,385	1,174,176
No. of Sheep in 1877 . . .	20,962,244	10,114,267
No. of Pigs in 1877 . . .	191,677	183,391
Estimated Population on Dec. 31, 1877.	662,212	860,787
Public Debt on Dec. 31, 1877 . .	11,724,419*l.*	17,018,913*l.*
Rate of Indebtedness per head of Population . : . .	17*l.* 14*s.* 1*d.*	19*l.* 15*s.* 5*d.*

ª Includes a private line of railway, forty-five miles in length.
ᵇ Could not be ascertained.
ᶜ For financial year ended June 30.
ᵈ The mean population for the year 1876-7 has been used, viz., 83
ᵉ There are also 5,158 acres in fallow, making the total und
105,049 acres.
ᶠ Not stated in return received from this colony.
ᵍ Exclusive of land in sown grasses (including hay, 45,090 acres)
of which were as follows :—In grass, after having been broken up,
grass, not previously ploughed, 1,531,385 acres.

COLONIES.

of the Australasian Colonies at the close of the Year 1877.

Queensland	Tasmania	Western Australia	Total	New Zealand	Total for Australasian Colonies
195,092	106,294	27,579	2,056,212	408,348	2,464,560
1,436,581*l.*	361,771*l.*	165,413*l.*	13,877,288*l.*	3,916,023*l.*	17,793,311*l.*
609,860*l.*	236,777*l.*	81,268*l.*	4,433,496*l.*	1,343,944*l.*	5,777,440*l.*
3*l.* 2*s.* 6¼*d.*	2*l.* 4*s.* 6½*d.*	2*l.* 18*s.* 11*d.*	2*l.* 3*s.* 4*d.*	3*l.* 5*s.* 9¾*d.*	2*l.* 7*s.* 0¾*d.*
4,068,682*l.*	1,308,671*l.*	362,707*l.*	41,334,469*l.*	6,973,418*l.*	48,307,887*l.*
20*l.* 17*s.* 1¼*d.*	12*l.* 6*s.* 2¾*d.*	13*l.* 3*s.* 0¼*d.*	20*l.* 2*s.* 0½*d.*	17*l.* 1*s.* 6½*d.*	19*l.* 12*s.* 0¼*d.*
4,361,275*l.*	1,416,975*l.*	373,352*l.*	39,061,639*l.*	6,327,472*l.*	45,389,111*l.*
22*l.* 7*s.* 1¼*d.*	18*l.* 6*s.* 7¼*d.*	13*l.* 10*s.* 9*d.*	18*l.* 19*s.* 11¼*d.*	15*l.* 0*s.* 10¾*d.*	18*l.* 8*s.* 4*d.*
8,429,957*l.*	2,725,646*l.*	736,059*l.*	80,396,108*l.*	13,300,890*l.*	93,696,998*l.*
43*l.* 4*s.* 2½*d.*	25*l.* 12*s.* 10*d.*	26*l.* 13*s.* 9¼*d.*	39*l.* 1*s.* 11¾*d.*	32*l.* 11*s.* 5¼*d.*	38*l.* 0*s.* 4¼*d.*
Miles 357	Miles 172½	Miles 68	Miles 2,498½	Miles 954	Miles 3,452½
168	—	25	1,007¾	219	1,226¾
5,033	621	1,567¼	20,167¼	3,307	23,474¼
6,778	843	[f]—	27,735	7,530	[k]35,265
—	55	—	—	—	—
—	55	—	2,178	—	2,178
[e]99,891	131,013	50,591	4,076,668	[g]641,833	4.718,501
140,174	22,195	30,691	835,044	[h]99,859	934,903
2,299,582	126,882	52,057	6,629,761	[h]494,917	7,124,678
6,272,766	1,818,125	797,156	46,062,917	[h]11,704,853	57,767,770
52,371	55,652	18,942	606,560	[h]123,921	730,481
203,084	107,104	27,838	2,098,115	[i]417,622	2,515,737
7,685,350*l.*	1,589,703*l.*	161,000*l.*	42,916,587*l.*	[j]20,691,111*l.*	63,607,698*l.*
37*l.* 16*s.* 10*d.*	14*l.* 16*s.* 10*d.*	5*l.* 15*s.* 8*d.*	20*l.* 9*s.* 1*d.*	49*l.* 10*s.* 10¾*d.*	25*l.* 5*s.* 8*d.*

[h] At the time the last Census was taken in March 1874.

[i] This estimate is a little over 3,000 in excess of the ascertained population on March 3, 1878; the difference being probably caused by unascertained departures from the colony since the Census of 1874.

[j] As the invested Sinking Fund amounted to 1,438,838*l.*, the total debt should be reduced by that amount to exhibit the net liability.

[k] The information for Western Australia is not included.

'During the sixteen years ending 1877, no less than 31,377,000*l.* worth of wool was exported from the colony. The export of 1862 was 674,000*l.* ; of 1877, 3,658,000*l.*

'Land has advanced in price from 1*l.* to 2*l.* an acre, to from 5*l.* to 12*l.* an acre, and excellent authorities maintain that for its productive powers it is well worth 20*l.* an acre. The official returns show that during 1876, the yield of wheat from 141,614 acres was 4,054,377 bushels, whilst in South Australia, one of the finest wheat-producing countries in the world, 183,732 acres only yielded 5,857,569 bushels.'

Victoria is the most populous colony in Australia. 'From 1851 to the end of 1877, it produced gold to the astounding amount of 189,568,000*l.*, and silver to the value of 2,100,000*l.*

'The estimated population of Victoria is about 840,000.

'Pastoral occupations flourish here as in the other colonies.

'The estimated value of the produce of the colony for 1876 was as follows:

				£
Value of agricultural produce	.	.	.	5,574,238
„ pastoral produce	.	.	.	10,069,570
„ mining produce	.	.	.	3,886,418
				£19,530,227

'During the seven years ending 1876, the exports of wool amounted to 31,000,000*l.*'

Tasmania is the sanatorium of Australia. The small mortality among children in that island is a most re-markable feature. Taking an average of five years, the proportion of children under five, who died, to 1,000 children of the same age living, was in England and Wales 67½, in Tasmania less than 27.

The table occupying pp. 264, 265 gives, in a convenient form, the latest and most complete statistical information relating to the Australian colonies.

Our colonists have not hitherto been diverted by a protectionist tariff from their legitimate sphere of agricultural development. Their demand for manufactured goods has hitherto been supplied, to the mutual advantage both of buyers and sellers, from the looms and foundries of the United Kingdom.

We have already seen how great has been the gain to our manufacturing industry. With the growth of the colonies in wealth and civilisation, a corresponding increase will follow in their demand for our productions. At the present time, railway enterprise is warmly supported in Australia. Seven lines are projected for South Australia, with a total length of 400 miles, at a cost of about 2,000,000*l.* In New Zealand, the Government propose to borrow about 1,300,000*l.* for railway extensions. The rails and rolling stock for these undertakings will be purchased in the United Kingdom.

It is evident, from the diminishing numbers leaving our shores for the United States, and from the increase in the numbers sailing to the Antipodes, that British emigrants appreciate the immunity the Australian colonies have hitherto enjoyed from the civil wars and financial crises, which have chequered the prosperity of the United States.

The following figures are taken from the Registrar-General's tables :

Average Annual Number of Emigrants of British Origin to

	United States	British North America	Australasia
5 years 1871–75	134,853	22,283	27,282
1876	54,554	9,335	32,196

In 1876 the Australasian emigration constituted 29 per cent. In the preceding period it was 14 per cent. In the five years 1866–70, it was 9 per cent. of the total. The Registrar-General reports that the number of emigrants to Australasia in 1877 was nearly the same as in the previous year, while the numbers to the United States and to British North America in 1877 were still less than the already greatly diminished numbers in the previous year. The emigrants to the several destinations, however, bore nearly the same proportions to the total as in 1876.

Table showing the Average Annual Number of Emigrants of British Origin to each of the undermentioned Places.

Period	To United States		To British North America		To Australasia		To all other Places		Total
	Average Annual Number	Per-cent-age of Total	Average Annual Number	Per-cent-age of Total	Average Annual Number	Per-cent-age of Total	Average Annual Number	Per-cent-age of Total	
Three years 1853–55	143,606	62	27,856	12	59,876	26	395	—	231,733
Five years 1856–60	74,956	61	7,968	6	37,136	30	3,437	3	123,497
„ 1861–65	93,208	65	9,548	7	37,268	26	3,535	2	143,559
„ 1866–70	133,317	78	16,514	10	16,204	9	4,772	3	170,807
„ 1871–75	134,853	70	22,283	11	27,882	14	8,889	5	193,907
Year 1876 . .	54,554	50	9,335	9	32,196	29	13,384	12	109,469
„ 1877 . .	45,481	48	7,720	8	30,138	32	11,856	12	95,195

Note.—No correction has been made in the above table for those whose nationality was not distinguished.

These are striking figures, and they fully justify the observation of Mr. Wells, that the rapid development of the British colonies in the South Pacific is one of the wonderful social and economic phenomena of the latter half of the nineteenth century.

The recent commercial recovery of the United States has once more stimulated the movement of emigration to the more accessible field of North America. Mr. Giffen observes, in his latest report on the returns of emigration, ' that of persons of British and Irish origin, 54,694 went to the United States in 1878 as compared with 45,481 in 1877, so that the United States had more than half the increase of 17,707 in the emigration. There was also a great increase of the emigration to Australia, viz. from 30,138 in 1877, to 36,479 in 1878; and an increase in the emigration to British North America from 7,720 in 1877, to 10,652 in 1878.'

We have dwelt at such length on the Australian colonies, that space forbids a detailed statement of the growth of our other dependencies. The readers of Mr. Wilson's pages will be aware that our colonies in South Africa have of late made remarkable strides. Since the discovery of diamonds, the export of precious stones has been enormous. The great Kimberley mine alone has furnished some 12,000,000*l*. The great need of the Cape is population.

The capabilities of Canada, especially of the Upper Canada Provinces of the Dominion, have been described in glowing terms by Mr. Wells in an article entitled, ' How shall the Nation regain Prosperity?' contributed to the ' North American Review ' in 1877. He says : ' North of Lake Erie and Ontario and the River St. Lawrence, east of Lake Huron, south of the 45th parallel, and included mainly within the present Dominion Province of Ontario, there is as fair a country as exists on the North American continent; nearly as large in area as New York, Pennsylvania, and Ohio combined, and equal, if not superior, as a whole, to these States in its agricultural capacity. It is the natural habitat on this continent of the combing-wool sheep, without a full, cheap, and reliable supply of the wool of which species the great worsted-manufacturing interest of the country cannot prosper, or, we should rather say, exist. It is the land where grows the finest barley, which the brewing interest of the United States must have if it ever expects to rival Great Britain in its present annual export of over 11,000,000 dollars worth of malt products. It raises and grazes the finest cattle, with qualities especially desirable to make good the deterioration of stock in other sections ; and its climatic conditions, created by the encirclement of the Great Lakes, especially fit it to grow men. Such a country is one of the greatest gifts of Providence to the human race, better than bonanzas of silver, or rivers whose sands contain gold.'

Mr. Wells does not seek to persuade his fellow countrymen to annex this fertile region : he asks them to utilise its resources, to the mutual advantage of the United States and the colony, by the abolition of protective duties.

It is stated by Mr. Alfred Bateman that nearly twelve millions of acres were under crop in Canada in 1870–71, and five millions under pasture. No less than 90,000,000 bushels of corn and grain were grown. The Dominion possesses 2,500,000 head of cattle, and 3,000,000 sheep. The annual value of the butter, cheese, and maple-sugar made in Canada has been estimated at 3,000,000*l.*; while the other agricultural products included 47,000,000 bushels of potatoes, besides hops, tobacco, and fruits.

The following remarks on the climate are taken from the Canadian official hand-book:

'If the climate of a country is to be measured by its productions, then Canada, either in the quality of her timber, grains, fruits, plants, and animals, not excepting man, must be accorded a front rank.

'Her extremes of cold, though of short duration, and her invaluable winter covering of snow, have given her an Arctic reputation—acquired in the past when the fur trade was her only export, and when the savage was " lord of the soil." Furs are suggestive of cold and snow, and these have obliterated from memory the heat of the Canadian summer, whereby the range of production is extended, in grains, from barley to maize; in fruits, from apples to peaches, grapes, melons, nectarines, and apricots; in vegetables, from turnips, carrots, and cabbages, to the egg plant and tomatoes.

'Snow and ice, however objectionable they may be in other countries, are no drawback to the Canadian winter. To Cánada they mean not only protection to her cultivated acres, almost as valuable as a covering of manure, but the conversion of whole areas, during several months in the year, to a surface upon which every man may make his own road, equal to a turn-pike, in any direction, over swamp or field, lake or river, and on which millions of tons are annually transported at the minimum cost,—whereby employment is

afforded for man and horse when cultivation is arrested
by frost.

'Intensity of winter cold has little effect upon the
agriculture of a country except the beneficial one of
pulverising the soil where exposed. High spring and
summer temperatures, with abundance of rain, secure
the certain ripening of maize and the melon in Canada.

'On the other hand (for the continent of America),
on the lines of latitude where frost and snow cease,
malignant fevers commence, and in the tropical zones
the trees become dwarfed by a rank growth of vegeta-
tion. In a country so extensive as Canada there is a
great difference in climate on the same lines of latitude.
which is due rather to longitude than to elevation above
the sea. Like Europe, the western coast is the warmest,
and for the same reason—warm winds and waters from
the adjacent ocean.'   ·

In addition to her agricultural resources, Canada
possesses most productive fisheries. In a recent paper
by Mr. Young we are informed that these fisheries give
employment to two hundred thousand men, a thousand
ships, and seventeen thousand smacks, manned by
seven thousand sailors and twenty-six thousand fisher-
men. The importance of the fisheries is growing every
year. The annual return from the fisheries increased
from 1,320,000*l.* in 1870, to 2,240,000*l.* in 1874.

The mineral production of Canada is not unimportant. Nearly a million tons of coal have been raised in
some years in Nova Scotia, and more than 150,000 tons
were raised in Vancouver in 1877.

The number of persons in the receipt of wages in

the Dominion was 188,000; their total earnings were more than eight millions sterling, or a weekly average of about 17s. 6d., a high rate, considering that a large number of females, and of persons under sixteen years, tend to lower the average.

Few of us in this country appreciate the rapidly growing commercial value of Canada. In 1876 the total imports of the Dominion were rather less than twenty millions sterling, of which more than eight millions were from England; and of sixteen millions of exports, the mother country received more than eight and a half millions.

Hitherto we have been considering emigration as a means of forming new nations in unpeopled regions, and as a means of creating an important outlet for external trade. But emigration tends to ameliorate the condition of the population at home by diminishing the competition for employment; in other words by increasing wages, or at least arresting the downward tendency consequent on an excessive growth of the population. It confers an equally essential benefit by the additional supplies it furnishes to a country depending largely on imported food. I have already alluded to the pastoral wealth of the Australian colonies. As their population increases they will doubtless become extensive growers of grain. The prospect of an increased supply of wheat from the colonies becomes especially valuable in view of the diminished growth of cereals at home. The acreage under wheat in the United Kingdom in 1867 was 3,367,876 acres. In 1877 it was reduced to 3,168,540

Emigration sustains wages at home.

T

Trade or Calling	New South Wales	Victoria	South Australia
Bookbinders . .	... ...	40s. to 60s. per week	45s. to 60s. per week
Compositors . .	1s. to 1s. 1d. per 1,000	1s. per 1,000	1s. 1d. per 1,000
Lithographers . .	... ...	55s. to 75s. per week	... ...
Carpenters . . .	9s. to 11s. per diem	10s. per diem (8 hours)	9s. to 10s. per diem (8 hours)
Stonemasons . .	11s.	10s. „	9s. to 10s. „
Bricklayers . . .	10s. to 12s. „	10s. „	9s. to 10s. „
Plasterers . . .	11s. to 12s. „	10s. „	10s. to 12s. „
Building labourers	8s. to 9s. „	7s. „	6s. to 7s. „
Painters and glaziers	9s. to 10s. „	9s. „	8s. to 12s. „
Joiners	10s. to 11s. „	... ...	... ...
Plumbers . . .	10s. to 12s. „ .	60s. per week	10s. to 12s. per diem
Gasfitters . . .	10s. „	... ...	40s. to 60s. per week
Blacksmiths . .	1s. 1d. to 1s. 5d. per hour (eight hours a day)	10s. to 13s. per diem	9s. to 12s. per diem
„ country	75l. per annum, with board	... ...	70l. to 80l. per an., with board and lodging
Blacksmiths' strikers	8d. to 9¾d. per hour	... ...	... ...
Iron-moulders and Turners	1s. 0½d. to 1s. 4½d. per hour	10s. to 13s. per diem	10s. to 11s. per diem
Boiler-makers . .	1s. to 1s. 6d. per hour	12s. to 13s. per diem	10s. to 12s. „
Engine-fitters . .	11d. to 1s. 4d. per hour	... ...	... ...
Furnacemen . .	1s. 1½d. to 1s. 3d. per hour	... ...	... ...
Brass-finishers & Moulders.	1s. 1d. to 1s. 3d. per hour	9s. to 12s. per diem	55s. to 65s. per week
Coppersmiths . .	1s. 1d. to 1s. 4½d. per hour	ditto	9s. to 12s. per diem
Brickmakers . .	22s. 6d. to 25s. per 1,000	... ...	13s. per 1,000, on the hack
Carriage-builders	1s. 1d. to 1s. 4d. per hour	50s. to 80s. per week	54s. to 70s. per week
Wheelwrights . .	70s. per week	... ...	8s. to 10s. per diem
Shipwrights . .	10s. to 12s. per diem	13s. per diem	... ...
Sawyers in Mill .	10d. to 1s. 3d. per hour	... ...	At pit, 13s. per 100 feet
Tailors	Paid by the piece, can average 50s. to 70s. per week	10d. to 1s. per hour	10d. to 1s. per hour
Shoemakers . .	50s. to 70s. per week	Piecework—riveting, 6d. to 1s. 3d.; finishing, 6d. to 1s. 3d.; Wellingtons, 10s.; elastics, 7s. 6d.	Piecework—Average earnings, 45s. to 60s. per week
Saddlers. . . .	45s. to 55s. per week	30s. to 55s. per week	7s. 6d. to 8s. 6d. per diem
Tinsmiths . . .	8s. to 11s. per diem	Can earn 40s. to 60s. per week at piece	9d. to 1s. per hour

the Australasian Colonies at the date of the last advices.

Queensland	Western Australia	Tasmania	New Zealand
60s. per week	By the job	... ...	10s. per diem (8 hours)
1s. to 1s. 3d. per 1,000	5s. to 8s. per diem	40s. to 60s. per week	10s. „
... ... 10s. per diem	... ... 6s. to 12s. per diem	... ... 7s. 6d. per diem	... . 8s. to 10s. per diem
10s. „	6s. to 8s. „	7s. 3d. „	8s. to 10s. „
11s. „	6s. to 9s. „	7s. 6d. „	8s. to 10s. „
11s. to 12s. „	6s. to 8s. 6d. „	6s. to 8s. „	6s. to 8s. „
7s. to 8s. „	4s. „	5s. to 6s. „	6s. to 8s. „
8s. to 10s. „	6s. to 9s. „	7s. 6d. „	6s. to 9s. „
... ... 10s. per diem	... ...	... ... 8s. per diem	... ...
... ... 10s. to 12s. per diem	6s. to 9s. per diem	6s. to 7s. per diem	... ... 8s. to 10s. per diem
50l. per annum, with rations	...	... ...	... ...
... ...	... ...	...	... ...
10s. to 14s. per diem	... ...	7s. per diem	8s. to 10s. per diem
... ...	... ...	... ...	... ...
...	... ...	9s. to 11s. 6d. per diem	... ...
... ...	... ...	... ...	... ...
... ...	... ...	... ...	... ...
... ...	... ...	10s. per diem	... ...
... ...	... ...	... ...	5s. to 6s. per diem
... ...	8s. to 10s. per diem	... ...	... ...
... ...	6s. to 9s. „	7s. 6d. per diem	6s. to 8s. per diem
10s. to 14s. per diem	... ...	8s. „	... ...
... ...	10s. per 100 ft.	6s. 6d. per 100 ft.	... ...
5s. to 7s. 6d. per diem	... ...	... ...	8s. to 10s. per diem
40s. to 60s. per week	6s. to 9s. per diem	5s. 6d. per diem	7s. to 8s. per diem
10s. to 12s. per diem	... ...	7s. „	40s. to 60s. per week
40s. to 60s. per week	... ...	25s. to 40s. per week	... ...

Trade or Calling	New South Wales	Victoria	South Australia
Coopers	12*s.* to 14*s.* per diem	10*s.* per day (10 hrs.)	8*s.* to 10*s.* per diem
Cabinetmakers	... ...	50*s.* to 70*s.* per week	9*s.* to 10*s.* „
Bakers	... ...	40*s.* to 60*s.* „	35*s.* to 60*s.* per week
Drapers' Assistants	... ...	50*s.* to 80*s.* per week	20*s.* to 60*s.* per week, and board
Milliners	... ...	35*s.* to 70*s.* per week	... ...
Hatters	... ...	Body makers, 12*s.* to 20*s.* per doz.; finishers, 12*s.* to 24*s.* per doz.; shapers, 4*s.* to 12*s.* per doz.	... ...
Jewellers and watchmakers	... ...	55*s.* to 100*s.* per week	50*s.* to 80*s.* per week
Butchers	20*s.* to 30*s.* per week, with board and lodging	35*s.* to 40*s.* per week	35*s.* to 50*s.* per week
Coal miners	... ...	... ...	... ...
Miners (Goldfields)	... ...	40*s.* to 50*s.* per week	... ...
Servants, &c.: Cooks (Private houses)	35*l.* to 65*l.* per an., with board, &c.	35*l.* to 60*l.* per an., with board, &c.	10*s.* to 20*s.* per week with board, &c.
Servants, &c.: Cooks (Hotels)	52*l.* to 65*l.* „	50*l.* to 100*l.* „	... ...
Servants, &c.: Laundresses	32*l.* to 45*l.* „	30*l.* to 40*l.* „	10*s.* to 16*s.* „
Servants, &c.: House, Nurse, and Parlour Maids	26*l.* to 35*l.* „	25*l.* to 35*l.* „	6*s.* to 12*s.* „
Servants, &c.: General Servants	26*l.* to 45*l.* „	30*l.* to 36*l.* „	10*s.* to 14*s.* „
Servants, &c.: Grooms and Coachmen	45*l.* to 65*l.* „	... ...	... ...
Servants, &c.: Gardeners	52*l.* to 65*l.* „	15*s.* to 25*s.* per week	6*s.* to 7*s.* per diem
Station and Farm Hands: Married couples	60*l.* to 75*l.* per an., with quarters and rations	40*l.* to 90*l.* per an., with quarters and rations	50*l.* to 75*l.* per an., with quarters and rations
Station and Farm Hands: Farm Labourers	35*l.* to 45*l.* „	40*l.* to 60*l.* „	16*s.* to 20*s.* per week, with board &c.
Station and Farm Hands: Team Drivers	40*l.* to 65*l.* „	60*l.* to 100*l.* „	25*s.* to 30*s.* „
Station and Farm Hands: Stockmen	40*l.* to 75*l.* „	60*l.* to 75*l.* „	40*l.* to 75*l.* per an.
Station and Farm Hands: Boundary Riders	40*l.* to 52*l.* „	... ...	17*s.* to 25*s.* per week
Station and Farm Hands: Shepherds	35*l.* to 40*l.* „	15*s.* to 20*s.* per week	17*s.* to 20*s.* „
Station and Farm Hands: Ploughmen	... ...	20*s.* per week	20*s.* to 25*s.* „
Station and Farm Hands: Useful boys	16*l.* to 30*l.* „	5*s.* to 6*s.* per week	4*s.* to 8*s.* „
Lumpers & Wharf Labourers	1*s.* to 1*s.* 3*d.* per hour	12*s.* per diem	...
Labourers (Corporation)	6*s.* 8*d.* to 7*s.* per diem	... ...	... ...
Labourers (General)	4*s.* to 6*s.* per diem	5*s.* to 7*s.* per diem	6*s.* to 7*s.* 6*d.* per diem
Labourers (Railway)	7*s.* to 9*s.* „	6*s.* 6*d.* „	...

In the case of country labourers, board and lodging usually consists of a dwelling, with
As a rule, it may be said that cottage accommodation for a mechanic and his family

Queensland	Western Australia	Tasmania	New Zealand
8s. to 10s. per diem	6s. per diem	8s. per diem	6s. to 8s. per diem
9s. per diem	... ...	... ...	8s. to 10s. ,,
... ...	... ...	... ...	5s. to 6s. ,,
40s. to 60s. per week	30l. to 100l. per an., with one week	5s. per diem	40s. to 100s. per week
... ...	... ...	... ...	... ...
... ...	... ...	... ...	... ...
... ...	... ...	... ...	8s. to 10s. per diem
7s. to 10s. per diem	5s. per diem	5s. to 6s. per diem	5s. to 6s. ,,
8s. to 10s. per diem	... ...	... ...	... ...
10s. to 20s. per week, with board, &c.	20l. per annum, with board, &c.	... ...	20l. to 30l. per an., board and lodging
Ditto	... ...	... ...	30l. to 40l. ,,
10s. to 16s. per week, with board, &c.	... ...	... ...	20l. to 30l. ,,
8s. to 12s. ,,	12l. to 20l. per an., board and lodging	20l. to 30l. per an.	20l. to 35l. ,,
8s. to 15s. ,,	Ditto	Ditto	20l. to 30l.
30l. to 60l. ,,	... ...	... ...	... ...
6s. to 8s. per diem	... ...	... ...	50l. ,,
52l. to 75l. with rations, &c.	... ...	... ...	50l. to 60l. ,,
5s. to 7s. per diem, with rations, &c.	20l. to 30l. per an., board and lodging	9s. to 10s. per week, with cottage and rations	25l. to 50l. ,,
45l. per annum, with board, &c.	24l. ,,	... ...	24l. to 30l. ,,
... ...	... ...	... ...	30l. to 50l. ,,
... ...	... ...	... ...	... ...
30l. to 35l. per an.	35l. to 40l. per an.	30l. per annum	24l. to 30l. ,,
20s. to 25s. per week	50s. to 60s. per month, with rations	30l. per annum, with quarters and rations	30l. to 50l. ,,
6s. to 8s. per week	50s. to 60s. per month, with board and lodging	10s. to 12s. per week, rations &c.	... ...
	... ...	... ...	... ...
} 6s. to 7s. 6d. per diem	... ...	... ...	...
	... ...	... ...	} 6s. to 8s. per diem
	... ...	... ...	

a ration of 12lbs. meat, 10 lbs. flour, 2 lbs. of sugar, and 4 ozs. of tea per week,
can be obtained in the Australasian colonies at from 5s. to 12s. a week.

PRICES OF PROVISIONS IN AUSTRALIA AND NEW ZEALAND

The following Return shows the Prices of the principal Articles of Provisions in the Australasian Colonies.

Article	New South Wales	Victoria	South Australia	Queensland	Western Australia	Tasmania	New Zealand
Bacon, per lb.	7d. to 10d.	10d. to 1s.	11d.	10d. to 1s.	9d. to 1s.	10d. to 1s.	3d. to 4½d.
Bread, per 2 lb. loaf	3½d. to 4½d.	3d. to 3½d.	4½d. to 5d.	4½d.	2d.	3d. to 3½d.	1s. to 1s. 6d.
Butter, Fresh, per lb	2s.	} 1s. to 1s. 4d.	{ 1s.	2s. to 2s. 6d.	1s. 6d. to 2s.	1s. 4d. to 1s. 8d.	1s.
Butter, Salt	1s. 3d.		1s.	1s. 6d. to 2s.	1s. to 1s. 6d.	1s. to 1s. 6d.	... ...
Candles	5d.	6d. to 1s. 4d.	7d. to 1s. 2d.	1s. 2d.	... ...	... ...	... ...
Cheese, Colonial	9d. to 1s. 2d.	8d. to 1s. 2d.	9d.	10d. to 1s.	1s. to 1s. 6d.	8d. to 1s.	6d. to 1s.
Cheese, English	1s. 6d. to 1s. 9d.	1s. 6d. to 2s.	1s. 3d. to 1s. 6d.	1s. to 1s. 6d.	1s. 6d.	... ...	... ...
Coffee	1s. 4d. to 1s. 6d.	1s. 4d. to 1s. 8d.	1s. 6d.	2s.	1s. 6d. to 2s.	1s. 6d.	1s. 2d. to 1s. 9d.
Eggs, per doz.	10d. to 1s.	1s. 9d. to 2s.	1s. 4d.	10d. to 1s. 6d.	1s. 6d. to 2s.	1s. to 1s. 6d.	1s.
Flour, per 100 lbs.	17s. to 18s.	13s. to 18s.	2½d. to 3d. per lb.	3d. per lb.	1½d. per lb.	1½d. per lb.	2½d. per lb.
Milk, per quart	6d.	4d. to 6d.	5d.	6d.	6d.	6d.	4d. to 6d.
Mutton, per lb.	2d. to 3d.	1½d. to 4½d.	3½d. to 6d.	2d. to 3d.	3d. to 6d.	5d. to 8d.	2d. to 4d.
Beef "	3d. to 6d.	3d. to 8d.	6d. to 10d.	3d. to 5d.	3d. to 8d.	4d. to 8d.	3d. to 6d.
Pork "	5d. to 8d.	8d. to 9d.	7d. to 8d.	... ...	8d. to 10d.	5d. to 8d.	... ...
Veal "	4½d. to 7d.	... ...	5d. to 9d.	... ...	... ...	6d. to 8d.	... ...
Potatoes, per cwt.	5s. to 6s.	4s. to 4s. 6d.	5s. to 6s.	7s. to 9s.	8s. to 12s.	3s. to 6s.	5s. to 10s.
Sugar, per lb.	3½d. to 4½d.	3d. to 5d.	3d. to 4½d.	3d. to 6d.	4½d.	4d. to 6d.	6d. to 1s.
Tea "	1s. 4d. to 2s. 6d.	2s. to 3s.	2s. to 2s. 6d.	2s. to 3s.	2s. to 3s.	2s. to 3s.	2s. to 3s.
Tobacco, American, per lb.	3s. 0d. to 4s. 6d.	} 4s. to 5s.	3s. to 3s. 6d.	3s. to 6s.	... ...	... ...	... ...
Tobacco, Colonial "	1s. 6d. to 2s. 6d.		... ...	... ...	... ...	... ...	... ...
Coal, per ton.	20s. to 25s.	31s. to 33s.	... ...	... ...	... ...	20s. to 32s.	... ...

Vegetables generally will be found somewhat dearer in Australia than in England, whilst many fruits are much cheaper.

PRICES OF CLOTHING IN AUSTRALIA AND NEW ZEALAND.

The following Return shows the Current Prices of Clothing &c. in the Australasian Colonies.

Article	New South Wales	Victoria	South Australia	Queensland	Western Australia	Tasmania	New Zealand
MEN'S.				About one-fourth more than in England		About one-fourth more than in England	About one-third more than in England
Boots, Strong, per pair	12s. 6d.	8s. to 20s.	7s. 6d. to 20s.		12s. to 18s.		
Coats, Tweed	12s. to 16s.	12s. to 20s.	20s.		15s. to 20s.		
Hats, Felt	2s. to 4s. 6d.	2s. 6d. to 7s.	3s. to 12s.		3s. 6d. to 5s.		
Hats, Straw	1s. to 3s.	1s. 6d. to 5s.	2s. 6d. to 9s. 6d.		4s. to 6s.		
Shirts, Cotton	2s. to 4s. 6d.	3s. to 5s.	3s. tn 10s.		2s. 3d. to 3s. 6d.		
Shirts, Crimean	3s. 6d. to 6s. 6d.	3s. 6d. to 6s.	7s. to 15s.		2s. to 3s.		
Trousers, Tweed	8s. to 12s.	10s. to 15s.	7s. 6d. to 20s.		9s. to 12s.		
Socks, Cotton, per pair	6d. to 10d.	1s. to 1s. 6d.	5d. to 2s. 6d.		} 8d. to 2s. 6d.		
Socks, Woollen	1s. to 1s. 6d.	1s. 6d. to 2s. 6d.	1s. 3d. to 3s.				
WOMEN'S.							
Calico, per yard	3d. to 7½d.	7d. to 1s. 6d.	4d. to 1s. 3d.		4d. to 1s.		
Flannel, per yard	10d. to 1s. 6d.	8d. to 2s. 6d.	1s. 6d. to 2s. 6d.		1s. 3d. to 2s. 6d.		
Print, per yard	3d. to 6d.	4d. to 8d.	... ...		... ...		
Merino, per yard	2s. to 6s.	3s. to 7s.	... ...		... ...		
Boots and Shoes, per pair	4s. 6d. to 6s.	3s. to 5s.	2s. 6d. to 7s. 6d.		3s. to 8s.		
Stockings, per pair	9d. to 2s.	9d. to 1s. 6d.	6d. to 1s. 6d.		1s. to 2s.		
Petticoats	2s. 6d. to 7s.	3s. to 12s.	2s. 6d. to 6s. 6d.		5s. to 6s.		
Hats, Bonnets	1s. to 3s.	1s. to 3s.	2s. 6d. to 10s.		3s. to 8s.		
Blankets, per pair	7s. 6d. to 15s.	6s. to 20s.	9s. to 30s.		10s. to 20s.		
Mattresses	12s. to 20s.	3s. to 7s. 6d.	4s. to 20s.		5s. to 10s.		
Palliasses	10s. to 16s.	4s. to 8s.	4s. to 6s.		... ...		

acres. The acreage under wheat in the Australian colonies and the Cape of Good Hope was 1,056,871 acres in 1867, and 1,513,419 acres in 1875. The average returns of produce per acre in New Zealand in the years 1875 and 1876 were : Wheat, nearly 30 bushels; oats, 36 bushels; barley, $32\frac{1}{2}$ bushels; hay, $1\frac{3}{8}$ ton ; potatoes, $4\frac{7}{8}$ tons.

Wages in colonies.   The advantage secured to the individual emigrant by his removal from an over-peopled country is sufficiently proved by the high wages paid in the colonies. The table of rates current in Australia, printed on pp. 274–7, is extracted from ' The Colonies' of January 1879.

Far be it from me to urge our working men to quit their native land in a mere spirit of restlessness and discontent. Progress and material development will be secured, almost with certainty, by emigration ; but the charms which belong to an ancient civilisation, the hallowed associations, the picturesqueness—these are the work of time, and are necessarily wanting in a new country :

> Across the gap made by our English hinds
> Amidst the Roman's handiwork, behold
> Far off the long-roofed church ; the shepherd binds
> The withy round the hurdles of his fold,
> Down in the foss, the river-bed of old,
> That through long lapse of time has grown to be
> The little grassy valley that you see.
> Rest here awhile. Not yet the eve is still,
> The bees are wandering yet, and you may hear
> The barley-mowers on the trenchèd hill,
> The sheep-bells, and the restless changing weir.
> All little sounds made musical and clear
> Beneath the sky that burning August gives,
> While yet the thought of glorious summer lives.[1]

[1] Morris, ' Earthly Paradise.'

But if the downward tendency of wages should continue, until it falls to a level which involves a real degradation in the condition of the workman; if his position in the old country is conspicuously inferior to that in which he knows he will find himself on his removal to a British colony or to the United States, emigration surely is the alternative which prudence and enterprise recommend. The Registrar-General speaks in terms of the highest satisfaction of the overflow of our surplus population into the fruitful regions of America and the Antipodes. No part of the social changes of the last forty years is more satisfactory, both to the mother country and the colonial and foreign countries, than this voluntary emigration, undertaken by the free choice, and paid for out of the savings, of the emigrants themselves.

The high wages in the colonies are due to the same causes which affect the labour market in the United States: they are governed by an economic law, concisely stated by the Registrar-General. 'The value of labour is greatest where there is the greatest facility for its profitable use, where there is a large area of fertile land unappropriated, and where all fertile land is not as yet fully cultivated and subject to the payment of rent.' It was mainly on colonisation and emigration that Mr. Mill relied as the effective remedy for the depressing influence on wages caused by overpopulation. But he hesitated to believe that even under the most enlightened arrangements ' a permanent stream of emigration could be kept up sufficient to take off, as in America, all that portion of the annual increase, when proceeding at its greatest rapidity, which, being in excess of the progress made during the same short period in the arts of life, tends to render living more difficult for every averagely situated individual in the community.'

Since the publication of Mr. Mill's treatise, more than thirty years ago, the facilities of communication with the colonies have been multiplied to a degree of which at that date no conception could have been formed. A journey to Canada, or even Australia, can now be made for a sum but slightly exceeding what it then cost to convey a traveller from New York to the Western prairies.

Value of colonies.

Writing more than a generation ago, when our colonies were in their infancy, and there was nothing to indicate the prospective growth on which we may now venture to rely, Mr. Porter opened the chapter on Colonies in his 'Progress of the Nation,' with these glowing words : ' If called upon to declare that circumstance in the condition of England which, more than all other things, makes her the envy of surrounding nations, it would be to her colonial possessions that we must attribute that feeling. In the eyes of foreigners, those possessions are at once the evidence of our power and the surest indicant of its increase.'

British capitalists seeking investment for their resources will best promote their own interests, and, what is far more important, the interests of the country, by judiciously fostering colonial enterprise. The promoters of railways in the United States offer the temptations of high rates of interest, and the capital they borrow in the European Exchanges is doubtless employed advantageously to mankind. But the British capitalist, who lends his money to the farmers in New Zealand or the graziers in Australasia, may both command a liberal return for his capital, increase the supplies of food at home, and confer a special benefit on his country, by helping to create a market for her manufactures.

After the interval of a single generation from the publication of Mr. Porter's essay, Mr. Graham, a not less competent observer, gives the same weighty testimony to the economic value of emigration. 'The emigrants,' says Mr. Graham, 'have sent to England wheat, cotton, wool, and gold, to the value of hundreds of millions. What is of still more importance, they grow into new nations; they multiply discoveries; by confederation they will be to the Anglo-Saxon race outposts of strength, across the Atlantic, in the Pacific, in South Africa, and in Australasia, on the flank of India.'

In a recent eloquent speech, Sir Hercules Robinson, Governor of New South Wales, advocated the federation of the colonies, and described the future increase of their populations. 'Assuming that the recent rate of increase in the United Kingdom is not diminished, and that for Australia is not augmented, the population of Australia will in 1955 be over thirty-eight millions, which was the population of the United States of America at the last census in 1870; and the population of this continent will then bear to that of the United Kingdom the proportion of thirty-eight to

Policy of federation.

sixty-three, instead of only two to thirty-three, as at present. Surely such a prospect of future greatness must suggest the necessity of now laying broad and deep the foundations for the development of this vast country, and for its corresponding advancement in civilisation.'

I earnestly hope that the warnings of Mr. Goldwin Smith in his essay ' On the Foundation of the American Colonies' may not be neglected. 'English statesmen, with all their greatness, have seldom known how to anticipate necessity; too often the sentence of history on their policy has been that it was wise, just, and generous, but " too late." Too often have they waited for the teaching of disaster.' They should make every effort to preserve the colonial connection. They should encourage emigration.

We cannot hope to concentrate within the narrow limits of the United Kingdom the productive industry of the world ; other lands must be found for the growth and expansion of the Anglo-Saxon race. The labours of one busy generation in the Antipodes have shown what the energy and administrative ability of our race can accomplish. Our teeming multitudes must find their way to the field of promise, whither an illustrious band of pioneers have gone before. Australasia, New Zealand, Tasmania, South Africa, and the Canadian Dominion, afford space for the dwellings of millions, and a fruitful soil, on which they may bestow their labours.

The strength of a nation is diminished, rather than fortified, by an excessive population. The necessary limits of population were accurately defined by Rousseau in the ' Contrat Social.' ' Ce sont les hommes qui font l'Etat, et c'est le terrain qui nourrit les hommes ; ce rapport est donc que la terre suffise à l'entretien de ses habitants, et qu'il y'ait autant d'habitants que la terre en peut nourrir. C'est dans cette proportion que se trouve le *maximum* de force d'un nombre donné de peuple.' [1]

The Englishman who emigrates is not an exile. He is in no real sense an exile, who remains a loyal subject of the Queen, and still lives beneath the flag of the old country. That flag is the guarantee to all who live beneath its folds, that they will be protected against foreign aggression by the strength of the United Empire. It is the symbol of something far more precious than the protection of the fleets and armies, which will not long be needed by the vigorous populations of the colonies. That flag is the symbol of the constitutional liberties, for which our fathers long contended, and of the inestimable privilege of a pure and equal administration of justice. Nor is it the least of the blessings it bestows, that it attracts to the colonial service of the Crown the ablest men from the ranks of our political and professional classes.

Links between the colonies and the mother country.

The future of our race depends on the love, which our ' kin beyond the sea ' will ever bear to the home of their fathers. Modern diplomacy has paid greater regard to nationalities than to dynasties. The kindred races of the Continent have been brought together, and nations have been formed, which, by mere superiority

[1] Rousseau, ' Contrat Social,' ch. x. p. 271.

of numbers, might crush the utmost forces of our narrow island, but for the support, on which we shall not trust in vain, of the rising nations which we have created.

I find these views put forth, with his usual felicity of expression, by a high authority, Lord Dufferin, who made use of the following words in a recent speech at Belfast : ' From his very earliest days he had always been a believer in our colonial future, and his official experience had convinced him that if only England would be true to herself and to those noble children whom she had sent forth to plant the laws, liberty, language, domestic peace, and manliness of England upon the earth ; if she would only encourage them to cling to their birthright as her sons ; if she would only treat them in a tender, sympathetic, and generous spirit, then this famous Empire of ours, which was daily asserting itself with ever-increasing power and vitality, in every hemisphere, and under every sun, instead of showing signs of disruption, would find its associated realms daily becoming prouder and prouder of their common origin, daily looking more fondly back upon their common antecedents, drawing more closely and closely together those bonds which united them to each other and to the mother country.'

The British confederation must be maintained on terms of equality to all its members. The bond which unites them is the bond of natural affection—a bond far closer and more enduring than any which can be formed by treaties of friendship and alliance between nations differing in race and language, and incapable of feeling those pervading and perpetual sympathies which unite the parent with the child. Secure in the strength she will derive from her colonies, the old country may be content to see the growth of her commerce arrested, and to leave the task of material development to the elastic energies of her sons. Her strength may be thrown into other spheres of human endeavour. Already the favoured retreat of successful colonists, England may rise to yet higher things. In the conduct of their domestic affairs the colonies may become absolutely independent; but the loss of political importance may be amply compensated to the old country if she becomes, in a larger sense than now, the social centre of the whole Empire, a seminary of learning for all her sons, the home of literature and the arts, the Athens of the Anglo-Saxon race.

From a political point of view my visits to our distant possessions in Hong Kong, the Straits Settlements, Ceylon, and Aden were perhaps the most satisfactory feature of my recent voyage round the world. The evidences of prosperity and good government in those scattered dominions of the Crown redound greatly to the honour of our country; and when I combine with these more recent experiences recollections of a former journey to Canada and the United States, I see the most reassuring indications of great and beneficent destinies for the Anglo-Saxon race. We cannot hope nor even desire for our densely crowded little island the monopoly of the trade of the world. We cannot wish to concentrate in our own metropolis the responsibility of governing the vast and growing communities of the

Confederacy of the Anglo-Saxon peoples.

Antipodes and the New World. We can, however, retain, and retain for ever, our proud position as the mother country of the great Anglo-Saxon brotherhood. If we help our children in a large and unselfish spirit, now, in the days of their youth, they will not forget old England, if she becomes less vigorous in the lapse of ages. I invite all those who are unnerved by their dread of Panslavism, or their fears of Teutonic ascendency on the Continent, to realise the grand but not impracticable vision of the power which might be created by a federation of all the Anglo-Saxon peoples. We are one in history, religion, and race ; and the sea, the great highway of nations and the cradle of our hardy northern ancestors, unites us. If all unworthy jealousies be repressed, and all our natural ties be cultivated in the spirit of sympathy and kindness, we shall never want an ally in the day of need.

CHAPTER XIV.

ON THE ACCUMULATION OF CAPITAL, AND THE LAW
OF WAGES.

Nothing generates discontent so much as fluctuation in profits and wages; for human nature is so constituted that a man will expect to have always what he has once received.—JOHNSON.

> Nessun maggior dolore
> Che ricordarsi del tempo felice
> Nella miseria.
>
> DANTE, *Inferno*, v. 121.

MANY false notions have been accredited by a terse and easily remembered phrase. The generally accepted, but ill-founded belief, that the poor are growing poorer and the rich richer, rests on this shallow foundation. If we look back to the beginning of the present century, and follow the improvements which have been effected in the dwellings, food, clothing, and education of the people, it will be evident that real progress has been secured in the social condition of the masses. Social progress of the masses.

We read in the 'Chapters on Socialism' by the late Mr. Mill, recently published in the 'Fortnightly Review,' that it has yet to be proved that there is any country in the civilised world where the ordinary wages of labour, estimated either in money or in articles of consumption, are declining; while in many they are, on the whole, on the increase; and an in-

U

crease which is becoming, not slower, but more rapid. There is much evidence of improvement, and none, that is at all trustworthy, of deterioration in the mode of living of the labouring population of the countries of Europe.

Unequal distribution of wealth.

While, however, we congratulate ourselves on the strides that we have made, we still see an inequality in the distribution of wealth, which would scarcely be accepted in any ideal scheme of society, and greater than is consistent with the degree of perfection, to which we may reasonably venture to hope that human institutions may be brought. These inequalities arise from differences of character, capacity, and opportunity. Some are inherent in human nature itself; others arise out of the conditions in which individuals are placed.

In an uninhabited country, where every man is free to take for himself as much land as he can cultivate, the same inequalities are observable as in an old country. They arise from the unequal strength and diligence of the cultivators, from the unequal fertility of the soil, from the division of the property of one man amongst numerous successors, and the devolution of the entire inheritance of another upon a single heir. 'The intelligence,' says Turgot, 'and activity, and especially the forethought of some, in contrast with the indolence, inaction, and dissipation of others, are most powerful causes of inequality in the condition of various individuals.'

Argentine Colonies.

I can speak of these things not only in theory, but by the light of practical experience gained by watching

the results of colonisation in the Argentine Republic.
Large numbers of colonists were sent out from all
parts of Europe. To each was allotted an equal area
of land; for each a house was built, a well dug, and
seeds and implements provided. Nature gave to each
an equal portion of sunshine and of rain; and at the
end of a short term of years you find some in penury,
many struggling to maintain a bare subsistence; a
few, but only a few, had prospered. The unsuccessful
naturally regard themselves as the victims of unde-
served misfortune, and view with envy the growing
prosperity of their neighbours.

In an old country, where the accumulations of past
generations devolve on a few fortunate individuals, the
inequality is far greater, and the seeming injustice
more flagrant. But when we come to examine the
process by which an accumulation of capital is commenced, we shall see reasons which should tend to miti-
gate the natural antagonism of labour and capital.

Usurers and money-lenders have been at all times
odious. It is so easy to borrow money; it is so hard
to be obliged to pay it back. The sense of relief from
pressing necessity soon passes away. The same want
is again felt. The former debt is still due. The
lender has parted with what was more or less a superfluity; to the borrower the loan seemed indispensable;
and though justice may incline wholly to the lender,
though he claims nothing more than his just debt,
humanity, and pity, and sympathy are always on the
side of the debtor.

In order, however, to do justice to capital, let us

*Accumu-
lations of
wealth
formed by
saving.*

trace, step by step, the process by which an accumulation is formed.

'All capital,' says Mr. Mill, 'was originally formed by saving.' It is the product of labour, but it is kept together by self-denial. In every nation those who desire to grow rich are far more numerous than the wealthy; and there is one way alone by which the former can acquire riches. It is by setting aside small sums, by foregoing simple pleasures, luxuries, and enjoyments, in which others have indulged. We respect these acts of self-denial so long as the individual remains poor : shall we condemn the conduct of one who perseveres in the same course, and gradually becomes a capitalist? Large fortunes could never have been amassed by those who have risen from poverty to wealth, if, in the commencement of their careers, they had spent all that they had earned—had lived, to use a familiar phrase, up to their incomes.

Popular illusion concerning capital employed in business.
In the 'Chapters on Socialism' Mr. Mill sought to dissipate a popular illusion with reference to capital employed in business. 'When a capitalist invests 20,000*l.* in his business, and draws from it an income of (suppose) 2,000*l.* a year, the common impression is as if he was the beneficial owner both of the 20,000*l.* and of the 2,000*l.*, while the labourers own nothing but their wages. The truth, however, is that he only obtains the 2,000*l.* on condition of applying no part of the 20,000*l.* to his own use. He has the legal control over it, and might squander it if he chose, but if he did he would not have the 2,000*l.* a year also. As long as he derives an income from his

capital he has not the option of withholding it from the use of others.'

Is it an advantage or a disadvantage to the working classes that large fortunes should be amassed? This problem will be most easily elucidated by taking some simple illustration of the use of capital in the development of industry, and in furnishing employment to the wage-earning classes. The process has been traced, in its application to agriculture, by M. Turgot, in his essay ' On the Formation of Wealth.' Use of capital in agriculture.

Advances are required to enable every kind of work, whether agricultural, industrial, or commercial, to be carried on. The man who tills his own land must sow before he reaps. He must live until the harvest is gathered. The more extensive and perfect the system of cultivation, the larger are the advances required. Cattle, implements, buildings to shelter the cattle and store up the grain, become necessary. Until the harvest is gathered in, a number of labourers, proportionate to the extent of the operations, must be paid and fed. It is only by means of a proportionate expenditure that large returns can be obtained. In every trade the workman must be furnished in advance with tools, and with a sufficient quantity of the raw materials of the industry in which he is engaged. He must be provided with the means of subsistence, until a market can be found for the produce of his labour.

In new countries, where a virgin soil is being brought for the first time into cultivation, and the settler is not burdened with heavy charges for rent, capital commands a higher rate of interest than in a country of older civilisation.

In his recent lectures, Mr. Leone Levi has given some remarkable figures showing the amount of capital required to carry on the industry of our own country. ' He estimates the number of acres under cultivation in the United Kingdom at 20,000,000, which, taken at 8*l.* per acre, would give a total of 160,000,000*l.* The very existence of a large number of industries depends on the constant flow of capital. No less than 80,000,000*l.* was required for the cotton trade, 30,000,000*l.* for the wool trade, 30,000,000*l.* for the iron trade, 70,000,000*l.* for the merchant marine. The vast total of 609,000,000*l.* was invested in railways ; and he could not say how much more had been invested in the numerous other public undertakings, such as water-works, gas-works, docks, banks, and insurance companies both at home and abroad.'

In an economical point of view, the larger the store of capital, the more prosperous will be the condition of the population. It is doubtless to be desired that the accumulated wealth of a country should be in the hands of many, rather than in the possession of a few, but in each case the acquisition of wealth is a question of the opportunities afforded to individuals. I do no injustice to my neighbour when I deny myself an indulgence ; and if I employ my resources, be they small or be they large, in industrial or commercial operations, I create employment and benefit the working man.

If, then, it be a benefit to the masses that capital

should be accumulated, and if the process, by which these accumulations are formed, involves more or less of self-denial, it is obvious, as Mr. Ricardo puts it, that no one will accumulate but with a view to make that accumulation productive. The farmer and the manufacturer can no more live without profit, than the labourer without wages. In proportion as you diminish profits you lessen the motive for accumulation; in proportion as you increase profits you increase the desire to accumulate.

If the command of capital at a low rate of interest is a source of wealth to a nation, it is certain that the use of money on moderate terms will be most easily obtained in a country where the supply of money is abundant, and the security afforded by the law, and by the high tone of the commercial classes, is most complete. These conditions have been combined in the United Kingdom in a higher degree than in any other country, and the average rate charged for interest at the Bank of England would have been considerably lower than elsewhere, but for the impetuous enterprise of the British nation, which leads to over-trading and over-production, and to ever recurring fluctuations from a state of inflation to one of depression, from a mania for speculation to a commercial crisis. We are more subject to these changes than other nations; and when credit is falling low, and the supply of capital is less copious, we are called upon to pay very high rates for the use of money.

Mr. Palgrave has recently published a careful analysis, showing the alterations in the Bank rate between January 1, 1844, and December 31, 1877. The result has been to show that the vast capital, which has been absorbed in the development of our colonies, in loans to foreign countries, and in enterprise of every kind at home, has been supplied at lower rates than those charged in the same period in any of the great monetary exchanges of Europe. We have seen more frequent changes, and the highest rates have been reached oftener, and maintained longer, in London than in Paris. On the other hand, low rates of interest are much more constant in London. A period of 12,170 days is included in Mr. Palgrave's tables. During a quarter of this period the rate of interest in England varied from 2 to $2\frac{1}{4}$ and $2\frac{1}{2}$ per cent. These low rates were not maintained in France for half the number of days, during which they were charged in England. In London 3 per cent. has been the usual rate of interest. During half of the whole period under review the rate has stood at 2, $2\frac{1}{4}$, $2\frac{1}{2}$, and 3 per cent. In France 4 per cent. has been the ordinary rate; and it was maintained during the half of the whole period. Before 1877, the Bank of France had never reduced the rate of interest so low as 2 per cent.

When the rate stands at or over 5 per cent., money can no longer be said to be cheap. If the rate rises above 6 per cent., it is an indication of commercial distress and famine. In France, in consequence chiefly of the financial pressure caused by the disastrous struggle with Germany, six per cent. has been demanded during a much longer period than with us.

On the other hand, we have had a more frequent experience than our neighbours of the panic rates of eight, nine, and ten per cent.

M. Leroy Beaulieu attributes these exceptional rates to two causes :—

(I.) To the rigorous restriction imposed by the law of 1844 on the issue of notes.

(II.) The insufficiency of the reserves of bullion maintained in England. No less than 80,000,000*l.* of bullion are stored up in the cellars of the Bank of France. But the money is not idle. In the form of bank notes it is in constant circulation, and the ample store, which it is thought expedient to keep in reserve, is a guarantee against the sudden and frequent fluctuations of the rates of interest experienced in England. The explanations suggested by M. Leroy Beaulieu do not, in my opinion, wholly account for the recurrence of panic rates more frequently in London than in Paris. Our rash spirit of adventure manifests itself in trade, as it does in other things, and is the cause of periodical crises.

Viewed as a working man's question, and with reference to the well-being of the masses, accumulations of capital, whether formed by profitable enterprise, or by the thrift of the wage-paying and wage-earning classes, have furnished a comfortable maintenance to multitudes, whose existence, even had they been content with the lowest standard of living, would have been impossible within the narrow limits of the United Kingdom, but for the creation of those great industries, in which so much of the national

Abundant supplies of capital a benefit to the whole population.

capital is invested. This store of capital has been the chief resource of the population. Its abundance has given an impetus to every kind of industry, and the low rate of interest, which has prevailed in London, may be taken as at once the result and the indication of the existence of abundant resources.

Low rate of interest. As a country progresses in civilisation, so the rate of interest tends to diminish. The reduction in the rate of interest is attributable to three causes :

(I.) The increased security with which all commercial transactions are conducted.

(II.) The constant accumulation of savings.

(III.) The diminished profit realised on the new employments of capital. Branch lines are less profitable than arterial lines of railway. The earlier irrigation works produce a more beneficial result than those subsequently undertaken.

Three causes are at work, on the other hand, which, although intermittent in their action, to a certain extent neutralise the effect of those influences, which tend to diminish the return upon capital. They are :

(I.) Industrial discoveries, such as railways, which create suddenly new and productive employments for capital.

(II.) The migration of capital from old to new countries.

(III.) The waste of capital in war, and in loans to bankrupt states.

It is further to be remembered by those who cherish sentiments of animosity towards capitalists in general, that the greatest undertakings of our age have been formed, not by a few bloated monopolists, but by the associated capital of multitudes of contributors. The capital of our railways and our joint-stock banks has been supplied by many poor annuitants, and has been gleaned from the hard earnings of people, whose labours have been remunerated at very moderate rates.

Not only has the capital been raised by the contributions of individuals, the great mass of whom are possessed of only moderate means, but the dividends realised by the railway shareholders have never exceeded a reasonable return upon a commercial enterprise.

The following summary of the rate of interest, which would have been received by the investor in Consols, and in the stocks of the London and North-Western Railway during the last thirty years, is taken from the 'Economist' of October 1877 :

Average Yield of Consols and London and North-Western Railway Ordinary Stock, in the following periods.

Period	Yield of Consols			Yield of London and North-Western Ordinary Stock		
	£	*s.*	*d.*	£	*s.*	*d.*
1846–50 . . .	3	6	0	5	0	0
1851–55 . . .	3	3	4	4	13	4
1856–60 . . .	3	3	4	4	18	6
1861–65 . . .	3	6	0	5	2	6
1868–70 . . .	3	5	0	5	3	9
1871–75 . . .	3	5	0	4	19	6
1876 . . .	3	2	6	4	12	6

I cannot pass from this subject without a brief allusion to the labour and responsibility undertaken by the directors of these great undertakings, without acknowledgment from the public, and often with a

A word in behalf of railway directors.

scanty return of thanks and gratitude from the shareholders, for whose interests they are more directly
concerned. For some years I held a seat at the Board
of one of our largest railways. I shall always esteem
it one of the great privileges of my life to have had an
opportunity of witnessing the untiring devotion of the
Chairman of that undertaking to the onerous duties,
with which he was charged. The administration of a
railway involves the most complex and difficult duties,
both to the public and to the shareholders. The head
of such an undertaking must be a man of many
qualifications and unwearied dilligence ; and he must
be content to see the fruits of his labours enjoyed
mainly by others, and slenderly shared by himself.

We have seen how capital is the result of saving,
in other words of self-denial. The instances are few,
in which fortunes have been acquired by any other
means. The exceptions are those of great inventors,
of such men as Arkwright or Stephenson in a former
generation, or of a few ingenious inventors among our
own contemporaries, whom it would be invidious to
mention by name.

Large profits have been generally made in time of
war by receiving information earlier than others of
the result of great battles, by which a sudden change
may have been caused in the value of securities; or,
again, by being first in the field in opening out a
new branch of industry. My father's success as a
railway contractor was due to this cause. In the
United States and in our own country immense fortunes have been realised by the growth of large towns,

*Excep-
tional op-
portunities
of amass-
ing wealth.*

and the consequent increase in the rentals of lands, which had formerly a mere agricultural value, but are now the site of docks, warehouses, and factories, or the fashionable quarters of a great city. Advantages gained suddenly, and by such exceptional causes, can never be retained. Competition will speedily bring down profits to a common level. The business, to which I am personally indebted, furnishes a striking illustration of the effects of competition in reducing profits. For a short time it was very profitable, but the competition for contracts soon became so keen that it was no longer possible to realise the ordinary rate of profit. Of my father's own experience it is sufficient to say that, during the last twenty years of his life, the profits upon his successful undertakings in the United Kingdom were quite insufficient to balance the losses sustained in other cases.

Where from time to time the average returns from trade and industry are increased, and a profit is realised, in excess of the amount necessary to pay the ordinary rate of interest, and to cover any special risk incurred, the working man will certainly reap his share of the benefit, from the rise of wages caused by the increased demand for labour. Whenever the returns from the sale of commodities are exceptionally profitable, a universal anxiety is created to augment the rate of production of such commodities. Hence the demand for labour, and the advance of wages.

Increased wages indirectly resulting from extra profits.

The rate of wages is determined by competition— by the competition of employers for workmen, and by the competition of workmen for employment. It is also determined by the price of the necessaries of life.

'Natural price' of labour.   What is called by Ricardo the natural price of labour is its price as regulated by the cost of the food and necessaries, which, according to the standard of living prevailing in the particular country, are deemed essential for the maintenance of the labourer and his family.

Mutual relation of prices and wages.   Modifications of prices have an important bearing on the question of wages. The value of a thing is relative rather than absolute. It depends mainly, says Ricardo, on the power of purchasing other goods which the possession of that object conveys. The price of things, according to M. Turgot, is only a term of comparison between their abundance, their value in use, and the supply of money. The apparent advantage of high wages may be completely neutralised by the high value of commodities. In the terse phrase of Mr. Mill, if wages could not rise without a proportionate rise in the price of everything, they could not, for any substantial purpose, rise at all. On the other hand, if the fall in prices is proportionate to the fall in wages, it may be possible that the lower wages will command as ample a supply of the necessaries and the comforts of life, as the higher wages obtained in a period of commercial inflation.

The rise of wages in the United States during and after the Civil War, was followed by an equally remarkable increase in the cost of living. Mr. Lowthian Bell, in his 'Notes of a Visit to the Coal and Iron

Mines of the United States,' gives the following comparative prices, on the authority of Professor Cox of Indiana :

	1850	1874
Wheat, per bushel of 60 lbs. .	1*s*. 2*d*.	4*s*. 1*d*.
Indian Corn, „ 56 lbs. .	5*d*.	2*s*. 2*d*.
Pork, per 100 lbs. . . .	4*s*. 8*d*. to 5*s*. 8*d*.	32*s*.
Beef, per lb.	1*d*.	5*d*. to 6*d*.

After the war, wages were reduced very rapidly. They had fallen at least 40 per cent. all round since 1873. During the same period, however, the cost of living had been decreased by at least 30 per cent. Hence the purchasing power of labour was only ten per cent. less than it was when labour was paid at the rate of three dollars a day.

If money wages remained the same, while the cost of living was reduced, the result would be equivalent to a rise of wages. The recent reductions must therefore be viewed as, to a large extent, an adjustment of wages to the changes in the cost of commodities.

Subject always to the universal condition that the workmen engaged in a competitive industry can maintain themselves in that industry, only so long as they are able to produce as cheaply and as well as their foreign competitors, it is from every point of view desirable that the labourer should seek to establish a high standard of living. Mr. Ricardo has most truly said : ' The friends of humanity cannot but wish that in all countries the labouring classes should have a taste for comforts and enjoyments, and that they should be stimulated by all legal means in their exertions to

Advantage to the labourer of a high standard of living.

procure them. There cannot be a better security against a superabundant population. In those countries where the labouring classes have the fewest wants, and are contented with the cheapest food, the people are exposed to the greatest vicissitudes and miseries. They have no place of refuge from calamity; they cannot seek safety in a lower station; they are already so low that they can fall no lower. On any deficiency of the chief article of their subsistence there are few substitutes of which they can avail themselves, and dearth to them is attended with almost all the evils of famine.' The recurrence of famines in India, and the potato famine in Ireland, are familiar and painful examples of the sufferings, to which a people are exposed, whose wages are scarcely sufficient to support life in ordinary seasons, and are therefore quite insufficient in a time of dearth.

The diligence, displayed by the factory operatives in the United States, is encouraged by the hope of an early improvement in their condition. To all who can put by a moderate accumulation, a prospect is afforded of exchanging a wearisome employment for the wholesome occupation of agriculture. They look forward to a position of independence, as free proprietors of the soil.

> Seldom despairing men look up to heaven,
> Although it still speak to 'em in its glories:
> For when sad thoughts perplex the mind of man,
> There is a plummet in the heart that weighs
> And pulls us living to the dust we came from.[1]

[1] Beaumont and Fletcher, 'The Laws of Candy,' iv. 1.

In the United Kingdom the price of labour is regu- Market price of lated—let us record the fact with thankfulness—not labour. by the cost of living, but by the market price; by the natural operation, to use the language of Mr. Ricardo, of the proportion between the supply and the demand. Labour is dear when it is scarce, and cheap when it is plentiful. The same law has been stated more fully by Adam Smith. ' The demand,' he says, ' for those who live by wages cannot increase but in proportion to the increase of the funds, which are destined for the payment of wages. When an annuitant or moneyed man has a greater revenue than what he judges suffi- cient to maintain his own family, he employs the whole or a part of the surplus in maintaining one or more menial servants. Increase this surplus, and he will naturally increase the number of those servants. When an independent workman has got more stock than what is sufficient to purchase the materials of his own work, and to maintain himself till he can dispose of it, he naturally employs one or more journeymen with the surplus. Increase this surplus, and he will increase the number of his journey- men.'

As, therefore, the price of labour depends on Wages raised by the demand, depends on the proportion between the capital increasing amount available for expenditure, whether produc- in greater ratio than tively or unproductively, and the number of working popula- men employed, the condition of the mass of the people tion. must be most favourable in that country, in which capital has increased in the most rapid ratio in relation to the increase of the population. That the economic

x

progress of the United Kingdom has been highly satisfactory in this regard, is clearly shown by the statistics collected by Mr. Giffen: 'If we look at the Income Tax Returns, we perceive that the gross income assessed rose in Great Britain from 115,000,000*l.* at the beginning of the century to 130,000,000*l.* in 1815, 251,000,000*l.* in 1843, 262,000,000*l.* in 1853, 308,000,000*l.* in 1855, 396,000,000*l.* in 1865, and 571,000,000*l.* in 1875. If the growth of every portion of the national income had only progressed at the same rate, the annual increase of capital all through, and especially of recent years, must have been enormous. The increase in the income assessed between 1865 and 1875 amounts to 175,000,000*l.*, which is equal to 44 per cent. of the income assessed in 1865. During the first decade subsequent to 1855 the increase of property must have been 30 per cent., and during the second decade the increase must have been 44 per cent. The addition, therefore, to the capital of the community has been immensely greater in proportion than the increase in its numbers. The increase of population has been about 1 per cent. per annum, but property has increased 3 to 4 per cent. and upwards.'

The rapid growth of capital affords an obvious explanation of the speculation in foreign bonds of an unreliable character. It has led to the too rapid extension of our manufacturing industries, and to extreme competition in mercantile transactions. The inflation is necessarily followed by a reaction in prices, and by that state of collapse, from which our industry and commerce have not yet recovered.

The following table compares the details of the increase:

Approximate Account of Capital as Property in United Kingdom in 1865 and 1875 compared.

	1865	1875	Increase in 1875	
			Amount	Per cent.
	Millions	Millions	Millions	
Lands	1,864	2,007	143	8
Houses	1,031	1,420	389	38
Farmers' profits	620	668	48	8
Public funds less home funds . .	211	519	308	146
Mines	19	56	37	195
Ironworks	7	29	22	314
Railways	414	655	241	58
Canals	18	20	2	11
Gasworks	37	53	16	43
Quarries	2	4	2	100
Other profits	55	84	29	53
Other income-tax income, principally trades and professions and public companies	659	1,128	469	71
	4,938	6,643	1,706	35
Trades and professions omitted . .	75	105	30	40
Income from capital of non-income-tax paying classes	200	300	100	50
Foreign investments not in Schedules C and D	100	420	300	300
Movable property not yielding income .	500	700	200	40
Government and local property, say .	300	400	100	33
	6,113	8,548	2,436	40

It has been said that during the last few years there has been little or no surplus of income over expenditure and losses, either in Europe or America. The accuracy of this statement is questioned by Mr. Giffen, because— State of income in relation to the present depression.

(I.) Even in dull years the investments in new houses are always going on actively.

(II.) The investments in railways, tramways, and

other works, as we know from the accounts of the
joint-stock companies, are not greatly affected by the
general depression in trade.

(III.) The investments in public works by local
authorities are now never less than 10,000,000*l.* a year.

In his presidential address to the Statistical Society,
Mr. Shaw Lefevre said: 'The Income Tax Returns
show for the decade an increase of income of 44 per
cent., as compared with 26 per cent. in the previous
decade, and 26 per cent. in the decade 1847 to 1857.
The income of trade under Schedule D shows an increase of 60 per cent. The property assessed to legacy
duty shows an increase of nearly 40 per cent. When
these increases are examined, it appears that they have
been far more steady, continuous, and sustained than
would be supposed by those who dilate on expansion
and depression. The increase of the Income Tax for
each of the ten years has been, in millions, 10, 7, 4,
10, 21, 17, 31, 30, 29, and 8; and that for the present
year is not yet published.'

Poverty a
result of
increase
of popu-
lation.

It may be said that the low condition of large
masses of our people is a proof that they have derived
no benefit from the fortunes which have been amassed
in England, and that the condition of the French
peasantry is far more favourable than that of the
English agricultural labourer; that the former are not
only the owners of the land they cultivate, but that it
was from their savings that the war indemnity of
200,000,000*l.* was paid to Germany. A wider and
more equal distribution of the wealth of the country
is much to be desired; but it is not through the ac-

cumulation of excessive wealth, in the hands of a limited number of individuals, that the condition of large masses of our population is depressed below the standard of living we should desire to see them maintain. The increase of the population, an increase far more rapid in England than in France, must necessarily tend to keep the masses poor. A given sum is available for distribution among the wage-earning classes, and the share of each individual must be increased or diminished in proportion to their numbers. Capital has increased in the United Kingdom in a greater ratio than the population, and the condition of the masses has been proportionately ameliorated. But population has increased far more rapidly in the United Kingdom than in France. Our marriage rate is much higher. A return of the persons married per thousand of the population gives the following comparison:

	1874	1875	1876
England and Wales .	17·1	16·8	16·7
France	16·6	16·4	15·8

Wages, as it has already been observed, are raised when the circulating capital of the country accumulates in a greater ratio than the increase of the population, and by the competition of employers in a time of exceptional prosperity in trade, or of exceptional scarcity of labour. A striking example of the enhanced value of labour from the latter cause is given in Green's 'Short History of the English People:'—'The most terrible plague which the world ever witnessed ad-

Effect of scarcity of labour in enhancing wages.

vanced from the East, and swooped, at the close of 1348, upon Britain. Of the three or four millions who then formed the population of England, more than one-half were swept away. The sudden rise of wages, consequent on the enormous diminution in the supply of free labour, rudely disturbed the course of industrial employments.

'A summary redress for these evils was found by the Parliament and the Crown in a royal ordinance which was subsequently embodied in the Statutes of Labourers. "Every man or woman . . . not serving any other, shall be bound to serve the employer who shall require him to do so, and shall take only the wages which were accustomed to be taken in the neighbourhood where he is bound to serve," two years before the plague began.

'The Statutes of Labourers were powerless for their immediate ends, either in reducing the actual rate of wages, or in restricting the mass of floating labour to definite areas of employment. A hundred years after the Black Death, the wages of an English labourer commanded twice the amount of the necessaries of life which could have been obtained for the wages paid under Edward III. "Labourers," Longland tells us, "that have no land to live on but their hands," disdained to live on penny ale or bacon, but demanded "fresh flesh or fish, fried or bake." The poet saw clearly that as population rose to its normal rate, times such as these would pass away. "Whiles Hunger was their master here, would none of them chide nor strive against *his* statute, so sternly he looked!"'

The effect of the competition by employers for labour was seen in the general rise of wages consequent on the augmented production in the United Kingdom, prior to the present crisis.

A similar advance of wages took place in the United States from the same cause. It was followed, as in England, by a reaction, which threw large numbers of hands out of employment. The American workmen wisely determined to bow to the inevitable. In his recent report, Mr. Victor Drummond, the secretary to the British Legation at Washington, says : ' Let the British workman take advice from the bearing of the workmen in the United States during this past year ; they calculated sensibly, for once at any rate, that to strike when many were out of employment, when many of the mills were only working on half time, would be too hazardous a proceeding, and determined to wait for better times, which have happily come in most places, although many here are at this moment working at a minimum rate of wages. The British workmen must, like the American workmen, accept a moderate wage until there is a revival of trade.'

Under the pressure of commercial depression both the masters and the operatives engaged in the cotton manufacture in the United States have made the most strenuous and successful efforts to restore prosperity to the trade. ' The present production per labourer employed, as compared with the same kind of production in 1860, as found from mill records, is fifty per cent. more in the coarser fabrics and sixty to sixty-five per cent. more in the finer, while the labour cost per pound is reduced only twenty-two to thirty per cent., and the weekly earnings of operatives are ten to twenty-five per cent. larger now than in 1860, and the cost of their living (of the same kind) is now less.'

Rise of prices and rise of wages.

Let us now proceed to trace the connection between the rise of prices and the rise of wages. In order of time it will be found that, after a period of depression, prices augment in more rapid ratio than wages, and that, on the other hand, after a period of inflation, the fall of prices is more rapid than the fall in wages.

Prices, like wages, are determined by competition, and by the varying relation between the demand and the supply. High profits, however, have much more effect than high wages in raising the cost of production. 'If,' says Adam Smith, 'the wages of the working people employed in producing an article are raised 2*d.* a day, the price of the article need only be raised by a number of twopences equal to the number of people that had been employed about it, multiplied by the number of days during which they had been so employed. But if the profits of all the different employers of those working people should be raised five per cent., the part of the price of the commodity which resolves itself into profit would, through all the different stages of manufacture, rise in geometrical proportion to this rise of profit. In raising the price of commodities, the rise of wages operates in the same manner as simple interest does in the accumulation of debt; the rise of profit operates like compound interest. Our merchants and master manufacturers complain much of the bad effects of high wages in raising the prices, and thereby lessening the sale of their goods both at home and abroad ; but they say nothing concerning the bad effects of high profits. They are silent with regard to the pernicious effects of their own gains : they complain only of those of other people.'

Mr. Lowthian Bell has traced the fluctuations in the cost of the raw materials, and the rates of wages, in the iron and coal trades in the United States. His narrative supplies a striking instance of the practical working of the law laid down by Adam Smith. Upon the imposition of prohibitory duties a general rise of prices ensued, and the cost of the raw materials used in the manufacture of pig-iron was raised in the proportions shown in the following table:

Manufacturers' profits from enhanced prices.

Cost per ton of Pig-iron	For Coal		Ore		Limestone		Labour		Sundries		Total	
	s.	*d.*	*s.*	*d.*	*s.*	*d.*	*s.*	*d.*	*s.*	*d.*	*s.*	*d.*
1860	24	4	11	1	0	4½	6	6	5	6	47	9½
1871	32	10	25	9	1	1	9	9½	8	6½	78	0
1874	41	8	34	7	1	4	10	4	8	6½	90	5½

The table shows that the increase in the cost of the labour, directly employed in the manufacture of pig-iron, constituted but a fraction of the aggregate increase of price; and that while the wages of miners rose very considerably during the period under review, the increased amount paid in respect of wages constituted a small proportion of the augmented price, which the consumer was required to pay for coals. Fabulous profits were realised by the iron manufacturers. The profit on the pig-iron made in a single year sufficed to pay the cost of the furnace in which it was manu-factured.

In the United Kingdom the rise in the price of iron in the year 1871 and the following year both preceded, and was greater in proportion than, the advance in wages. The following tables, taken from Mr. Bevan, give the amount of pig-iron produced from year to year, while prices were increasing, and the quantity and value of the pig-iron exported. They supply data, from which an appreciation may be formed as to the proportions, in which the increased prices, paid by the consumers, were shared between the operatives and the manufacturers.

Production of Pig-iron.

	Tons
1870	5,963,000
1871	6,627,000
1872	6,742,000
1873	6,566,000
1874	5,991,000

Quantity and Value of Pig-iron exported from year to year.

	Quantities exported	Value
	Tons	£
1870	753,000	2,229,000
1871	1,057,000	3,220,000
1872	1,332,000	6,322,000
1873	1,142,000	7,118,000
1874	776,000	3,673,000

A table giving the prices of iron and of puddling from 1863 down to the present time has been published in the 'Statist.' It shows that the manufacture of iron by the processes actually in use yields to the working puddler the value of one ton for every sixteen tons which he produces. The investigation established another deduction which, in justice to the workmen, it is important to bring into view, namely this, that wages at the present time are at least as low as they were ten years ago. In 1868, when the price of iron stood at 6*l*. 5*s*. 5*d*. per ton, the price paid for puddling ranged from 8*s*. to 6*s*. 6*d*. per ton; in 1878, when the price of iron was 6*l*. 0*s*. 5*d*., the price paid for puddling was reduced to seven shillings. 'All the rates from time to time fixed by the Board of Arbitration in the North of England iron trade,' as it is pointed out by the 'Engineer,' 'bear a rough general approximation to the old rule of the puddler, which defined the relation of wages to prices as "shillings to pounds and a shilling over."'

Messrs. Fallows, in their latest circular, state that 'labour has followed in the wake of prices, and is now lower than for many years past. Ironworkers' wages have been reduced 52½ per cent. since 1873, and colliers have suffered in some cases a still greater reduction. In Scotland miners' wages now range from 2*s*. 6*d*. to 3*s*. per day.'

The relation between prices and wages in the iron trade is clearly traced in an article, published in 'Engineering,' from which the following details have been borrowed:

After 1868 the rate of puddlers' wages in the North of England rose from 8*s*. per ton to 13*s*. 3*d*., from which latter figure it declined step by step until it is now fixed at 7*s*. per ton, the increase and decrease reflecting in very great degree the rise and fall in the price of manufactured iron.

The fluctuations in the price of iron and the wages of the puddlers are given in the following table:

	Average Price per ton	Puddlers' Wages per ton
	£ *s.* *d.*	*s.* *d.*
1868	6 11 3	8 0
1873	11 8 4	13 3
1874.	10 18 11	11 6
1875	7 10 4	8 3
1877	6 17 1	8 3
1878	6 7 4	7 6
1879	5 18 7	7 0

Mr. Shaw Lefevre, in his recent address to the Statistical Society, gave the following comparative statement of the prices of pig-iron and the wages of the workmen : ' The average price of pig-iron rose from 60*s.* in 1869 to 102*s.* in 1872 ; 117*s.* in 1873 ; then fell to 65*s.* in 1875 ; and to 53*s.* in 1878. The wages rose from 3*s.* 9*d.* a day in 1869, to 7*s.* 3*d.* in 1872, and 8*s.* 6*d.* in 1873 ; then fell to 4*s.* 6*d.* in 1876, and 2*s.* 9*d.* in 1878.'

Wages in collieries.

The fluctuations in wages in the coal trade in the years 1871–74 are shown in the following table, taken by Mr. Bevan from returns, prepared by Mr. Bunning, of Newcastle, for the American Government:

Date	Advance per cent.	Reduction per cent.	Total Advance per cent. since 1871	Average Daily Earnings
				s. *d.*
1871	—	—	—	4 9
1872	—	—	38	6 6
1873	15	—	58·7	7 3
1874	—	19	30	6 3

Sir George Elliott, M.P., has kindly supplied the following statement of the average earnings of the workmen and of the cost of raising coal for the year 1878, as compared with 1873 : 'In South Wales the cost of getting the coal was rather higher in 1874 than in 1873, and averaged 12*s.* 6*d.* per ton, the wages being 7*s.* 6*d.* per ton. During 1878 the total cost was 5*s.* 6*d.* per ton, wages 3*s.* 4*d.* per ton. The highest price realised for coal in 1873 was 30*s.*, free on board, as compared with 10*s.* per ton in 1878.'

The writer of these pages is painfully sensible that they offer nothing to charm and delight the imagination. He sympathises with the reader's weariness of such an accumulation of details. The subject of wages, however, is one on which the wage-earner feels deeply, though he often acts ignorantly. It cannot be disposed of by mere argument nor by invective. The rate of wages for large masses cannot be raised by the force of sympathy, nor depressed by class prejudice. The student of these questions from an economic point of view may perhaps be conciliated by the conviction that if the work, which he is perusing, is destitute of literary attractions, it may add something to his knowledge. The author of 'Rasselas' has wisely said that 'Knowledge is certainly one of the means of pleasure, as is confessed by the natural desire, which every mind feels, of increasing its ideas. Ignorance is mere privation, by which nothing can be produced: it is a vacuity in which the soul sits motionless and torpid for want of attraction ; and, without knowing why, we always rejoice when we learn, and grieve when we forget.' We return to our figures.

The cost of getting coal in 1873, per ton at the

pit's mouth, was 13*s.* The cost in 1878 was 5*s.* 6*d.* per ton. The final reduction in the cost of extraction was due to a sudden reduction in the establishment by one-third. This had the effect of increasing the diligence of the miners to such an extent that the cost of getting was diminished by 2*s.* per ton. At the same time, the selling price was reduced by 1*s.* 6*d.* The price of coal in 1873 was 30*s.* per ton; in 1878 it was 9*s.* 6*d.* per ton.

A similar return, prepared by the South Wales Collieries Association, is appended:

Average Weekly Earnings in the year 1873, and three months of 1878.

Description	Average Weekly Earnings in 1873	Average Weekly Earnings from February 24 to May 18, 1878	Remarks
	s. d.	*s. d.*	
Hewers .	48 9	19 1½	In 1873 the pits were working full time, but in the three months of 1878 they only worked on an average nine days per fortnight.
Timbermen.	53 4	23 6	
Hauliers .	31 6	16 11	
Landers .	36 9	18 8¼	
Labourers .	24 0	14 9½	
Average .	36 8	18 10½	

	1873	1878
Cutting price per ton of 4 feet .	2*s.*	1*s.* 3*d.*
„ „ 6 „ .	2*s.* 5*d.*	1*s.* 6*d.*
„ „ 9 „ .	2*s.* 5*d.*	1*s.* 6*d.*
Hewers, per day . . .	Contract work	Contract
Timbermen „	„	4*s.* 9*d.*
Hauliers „	5*s.* 3*d.*	3*s.* 3*d.*
Landers „	5*s.* 3*d.*	3*s.* 6*d.*
Labourers „	4*s.* 2*d.* to 4*s.* 4*d.*	2*s.* 6*d.* to 2*s.* 10*d.*

The rise from 1871–74 was very remarkable; but, as Mr. Morley reminds us, while the price of coal at the pit's mouth had gone up by 15*s.* 5*d.* per ton, wages only went up 1*s.* 1½*d.* per ton. The aggregate increase in the earnings of the colliers was calculated at 15,000,000*l.*, but the increased profits in the same year amounted to 60,000,000*l.*

The downward movement in the wages of miners, from the inflation of 1873, has been unprecedented, both in extent and in the rapidity of the change. In a recent article in the ' Times ' we read : ' It is difficult indeed to form even an approximate idea of the extent to which the wages of coal miners have been reduced all round since the trade began a downward course ; but the aggregate must be enormous. Mr. A. Hewlett informed the Coal Committee of 1873 that in some of the mines under his charge during April of that year one man was making 24*s.* 1*d.* per day, another 26*s.* 10*d.*, and so on. Mr. Isaac Booth proved that in the Oldham district the average rate of wages had advanced from 7*s.* 3*d.* to 12*s.* 11*d.* per day. Mr. R. Tennant, M.P., quoted figures to show that the average had gone up in West Yorkshire from 3*s.* 7*d.* to 7*s.* 1*d.* per ton. In Northumberland, according to Mr. George Baker Forster, there was an advance all round of 66 per cent. Mr. Lindsay Wood spoke to an average rise in Durham from 4*s.* 8*d.* to 7*s.* 9*d.*; and in other districts the same, or a still larger, rate of advance occurred. But wages are now on an average below the range of 1871—in some cases they are even 20 per cent. lower ; and we shall therefore be justified in assuming that, taking one district with another, the miners are not now earning much more than one-half what they did in 1873. In

Scotland, miners' wages now range from 20*s*. 6*d*. to 30*s*. a day. The average rates in Wales are about the same.'

Reduction of numbers employed.
If we allow, with the writer in the 'Times,' an average reduction of only 20*s*. per week in the wages of each miner employed, we shall arrive at the vast sum of 25,688,000*l*. as the annual difference between the earnings of the whole body in the year 1873 and in 1878.

While an unprecedented fall has taken place in wages, the fluctuations in the numbers employed have been equally remarkable. The total number of male persons employed in our coal mines was 370,000 in 1871, 477,000 in 1873, 536,000 in 1875, and 494,000 in 1877.

Behaviour of the miner in adversity.
The privations endured by the working population in the mineral districts, from the sudden fall in wages and cessation of employment, should entitle them to the heartfelt sympathy of the public. The conduct of the ignorant miner must not be judged too hastily. The responsibility for our commercial disasters rests with the capitalists and employers rather than the workmen. The comparatively small increase in pauperism reflects honour on the population, which has struggled against adversity with so much fortitude, and borne without a murmur or complaint such bitter distress and privation.

The fluctuations in wages in the iron and coal trades in the last decade afford conclusive proof that the price of labour depends on competition. There is competition among employers for workmen when trade is brisk, and competition among workmen for employment when trade is languishing. It is by striking a balance between demand and supply, and not by the strategy, too often of a highly objectionable character, of masters' and workmen's associations, that the reward of labour is finally adjusted.

In the cotton, as in the metallurgical industries, the rise of wages followed the rise in prices in the years of prosperity, and wages have slowly fallen in proportion to the fall of prices during the subsequent reaction. *Wages in textile industries.*

In the latest manifesto on behalf of the operative cotton spinners, Mr. Mawdsley remarks that ' during the six or seven years subsequent to 1869, the cotton trade, in conjunction with other trades, enjoyed a period of exceptional prosperity ; but instead of adopting the tactics of most of the other sections of working men, factory workers, in the main, allowed the prices paid for their work to remain stationary ; and in a large proportion of cases they were even paid a less price during the whole of that period than they were three or four years previous, while other trades were obtaining advances varying from 10 to 50 per cent.'

The operatives, it is urged, relied on the manufacturers to compensate them by keeping up wages after the tide had turned against the trade. To assume that manufacturers would be contented to produce goods for an extended period at a serious loss, that they would be ready to manufacture without profit during four consecutive years, because they had realised twenty per cent. during the preceding period of four

Y

years, was an expectation altogether inconsistent with
the ordinary experience of human nature.

Wages
must
follow
prices.

When, after a long depression, trade begins to recover, an upward movement in wages will shortly follow. As soon as the first ray of light begins to pene-
trate the gloom, the operatives hail the promise of
improvement with thankfulness. They are not curious
to ascertain whether their employers might have given
a larger advance ; it is sufficient for them that a reaction has commenced. Presently the competition of
employers begins to tell on the price of labour, and
the advance of wages, already described, commences.
The upward movement will probably continue, until
the improvement in pay becomes fully proportionate
to the rise of prices. The vigilance of those, who
guide the conduct of the operatives, might often secure
a more immediate participation in the improving returns from industry. Their influence is pernicious,
rather than beneficial, when the operatives are urged
to make a stand against a reduction, at a time when
the interest of every coal owner and manufacturer
would be promoted by an absolute and prolonged
cessation of production. It is the wrong moment to
fight a battle. It is when trade is profitable, and employers would lose money by suspending operations,
that an organised pressure may produce concessions to
the working people. In point of fact, a reduction of
wages is generally postponed by employers as long as
possible. It is an economy, to which they have recourse with reluctance, and only in the last resort.
Regrettable as they are, we must still look in the future

for a repétition of the same oscillations in prices and wages, which have been so frequent in recent years. Trade has now become international, in a larger sense than before. The fluctuations in prices depend on the state of foreign markets, and foreign politics, and on the stability of governments, which do not rest on the solid foundations, on which our liberal and venerable constitution has been reared. Trade is now organised on such a scale as to admit of the influx of vast and uncertain amounts of loose capital, whenever the course of prices turns in favour of any particular branch of industry, and renders it for the time being exceptionally profitable. As prices and profits vary, so there must be a continual higgling in the labour market. When trade is less busy, wages will fall. We see this occur more frequently in England and Belgium than in France. In the latter country many branches of trade are monopolised by a few large firms, who are not easily lured by an ephemeral prosperity to excessive competition and to over-production. So, too, when the trade is limited to the home market, and goods are chiefly made to order, accumulations of stock will be less frequent than where large quantities of goods are manufactured on speculation and for the foreign markets.

Many alternations of poverty and abundance have been experienced by the working classes of England during the whole course of the present century. The following fluctuations in wages have been taken from Mr. Porter's ' Progress of the Nation : '

Fluctuations in wages.

Greenwich Hospital.

Dates	Carpenters		Bricklayers		Masons	
	s.	*d.*	*s.*	*d.*	*s.*	*d.*
1800	18	0	18	0	17	0
1805	27	0	29	0	30	0
1810	34	0	31	0	31	6
1815	33	0	30	6	34	6
1816	31	0	30	6	31	6
1825	30	0	29	0	30	0
1826	34	6	—		33	0
1834	32	6	28	6	31	6
1835	29	3	26	5	29	1½

Use of capital as affecting the workman's condition.   The fluctuations in the wages of hand-loom weavers at the commencement of the century may be examined with advantage by the operatives of the present day, employed in large concerns, carried on by the application of more or less considerable amounts of individual or associated capital. It will be manifest how beneficent is the influence of capital in tempering the severity of adverse seasons, in equalising the condition of the operatives, and in shielding them from the rude shock of a sudden revulsion in the commercial value of the commodity produced by their industry and skill. The wages of the hand-loom weavers of Bolton are taken from Mr. Porter's treatise :—

Date	Wages per week		Date	Wages per week	
	s.	*d.*		*s.*	*d.*
1800	25	0	1817	9	0
1810	19	6	1825	8	6
1811	14	0	1826	7	0
1814	24	0	1828	6	0
1815	24	0	1829	5	6

The accumulation of capital has the same beneficent effect in modifying sharp fluctuations in prices. The operations of speculative merchants, who buy when goods are cheap, and sell when they are dear, tend to equalise prices. In truth, as Mr. Greg so forcibly puts it, large employers virtually and practically save for the operatives, and bear the fluctuations for them : a signal benefit is thus secured to the working class. On the other hand, the imprudent speculations of capitalists are the cause of over-production. They honeycombed the black country with new furnaces, which so completely overtook the demands of the market, that in five years no less than 30,000 men have been driven out of the trade. It was through the recklessness of capital that the dislocation of the cotton trade occurred.

The consequences are sad for the working classes, who, from no fault of their own, are exposed suddenly and unexpectedly to the loss of the larger proportion of their incomes. Many painful reflections must occur to men suffering from these vicissitudes. They were vividly described by Mrs. Gaskell in the melancholy tale of ' Mary Barton : ' Consequences of over-production to the workman.

' At all times it is a bewildering thing to the poor weaver to see the employer removing from house to house, each one grander than the last, till he ends in building one more magnificent than all, or withdraws his money from the concern, or sells his mill, to buy an estate in the country ; while all the time the weaver, who thinks he and his fellows are the real makers of this wealth, is struggling on for bread for his children, through the vicissitudes of lowered wages, short hours, fewer hands employed, &c. . . . He would bear and endure much without complaining, could he also see that his employers were bearing their share. He is, I

say, bewildered, and (to use his own word) "aggravated" to see that all goes on just as usual with the
mill-owners. . . . Carriages still roll along the streets,
concerts are still crowded by subscribers, the shops for
expensive luxuries still find daily customers. . . . The
contrast is too great. Why should he alone suffer from
bad times?'[1] The change from good times to bad
times must be far more keenly felt by the working
man than by the capitalist, who is enabled to maintain
his habitual standard of living irrespective of the
fluctuating results of trade. The constant recurrence
of unmerited and unanticipated misfortune reduces the
bravest hearts at last to a state of prostration and exhaustion, which has been described by Mr. Matthew
Arnold in touching verses, in 'The Scholar Gipsy:'

> For what wears out the life of mortal man ?
> 'Tis that from change to change his being rolls,
> 'Tis that repeated shocks, again, again,
> Exhaust the energy of strongest souls,
> And numb the elastic powers.

Socialist feeling excited by tyranny of property. Mr. Green has condensed in a few graphic phrases
the speeches of John Ball, which were the knell of
feudalism in England. ' " By what right," said he, " are
they whom we call lords greater folk than we ?
They are clothed in velvet, and warm in their furs
and their ermines, while we are covered with rags.
They have wine and spices and fair bread ; and we,
oat-cake and straw, and water to drink. They have
leisure and fine houses ; we have pain and labour, the
rain and the wind in the fields. And yet it is of us

---

[1] 'Mary Barton,' ch. iii.

and of our toil that these men hold their state."
It was the tyranny of property that then, as ever,
roused the defiance of Socialism. A spirit, fatal to
the whole system of the Middle Ages, breathed in the
popular rhyme which condensed the levelling doctrine
of John Ball : " When Adam delved and Eve span,
who was then the gentleman ? " '

The committee of the Cotton Spinners' Association, in a paper issued in December last, refer to the hostile tariffs and the devastating wars, from which the trading communities have lately suffered, as main causes of the present depression ; but they very fairly attribute some share of the falling away in trade to the altered habits of the employers. ' Let the moral attitude,' they say, ' of masters and workpeople, as compared with that of former days, be regarded. The older cotton spinners cannot but remark upon the contrast in the business habits and style of living between the cotton spinner of thirty and forty years ago with the cotton spinner of to-day. To a degree which is very conspicuous the old plodding, constant, steady working millowner, having and taking a personal interest in all and each of his hands, and living carefully but in ample comfort, is in a great measure replaced by men somewhat intermittent in the exercise of their energies, demanding that their money should come easy to them, having little or no·personal knowledge of or personal interest in their hands, and living at a heavy personal expenditure in the enjoyment of constantly augmenting and exciting luxuries.'

(Altered habits of employers.)

The excess of luxury, the growing extravagance in

Force of
example.

the houses, the dress, the tables of the wealthy, has set a pernicious example before the mass of the people, whose duty it is to live not meanly but with simplicity. The ladies of England are very responsible in this matter. They must exercise a censorship over themselves and their household. They must learn to resist the temptations and extortions of tradesmen, who seem to think that they have suffered a wrong because the public have sought to protect themselves by establishing co-operative stores. There is no isolation of classes in our happily constituted society. Each may contribute by its virtues to raise, and by its follies to lower, the moral tone of the whole people. The strength of our nation consists in the social union we enjoy, in a degree, which is indeed remarkable, when we consider how unequal is the distribution of wealth and social advantages. Let us be thankful for the strong mutual sympathies which bind class and class together. Let each work in concert with the other for the common welfare, the rich to ease the burden of the poor, the poor in grateful acknowledgment of the kindness and the help which they in turn receive.

CHAPTER XV.

THE IMPROVED CONDITION OF THE PEOPLE.

The more carefully we examine the history of the past, the more reason shall we find to dissent from those who imagine that our age has been fruitful of new social evils. The truth is that the evils are, with scarcely an exception, old. That which is new is the intelligence which discerns and the humanity which remedies them.—MACAULAY, *History of England.*

A decent provision for the poor is the true test of civilisation. Gentlemen of education are pretty much the same in all countries: the condition of the lower orders, the poor especially, is the true mark of national discrimination.—BOSWELL, *Life of Johnson.*

HAVING considered the qualities of the workman, let us endeavour to ascertain what progress has been made in ameliorating his condition. The 'British Quarterly' Reviewer gives gratifying assurances on this point. He refers to the improvements in the dwellings of the people, and quotes some highly satisfactory statistics. 'In 1801 England and Wales contained nine millions of people, living in one and a half million of houses. In 1873 there were twenty-three millions in four and a quarter millions of houses; and it is quite certain that the twenty-three (now in 1877 become at least twenty-four) millions of people are far better fed, clothed, taught, and occupied, and the four and a quarter millions (now become four and a half millions) of houses are in all respects better constructed and appointed in 1877 than they were in 1800, nearly

[margin note: Progress of improvement in the workman's condition.]

three generations ago.' He compares the slow growth of the population in the interval between William I. and William III., a period of six hundred years, during which time it barely doubled itself, with the recent increase in the population, as an evidence of the superior well-being of later generations. The comparative condition of the masses of the population in her Majesty's happy reign and in the age of the Stuarts was carefully investigated by Lord Macaulay. The results were summarised in the celebrated third chapter of his history.

' During several generations the Commissioners of Greenwich Hospital have kept a register of the wages paid to different classes of workmen who have been employed in the repairs of the building. From this valuable record it appears that, in the course of a hundred and twenty years, the daily earnings of the bricklayer have risen from half-a-crown to four and tenpence ; those of the mason from half-a-crown to five and threepence ; those of the carpenter from half-a-crown to five and fivepence ; and those of the plumber from half-a-crown to five and sixpence.

' It seems clear, therefore, that the wages of labour, estimated in money, were, in 1685, not more than half of what they now are ; and there were few articles important to the working man of which the price was not, in 1685, more than half of what it now is. Beer was undoubtedly much cheaper in that age than at present. Meat was also cheaper, but was still so dear that hundreds of thousands of families scarcely knew the taste of it. In the cost of wheat there has been very little change. The average price of the quarter, during the last twelve years of Charles the Second, was fifty shillings. Bread, therefore, such as is now given to the inmates of a workhouse, was then seldom seen, even on the trencher of a yeoman or of a shopkeeper. The great majority of the nation lived almost entirely on rye, barley, and oats. The produce of tropical countries, the produce of the mines, the produce of machinery was positively dearer than at present. Among the commodities for which the labourer would have had to pay higher in 1685 than his posterity pay in 1848 were sugar, salt, coals, candles, soap, shoes, stockings, and generally all articles of clothing and all articles of bedding. It may be added that the old coats and blankets would have been not only more costly, but less serviceable, than the modern fabrics.'

A numerous population is an important element of our industrial prosperity. Our ability to compete with foreigners in part depends upon an abundant supply of labour. In the interval between 1838 and 1876, during which a complete system of registration has been opened, the increase of the population of the United Kingdom, according to the last report of the Registrar-General, was 7,619,759. The increase in the last ten years was at the rate of 0·94 per cent. per annum. During the whole period embraced in the review the increase was at the rate of 0·66 per cent.

Population an element of industrial prosperity.

A calculation by M. Toussaint Loua, showing the probable time required to enable the present populations of the several countries of Europe to double themselves, gives the following results :

England .	.	. 72 years	Belgium .	.	. 95 years
Finland .	.	. 73 „	Greece .	.	. 112 „
Russia	.	. 76 „	Ireland .	.	. 113 „
Scotland .	.	. 81 „	Switzerland	.	. 148 „
Norway .	.	. 81 „	Austria .	.	. 155 „
Sweden .	.	. 83 „	Italy	.	. 100 „
Germany .	.	. 83 „	France .	.	. 263 „
The Netherlands	.	86 „	Roumania	.	. 288 „
Denmark .	.	. 93 „	Hungary (gradually diminishing)		

Economic value of the population.

The economic value of the population is the most important element of the capital of the United Kingdom. Mr. Graham, the present Registrar-General, in his penultimate report published an elaborate calculation of the enormous value inherent in the people. Taking as his basis the average wages of agricultural labourers at different ages, determining their value by the life table at five per cent. interest, and multiplying the numbers living by those values, he fixes the mean gross value at all ages at 349*l*. Deducting 199*l*., being the mean value of the subsistence of the labourer, the mean net value of the male population is estimated at 150*l*. Extending this value to the whole population, including females, the standard is reduced to 110*l*. per head ; and, multiplying the whole population by that figure, the aggregate value is 3,640,000,000*l*.

The aggregate incomes of the classes subject to income tax under Schedules D and E amount to 306,000,000*l*. a year. Deducting the half of this revenue as due to external capital and as required for the necessary sustenance of farmers, tradesmen, and professional men, there remains 186,500,000*l*. as pure profit, which, capitalised at ten years' purchase, makes the value of these incomes 1,865,000,000*l*. After deduction of the incomes previously valued in the aggregate of 3,640,000,000*l.*, no less than 1,610,000,000*l.* remains, which gives the total of 5,250,000,000*l.* as the value of the earnings, fees, salaries, and wages of the mercantile, trading, and working classes. This amount may be fairly added to the national capital in the form of realised property, such as land, houses, cattle, or stock.

It must be further borne in mind, as Mr. Graham remarks, that the value under Schedule A is dependent upon population. Where there is little population, land and house property is of little value ; railways yield no profit, mines cannot be worked. Should the population decay, the value of capital might diminish to the vanishing point.

The efforts lately made to extend the blessings of education to the entire population will ultimately add much to their industrial capabilities. Mr. Graham truly says : ' The clever artisan is worth more than the rude labourer. The art of reading and writing is not a proof of complete education or technical training ; but it is a proof that men are prepared to enter on the inheritance of knowledge bequeathed to them from past ages.' In 1837 not more than fifty-eight in one hundred, at the present time eighty-one in one hundred, can write their names in the marriage register. *Extended education.*

Improved sanitary measures contribute most materially, not only to the national happiness, but to its wealth. The mean lifetime, by the English life table, was 40·86 years ; by the healthy life table it is 49·0 years ; and this average is attainable in every well-organised state. To add one-fifth to their lifetime is to add one-fifth to the economic value of the population. In the United Kingdom this would repre- *Sanitary improvements.*

sent an addition of not less than 1,050,000,000*l.*
to the national wealth.

In comparison with other European states, England
holds a not unsatisfactory position. We stand at the
head of European nations in the rapidity of the increase of our population. The Improved Dwellings
Act, a measure which is largely due to the advocacy of
Sir Ughtred J. K. Shuttleworth, my colleague in the
representation of Hastings, will ensure henceforward a
continuous improvement in the habitations of the poor.
The increase in the numbers of the people depends in
a great measure on the sanitary conditions under
which they live. The Legislature and the local authorities of the United Kingdom may claim a high
meed of praise for the attention recently bestowed on
these subjects. The result is seen in the steady improvement in the Registrar-General's returns. The
Reduced death-rate per thousand for England and Wales has
death-rate. fallen from 22·4 in 1853–72 to 21·0 in 1876. We
are still behind both Denmark and Sweden, where the
rate was 20·0 and 19·5 per thousand respectively;
but we are more favourably situated than any other
European country.

The following table gives the death-rate for the
principal countries of Europe :

	Deaths per Thousand Population	
	1853–72	1876
England and Wales . . .	22·4	21·0
Austria	31·9	29·4
German Empire	—	26·3
France	24·4	22·7
Italy	30·2	28·7
Denmark	20·3	20·0
Sweden	20·4	19·5

We may look for a further reduction from the labours of the Health Commission recently appointed, and from the continuous attention of a properly constituted department to the subject.

The latest return of the Registrar-General contains some valuable remarks on the sanitary results of overcrowding in our great cities. The economic value and the moral condition of the population would be seriously impaired if it were more concentrated. Our aim should be dispersion, rather than concentration. 'The advantage of residence in towns—of proximity of people to each other—is evident. Man is a sociable animal, and naturally in his workshop meets his fellowman. But there are countervailing disadvantages to which I now invite your attention. The first disadvantage strikes every one that comes from the country, and is embodied in Cowper's line—

> God made the country, and man made the town.

In the country you are surrounded by fields, by trees—in hill or vale; there the breezes coming from sea, shore, or mountain have free play. The atmosphere is redolent of ozone. In the town, this is wanting. Angus Smith, by chemical tests, proves the air is different. This atmosphere becomes in certain proportions deleterious, and I will proceed to show that as the population becomes more dense—within certain limits—this deleteriousness is expressed by the mortality. Excluding the London districts, about which there is some difficulty, we have seven groups of districts where the mortality ranges thus: 17, 19, 22,

Marginal note: Overcrowding relieved by suburban railways.

25, 28, 32, and 39. In the same districts the numbers of persons to a square mile are—166, 186, 379, 1,718, 4,499, 12,357, and 65,823. Thus in Liverpool, the densest and the unhealthiest district in England, there were 65,823 persons to a square mile, of whom 39 per 1,000 died annually.' Suburban railways are an invaluable means of relieving the pressure of population in the heart of great cities.

The Factory Acts.

By wise and beneficent legislation in another direction a most gratifying amelioration has been effected in the condition of our factory population. The Factory Acts, for which the operatives are indebted to Lord Shaftesbury, have put an end to the former inhuman treatment of children, compelled to toil beyond their strength, and cruelly beaten for the smallest fault or inattention to their work. The hours were almost incredibly long, during which the children were suffered to toil by their hard-hearted parents and employers. Cases were brought before the Factory Committee of 1833 of children, who had only returned home from their work at 11 p.m., being sent out to work again at two o'clock in the morning.

Every effort should be made to improve as far as possible the condition of factory labourers. Constant employment in a close heated atmosphere is exhausting to the constitution, and often leads to excessive indulgence in stimulants. The degeneracy of the factory population would be a national calamity of the gravest character in the United Kingdom, where such vast numbers are employed in the textile industries. The operations of several of our leading firms are conducted in palatial buildings, in which the operatives are supplied with air and light in a far more ample measure than is possible in small and more crowded buildings. A considerable difference is observable between the various branches of the textile industry in reference to health. The woollen manufactures are the most healthy; the cotton and the flax trades are the least favourable to the health of the operatives.

In the iron manufactures the workmen are not exposed to the deleterious atmosphere of the cotton mill, though their labours are arduous and sometimes dangerous. For the most laborious process in iron-making, that of puddling, serious and not unpromising efforts are being made to substitute mechanical agency for human labour.

Turning from iron to coal, the colliery-workers, who are 450,000 in number, follow an occupation which cannot be condemned as unhealthy. Their condition has been much improved by recent legislation. Women can no longer be employed, and boys, under thirteen, only by permission of the Secretary of State.

Mr. Redgrave gives a highly satisfactory report of the results attending the introduction of the Factory Acts into London in 1877. 'Ten years ago,' he says, 'I made the first effort to introduce the Factory Acts into London. There has been quite a revolution during that period in the conditions on which seamstress work is carried on in the metropolis; the employment of them in workshops and factories has increased enormously, but I can find no employer willing to commit himself to the opinion that in their respective classes

Mr. Redgrave's report on their beneficial working.

z

there has been any deterioration in the character and the conduct of the workpeople. All the evidence, indeed, which I have obtained, goes to establish the contrary. Those engaged in the higher branches of dressmaking and millinery, and who chiefly board their employées, acknowledge that since the enforcement of the factory regulations they have less difficulty than ever in getting apprentices of a superior class to engage with them. The relatives and friends of these young people, knowing that their health is protected by the limitations imposed upon the hours of work by the Factory Acts, have less hesitation in allowing them to go to work, and within the few years during which I have acted as inspector of the West end of London I have observed a remarkable improvement in the accommodation and treatment provided for this class of people. I have never met with any evidence which would encourage the idea that the morals of the seam-stresses of London as a class are so low that they could not be trusted with a moderate amount of leisure for amusement and recreation. They always appeared to me, as a rule, to be a most industrious and steady class of workpeople, who fight the battle of life bravely under circumstances at times of great discouragement. The argument that the tendency of the Factory Acts is to place an artificial restriction on the employment of women, and thus to depreciate the market value of their labour, is refuted on every hand by practical experience in the textile manufactories. Here the restrictions upon women's work are the most stringent, and yet the tendency for a long series of years has been the opposite : the proportion of women employed has steadily increased. The same observation applies to many of the trades and occupations carried on in London. As for the rate of wages paid, there is not an employer in the metropolis who will hesitate to acknowledge that there has been during the last ten or fifteen years a very substantial and important advance in the remuneration given to women for their work.'

The increased consumption of food is a sure indication of the condition of the people. Our national taste for roast beef is proverbial. A table, showing the annual consumption of meat in the several countries in Europe, has been published by M. Maurice Block in his treatise on Statistics. It gives the following figures per head of the population :

Consumption of food.

United Kingdom	86·68 lbs.
France	66·0 ,,
Russia	44·0 ,,
Prussia	41·58 ,,
Belgium	39·6 ,,
Italy	28·6 ,,
Spain	28·38 ,,

Observe how low the consumption falls in Belgium, the country whose competition some regard as so much to be dreaded ! I have no faith in the working capabilities of an ill-paid and badly fed population. Under the sunny skies of Spain and Italy meat is unnecessary, and the supplies of fruit and other substitutes for meat are plentiful. The climate offers no compensation to the working classes in Belgium for their meagre dietary.

While the English consume more meat than any other population, they have enjoyed exceptional advantages in the comparative cheapness of bread. Partly owing to the abolition of the Corn Laws, partly owing to the great facilities that we command for the importation of foreign wheat, the present generation have seen a considerable reduction, while on the Continent prices have risen in some cases to double the former rates. In the interval between 1830 and 1870 the price of wheat, according to M. Leroy-Beaulieu, has fallen by 14 per cent. in Great Britain, while it has risen in France 17 per cent., and even more in Belgium. The average price of 64 gallons of wheat was 40*s.* 7*d.* in the seventeenth century, 40*s.* 6*d.* in the eighteenth century. It is quoted at 39*s.* 7*d.* at the present time.

Mr. Howell's hints on economic feeding.

On this subject, Mr. George Howell remarks: 'There is one lesson which the working classes have yet to learn, namely, how to make the most of their food. Sometimes a pennyworth of good food is thrown away, when an expenditure of a halfpenny would make it palatable for another meal. Then again there is a prejudice against some articles, such as Scotch meal, or porridge. This is not only unreasonable, but very disastrous, as it possesses qualities, not to be found in any other article of domestic use, which are especially valuable to growing children. The same holds good in regard to rice; they cook it badly, and do not get its full nutriment. Oftentimes they will buy sausages at 10*d.* per lb., one-third of which consists of bread, and one-third of gross fat, and only one-third meat, and that of inferior quality; if the same amount were spent in good buttock-steak, it would make a beefsteak pudding large enough for a family of five persons.'

In England the working classes have made a successful effort to husband their resources by the establishment of co-operative stores for the distribution of
commodities. The value of these associations may be,
appreciated from the information collected by M. de
Foville, showing the average profits of the retail trade
in Paris. The results were published in an article in
the ' Economiste Français.'

X., in the subjoined table, sells in quantities of not
less than five kilogrammes. Y. is a retail grocer, on
the left bank of the Seine. The following table
exhibits the differences in the prices charged at the
two establishments :

Article sold	Wholesale price charged by X.	Retail price charged by Y.	Proportionate difference
	Francs	Francs	
Fine flour, per kilog	0·60	0·90	50 per cent.
Rice (superior), per kilog	0·80	1·20	50 „
Tapioca, per kilog	2·00	2·80	40 „
Semolina, „	0·60	1·20	100 „
Vermicelli macaroni, per kilog.	1·00	1·40	50 „
Dried haricots, per litre	0·60	0·70	17 „
„ peas, per litre	0·60	0·70	17 „
Lentils, per litre	0·70	0·90	28 „

Commenting upon these figures, M. de Foville
remarks that if a difference of from seventeen to one
hundred per cent. is observable in the prices charged
in two establishments not far separated in locality and
in the scale of their operations, the excess of one
hundred per cent. in the retail over the wholesale
prices would be found to be the rule, rather than the
exception, among the small retailers in the suburbs of
Paris. The small grocer renders a less amount of

service to his customers.   He offers a less varied
assortment of articles.   He does not keep a staff of
porters to deliver to his customers the goods purchased.
But his general expenses, increasing in proportion as
the amount of business diminishes, compel him either
to close his shop or to bleed his humble clients to death.
Nothing can be more disappointing or more disheartening than to see the workman paying 30, 40, or 50 per
cent. dearer than his employer for the necessaries of life.

No better illustration could be given of the practical
genius of the English people than their success in establishing these societies; while the French, remarkable
as they are for the gift of organisation in other departments, have done nothing more than indulge in vague
denunciations of the order of things which exists, which
they do nothing to improve, and for which, indeed,
their only remedies are upheaval and destruction.

Saving of labour effected by machinery. An incalculable economy of human labour has been
effected by machinery and by improved methods of
communication.   The Suez Canal has shortened the
communications between the East and the West certainly by one half.   Capital is thereby economised; there
is less need to accumulate stocks in Europe in anticipation of the demand.   The addition to our manufacturing
capabilities obtained by the application of steam-power
is incalculable.   It has been estimated that France
possesses steam machinery of 580,000 horse-power,
and that the aggregate mechanical power represents
the labour of twelve millions of slaves.   All improvements in machinery tend to cheapen the clothing or
lodging of the people.   They can enjoy more comforts
without increasing their expenditure.

That the accumulation during past years of pro- Accumulation
sperity has been very considerable, is abundantly proved proved by
by the permanent increase in the rateable value of increased rateable
property, even in those districts which have suffered value of property.
the most severely from the commercial depression.
The following observations on this subject were published in the 'Leeds Mercury: ' ' The condition of the
South Wales coal and iron districts is really in some
respects a marvel to the inhabitants themselves. In
the Merthyr Tydfil district, for instance, notwithstanding the stoppage of two ironworks which between them
gave employment to between 6,000 and 7,000 hands,
and although only one new colliery has been opened
in the neighbourhood, still the number of occupied
houses in the parish is not less to-day than it was when
those great ironworks were in full operation ; the
rateable value of the parish is maintained at its old
figure, although these great establishments are only
assessed as warehouses for machinery, and the rates of
all descriptions are collected with extraordinary close-
ness. The last poor-rate, amounting to over 6,000*l.*,
was collected in three months to within 20*l.*, and a
local board of health rate for 7,500*l.* has been collected
in four months to within 76*l.*, which represents the total
amount of arrears brought forward during the last nine
years in a collection of over 160,000*l.* These are vital
facts in their bearing upon the condition of the middle
classes, the tradesmen, professional gentlemen, cottage
proprietors, and others who come directly into contact
with the rate collectors. Their means have not yet
failed them, and these statistics, which have just been

published, have shown the people of that town that they are not quite so badly off as they imagined themselves to be.'

The future of the wage-earning classes depends on themselves. They must learn to be more thrifty. The British workman is distinguished for courage, industry, and prodigality. The first are noble qualities. Pity it is that the reward, which is their due, should be squandered in thoughtless self-indulgence! The working people will be greatly encouraged by the good example of their employers. Mr. Smiles quotes a wise observation by M. Alexandre Dumas. 'All the world cries, " Where is the man that will save us? " We want a man! Don't look so far for that man. You have him at hand. This man—it is you, it is I, it is each one of us! How to constitute oneself a man? Nothing harder, if one knows not how to *will* it; nothing easier, if one wills it.'

Mr. Smiles' work on 'Thrift' is full of warning, derived from his own experiences, and those of the many philanthropists, who have laboured for the welfare of the masses, whom he quotes. St. James's and St. Giles's, as he reminds us, lie close together. 'In the parks of London you may see how gold is worshipped ; in the East end of London, you may see to what depths human misery may fall. But the people, as the late Edward Denison, M.P., has said, create their destitution and their disease. Probably there are hardly any of the most needy, who, if they had been only moderately frugal and provident, could not have placed themselves in a position to tide over the occasional months of want of work, or of sickness, which there always must be.' Mr. Smiles, commenting on the unhappy picture which he had drawn in several preceding pages, thus expresses his view of the qualities of the British workman: 'No one can reproach the English workman with want of industry. He works harder and more skilfully than the workman of any other country; and he might be more comfortable and independent in his circumstances, were he as prudent as he is laborious. But improvidence is unhappily the defect of the class.'

Professor Levi, while·giving a reassuring view of the improvement in the material condition of the working classes, accompanies his observations with a warning against the habits of extravagance, in which a large proportion of their number have indulged. A considerable part of the extra amount earned from 1871 to 1873 was wasted in an excessive expenditure for eating, drinking, and smoking.

The consumption of the following imported and exciseable articles of food and drink per head of the population in 1866 and 1877 was as follows:

Articles	1866	1877	Increase
Bacon and ham . . .	2·13	8·04	277 per cent.
Wheat, per lb. . . .	104·50	208·26	94 ,,
Sugar, per lb.. . . .	21·21	64·96	57 ,, .
Tea, per lb.	3·42	4·52	32 ,,
Tobacco, per lb. . . .	1·39	1·49	10 ,,
Spirits, gallons . . .	1·01	1·23	21 ,,
Malt, bushels	1·82	1·92	5 ,,

'In no other country,' as the 'Economist' truly remarks, 'are the wages more liberal, but in no other

[margin note: Professor Levi's warning against extravagance.]

country are they more wastefully used, than in the
United Kingdcm.' From the high wages earned
during a period of exceptional prosperity an accumulation should be made, as a provision for the cycle of
years of · depression which will surely follow, the
intensity and duration of the crisis being generally
proportionate to the height of prosperity which had
preceded the reaction.

Evidences of thrift among the people. Mr. Levi's admonitions are not superfluous. It is
gratifying, however, to be able to show unmistakable
evidence that the virtues of thrift and forethought
prevail widely among the masses. In February last
771,772 paupers were in receipt of relief, being an
increase of 61,858 over the corresponding date in the
previous year. The increase had taken place chiefly
in the manufacturing districts. The severity of the
winter and the depression of trade had probably
proved an insupportable burden to the lowest classes
of the population. The general well being, however,
of the people, notwithstanding the lifeless condition of
several of our greatest industries, is indicated in the
steady increase in the deposits in the savings-banks.

Mr. Morley has published some remarkable returns
showing what considerable progress has already been
made by the·operatives in the Manchester district in
this direction.

Building societies. Of a total number of 114 local building societies
75 sent in returns as to the condition of their accounts.

Total number of members	50,690
Annual income	£6,584,300
Share deposits	£4,125,500

Loans with interest	£6,159,100
Mortgage securities	£10,471,500
Contingent reserve fund	£239,231

These are encouraging statistics. The more general the ownership of property, especially of property consisting of a house or a plot of. land, however small, the more strongly the fabric of society is cemented together.

The savings-banks had a capital of 53,000,000*l.* at Savings banks. the beginning of 1871. It was increased by 8,610,231*l.* in the three succeeding years. The accumulation continued, as we learn from the report of the Registrar-General, even in the three succeeding years of flagging industry, during which 8,612,236*l.* were laid by, chiefly by the working classes.

In his recent speech at Westminster, Mr. Smith said : ' On January 11, 1877, the deposits in the savings-banks were 70,963,555*l.* ; in January 1878, 73,534,000*l.*—that is to say, in the year 1878 an additional 2,600,000*l.* had been deposited in the savings-banks. Well, on January 11, 1879, after a year of very great depression, the working classes had managed to increase these deposits by 1,300,000*l.*—that is to say, the deposits, which were in 1878 73,534,000*l.*, were in January, 1879, 74,637,000*l.* I think that is a very significant fact. It shows that after all, though there is great distress, there is also a considerable amount of what I call local wealth. Seventy-four millions represent the savings of the working classes. The increase of 1,300,000*l.* represents the amount which they could afford to put by after having spent all that was necessary for their own comfort, after having withdrawn all that was necessary to keep them alive. That was going on this year since January 11 in a very remarkable manner. I have tables from the Post Office, which form only a portion of these figures, showing that on January 18 the deposits were 266,000*l.* for the week against withdrawals of 178,000*l.*, being an increase of deposits of upwards of 88,000*l.* On January 25 the deposits were 276,000*l.* against withdrawals 174,000*l.* ; so that the difference in favour of deposits was 93,000*l.*; and on February 1 the deposits were 312,000*l.* against 136,000*l.* withdrawals, so that the deposits were more than double the amount of the withdrawals. Now, I think that fact should show you that, although there is distress, there is a very considerable number of persons who are fairly well off in this country, belonging to the working classes, and the times are not universally so bad as they are said to be.'

According to the ' Industrial Review,' at the end of 1871 the total sum due to savings-banks depositors was 55,845,000*l.*, in round numbers ; the Post Office banks owing 17,025,000*l.*, the trustee banks 38,820,000*l.* At the close of 1877 the grand total due was 72,979,000*l.* ; Post Office, 28,741,000*l.* ; and the older banks, 44,238,000*l.* The six years' accumulations, made up of money saved and interest allowed thereon, reached 17,135,000*l.*, the mean annual accumulations being 2,856,000*l.* The increments at the postal banks were in sum more than twice those effected at the trustee savings-banks—the respective amounts being 11,716,000*l.* and 5,419,000*l.*

It has been highly satisfactory to be able to bring together, in this brief review of the material progress of the population, such indications of improvement both in the earnings and in the comfort enjoyed by the masses of the people. Wages, notwithstanding the too frequent fluctuations in their amount, tend, and ought to tend, to become more and more liberal. We may venture to hope that the supply of food may for a considerable period increase more rapidly than the population.

The material condition of the people tells directly on their moral and social progress. 'Better motives,' said Mr. Bagehot, 'better impulses rather, come from a good body; worse motives or worse impulses come from a bad body; improper conditions tend to improper human action; deteriorated conditions tend to deprave human action.' We do not expect as much from St. Giles's as from Belgravia. Canon Farrar, in the preface to his noble sermons on 'Eternal Hope,' has given expression to the same sentiments. ' Clergymen of all denominations,' he says, ' bewail their utter inability to prevent the spread of materialism and infidelity. I, for my part, cannot be surprised at this, when I feel within me the revolt of an indignant conscience against much which is taught as an essential part of a gospel of salvation. It was the doctrine of endless torments which made an infidel of the elder Mill. Does the reader suppose that in this respect he stood alone? Those who work among our London artisans know well the effect that the doctrine has on them. Never was there a wilder and more monstrous

Moral and social progress of the people influenced by their material condition.

delusion than that it is efficacious in deterring them from sin! "I am but thirty-two; I am a coke-burner, which has injured my lungs. I have worked seven days and seven nights, on and off. You see I haven't had my chance," said a poor man to Mrs. Marie Hilton. "Do you really think, master, that God Almighty will put me in fire for ever and ever, after putting me in this here mud all my lifetime?" asked a rough navvy of a City missionary, not long ago.' In the social and the material order of things, no less than in the spiritual, hope inspires, despair discourages exertion.

In bringing about the improvements which we have been able to record, Parliament has done its part. The recent Acts relating to trades unions, conspiracy, and arbitration have been described by Mr. Howell, in his recent volume, as the charters of the social and industrial freedom of the people.

In their immunity from the conscription the working men of the United Kingdom enjoy an enviable advantage. Our country is safely guarded by the sea and by its volunteer defenders. The subjects of the military despots on the Continent look with envy on our military system, which secures an army strong enough for our defence, but which numbers no reluctant conscript in its ranks, no soldiers forcibly torn away from homes that can ill afford to lose them.

CHAPTER XVI.

SOCIAL AND MORAL CONDITION OF THE PEOPLE.

Perfection consists in becoming something rather than in having something.... Conscience and self-renouncement are righteousness.—MATTHEW
ARNOLD, *Culture and Dogma.*

Riches do not gain hearty respect: they only produce external
attention. Promiscuous hospitality is not the way to gain real influence
you offend more people than you please.—DR. JOHNSON.

> Nous ne recevons l'existence
> Qu'afin de travailler pour nous ou pour autrui.
> De ce devoir sacré quiconque se dispense
> Est puni par la Providence,
> Par le besoin, ou par l'ennui.—FLORIAN.

> The poor, inured to drudgery and distress,
> Act without aim, think little, and feel less,
> And nowhere, but in feign'd Arcadian scenes,
> Taste happiness, or know what pleasure means.—COWPER.

No man is obliged to do as much as he can do. A man is to have a
part of his life to himself.—DR. JOHNSON.

> Sweet recreation barr'd, what doth ensue
> But moody and dull melancholy,
> Kinsman to grim and comfortless despair,
> And at her heels a huge infectious troop
> Of pale distemperatures and foes to life?
> *Comedy of Errors,* act v. sc. 1.

The temper of the Puritan gentleman was just, noble, and self-con-
trolled. The larger geniality of the age that had passed away shrank into an
intense tenderness within the narrower circle of the home. 'He was as
kind a father,' says Mrs. Hutchinson of her husband, 'as dear a brother,
as good a master, as faithful a friend as the world had.' Passion was replaced by a manly purity. The new sobriety and self-restraint marked
itself even in his change of dress. Colonel Hutchinson 'left off very early

the wearing of anything that was costly, yet in his plainest negligent habit appeared very much a gentleman.' 'He had a loving and sweet courtesy to the poorest, and would often employ many spare hours with the commonest soldiers and poorest labourers.' 'He never disdained the meanest, nor flattered the greatest.'—GREEN, *Short History of the English People.*

I will neither always be busy and doing, nor ever shut up in nothing but thoughts. Yet that which some call idleness, I will call the sweetest part of my life, and that is my thinking.—OWEN FELTHAM, *Resolves.*

Everyone must seek to secure his independence, but he need not be rich. The old Confucius in China admitted the benefit, but stated the limitation: 'If the search for riches were sure to be successful, though I should become a groom with whip in hand, I will do so. As the search may not be successful, I will follow after that which I love.'—LONG-FELLOW, *Notes to Translation of Dante.*

Chacun doit se défier de ce qu'il y a d'exclusif et d'absolu dans son esprit. . . .' Pour moi, je m'irriterais d'un monde où tous mèneraient le même genre de vie que moi. Comme vous, je me suis imposé, en qualité d'ancien clerc, d'observer strictement la règle des mœurs ; mais je serais désolé qu'il n'y eût pas des gens du monde pour représenter une vie plus libre. Je ne suis pas riche ; mais je ne pourrais guère vivre dans une société où il n'y aurait pas de gens riches.'—RENAN.

Social influences more valuable than legislation.
I HAVE faithfully endeavoured to describe the actual condition of trade, and the relations between labour and capital, as they are in our country at the present time. There has been much on which we may congratulate ourselves, though some dark clouds are still gathering in the sky. It is a maxim of our law that there is no wrong without a remedy. We cannot contemplate the existence of an evil and not desire to remove it; but the remedies for the avoidable imperfections of our commercial and industrial organisation are to be provided rather by good social influences than by legislation. The legislator has done his part by removing the shackles from industry, and by placing the workman and his employer on an equal footing in the

courts of law. The work begun in the legislature must be followed up by social reforms.

The altered and less friendly relations between capital and labour were attributed by many witnesses before the French Commission of Inquiry into this subject, to the rapid extension of Paris, and to the separation of the various classes of society in distinct quarters of the city. The development of modern industry tends more and more to the concentration of operations in large establishments, equipped with costly machinery, and requiring a considerable capital. Such changes necessarily widen the gulf between the workman and his master.

A witness before the Commission gave the follow- *Separation of workmen and employers.* ing testimony : ' Formerly we were twenty in number in the workshop of ——. We were all friends together, and in the evening we sat down to supper with our employers by the light of a candle. To-day 400 men are employed in the same workshop, and they are gathered together from every quarter. You have pushed us away into the outskirts of Paris. Formerly mutual courtesies, and, if need were, mutual kindnesses and good offices, were exchanged between the workmen living on the fourth story and the more favoured dwellers on the first floor. The mother of the family on the first floor set a good example to the matron on the fourth story. The social relation between them was that of patron and client. To-day we are penned up in separate quarters of a great city, and the influence of a good example in our superiors is no longer felt.'

A A

Report of
the French
Commis-
sion on the
relations
between
employers
and work-
men. The conclusions formed by the committee, after hearing much evidence to the same effect, are embodied at length in their report. The workshop has ceased to be the workman's home : it is now a sort of neutral ground, in which persons jointly concerned in the production of some useful commodity are temporarily located. The distribution and division of the value created during this temporary partnership can no longer be made the subject of a friendly agreement as in the old days, when these things were settled by a sort of family compact.

M. Jules
Favre's
report. In his separate report to the French Commission M. Jules Favre insists in forcible terms on the general duty of masters to maintain kindly personal relations with their men. Taking a general view of the intercourse between men and their masters, not only in Paris, but throughout France, he declares himself convinced that the prevailing uneasiness and distrust are the result of a misunderstanding rather than a real antagonism, and that an agreement, based on an appreciation of the interests, which they have in common, might be established, if employers would but appreciate their social duties to their workmen.

The population of Paris has ever been largely recruited from the provinces. Its most valuable as well as its most dangerous elements are supplied by the adventurous spirits, who crowd into the capital with hopes which must be too often disappointed.

> Dans la confusion que ce grand monde apporte
> Il y vient de tous lieux des gens de toute sorte :
> Et dans toute la France il est fort peu d'endroits
> Dont il n'est le rebut aussi bien que le choix.[1]

[1] Corneille, 'Le Menteur.'

In the present day the employer may be a joint-stock company, managed by directors whose salaries depend upon the profits realised, and whose demands upon the workmen can only be resisted by combined action. The free workman, even under the actual organisation of industry, has, it is needless to say, unspeakable advantages over men who labour in a state of bondage. The difference between the conditions of labour on a large and a small scale is to some extent illustrated in the following remarks of the late Mr. Bagehot. 'The slavery,' he says, 'in which a master owns a few slaves, whom he well knows, and daily sees, is not an intolerable state. Wholesale slavery, under a great owner, who, so far from knowing each slave, can hardly tell how many gangs of them he works, is an abominable state.'

[margin note: Effect of the concentration of industry.]

In Great Britain both the ownership of land and of the capital invested in industry is far more concentrated than in France, Switzerland, Germany, and the United States. The 33,000,000 acres of land in England and Wales are owned by 932,000 proprietors, and produce a gross estimated rental of 99,352,000*l.* We have 1,815 owners of from 2,000 to 5,000 acres, and 875 owners of estates exceeding 5,000 acres. The total rental of the estates exceeding 5,000 acres amounts to 22,000,000*l.* One single individual is returned as owner of estates exceeding 100,000 acres, producing a rental of 162,000*l.* Turning to the other end of the scale, the total number of owners of less than one acre is 703,289, and their rental produces a comparatively unimportant amount.

[margin note: Distribution of ownership in land.]

Commenting on the Doomsday Book, lately prepared at the instance of Mr. Bright, Mr. Shaw-Lefevre points out that from the total of 301,378 entries of proprietors in the United Kingdom above one acre, great reductions must be made, and after deducting owners of house property, duplicate entries, holders of glebe lands, and corporate bodies and charities, the most liberal estimate cannot put the number of landowners at more than 200,000, of which the owners in England are less than 170,000, of Ireland 20,000, and Scotland under 10,000.

The agricultural population of France numbers 18,500,000. Of these 3,141,000 are farmers renting land, and 3,250,000 are workmen employed by the day, or rather, taking other employment, when not engaged in the cultivation of their own patrimony.

The annual product of French industry has been valued by M. Maurice Block at twelve milliards of francs, of which commodities of the value of 6,360,000,000 francs are produced by industry organised on a large scale, and 6,442,000,000 francs by small industrial establishments.

Sympathy between various classes in England.

The concentration of wealth and administrative authority in our own country would have led to greater social evils, but for the counteracting sympathies exhibited by many privileged persons for their humbler neighbours. I do not speak of public subscriptions, but of that sincere solicitude for the welfare of others which is found in the highest ranks, which flows from the pen of the man of letters, which sends forth young men of rank and wealth on self-denying missions to the lowly dwellings of the poor, and which leads so many ladies to convert a life of leisure into one of unceasing ministration to necessity.

Let me give an instance. The custom prevails in Kent of employing the migratory population of St. Giles to pick the hops, for which the county is renowned. These people come from a distance to their work, miserably equipped with the means of preparing food. Their lodgings are of the rudest. Their earnings are adequate, but their lives are singularly comfortless, especially in rainy weather. Hop-picking in Kent.

During a short visit last autumn in Kent, I had an opportunity of watching the efforts of certain ladies, who had no personal interest in the result of the hop-picking, but who, out of pure kindness of heart, provided hundreds of hop-pickers, at cost price, with tea and soup, meat-pies and bread—in short, with all the necessaries of life. The labours of these benevolent ladies were most arduous. They were wrought in the seclusion of a rural district, not to be seen of men, nor yet as a reward to dependants and followers for their faithful services. The recipients of these favours were 'wanderers from afar, and sympathy with strangers, whose lot seemed hard, was the only motive which actuated their benefactors. It is gladdening to turn aside from the recent strike of the agricultural labourers to a scene such as I have so imperfectly described.

The Rev. Baldwin Brown has lately given this encouraging testimony: 'The more I see of classes in which at first sight selfishness seems to reign, the more am I struck with the measure in which daily thought for others, and work for others, enter into their lives.'

Let us acknowledge gratefully the many admirable efforts to civilise the masses and relieve the necessities of the poor to which the ladies of England devote themselves. It is in the schoolroom, at the cottage door, and by the uneasy pallet of the sick and suffering, that the hearts of the people are won, and the best social influences are created. M. Renan has enlarged with touching eloquence on the profound importance of the influence of women on education and the moral tone of society :

‘ L'éducation, c'est le respect de ce qui est réellement bon, grand et beau ; c'est la politesse, charmante vertu, qui supplée à tant d'autres vertus ; c'est le tact, qui est presque de la vertu aussi. Ce n'est pas un professeur qui peut apprendre tout cela. . . . Ces choses-là s'apprennent dans l'atmosphère où l'on vit, dans le milieu social où l'on est placé : elles s'apprennent par la vie de famille, non autrement.

‘ La femme profondément sérieuse et morale peut seule guérir les plaies de notre temps, refaire l'éducation de l'homme, ramener le goût du bien et du beau. Il faut pour cela reprendre l'enfant, ne pas le confier à des soins mercenaires, ne se séparer de lui que pendant les heures consacrées à l'enseignement des classes, à aucun âge ne le laisser tout-à-fait séparé de la société des femmes.'

One or two further questions still demand consideration in relation to the subjects which we have passed under review. And, first, let us ask ourselves,

What should be the final aim of our industrial organisation? Have we made any real progress, morally and socially, if the mass of the population is increasing in numbers only, and not in comfort and civilisation?

The eloquent workman Finance, whose speech has been translated by Mr. Harrison, reminded the Workmen's Congress at Lyons of a saying by Pierre Lafitte, to the effect that 'to produce furiously that we may consume indefinitely seems the one ideal that men imagine for human life.' To read the letters addressed by some of their correspondents to the daily journals, it would seem as if they too thought that to secure the most economical production of commodities is the highest aim of a nation. It is certain that the conditions under which alone competition in trade can be successfully conducted must be respected. We shall find no sale for our goods in neutral markets, if the same goods can be purchased more cheaply elsewhere. But at least a reduction in wages should be regarded as a regrettable necessity; and every step in advance, which the workman can make without injustice to his employers, should be hailed with satisfaction.

A land overcrowded with a dense mass of ill-fed, ill-clothed, and poorly-housed inhabitants, is surely a miserable spectacle. Morality is depressed in the dismal alleys of our great cities, where sharpness of wit is dearly purchased by the loss of rural simplicity. It is, to quote the admirable verse of Milton:

> Knowledge of good bought dear by knowing ill.[1]

[1] 'Paradise Lost,' ii. 222.

Modern Europe contains, alas! populations in whom it might almost seem that the Mosaic prediction had been fulfilled : 'In the morning thou shalt say, Would God it were even! and at even thou shalt say, Would God it were morning!'[1]

And yet if low wages were a means to cheap production—which, however, I do not admit—and if cheapness of production be the ultimate aim of industry, it is towards such a condition that we ought to desire to see ourselves reduced. Numbers are indeed a source of strength, but only so when their reasonable physical wants are supplied, and when they have been sufficiently educated to be enabled to ascend from the drudgery of their daily toil to the nobler concerns of life. It is the lot of man to labour, but his labour should not be so incessant or so exacting as to leave no space for thought. As Mr. Bagehot said, ' Refinement is only possible when leisure is possible.' To work hard sixteen hours a day may be good for trade, but not for humanity.

Need of recreation.
Throughout his ' Political Economy ' Mr. Mill was remorseless in the close limits he placed on the kind of labour he was prepared to accept as productive ; but when he came to deal with the moral and social aspects of human life he pleaded in glowing terms for leisure, and space, and wholesome recreation. I have endeavoured to press the importance of recreation in a paper originally read before the Co-operative Congress at Halifax, and recently republished.

Music for the poor.
I am glad that attention has been invited to this

---

[1] Deut. xxviii. 07.

subject in a recent paper by Professor Jevons. The sweet sounds of music give a delightful sense of repose to an audience tired with the labours of the day, and which needs rest for mind and body. The Government and the municipalities should make an effort to give to the poor denizens of our vast cities this most innocent source of enjoyment.

All who care for the welfare of the masses, and desire to foster sentiments of mutual regard and kindness among all classes of society, will recognise and warmly acknowledge the admirable efforts made by a number of accomplished persons to provide musical entertainments for the poor. We ought to be grateful for the courage and self-devotion, with which they have sallied forth into the dingiest rookeries of the metropolis, on their truly charitable and humanising mission.

Bands and libraries can be best supplied by the combined efforts of an urban population ; but the inhabitants of great towns are never so truly happy as when they can exchange their crowded and monotonous alleys for the freshness, the beauty, and the solitude of the country. Let us be grateful to the zealous defenders of our parks and forests, our commons and open spaces. I remember to have heard the fervid denunciation of a working man at a conference of the Labour Representation League, in which the number of acres in Scotland not under cultivation was quoted as a ground of complaint against the Land Laws. The orator had perhaps forgotten that the moors he grudged to see surrendered to the sheep, the

Access to open spaces.

grouse, the·deer, and the tourist, are covered with snow during a prolonged winter. An agriculturist in search of a farm would direct his attention far more profitably to the prairies, or the valleys of New Zealand, than towards the hoary summits of the Grampians.

The same question was revived on a more recent occasion by the proposal for supplying water to Manchester from Thirlmere. A great city must be secured from drought; but the invasion of one of the few districts of the kingdom, which are still preserved inviolate for the lover of nature, was a lamentable necessity. Mr. Mill has enforced the arguments urged by Mr. Forster against the dreaded projects of the engineer in an admirable passage : ' A world from which solitude is extirpated is a very poor ideal. Solitude, in the sense of being often alone, is essential to any depth of meditation or of character ; and solitude in the presence of natural beauty and grandeur is the cradle of thoughts and aspirations, which are not only good for the individual, but which society could ill do without. Nor is there much satisfaction in contemplating the world with nothing left to the spontaneous activity of nature ; with every rood of land brought into cultivation which is capable of growing food for human beings; every flowery waste or natural pasture ploughed up, all quadrupeds and birds which are not domesticated for man's use exterminated as his rivals for food ; every hedgerow or superfluous tree rooted out, and scarcely a place left where a wild shrub or flower could grow without being eradicated as a weed in the name of improved agriculture.'

Let me ask one more question as to the most bene- Employ-
ment of
ficial application of their resources by those who have large for-
the command of wealth.   No doubt the exceptionally tunes in
the most
rich are comparatively few in number, and their united beneficial
way.
accumulations produce no sensible influence on the
economic progress of a great country.   But rich men
are too conspicuous to be able to live in unenvied and
unquestioned enjoyment of their wealth.   It is not
unimportant, therefore, to show that large fortunes may
possibly be used for the mutual benefit of the capitalist
and of society at large.   Questions of legal right apart,
can it under any circumstances be made better for
society that an income of 100,000*l.* a year should be
concentrated in the hands of a single individual rather
than distributed in equal proportions among twenty or
fifty heads of families?

Under no circumstances is it good for the country
that there should be a large number of individuals
enjoying exceptional fortune, in painful contrast with
the less favoured condition of their neighbours.

> Where, then, ah! where shall poverty reside
> To 'scape the pressure of contiguous pride?

On the other hand, more numerous examples of
grasping selfishness will probably be presented among
the small owners of cottage property than among the
larger proprietors.   The working classes are very
generous to one another; but working men, who have
advanced to the dignity of employers, are often the
most exacting in their dealings with labour.

In a social and intellectual point of view there can
scarcely be a doubt as to the answer that we ought to

give to the question I have ventured to propose.
For the diffusion of culture, and science, and art, for
carrying on works of beneficence, the labours of twenty
or fifty persons must be more effective than the labours
of a single individual. On the other hand there are
operations, such as the beautifying and improvement
of great cities, the development of the agricultural
resources of a considerable district, or the creation of
facilities of communication by sea and land—the Menai
Bridge, the Mont Cenis Railway, the first Atlantic Cable,
the Crystal Palace, are examples—where the object
sought to be attained, while conducive to the well-
being of society, is one which cannot prove remunerative to the promoters until after an interval of many
years. Under such circumstances the capital required
can only be furnished by the State, or by men whose
incomes are in excess of their immediate wants. The
resources employed in carrying out undertakings of
the kind indicated will probably be admitted to be of
some use to the world.

Adam Smith points with approval to another mode
of expending a large fortune.   ' Noble palaces,' he says,
' and great collections are frequently an ornament and
an honour, not only to the neighbourhood in which
they are placed, but to the whole country. Versailles
is an ornament and an honour to France ; Stowe and
Wilton to England.'

A society in which, by a rigorous code of sump-
tuary laws, every individual was kept on the same
level as regards external display, might perhaps be dull
and displeasing by such exact uniformity.

While the sanction of Adam Smith may be claimed for the encouragement of the arts, the great economist would not have viewed with the same indulgence the marshalling together of that useless array of 42,000 indoor male servants, who are said to have been thrown out of employment during the present crisis. Would that the usages of society might be so far modified as to prevent the reassembling of these useless symbols of our social pride !

It is almost superfluous to point out how much the progress of the higher education in every country has been promoted by the judicious assistance of the wealthy. The work begun by the founders of the colleges in our most venerable seats of learning has been followed up with no stinting hand by some of our own contemporaries.

It is in helping others to help themselves, and in the encouragement of spontaneous efforts for improvement, that the most fruitful employment of affluence may be found. The results brought about by a lax administration of the Poor Laws have given a warning, which cannot be neglected, of the mischief done by indiscriminate charity. Large gifts are a small sacrifice to a man of superfluous wealth. The duties of charity, rightly understood, demand a more serious act of self-sacrifice than a mere gift of money. The donor is responsible that his alms are judiciously applied ; and he must employ some portion of his time in seeing to their appropriate distribution. The gifts which involve a real act of self-sacrifice are gifts of things, the loss of which we feel in our own persons, whether in physical

True charity.

suffering, or in toil and labour unselfishly bestowed in ministering to others.   An illustrious example of self-devotion is recorded by Mr. Green in his 'History of the Reign of Queen Elizabeth.'   Sidney, the nephew of Lord Leicester, the idol of his time, flung away his life to save the English army in Flanders.   As he lay dying they brought a cup of water to his fevered lips. Sidney bade them give it to a soldier who was stretched on the ground beside him.   'Thy necessity,' he said, 'is greater than mine.'

I bring these papers to a close at a time of sore discouragement for British industry and commerce, a time when gaunt hunger and brooding discontent are stalking abroad, a time when the inequalities of fortune embitter the miseries of commercial failure and discredit.   Those who have seen their resources dwindling away in a succession of adverse years, may perhaps find some comfort in the conviction that many disappointments await the founders of great fortunes.

The burden of wealth.   The sumptuous mansion, lately risen from the ground, which has no associations, and cannot be occupied without a change in the habits and customs of a lifetime, is often found a burden rather than a satisfaction to its possessor.

> Cur invidendis postibus et novo
> Sublime ritu moliar atrium?
> Cur valle permutem Sabinâ
> Divitias operosiores?

A powerful French writer of fiction has put into the mouth of the hero of his story a description of his experiences.   In a less exaggerated degree, those expe-

riences are shared more widely than is commonly
supposed.   It is thus that the 'Nabab,' in defending
his election for Corsica, is represented as addressing
the assembled deputies of the French Republic.   'Ah!
I have known what it is to fight with misery, hand to
hand, and it is a dire struggle.   But to contend with a
superfluity of riches, to defend one's happiness, honours,
and peace of mind, behind a crumbling heap of gold,
that crushes you as it falls, is a far more repugnant
and disheartening struggle.   Never, in the darkest hour
of poverty, have I suffered the weariness, the agony,
the sleepless anxieties, which wealth has brought upon
me—wealth, that dreaded, hated, choking burden.'

Mr. Carlyle has depicted with powerful touches
the superior felicity of a life begun and ended in the
same station, and amid the scenes, which have been
familiar from infancy:

'The wealth of a man is the number of things
which he loves and blesses, which he is loved and
blessed by.   The herdsman in his poor clay shealing,
where his very cow and dog are friends to him, and
not a cataract but carries memories for him, and not a
mountain-top but nods old recognition; his life, all
encircled in blessed mother's-arms, is it poorer than
Slick's, with the ass-loads of yellow metal on his
back?'

The trained and philosophic mind finds, indeed,
deep pleasures in a contemplative existence.   To the
active, anxious, practical man of business a life of ease
can seldom prove a life of happiness.   He regrets, when
it is too late, the power, authority, and influence which

he formerly wielded, and which he lost by his retirement from the sphere of his successful labours. The hopes he would fain rest on his successor are dashed aside by repeated examples of riches misapplied. The inheritance of wealth has rarely proved the source of pure and unalloyed happiness. It exposes the feeble to temptation ; it casts on stronger natures a heavy load of responsibility.

369

CHAPTER XVII.

MR. CHAPLIN'S MOTION FOR A ROYAL COMMISSION ON
AGRICULTURAL DEPRESSION.

I KNOW not what kindly motive it was which induced Mr. Chaplin to pay me the compliment of asking me to second the motion for the appointment of a Royal Commission to inquire into the causes of, and the remedies for, the distressed condition of British agriculture which he recently submitted to the House of Commons in an able speech; but it so happens that while he is specially identified with the proprietors of land, I am connected perhaps more closely than any other member of the House by tradition and family ties with that less distinguished, but interesting and fast disappearing class, the yeomen farmers of the northern counties. I felt the greater satisfaction in seconding the motion for a Royal Commission, because I was anxious that the farmers and the landed interest generally should be assured that they had friends on both sides of the House, and that any reasonable proposal for their welfare would receive the full and impartial consideration of Parliament.

The case for a Royal Commission was very fairly stated in the 'Economist' newspaper. 'We are,' said the writer, 'in the midst of the most extended and

The agricultural question in Parliament.

B B

severe agricultural distress which has prevailed in this country for perhaps thirty years, and it becomes necessary to investigate the development of an industry, which is the largest and most powerful and diffused of any in the United Kingdom.'

The farmer's difficulties in face of competition.

If the difficulties of the British farmer were such only as are incidental to a succession of rainy seasons, it would be absurd to ask for a Royal Commission. The Meteorological Office would be the proper authority to consult, and we know how little their science can do for us in the way of prediction; but the landed interest of this country is now, for the first time, brought face to face with a most extensive and vigorous competition. It is a competition which it is the interest of the consumer to encourage, and one with which the Legislature will be too wise to interfere, but it is also a competition which must have very serious effects on the agriculture of this country, and which may possibly result in throwing some of our inferior lands permanently out of cultivation.

It cannot be said that English agriculture, under the conditions which have until lately prevailed, has been unsuccessful or unskilful. Monsieur Léonce de Lavergne, in his able work on English Agriculture, has done full justice to the ability and enterprise of our farmers. Our land, though on the whole inferior, has yielded more wheat per acre than that of any other country, and, taking sheep and cattle together, more animals are raised for the butcher in England than in any part of the Continent. The practical skill of the British farmer has been conspicuous in the management of sheep. The improvements in the breed were commenced in Leicestershire by Mr. Bakewell, and the results in the increased production of mutton are signally illustrated by M. de Lavergne. He says that assuming that France and the United Kingdom each possess an equal number of sheep, which number he took at 35,000,000—it is actually 32,500,000—each country would obtain from its flocks an equal quantity of wool, but the weight of mutton, assuming 8,000,000 sheep to be slaughtered annually, would be, in France, 39,600,000; in England, 99,000,000 stone.

The United States, however, have lately poured into our markets such copious and increasing supplies of wheat and animal food, that it has become evident that our old-established systems of cultivation, however perfected they may be by the expenditure of the capital of the landlord, and by the skill of the occupying tenantry, must undergo a very serious change. It is most important, therefore, that the landed interest of this country should be informed, through the inquiries of the proposed Commission, as to the probable course of trade with the United States in agricultural produce. What are the articles in which it is hopeless to undertake a competition with the superior natural resources of the great Continent of the West? What are the articles in which our soil and climate and vicinity to our own markets give us the greatest advantage? What steps should be taken to relieve a landowner, whose resources are exhausted, of the responsibility of ownership? Are our arable lands rented too high? What additional securities should be given to tenants? Are the usual conditions in leases too stringent? On all these subjects we may look for valuable suggestions from the report of the Commission. And first as to the mode of cultivation.

Wheat-growing capabilities of the United States.

The recent development of foreign importations has been so remarkable, and it has so direct a bearing on the subject of Mr. Chaplin's motion, that I shall venture to offer a few details extracted from the mass of information on the subject, which has been placed in my hands by Mr. Lee Higginson, of Boston, Mr. Clutton, Mr. Dunlop, and others. The natural resources of the United States for the growth of wheat are unbounded. So long ago as 1871, after a most extended journey through the United States, Mr. Dunlop informs me that he felt convinced that as growers of wheat the Americans would run us hard. Their success is due, not to superior husbandry, nor yet to the stimulus of ownership, not to superior science, not to the more advantageous distribution of the land in respect to the acreage occupied by individual holders. The one pre-eminent advantage of America over the United Kingdom consists in an almost boundless tract of fertile soil. In the greater part of their wheat-growing country, the cultivation is done in the rudest fashion. The straw is left to rot on the ground, and so long as the ground retains its primitive fertility, no rotation of crops is necessary, and no manure is required. When the land becomes exhausted, which it does in four or five years, it is abandoned, and the farmer moves on to another allotment of the same virgin soil, in all probability perfectly level, with no stones, no roots, nothing to interfere with the operations of the rude husbandry practised in those regions. It is by their agricultural resources that the United States have at length recovered from five years of unparalleled depression. Thousands of artisans, thrown out of employment in the ironworks and factories of New England, have permanently changed their occupation from manufactures to agriculture, and found these fertile lands ready to receive them. The new lands settled in 1878 may be estimated, according to Mr. Victor Drummond, at twenty millions of acres, and half a million souls have changed their locations, and to a great extent their vocations, within the year. Meanwhile, the production of wheat has increased from 287,745,000 bushels in 1869 to 365,094,000 bushels in 1877. It is a remarkable circumstance that while the commercial depression, which has led to this extensive migration westwards, is mainly due to the too rapid extension of railways, it is by those same railways that the new settlers are now enabled to send their produce from the far West to the Eastern States, and even to European markets. Not only has the acreage under wheat in the United States been increased in extraordinary proportions, but the weather in recent years has been exceptionally favourable.

The extra growth has been further stimulated by the progressive rise of prices in this country from 45s. 11d. per quarter in 1869–70 to 61s. 3d. in

1873–74.   The result has been a rapid increase in our importations.   We now derive half our bread from foreign lands.   .

In view of the various circumstances to which I have adverted, we can scarcely resist the conclusion that, as a wheat-growing country, the prospects of the United Kingdom are shadowy in the extreme, and that, except for the production of straw, it would scarcely be worth while to continue the cultivation of wheat.   This is one of those subjects which demand consideration more especially in relation to the prospects of foreign supply, and the aid of a Royal Commission will be valuable in collecting information and interrogating the most competent advisers.

Modifica-
tion of
produce to
meet the
crisis.

This question of the description of produce to which English agriculture should be especially directed is of the last importance both to owners and occupiers. It is said that the English farmer can afford to pay a rent equal in amount to the freight and railway charges on produce imported from America, but this can only be true when the land which he cultivates is equal in point of fertility to the soil cultivated by his American rival rent free, or the article which he is producing is protected from competition by difficulties of transport.   For example, our consumption of milk might be largely increased, and the supply of milk must be a monopoly in the hands of the British farmer.   Where, however, the land is inferior, and it can only be used for cultivating the same produce which the American farmer is sending into our market from land of higher fertility, for which he pays nothing, the British landowner can no longer obtain a rent from the occupier equal to the full amount of the freight on American produce.

Turning from wheat to animal food, we find that the importations from abroad have increased in a still more rapid ratio. According to Mr. Caird the value of our importations of animal food has risen in the period 1857–76 from 7,000,000*l.* sterling to 36,000,000*l.* It seems probable that the trade will be prosecuted with ever-increasing activity. A recent writer in the ' Economist ' points out that the shipments of live stock across the Atlantic have increased tenfold within the last two years. ' With meat,' he says, ' at present prices, and maize fetching only a guinea a quarter in Liverpool, an Illinois farmer has no difficulty in deciding which business will pay best.' According to a calculation published by Mr. Clark in the Journal of the Royal Agricultural Society, the average meat supply of the United Kingdom in 1876 was in the following proportions: Meat from home animals, 79 per cent. ; meat from imported live animals, 6¼ per cent. ; imported fresh meat 2, and imported salt meat 13 per cent. The importations of fresh meat were doubled in 1877. It is a very important subject for inquiry by the proposed Commission, whether this importation is likely to continue and to increase in the same ratio as it has lately done. The answer must depend on the cost of rearing stock in the United States, on the rates of freight, and on the extent of loss by deterioration in transit.

First as to the cost of rearing cattle. I have lately

been in correspondence with some friends in Boston, from whom I have derived much interesting information. The business of the herdsman in the far West is conducted on a vast scale. There are herdsmen owning herds of not less than 75,000 head. They feed their cattle on the eastern slope of the Rocky Mountains. The country is very dry, and cannot therefore be cultivated. The herdsmen hold the land under the United States Government, and let their cattle roam over a vast extent of country, where they feed all the winter out of doors. They are making every effort to improve the quality of their stock, and meanwhile fill up their herds with large numbers of cattle from Texas. I am informed that the loss of cows is only about one per cent., and the loss of steers about half per cent., annually. It costs six dollars, or 25s., to bring into the world and raise a four-year-old steer. Such an animal is worth at Chicago from 35 to 45 dollars, and the cost of transport to Chicago is only eight dollars. At the present prices the herdsmen realise profits of from 25 to 40 per cent.

I have stated the facts as to the cost of rearing cattle in the United States at the present time from a source of information on which I can very confidently rely; but it is essential for the guidance of the agricultural interest that a more extended inquiry should be made by the instrumentality of a Royal Commission.

In considering the expediency of laying down arable land in pasture, it is important to ascertain whether the importation of American cattle is likely

to continue, and to increase at anything like the
present rate of development. It is said that beasts are
becoming scarce in Canada. Railways will not long
continue to carry cattle at the rates they have been
willing to accept in a time of severe commercial
depression. Mr. Dunlop, to whom I have already
referred, is of opinion that the cattle now being exported represent, as it were, an accumulation of several
years. They have been kept hitherto, like the cattle
of the Argentine Republic, for their fat, their hides,
and their horns. It is a question again whether the
United States Government will not levy a charge for
pasturage on the public lands, when the trade has
been developed, and is known to be lucrative to the
keepers of stock. A rent of one shilling an acre would
materially affect the cost of breeding and rearing
cattle, which roam over such vast territories. The
effect of any such charge might be the more seriously
felt, because the Americans cannot put an animal on
the market in less than from four to five years. A
grass-fed animal cannot be fit for sale in a shorter
period.

Having referred to the expense of rearing cattle in
the United States, I turn to the cost of transport to
this country. On this subject Mr. Caird remarks:
'Under any circumstances the English producer has
the advantage of at least a penny a pound in the cost
and risk of transport against his Transatlantic competitor. It is an advantage equal to 4*l.* on an average
ox. Of this natural advantage nothing can deprive
him, and with this he may rest content.' It is impor-

Cost of
transport
to Eng-
land.

tant, however, to observe that the cost of transporting live animals across the Atlantic has been very rapidly reduced since the publication of Mr. Caird's book. I am informed by my friend Mr. Beazley, the well-known shipowner of Liverpool, that while the steamers at first obtained freights of about 6*l.* per head the rates have gradually been reduced, until now they are only 2*l.* 10*s.* to 3*l.* per head. I have received from Liverpool further particulars, which show that the loss of cattle during the voyage is being rapidly diminished by the improved appliances, which are being perfected by experience. The following figures give the importation of cattle into Liverpool from the United States during the past year:—In February, out of 4,828 oxen shipped, 468 were lost on the passage. Of 1,277 sheep, 120 died. In March the importation was reduced by 2,000 head—1,829 oxen were shipped, but only 9 lost; 1,236 pigs were shipped, and 75 lost; 1,454 sheep were embarked, and 143 lost. In April 1,993 oxen were shipped, and only 8 lost; of sheep the number embarked was 8,818, and the loss 164. The number of pigs shipped was 2,925, and the loss 447. In May a great increase took place in the numbers of cattle landed in Liverpool from the United States, and the loss was comparatively small. There were shipped 6,281 head of cattle, and 187 lost; of sheep 13,064 were embarked, and 217 lost; of pigs 5,834 were shipped, and 418 lost.

Prices realised for imported cattle.

With regard to the prices realised for the imported cattle Mr. Beazley has furnished me with the following details. 'They find it,' he says, 'better to kill immediately after arrival, as the animals are shipped fat and in good condition, and as a rule, in the regular traders fitted for the purpose, arrive in fair condition.' He informs me that '422 head from Montreal, not in particularly good condition, sold at an average of 22*l.* 8*s.*; 349 head from Montreal in better condition sold at an average of 24*l.* 2*s.*; six superior beasts fetched 31*l.* per head; 440 beasts sold in London on June 2 at an average of 24*l.* 1*s. ex* " City of London," This steamer only lost six out of 600.'

I venture to say that such facts as those which I have quoted, facts relating to the probable cost of transport by railway in America and by steamer over the Atlantic, are facts which it is very difficult for any private individual connected with the landed interest to collect; but they have a most important bearing on the prospects of the British farmer. It is, indeed, impossible to devise a satisfactory system for the treatment of the soil of England, if our inquiry is limited to what is taking place in our own country. We must extend our survey to foreign countries, and a Royal Commission would greatly assist in completing and perfecting the investigation. *Value of information on foreign farming:*

Agriculture, again, is suffering in East Sussex from the serious fall in the value of hops, the fall being due to over-production on unsuitable land. Some fourteen years ago, the excise duty on hops was repealed. It was announced at the same time by Mr. Gladstone that the Custom House duty must be repealed. But although hops were thenceforward exposed to unrestricted competition from abroad, the foreign *as instanced in the case of hop cultivation.*

trade necessarily required a certain interval of time for its development. In the meanwhile, through a period of about four years, the growers of hops were in the happy but ephemeral position of emancipation from the Excise, while foreign competition was not yet felt. Farmers were making every year a profit on hop cultivation equal to the fee simple of their lands. Such a state of prosperity could not possibly endure. It attracted a severe foreign competition, and sent down the price of hops. Meanwhile the high profits had encouraged farmers to extend the cultivation of hops to land not at all adapted for the purpose. The only remedy must be to convert some of the hop-gardens into orchards. Farmers, however, are hanging on in the hope of a return to the old prices and the old profits. We know very well that this can never take place in the teeth of foreign competition; and the sooner the illusion is dispelled by the report of the Commission, the better it will be for the landlords and the occupiers of land. Not only are hop gardens very suitable for conversion into orchards, they are well adapted for market gardening. A far larger supply of vegetables could be absorbed in the English market, and the returns upon this description of produce grown in rotation with farm crops would be found very satisfactory. Market gardening might be widely extended by growing vegetables alternately with regular farm crops. Bedfordshire, Gloucestershire, Worcestershire, Herefordshire, contain a large area of land suitable for fruit. Cheshire is famous for its damsons;

and I find among my own tenants a general desire for the extension of their orchards.

Some may perhaps regard the proposed Commission with suspicion as a compromise with and an encouragement to the Protectionist party. But the Government know too well the almost universal feeling of the country to allow the door to be open to any such misunderstanding. If the Commission be appointed, care will, I am sure, be taken to exclude even the discussion of the exploded doctrines of protection. There are Protectionist countries which have flourished, not because, but in spite of protection. But we are not in that position. A large proportion of our population can only live by successful competition in the neutral markets with the rival industries of foreign nations. We can hold our own only by the cheapness of our productions. More than one-fourth of our total consumption of agricultural produce is supplied by foreign importations; and, if we make the workman pay dearer prices for his food and admit, as we must, unless we contemplate a gross injustice, that wages must be proportionately advanced, we shall raise up an obstacle to the success of our export trade which may prove fatal to its prosperity. In a recent powerfully-written appeal to the Protectionist party in France Monsieur Leroy Beaulieu has used arguments, which might be addressed with equal propriety to the Protectionists in this country. 'People,' he says, 'are talking of the national beef, the national mutton, and the national pork. Are then the wheat, the mutton, the beef, and the pork the only things which are

Freedom of the Commission from Protectionist tendencies.

national in France? Are not the stomachs of Frenchmen national also?' Happily the repeated and earnest exhortations addressed by M. Beaulieu to his Protectionist fellow-countrymen are not needed in this country. We have long since accepted the greatest happiness of the greatest number as the aim of our financial policy, and we shall not be shaken in our faith by the temporary misfortunes of any interest, however important, however solicitous we may be for its welfare and prosperity. Protection is proposed in the interest of the tenant farmers, but a reference to the debates in Parliament, during the period when the corn duties were imposed, will show that the advantage of the higher prices secured by the imposition of those duties was appropriated wholly by the landlords. The competition of the occupiers is stimulated by protective duties, while it is diminished by the increased local charges upon land. It is the landlord and not the farmer who benefits by protection, and bears the burden of the rates. The high prices had yielded no extra profits to the farmer and no extra wages to the labourer. They had been absorbed in increased rents.

Precedents for such an inquiry: Very numerous precedents may be cited for an inquiry, not with the view to legislation, but to the accumulation of valuable information for the guidance of the industry and the commerce of this country. Mr. Fawcett in his recent volume on free trade, has enumerated five parliamentary inquiries into agricultural distress between 1815 and 1845. Inquiries bearing upon our trade and commerce have been equally numerous, and I will refer to a very recent example. In 1866 a Royal Commission was appointed the Coal Supply Commission; to investigate the resources of the coalfield of the United Kingdom. In 1871 they presented a voluminous report on this subject. That report related mainly to questions in which the interests of the producer of coal were concerned. Again, in 1873, when the consumers were alarmed by the increase in the price of coal, Parliament undertook another inquiry. A Select Committee was appointed, which collected a most valuable body of evidence, bearing not only on the economic but also on the commercial aspect of the question. The committee concluded their report with an emphatic declaration that the true policy of the country, and the best inducement for the proper conduct of business, as well as the greatest stimulus to a return to a more just balance between supply and demand, was to leave trade free and to maintain an inflexible resolution of non-interference on the part of the State. It is not desired that there should be such legislative interference, on the part of the State, with the supply of agricultural produce, but it was urged by those who supported this motion for a Royal Commission, that, when a great interest is in difficulty, it may fairly appeal to the Legislature to assist in collecting information for its guidance. Turning from our the *enquête agricole* of France. own country to foreign nations, I find that in 1868 a full report was presented to the ·French Government on the state of agriculture in France. This *enquête agricole* was conducted by M. Monny de Mornay, and embraced every question connected with the land, such as inheritance, registry, advances of money for improvements, labour, drainage, railway and road communications, and protective duties.

Relief to
the farmer
a certain
result of
the Com-
mission.
Whatever the result of its appointment may be, the Royal Commission will in any case assist the agricultural interest to tide over a period of extreme depression and anxiety, and relieve the farmer from the impending gloom. He is depressed because he is brought for the first time into competition with foreign producers, of whose resources and capabilities he is very ignorant. It will be a solace to him to know that his difficulties are receiving the careful and impartial consideration of statesmen, whom he can trust, and to whose matured opinions, as embodied in the report of the Royal Commission, both the owner and the occupier of the soil will look with confidence for guidance. If we want the advice of the ablest and the most experienced of our own agriculturists, we know very well that many gentlemen who are peculiarly qualified to give advice and information in a time of emergency will readily answer the interrogatories of a Royal Commission, who would not undertake to write books on the subject. The report of a Royal Commission has this further advantage over the writings, however able, of a private individual on a controverted subject, that it is known to be the result of a comparison of many views and the conference and consultation of many minds.

I shall not venture to anticipate the conclusions which may be reached by a Royal Commission after an exhaustive inquiry, but it is impossible to have had under consideration the lamentable condition to which agriculture has been reduced in many parts of the country, without formulating some ideas as to the policy which ought to be adopted in the treatment of the land. The mode of cultivation I believe to be a far more important question for the future than a reduction of rent.

We have traced the changes, which have lately passed on the formerly prosperous agricultural interest, to the foreign importations; and the obvious deduction must be that the British farmer should throw his strength henceforward into the cultivation of those articles of produce, which suffer the greatest amount of deterioration from a long sea voyage, and which involve the heaviest charges for freight. It is shown in the return which has been obtained by the Member for East Retford, Mr. Foljambe, that, while the price of wheat has been kept down by extensive foreign importations—the average quotation, for example, for 1858, being given at 44*s.* 3*d.*, and for 1878 at 46*s.* 5*d.* per quarter—a great and sustained advance has taken place in the price of meat. Taking, for the purposes of comparison, the inferior sorts only, we find the price of beef advanced from 3*s.* 3*d.* per stone of 8 lbs. in 1858, to 4*s.* 8¾*d.* in 1878, while mutton rose from 3*s.* 4½*d.* to 5*s.* 6½*d.* in the same interval. *Mode of cultivation.*

These figures point very clearly to the extension of pasture rather than arable land. Another fact, quoted by Mr. Caird, leads us to a like conclusion. The gross annual value, he tells us, of the land of Great Britain assessed to the Income-Tax increased from 55,856,000*l.* in 1857, to 66,911,000*l.* in 1875. In *Conversion of arable land into pasture.*

the purely corn districts, and on the chalk and sands, where the grass does not thrive, the increase has been small.   On the poor clays there has been no increase. It has been greatest in the grazing counties and in the West and North.   Mr. Caird's analysis of the total value of the home and foreign agricultural produce shows very clearly where the British farmer is best protected by advantages of situation against foreign competition.   Of wheat, cheese, and butter, we import a quantity about equal to our home production.   Our main supplies of wool are from abroad.   Our chief supply of barley, oats, and beans, is drawn from home. In a few important articles, however, our home farmers have an undisputed monopoly, and these items include potatoes, of which the annual production is valued at 16,650,000*l.* sterling ;   milk,   26,000,000*l.*   sterling ; hay, 16,000,000*l.* ; and straw for town consumption, 6,000,000*l.*   The agricultural interest depends not on wheat, but on meat, butter, and hay, which still fetch a good price.

The disposition to convert arable land into pasture, already widely prevailing, will doubtless become more general after our recent experiences.   Such changes, however, as Mr. Clutton remarks, must be made with caution.   Much of our arable land is ill-adapted for permanent pasture.   Poor land, used as permanent pasture, yields no return whatever.   Inferior land yields the least unsatisfactory return, when used as arable land with occasional crops of wheat, and growing in rotation green crops for the production of beef and mutton.

The question of large and small farms and peasant proprietorship offers another subject, concerning which it would be very desirable that some information should be collected by the Commission. As a matter of fact, we know that on the Continent the land is cultivated in much smaller parcels than is customary in this country. According to M. de Lavergne, 50,000 proprietors in France possess each an average of 750 acres; 500,000 have an average of 75 acres; and 5,000,000 an average of $7\frac{1}{2}$ acres. Mr. Kay, however, is of opinion that the average acreage of the smaller proprietors in France is considerably above the figure quoted by M. de Lavergne. In Belgium, where the land is even more minutely subdivided than in France, the average area of separate plots is given by Sir Henry Barron at 1·36 acre.

Areas of farms in relation to profitable cultivation.

We have a complete store of information on the tenure of land in North Germany, through the able report prepared by Mr. Harris-Gastrell in 1867–70 in compliance with instructions issued by Lord Clarendon. The greater part of the land in what was then the kingdom of Prussia is cultivated by the owners themselves. While the number of tenants wholly engaged in agriculture was only 30,000, there were no less than 1,000,000 proprietors similarly occupied. Of these more than half belonged to the class of yeomen or team-owning peasants. The area of land owned and cultivated by the so-called 'team-owning' peasant varies from 33 acres in Silesia, to 66 acres in Saxony, and 81 in the province of Prussia.

North Germany.

It will be interesting to compare the results attained

on the Continent with the agriculture of the United Kingdom. In Prussia, the productive area yields an inferior return relatively to the productive area of this country. Really high farming is rare. It does not appear to be as profitable as medium farming, and the peasant proprietor will not adopt it. He cannot afford the luxury of maximum crops at a less return to himself. In North Germany garden cultivation is renowned for its care and intelligence.

France.

We have seen from the statement of Sir H. Barron how minute is the cultivation in Belgium, and the quantities of fruit, meat, eggs, and potatoes shipped to England are really prodigious. We draw similar produce in large quantities from France. Reichensberger, in his work ' Die Agrafrage,' quoted by Mr. Kay, asserts that the prosperity of France since 1790, notwithstanding the tremendous wars and revolutions through which that country has passed, is entirely due to the laws, which have led to a more minute subdivision of the land. The population of France has increased in the interval from 25,000,000 to 34,000,000. A larger population derives far more nourishment from the land of France in the present day than was obtained under the former *régime.* The people pay, with less taxes, 1,300,000,000 francs, while the old Monarchy fell because it attempted to raise 500,000,000 francs annually.

United Kingdom.

In the United Kingdom, the average acreage of holdings is 56 acres. Of the tenant farmers, 560,000 in number, 70 per cent. occupy farms under 50 acres each ; 12 per cent. between 50 and 100 acres ; 18

per cent. farms of more than 100 acres each. These figures are quoted from Mr. Caird. Should we be more independent of the supplies we now draw from the Continent, if a greater acreage of our own land were cultivated with the minute care of the smaller tenantry and peasant proprietors of the Continent?

Perhaps I may venture to refer to a highly success- Experi-
ful operation in the line of agricultural improvements, Middleton.
in which I have been personally interested. The estate in question was situated at Middleton, midway between Rochdale and Manchester. In a period of twenty-five years, at an expenditure of about 8*l.* an acre, the average rent was increased by about 1*l.* per acre, the land finally yielding an average rent of from 45*s.* to 50*s.* When the improvements were begun, the holdings varied from four to five to from ten to fifteen acres. Twelve miles of fences were removed, and the farms were consolidated into holdings varying from 25 to 80 acres. The tenants were encouraged to devote their attention to dairy-farming. At first they took it up with reluctance, but experience soon showed that it paid them better than arable cultivation.

Moderate holdings seem peculiarly adapted for oc- Poultry.
cupiers who are prepared to devote attention to the secondary produce of the farm. The rearing of poultry has hitherto been too much neglected in this country. When we look to the fact that eggs are selling in Manchester for 2*d.* each, while foreign eggs are being imported at the rate of 2,000,000 a day, the retail price of which may be computed at 16,000*l.*, it is evident that the English farmers and their families

are allowing a most important source of revenue to be too extensively appropriated by the foreign producer. I have no hesitation in saying that, with good management, the sale of eggs and poultry on a small farm should go very far towards the payment of rent.

Example afforded by the cheese manufacture.   As an illustration of the great importance of this question of large and small holdings, I would specially refer to the manufacture of cheese. The total quantity of cheese manufactured in the United Kingdom is estimated at two millions of cwts. ; the importations in 1876 amounted to one and a half millions of cwts. The value of the annual home product is estimated by Mr. Clarke, in a recent paper in the Agricultural Society's Journal, at 3*l.* 15*s.* per cwt., or 8,370,000*l.* The finer qualities are produced in only a small proportion of the dairies of England. For cheese of superior quality excellent prices are still obtainable, but I am informed by an agricultural relative in Cheshire that large quantities of the cheese made last year have not sold for more than 30*s.* or 40*s.* for 120 lbs., while the best qualities fetch from 70*s.* to 80*s.* The same experiences have been obtained in all parts of the country. The question, therefore, that we have to consider, and which I should like to see examined by the Royal Commission, is, whether the acreage of farms in the dairy counties has been judiciously apportioned, and whether the farmers themselves have anything to learn from the processes of manufacture adopted in the United States.

In Derbyshire and Cheshire you will find multitudes of small farmers. On farms of less than a hundred acres, during a large part of the year, not more than one cheese can be made every other day. Cheese made from a succession of milkings is inferior in quality. At my own farm, where the high prices already quoted have been obtained, they always make one cheese and in summer two cheeses a day. In order to produce a high quality of cheese, not less than forty cows and a farm of from 200 to 250 acres are required. It will be necessary, accordingly, to combine operations according to the American plan, or to throw the smaller holdings together. It is easy to understand the landlord's objections to the latter alternative. A large number of buildings will become unavailable, and a lower rent will be obtained. These are changes of which the landlords are not likely to approve. Is it not desirable, therefore, to give information to the small farmers of Cheshire on the superior methods and organisation of dairy farming in America, and to show them the advantages of combination in the manufacture of cheese?

The increase in the manufacture of butter and cheese in the Eastern States of America has been most remarkable. Mr. Victor Drummond in his recent report gives the value of the cows in the different States at 62,000,000*l.* sterling, and the value of the cheese and butter which they produce at an equal amount. The production has increased 33 per cent. within the past year. The exportations of 1878 paid more than a quarter of a million sterling for freight to Europe. The introduction of what is called the factory system has had the effect of materially increasing the production. The Americans work on the co-operative plan. All the farms within a radius of perhaps four miles send their milk to the same dairy, where the production of cheese is carried on even by small occupiers on the most extensive scale, and upon the most scientific and economical system. Mr. Drummond gives details as to the processes of making butter and the milking of cows by a mechanical process, which deserve the attentive study of our own farmers ; and I look to the report of the Royal Commission to bring its discoveries in a prominent manner under their notice.

Under a system of large holdings you get a large produce to the acre, the result of a liberal and scientific application of capital. The smaller holder is more successful in enforcing strict economy in every item of expenditure. The larger farmer realises his profit by the abundant produce which he obtains from the soil. The small farmer makes a profit because he spends little. He feels the rent less seriously than the large farmer. The aggregate amount is less. He has but a small sum to pay for labour, and a larger proportion of the humble fare on which he lives is produced on his own farm. Hence the wave of agricultural depression seems to beat less heavily on the small farmer than on those who cultivate on a larger scale, and farm highly.

Small holdings, again, are best on inferior soil, and in these, vegetables might be grown more freely, an increased number of pigs might be kept, and poultry might be reared more extensively.

The subject is one which demands thorough investigation by a Royal Commission, and the experience acquired on the Continent, and especially in France, where both high farming and cheap farming have been thoroughly developed, cannot fail to afford useful hints for our guidance on this side of the Channel.

The question of peasant proprietorship is closely connected with that of small holdings. The valuable social and political influences exercised by the peasant proprietors in France, in the preservation of social order in a society of strong democratic tendencies, has been acknowledged by every writer on these questions. The peasant proprietor has inducements to undertake the most laborious toil which could not be felt by any labourer for daily wages. It is asserted by M. Laveleye that the barren tracts, which have been brought into cultivation in Belgium and Holland, could never have been reclaimed by large capitalists, requiring an annual interest upon their investments. What is true of Belgium and Holland is equally true of Scotland. The worst lands that have been brought into cultivation in that part of the kingdom have been held by the small cottiers. Peasant proprietorship.

Peasant proprietorship has been lately discussed, with his usual clearness, by Lord Derby, and we shall generally share in his conclusion, that while every occupier would be glad to be freed from the obligation to pay rent, the purchase of land at the present prices in England would seldom be regarded as a tempting speculation by the smaller capitalists.

Tested by its fruits, our mixed system seems to

have secured a more ample return from the land than has been realised in any other country. The one important condition, from an agricultural point of view, is not so much the acreage of an estate as the fact of its being in the hands of a substantial proprietor. The best organisation of rural property, says M.de Lavergne, is that which attracts to the soil the most ample supply of capital, whether because the proprietors are more wealthy in proportion to the extent of land which they cultivate, or because they are induced to expend upon it a larger proportion of their wealth. The general conclusion would seem to be that, in the experience of the continental countries, the minimum quantity of land required to support a labourer and his family varies from 7 to 20 acres. Whether as tenants or proprietors, the class of small independent cultivators occupy a very superior position to that of the day labourer. When, however, you ascend beyond the acreage which can be cultivated without the assistance of hired labourers, it seems desirable to distribute the land into large holdings, which will attract men of skill and capital to engage in agriculture.

Limited ownership of land.   One other subject it seems inevitable that any Royal Commission appointed to inquire into the causes of our agricultural distress must consider. I refer to the effect upon cultivation of the limited ownership of a large part of the soil of this country. We have it on the authority of the noble lord, the leader of the Opposition, that it is impossible to place a limited owner in as good a position, as regards the management of an estate, as an absolute owner. The well-known report of Mr. Pusey's Committee refers to this question. The Committee reported that it seemed very desirable that estates under settlement should be endowed with every practicable privilege for their advantage, which is attached to absolute property.

Mr. Wren Hoskyns, in his paper on the land laws of England, lately published by the Cobden Club, quotes the statement of Mr. Caird, that ' much of the land of England, a far greater proportion than is generally believed (by the evidence before Mr. Pusey's Committee, the estates under settlement were estimated at two-thirds of the kingdom), is in the possession of tenants for life, so heavily burdened with settlement encumbrances, that they have not the means of improving the land which they are obliged to hold. Such a property must be overborne in unrestricted competition with farmers of capital, cultivating land, where every accommodation, which an unencumbered landlord finds it his interest to give, is supplied. Still more certainly must such a property be overborne when brought into competition with the virgin and rent-free soil of the great States of Western America.' The necessity for giving increased facilities to limited owners for raising money for agricultural improvements has been established, whenever an inquiry has been instituted into agricultural affairs.

According to Mr. Bailey Denton's evidence, quoted in the Report of the Lords' Committee on the Improvement of Land, out of 20,000,000 acres requiring drainage in England and Wales, only 3,000,000 have as yet been drained. The importance of this question from a public point of view is fully recognised in the report of the Committee. The improvement of land, they say, in its effect upon the dwellings of the poor and the price of food, is a matter of public interest; but as an investment it is not sufficiently lucrative to offer much attraction to capital, and therefore even slight difficulties have a powerful influence in arresting it. The net income from agricultural land has varied from 2 to $4\frac{1}{4}$ per cent. If a further reduction takes place, it will be increasingly difficult for individuals, with limited means in proportion to the extent of land in their possession, to do all that is required to develope its resources.

The average payment upon the outlay on agricultural improvements is seven per cent., while the landlord receives from the tenant only five per cent. Drainage and cottage building are more costly operations than they were. Hence it is important to examine whether any alteration can lessen the difficulties to which limited owners are liable who desire to make capital expenditure on their estates.

Prohibition of settlements would be of little avail in the opinion of the Lords' Committee, because the landowner is led to make improvements more by solicitude for his descendants than by hope of personal gain. Mortgages, which prevent the landowner from giving a prior charge on his estate, are a still greater hindrance than settlements to the expenditure of capital for improvements.

The Committee suggest that trustees should be empowered to advance trust money, accumulated for younger children, upon the improvement of the family estates on redeemable mortgage. They further recommend that limited owners should be allowed to spread the repayment of a charge for improvements over a longer period than the twenty-five years, to which they are restricted under the Act of 1864. They recommend that the period should be extended to ten years more than their own expectation of life according to tables to be selected ; and so that no such term might be less than twenty-five or more than forty years.

The recommendations of the Lords' Committee have been too long neglected, and they will doubtless be confirmed by the proposed Commission. But the embarrassments of many owners are such that they can only be relieved by the sale of the whole or a part of their estates. When a landowner is overwhelmed by the interest on mortgages, and charges under family settlement, he cannot undertake any costly improvements on a long-neglected estate. I have alluded to the expediency of converting a certain extent of our wheat land into permanent pasture. The process is tedious, and it costs at least 5*l.* an acre to make a good meadow. The change entails upon the landlord the erection of buildings, and a large expenditure is required on the part of the tenant in the purchase of stock. In many cases it must be necessary to suspend the collection of rents while the change in the cultivation is in progress. Mr. Caird is of opinion that settlements of land should be limited to lives in being with large powers of sale. He illustrates his view by an example. Take a limited owner of 10,000 acres,

Relief to owners by giving powers of sale.

yielding a gross rent of 10,000*l.* If he were enabled
to sell 2,000 acres at a residential price of 100*l.* per
acre, or 200,000*l.*, retaining his family seat and 8,000
acres, his rental would then be 8,000*l.* plus the interest at 4 per cent. on 200,000*l.*, equal to 8,000*l.*
His income would thus be 16,000*l.*, or 60 per cent.
more than he had before. The fortunate proprietors
in the vicinity of the great towns and manufacturing
districts, whose property is advancing from an agricultural value of perhaps 40*l.* an acre to 800*l.* when
sold as building land, have no difficulty in raising the
capital required for the improvement of their estates,
but those whose property lies in a purely agricultural
district are in a less favourable position. What we
want is an Encumbered Estates Court. I should be
sorry to advocate any legislation, which seemed calculated to impair the valuable political and social influence of the hereditary families of this country ; but
the position of an owner, who cannot do justice to his
property, is miserable to himself, and a public calamity.
Such an individual may derive immense advantage
from the conversion of a portion of his landed property into personalty, and the law allows personal
property to be tied up in settlement under trustees for
as long a period as an entailed estate in land.

Greater
security of
tenure for
the tenant.

The recommendations of the committee of the
present session for simplifying the transfer of land
will doubtless be adopted. They will afford additional
facilities for the application of capital to agriculture.
While the owner requires larger powers of sale, the
tenant requires greater security of tenure. In the

speech, in which he moved for a committee of inquiry in 1845, Mr. Cobden stated that the primary cause of the distressed condition of agriculture was the deficiency of capital in the hands of the farmers. That deficiency of capital he attributed to insecurity of tenure. He quoted many witnesses, and relied particularly on one whose authority will be acknowledged by members of the Conservative party. At a late meeting in Liverpool, Lord Stanley had spoken as follows : 'I say, and as one connected with the land I feel myself bound to say it, that a landlord has no right to expect any great and permanent improvement of his land by the tenant, unless he shall be secured the repayment of his outlay, not by the personal character and honour of his landlord, but by a security which no casualties can interfere with—the security granted him by the terms of a lease for years.' An attempt has been made to attain this object in the Agricultural Holdings Act. The provisions of that measure, with two instead of one year's notice, would, in the opinion of Mr. Caird, be a vast improvement on the common practice of yearly tenancy. 'Writing with the responsibility of a practical experience of forty years, I say with confidence that the system of a yearly tenancy will not for many years longer be able to withstand the pressure of competition, and that the relation between landlord and tenant must become one of business.' The future of English agriculture depends in part on the prosecution of farming enterprise in the line in which such men as Mr. Lawes and Mr. Prout have led the way. Mr. Lawes has succeeded in trebling the natural produce of grass land. Mr. Prout has obtained a return of more than 10*l.* per acre, as against the average product of the United Kingdom, which is estimated at 6*l.* 10*s.*, and he has realised a handsome profit on his outlay. These results, however, could not have been obtained without a large expenditure. Mr. Cobden speaks of 10*l.* an acre as the minimum, and Mr. Prout has expended 16*l.* an acre on improvements. If we wish to see high farming extended in this country, it is evident that it can only be done under the stimulus of proprietorship, or by greater security of tenure.

Payment of farm labour by the piece.

The question of labour is intimately connected with peasant proprietorships and small holdings. Where the holdings exceed the acreage which can be properly cultivated by the occupier and his family, you have the disadvantage of hired, and therefore less energetic and industrious labour. When the occupier does not engage in manual labour himself, an additional charge is thrown upon the land for the maintenance of an individual, who is no longer directly employed as a producer. The proportion of individuals, whose task is limited to the superintendence of the labours of others, is probably far larger in the agriculture of the United Kingdom than in that of any other country. The cost of labour has not increased in recent years. Wages are higher, but machinery has been more extensively used. Farmers should resort more generally to piecework. No system of paying labour can be more truly extravagant and costly in its results than that of low wages at fixed rates.

Among the farmers, as indeed in every class of the community, there are to be found many who are neither liberal-minded nor progressive. They have failed to realise the importance of the system of payment by the piece. Resistance to piecework is one of the gravest errors of the Trades Unions. I know not what are the rules adopted by the National Agricultural Labourers' Union on this subject. It cannot, however, be too emphatically stated that agriculture can only be successful when the labourer is industrious. Many employers are to be found who, having assigned a certain price to the work to be done, and finding that the labourer, when paid by the piece, earns an amount by the day or the week, far in excess of what they have been accustomed to pay, are so foolish as to believe that the cost of labour must be excessive, because the workmen's earnings have increased. If a farm labourer could succeed in earning 24*s.* or 30*s.* a week on a system of piecework, his earnings would be grudgingly paid by many agricultural employers, however great the industry of the workman, and however moderate the cost of the task on which he was engaged.

In urging the necessity for the appointment of a Royal Commission, it has been my duty to dwell only on the gloomier circumstances that affect British husbandry at the present time, and indeed it seems not improbable that for some years to come the land-owner may suffer a loss of income. But I do not despair of the future. It is not the way of the British nation to surrender to difficulties. We have been

Future of British husbandry.

D D

successful in raising agriculture to a high pitch of perfection. If we are to depend on the foreign supply of wheat, the cultivation of our soil will require readjustment, and the period of transition may be a severe trial, but by the united action of landowners and tenants, and by relieving agriculture of the trammels of an antiquated system of land laws, we shall triumph in the end.

There is always in favour of the landed interest what M. Léonce de Lavergne has designated the Economic Reaction. If the agricultural industry could have been destroyed, it would have been destroyed a hundred times. It owes its preservation to the fact that it is necessary—that it is indispensable. The labourer was never in a more favourable position than now, he has always the resource of emigration, and if he retains in a foreign land, or in one of the colonies of the Empire, that affection for the mother country, which makes the whole Anglo-Saxon race speak of England in terms of endearment as their home, neither the greatness nor the influence of this country will be diminished by the gradual migration of a portion of the agricultural population. The present difficulties of the tenant farmer will be finally adjusted by competition. If the profits derived from the cultivation of the soil are diminished, the rents must be proportionately reduced. In unprosperous times the owners are more dependent upon the cultivators than are the cultivators upon the proprietors of the soil. Meanwhile the landowner may take comfort in the conviction that his property is the one exchangeable article which admits of no increase, and that the accumulation of capital, which diminishes the profits of the merchant, will increase the competition for land. In the improbable event of the recurrence of adverse seasons the agricultural value may be diminished, but the steady growth in residential value will not be interrupted. The action of economic laws may be impeded by narrow and illiberal legislation, but the only laws by which the value of the land will be enhanced are those which promote the happiness of the people.

INDEX.

414

LONDON: PRINTED BY
SPOTTISWOODE AND CO., NEW-STREET SQUARE
AND PARLIAMENT STREET

* E E

WORKS BY THOMAS BRASSEY, M.P.

39 PATERNOSTER ROW, E.C.

LONDON, *July* 1879.

GENERAL LIST OF WORKS

PUBLISHED BY

MESSRS. LONGMANS, GREEN & CO

—◦◦⟩⦿⟨◦◦—

HISTORY, POLITICS, HISTORICAL MEMOIRS, &c.

A History of England from the Conclusion of the Great War in 1815. By SPENCER WALPOLE, Author of 'Life of the Rt. Hon. Spencer Perceval.' VOLS. I. & II. 8vo. 36*s*.

History of England in the 18th Century. By W. E. H. LECKY, M.A. VOLS. I. & II. 1700–1760. 2 vols. 8vo. 36*s*.

The History of England from the Accession of James II. By the Right Hon. Lord MACAULAY.

STUDENT'S EDITION, 2 vols. cr. 8vo. 12*s*.
PEOPLE'S EDITION, 4 vols. cr. 8vo. 16*s*.
CABINET EDITION, 8 vols. post 8vo. 48*s*.
LIBRARY EDITION, 5 vols. 8vo. £4.

Critical and Historical Essays contributed to the Edinburgh Review. By the Right Hon. Lord MACAULAY.

CHEAP EDITION, crown 8vo. 3*s*. 6*d*.
STUDENT'S EDITION, crown 8vo. 6*s*.
PEOPLE'S EDITION, 2 vols. crown 8vo. 8*s*.
CABINET EDITION, 4 vols. 24*s*.
LIBRARY EDITION, 3 vols. 8vo. 36*s*.

Lord Macaulay's Works. Complete and uniform Library Edition. Edited by his Sister, Lady TREVELYAN. 8 vols. 8vo. with Portrait £5. 5*s*.

The History of England from the Fall of Wolsey to the Defeat of the Spanish Armada. By J. A. FROUDE, M.A.

CABINET EDITION, 12 vols. cr. 8vo. £3. 12*s*.
LIBRARY EDITION, 12 vols. 8vo. £8. 18*s*.

The English in Ireland in the Eighteenth Century. By J. A. FROUDE, M.A. 3 vols. 8vo. £2. 8*s*.

Journal of the Reigns of King George IV. and King William IV. By the late C. C. F. GREVILLE, Esq. Edited by H. REEVE, Esq. Fifth Edition. 3 vols. 8vo. price 36*s*.

The Life of Napoleon III. derived from State Records Unpublished Family Correspondence, and Personal Testimony. By BLANCHARD JERROLD. In Four Volumes, 8vo. with numerous Portraits and Facsimiles. VOLS. I. to III. price 18*s*. each.

The Constitutional His-tory of England since the Accession of George III. 1760–1870. By Sir THOMAS ERSKINE MAY, K.C.B. D.C.L. Fifth Edition. 3 vols. crown 8vo. 18*s*.

Democracy in Europe; a History. By Sir THOMAS ERSKINE MAY, K.C.B. D.C.L. 2 vols. 8vo. 32*s*.

A

Introductory Lectures on Modern History delivered in 1841 and 1842. By the late Rev. T. ARNOLD, D.D.   8vo. price 7s. 6d.

On Parliamentary Government in England; its Origin, Development, and Practical Operation. By ALPHEUS TODD.   2 vols. 8vo. price £1. 17s.

History of Civilisation in England and France, Spain and Scotland.   By HENRY THOMAS BUCKLE.   3 vols. crown 8vo. 24s.

Lectures on the History of England from the Earliest Times to the Death of King Edward II. By W. LONGMAN, F.S.A.   Maps and Illustrations.   8vo. 15s.

History of the Life & Times of Edward III. By W. LONGMAN, F.S.A.   With 9 Maps, 8 Plates, and 16 Woodcuts.   2 vols. 8vo. 28s.

History of the Life and Reign of Richard III.   To which is added the Story of PERKIN WARBECK, from Original Documents.   By JAMES GAIRDNER.   With Portrait and Map. Second Edition.   Crown 8vo. 10s. 6d.

Memoirs of the Civil War in Wales and the Marches, 1642-1649.   By JOHN ROLAND PHILLIPS, of Lincoln's Inn, Barrister-at-Law.   Second Edition, in One Volume.   8vo. 16s.

The Life of Simon de Montfort, Earl of Leicester, with special reference to the Parliamentary History of his time.   By G. W. PROTHERO.   Crown 8vo. Maps, 9s.

History of England under der the Duke of Buckingham and Charles I. 1624-1628.   By S. R. GARDINER.   2 vols. 8vo.   Maps, 24s.

The Personal Government of Charles I. from the Death of Buckingham to the Declaration in favour of Ship Money, 1628-1637.   By S. R. GARDINER.   2 vols. 8vo. 24s.

Popular History of France, from the Earliest Times to the Death of Louis XIV.   By ELIZABETH M. SEWELL.   With 8 Maps. Crown 8vo. 7s. 6d.

The Famine Campaign in Southern India, (Madras, Bombay, and Mysore,) in 1876-78.   By WILLIAM DIGBY, Secretary of the Madras Famine Committee.   With Maps and many Illustrations.   2 vols. 8vo. 32s.

A Student's Manual of the History of India from the Earliest Period to the Present.   By Col. MEADOWS TAYLOR, M.R.A.S.   Third Thousand.   Crown 8vo. Maps, 7s. 6d.

Indian Polity; a View of the System of Administration in India. By Lieut.-Col. G. CHESNEY. 8vo. 21s.

Waterloo Lectures; a Study of the Campaign of 1815.   By Colonel C. C. CHESNEY, R.E. 8vo. 10s. 6d.

The Oxford Reformers— John Colet, Erasmus, and Thomas More; a History of their Fellow-Work. By F. SEEBOHM.   8vo. 14s.

General History of Rome from B.C. 753 to A.D. 476.   By Dean MERIVALE, D.D.   Crown 8vo. Maps, price 7s. 6d.

The Fall of the Roman Republic; a Short History of the Last Century of the Commonwealth.   By Dean MERIVALE, D.D.   12mo. 7s. 6d.

Carthage and the Carthaginians.   By R. BOSWORTH SMITH, M.A.   Second Edition.   Maps, Plans, &c.   Crown 8vo. 10s. 6d.

History of the Romans under the Empire.   By Dean MERIVALE, D.D.   8 vols. post 8vo. 48s.

The History of Rome. By WILHELM IHNE.   VOLS. I. to III. 8vo. price 45s.

The Sixth Oriental Monarchy; or, the Geography, History, and Antiquities of Parthia. By G. RAWLINSON, M.A. With Maps and Illustrations. 8vo. 16s.

The Seventh Great Oriental Monarchy; or, a History of the Sassanians. By G. RAWLINSON, M.A. With Map and 95 Illustrations. 8vo. 28s.

The History of European Morals from Augustus to Charlemagne. By W. E. H. LECKY, M.A. 2 vols. crown 8vo. 16s.

History of the Rise and Influence of the Spirit of Rationalism in Europe. By W. E. H. LECKY, M.A. 2 vols. crown 8vo. 16s.

The History of Philosophy, from Thales to Comte. By GEORGE HENRY LEWES. Fourth Edition. 2 vols. 8vo. 32s.

Zeller's Stoics, Epicureans, and Sceptics. Translated by the Rev. O. J. REICHEL, M.A. Cr. 8vo. 14s.

Zeller's Socrates & the Socratic Schools. Translated by the Rev. O. J. REICHEL, M.A. Second Edition. Crown 8vo. 10s. 6d.

Zeller's Plato & the Older Academy. Translated by S. FRANCES ALLEYNE and ALFRED GOODWIN, B.A. Crown 8vo. 18s.

Epochs of Modern History. Edited by C. COLBECK, M.A.

Church's Beginning of the Middle Ages, 2s. 6d.

Cox's Crusades, 2s. 6d.

Creighton's Age of Elizabeth, 2s. 6d.

Gairdner's Houses of Lancaster and York, 2s. 6d.

Gardiner's Puritan Revolution, 2s. 6d.

———— Thirty Years' War, 2s. 6d.

Hale's Fall of the Stuarts, 2s. 6d.

Johnson's Normans in Europe, 2s. 6d.

Ludlow's War of American Independence, 2s. 6d.

Morris's Age of Anne, 2s. 6d.

Seebohm's Protestant Revolution, price 2s. 6d.

Stubbs's Early Plantagenets, 2s. 6d.

Warburton's Edward III. 2s. 6d.

Epochs of Ancient History. Edited by the Rev. Sir G. W. COX, Bart. M.A. & C. SANKEY, M.A.

Beesly's Gracchi, Marius & Sulla, 2s. 6d.

Capes's Age of the Antonines, 2s. 6d.

———— Early Roman Empire, 2s. 6d.

Cox's Athenian Empire, 2s. 6d.

———— Greeks & Persians, 2s. 6d.

Curteis's Macedonian Empire, 2s. 6d.

Ihne's Rome to its Capture by the Gauls, 2s. 6d.

Merivale's Roman Triumvirates, 2s. 6d.

Sankey's Spartan & Theban Supremacies, 2s. 6d.

Epochs of English History. Edited by the Rev. MANDELL CREIGHTON, M.A. Fcp. 8vo. 5s.

Browning's Modern England, 1820-1874, 9d.

Cordery's Struggle against Absolute Monarchy, 1603-1688, 9d.

Creighton's (Mrs.) England a Continental Power, 1066-1216, 9d.

Creighton's (Rev. M.) Tudors and the Reformation, 1485-1603, 9d.

Rowley's Rise of the People, 1215-1485, 9d.

Rowley's Settlement of the Constitution, 1688-1778, 9d.

Tancock's England during the American & European Wars, 1778-1820, 9d.

York-Powell's Early England to the Conquest, 1s.

Creighton's Shilling History of England, introductory to the above. Fcp. 8vo. 1s.

The Student's Manual of Modern History; the Rise and Progress of the Principal European Nations. By W. COOKE TAYLOR, LL.D. Crown 8vo. 7s. 6d.

The Student's Manual of Ancient History; the Political History, Geography and Social State of the Principal Nations of Antiquity. By W. COOKE TAYLOR LL.D. Cr. 8vo. 7s. 6d.

BIOGRAPHICAL WORKS.

Memoirs of the Life of
Anna Jameson, Author of 'Sacred and Legendary Art' &c. By her Niece, GERARDINE MACPHERSON. 8vo. with Portrait, price 12*s*. 6*d*.

Memorials of Charlotte
Williams-Wynn. Edited by her Sister. Crown 8vo. with Portrait, price 10*s*. 6*d*.

The Life and Letters of
Lord Macaulay. By his Nephew, G. OTTO TREVELYAN, M.P.

CABINET EDITION, 2 vols. crown 8vo. 12*s*.
LIBRARY EDITION, 2 vols. 8vo. 36*s*.

The Life of Sir Martin
Frobisher, Knt. containing a Narrative of the Spanish Armada. By the Rev. FRANK JONES, B.A. Portrait, Maps, and Facsimile. Crown 8vo. 6*s*.

Gotthold Ephraim Les-
sing, his Life and Works. By HELEN ZIMMERN. Crown 8vo. 10*s*. 6*d*.

The Life, Works, and
Opinions of Heinrich Heine. By WILLIAM STIGAND. 2 vols. 8vo. Portrait, 28*s*.

The Life of Mozart.
Translated from the German Work of Dr. LUDWIG NOHL by Lady WALLACE. 2 vols. crown 8vo. Portraits, 21*s*.

Life of Robert Frampton,
D.D. Bishop of Gloucester, deprived as a Non-Juror in 1689. Edited by T. S. EVANS, M.A. Crown 8vo. 10*s*. 6*d*.

The Life of Simon de
Montfort, Earl of Leicester, with special reference to the Parliamentary History of his time. By G. W. PROTHERO. Crown 8vo. Maps, 9*s*.

Maunder's Biographical
Treasury; a Dictionary of Universal Biography. Latest Edition, thoroughly revised and for the most part re-written, with over Fifteen Hundred additional Memoirs, by WILLIAM L. R. CATES. Fcp. 8vo. 6*s*.

Felix Mendelssohn's Let-
ters, translated by Lady WALLACE. 2 vols. crown 8vo. 5*s*. each.

Autobiography. By JOHN
STUART MILL. 8vo. 7*s*. 6*d*.

Apologia pro Vitâ Suâ;
Being a History of his Religious Opinions by JOHN HENRY NEWMAN, D.D. New Edition. Crown 8vo. 6*s*.

Isaac Casaubon, 1559-
1614. By MARK PATTISON, Rector of Lincoln College, Oxford. 8vo. 18*s*.

Leaders of Public Opi-
nion in Ireland; Swift, Flood, Grattan, O'Connell. By W. E. H. LECKY, M.A. Crown 8vo. 7*s*. 6*d*.

Essays in Ecclesiastical
Biography. By the Right Hon. Sir J. STEPHEN, LL.D. Crown 8vo. 7*s*. 6*d*.

Cæsar; a Sketch. By JAMES
ANTHONY FROUDE, M.A. formerly Fellow of Exeter College, Oxford. With Portrait and Map. 8vo. 16*s*.

Life of the Duke of Wel-
lington. By the Rev. G. R. GLEIG, M.A. Crown 8vo. Portrait, 6*s*.

Memoirs of Sir Henry
Havelock, K.C.B. By JOHN CLARK MARSHMAN. Crown 8vo. 3*s*. 6*d*.

Vicissitudes of Families.
By Sir BERNARD BURKE, C.B. Two vols. crown 8vo. 21*s*.

MENTAL and POLITICAL PHILOSOPHY.

Comte's System of Positive Polity, or Treatise upon Sociology :—

VOL. I. General View of Positivism and Introductory Principles. Translated by J. H. BRIDGES, M.B. 8vo. 21s.

VOL. II. The Social Statics, or the Abstract Laws of Human Order. Translated by F. HARRISON, M.A. 8vo. 14s.

VOL. III. The Social Dynamics, or the General Laws of Human Progress (the Philosophy of History). Translated by E. S. BEESLY, M.A. 8vo. 21s.

VOL. IV. The Theory of the Future of Man ; with COMTE'S Early Essays on Social Philosophy. Translated by R. CONGREVE, M.D. and H. D. HUTTON, B.A. 8vo. 24s.

De Tocqueville's Democracy in America, translated by H. REEVE. 2 vols. crown 8vo. 16s.

Analysis of the Phenomena of the Human Mind. By JAMES MILL. With Notes, Illustrative and Critical. 2 vols. 8vo. 28s.

On Representative Government. By JOHN STUART MILL. Crown 8vo. 2s.

On Liberty. By JOHN STUART MILL. Post 8vo. 7s. 6d. crown 8vo. 1s. 4d.

Principles of Political Economy. By JOHN STUART MILL. 2 vols. 8vo. 30s. or 1 vol. crown 8vo. 5s.

Essays on some Unsettled Questions of Political Economy. By JOHN STUART MILL. 8vo. 6s. 6d.

Utilitarianism. By JOHN STUART MILL. 8vo. 5s.

The Subjection of Women. By JOHN STUART MILL. Fourth Edition. Crown 8vo. 6s.

Examination of Sir William Hamilton's Philosophy. By JOHN STUART MILL. 8vo. 16s.

A System of Logic, Ratiocinative and Inductive. By JOHN STUART MILL. 2 vols. 8vo. 25s.

Dissertations and Discussions. By JOHN STUART MILL. 4 vols. 8vo. price £2. 6s. 6d.

Philosophical Fragments written during intervals of Business. By J. D. MORELL, LL.D. Crown 8vo. 5s.

The Philosophy of Reflection. By S. H. HODGSON, Hon. LL.D. Edin. 2 vols. 8vo. 21s.

The Law of Nations considered as Independent Political Communities. By Sir TRAVERS TWISS, D.C.L. 2 vols. 8vo. £1. 13s.

A Systematic View of the Science of Jurisprudence. By SHELDON AMOS, M.A. 8vo. 18s.

A Primer of the English Constitution and Government. By S. AMOS, M.A. Crown 8vo. 6s.

A Sketch of the History of Taxes in England from the Earliest Times to the Present Day. By STEPHEN DOWELL. VOL. I. to the Civil War 1642. 8vo. 10s. 6d.

Principles of Economical Philosophy. By H. D. MACLEOD, M.A. Second Edition in 2 vols. VOL. I. 8vo. 15s. VOL. II. PART 1. 12s.

The Institutes of Justinian ; with English Introduction, Translation, and Notes. By T. C. SANDARS, M.A. 8vo. 18s.

Lord Bacon's Works, collected & edited by R. L. ELLIS, M.A. J. SPEDDING, M.A. and D. D. HEATH. 7 vols. 8vo. £3. 13s. 6d.

Letters and Life of Francis Bacon, including all his Occasional Works. Collected and edited, with a Commentary, by J. SPEDDING. 7 vols. 8vo. £4. 4s.

The Nicomachean Ethics

of Aristotle, translated into English by R. WILLIAMS, B.A. Crown 8vo. price 7s. 6d.

Aristotle's Politics, Books

I. III. IV. (VII.) Greek Text, with an English Translation by W. E. BOLLAND, M.A. and Short Essays by A. LANG, M.A. Crown 8vo. 7s. 6d.

The Politics of Aristotle;

Greek Text, with English Notes. By RICHARD CONGREVE, M.A. 8vo. 18s.

The Ethics of Aristotle;

with Essays and Notes. By Sir A. GRANT, Bart. LL.D. 2 vols. 8vo. 32s.

Bacon's Essays, with An-

notations. By R. WHATELY, D.D. 8vo. 10s. 6d.

Picture Logic; an Attempt

to Popularise the Science of Reasoning. By A. SWINBOURNE, B.A. Post 8vo. 5s.

Elements of Logic. By

R. WHATELY, D.D. 8vo. 10s. 6d. Crown 8vo. 4s. 6d.

Elements of Rhetoric.

By R. WHATELY, D.D. 8vo. 10s. 6d Crown 8vo. 4s. 6d.

On the Influence of Au-

thority in Matters of Opinion. By the late Sir. G. C. LEWIS, Bart. 8vo. 14s.

The Senses and the Intellect. By A. BAIN, LL.D. 8vo. 15s.

The Emotions and the

Will. By A. BAIN, LL.D. 8vo. 15s.

Mental and Moral Sci-

ence; a Compendium of Psychology and Ethics. By A. BAIN, LL.D. Crown 8vo. 10s. 6d.

An Outline of the Neces-

sary Laws of Thought; a Treatise on Pure and Applied Logic. By W. THOMSON, D.D. Crown 8vo. 6s.

Essays in Political and

Moral Philosophy. By T. E. CLIFFE LESLIE, Hon. LL.D. Dubl. of Lincoln's Inn, Barrister-at-Law; late Examiner in Polit. Econ. in the Univ. of London; Prof. of Jurisp. and Polit. Econ. in the Queen's University. 8vo. price 10s. 6d.

Hume's Philosophical

Works. Edited, with Notes, &c. by T. H. GREEN, M.A. and the Rev. T. H. GROSE, M.A. 4 vols. 8vo. 56s. Or separately, Essays, 2 vols. 28s. Treatise on Human Nature, 2 vols. 28s.

The Schools of Charles

the Great, and the Restoration of Education in the Ninth Century. By J. BASS MULLINGER, M.A. 8vo. price 7s. 6d.

MISCELLANEOUS & CRITICAL WORKS.

The London Series of

English Classics. Edited by JOHN W. Hales, M.A. and by CHARLES S. JERRAM, M.A. Fcp. 8vo.

Bacon's Essays, annotated by E. A. ABBOT, D.D. 2 vols. 6s. or in 1 vol. without Notes, 2s. 6d.

Ben Jonson's Every Man in His Humour, by H. B. WHEATLEY, F.S.A. Price 2s. 6d.

Macaulay's Clive, by H. C. BOWEN, M.A. 2s. 6d.

Marlowe's Doctor Faustus, by W. WAGNER, Ph.D. 2s.

Milton's Paradise Regained, by C. S. JERRAM, M.A. 2s. 6d.

Pope's Select Poems, by T. ARNOLD, M.A. 2s. 6d.

Miscellaneous Writings

of J. Conington, M.A. Edited by J. A. SYMONDS, M.A. 2 vols. 8vo. 28s.

Selected Essays, chiefly

from Contributions to the Edinburgh and Quarterly Reviews. By A. HAYWARD, Q.C. 2 vols. crown 8vo. 12s.

Literary Studies. By the
late WALTER BAGEHOT, M.A. and
Fellow of University College, London.
With a Prefatory Memoir. Edited by
R. H. HUTTON. 2 vols. 8vo. with
Portrait, 28s.

Short Studies on Great
Subjects. By J. A. FROUDE, M.A.
3 vols. crown 8vo. 18s.

Manual of English Lite-
rature, Historical and Critical. By
T. ARNOLD, M.A. Crown 8vo. 7s. 6d.

Lord Macaulay's Miscel-
laneous Writings :—
LIBRARY EDITION, 2 vols. 8vo. 21s.
PEOPLE'S EDITION, 1 vol. cr. 8vo. 4s. 6d.

Lord Macaulay's Miscel-
laneous Writings and Speeches.
Student's Edition. Crown 8vo. 6s.

Speeches of the Right
Hon. Lord Macaulay, corrected by
Himself. Crown 8vo. 3s. 6d.

Selections from the Wri-
tings of Lord Macaulay. Edited,
with Notes, by G. O. TREVELYAN,
M.P. Crown. 8vo. 6s.

The Wit and Wisdom of
the Rev. Sydney Smith. Crown
8vo. 3s. 6d.

Miscellaneous and Post-
humous Works of the late Henry
Thomas Buckle. Edited by HELEN
TAYLOR. 3 vols. 8vo. 52s. 6d.

Miscellaneous Works of
Thomas Arnold, D.D. late Head
Master of Rugby School. 8vo. 7s. 6d.

German Home Life; a
Series of Essays on the Domestic Life
of Germany. Crown 8vo. 6s.

Realities of Irish Life.
By W. STEUART TRENCH. Crown
8vo. 2s. 6d. boards, or 3s. 6d. cloth.

Max Müller and the
Philosophy of Language. By
LUDWIG NOIRÉ. 8vo. 6s.

Lectures on the Science
of Language. By F. MAX MÜLLER,
M.A. 2 vols. crown 8vo. 16s.

Chips from a German
Workshop ; Essays on the Science of
Religion, and on Mythology, Traditions
& Customs. By F. MAX MÜLLER,
M.A. 4 vols. 8vo. £2. 18s.

Language & Languages.
A Revised Edition of Chapters on Language and Families of Speech. By
F. W. FARRAR, D.D. F.R.S. Crown
8vo. 6s.

The Essays and Contri-
butions of A. K. H. B. Uniform
Cabinet Editions in crown 8vo.

Recreations of a Country Parson, Three
Series, 3s. 6d. each.

Landscapes, Churches, and Moralities,
price 3s. 6d.

Seaside Musings, 3s. 6d.

Changed Aspects of Unchanged
Truths, 3s. 6d.

Counsel and Comfort from a City
Pulpit, 3s. 6d.

Lessons of Middle Age, 3s. 6d.

Leisure Hours in Town, 3s. 6d.

Autumn Holidays of a Country Parson,
price 3s. 6d.

Sunday Afternoons at the Parish
Church of a University City, 3s. 6d.

The Commonplace Philosopher in
Town and Country, 3s. 6d.

Present-Day Thoughts, 3s. 6d.

Critical Essays of a Country Parson,
price 3s. 6d.

The Graver Thoughts of a Country
Parson, Three Series, 3s. 6d. each.

DICTIONARIES and OTHER BOOKS of REFERENCE.

Dictionary of the English Language. By R. G. LATHAM, M.A. M.D. Abridged from Dr. Latham's Edition of Johnson's English Dictionary. Medium 8vo. 24*s*.

A Dictionary of the English Language. By R. G. LATHAM, M.A. M.D. Founded on Johnson's English Dictionary as edited by the Rev. H. J. TODD. 4 vols. 4to. £7.

Roget's Thesaurus of English Words and Phrases, classified and arranged so as to facilitate the expression of Ideas, and assist in Literary Composition. Revised and enlarged by the Author's Son, J. L. ROGET. Crown 8vo. 10*s*. 6*d*.

English Synonymes. By E. J. WHATELY. Edited by R. WHATELY, D.D. Fcp. 8vo. 3*s*.

Handbook of the English Language. By R. G. LATHAM, M.A. M.D. Crown 8vo. 6*s*.

Contanseau's Practical Dictionary of the French and English Languages. Post 8vo. price 7*s*. 6*d*.

Contanseau's Pocket Dictionary, French and English, abridged from the Practical Dictionary by the Author. Square 18mo. 3*s*. 6*d*.

A New Pocket Dictionary of the German and English Languages. By F. W. LONGMAN, Ball. Coll. Oxford. Square 18mo. 5*s*.

A Practical Dictionary of the German and English Languages. By Rev. W. L. BLACKLEY, M.A. & Dr. C. M. FRIEDLÄNDER. Post 8vo. 7*s*. 6*d*.

A Dictionary of Roman and Greek Antiquities. With 2,000 Woodcuts illustrative of the Arts and Life of the Greeks and Romans. By A. RICH, B.A. Crown 8vo. 7*s*. 6*d*.

The Critical Lexicon and Concordance to the English and Greek New Testament. By the Rev. E. W. BULLINGER. Medium 8vo. 30*s*.

A Greek-English Lexicon. By H. G. LIDDELL, D.D. Dean of Christchurch, and R. SCOTT, D.D. Dean of Rochester. Crown 4to. 36*s*.

Liddell & Scott's Lexicon, Greek and English, abridged for Schools. Square 12mo. 7*s*. 6*d*.

An English-Greek Lexicon, containing all the Greek Words used by Writers of good authority. By C. D. YONGE, M.A. 4to. 21*s*.

Mr. Yonge's Lexicon, English and Greek, abridged from his larger Lexicon. Square 12mo. 8*s*. 6*d*.

A Latin-English Dictionary. By JOHN T. WHITE, D.D. Oxon. and J. E. RIDDLE, M.A. Oxon. Sixth Edition, revised. 1 vol. 4to. 28*s*.

White's College Latin-English Dictionary, for the use of University Students. Medium 8vo. 15*s*.

A Latin-English Dictionary for the use of Middle-Class Schools. By JOHN T. WHITE, D.D. Oxon. Square fcp. 8vo. 3*s*.

White's Junior Student's Latin-English and English-Latin Dictionary. Square 12mo. ENGLISH-LATIN DICTIONARY, 5*s*.6*d*. LATIN-ENGLISH DICTIONARY, 7*s*.6*d*. COMPLETE, 12*s*.

M'Culloch's Dictionary of Commerce and Commercial Navigation. Re-edited by HUGH G. REID. With 11 Maps and 30 Charts. 8vo. 63*s*.

Keith Johnston's General Dictionary of Geography, Descriptive, Physical, Statistical, and Historical; a complete Gazetteer of the World. Medium 8vo. 42*s*.

The Public Schools Atlas of Ancient Geography, in 28 entirely new Coloured Maps. Edited by the Rev. G. BUTLER, M.A. Imperial 8vo. or imperial 4to. 7*s*. 6*d*.

The Public Schools Atlas of Modern Geography, in 31 entirely new Coloured Maps. Edited by the Rev. G. BUTLER, M.A. Uniform, 5*s*.

ASTRONOMY and METEOROLOGY.

Outlines of Astronomy.
By Sir J. F. W. HERSCHEL, Bart. M.A. Latest Edition, with Plates and Diagrams. Square crown 8vo. 12s.

Essays on Astronomy.
A Series of Papers on Planets and Meteors, the Sun and Sun-surrounding Space, Star and Star Cloudlets. By R. A. PROCTOR, B.A. With 10 Plates and 24 Woodcuts. 8vo. 12s.

The Moon; her Motions,
Aspects, Scenery, and Physical Condition. By R. A. PROCTOR, B.A. With Plates, Charts, Woodcuts, and Lunar Photographs. Crown 8vo. 10s. 6d.

The Sun; Ruler, Light, Fire,
and Life of the Planetary System. By R. A. PROCTOR, B.A. With Plates & Woodcuts. Crown 8vo. 14s.

The Orbs Around Us;
a Series of Essays on the Moon & Planets, Meteors & Comets, the Sun & Coloured Pairs of Suns. By R. A. PROCTOR, B.A. With Chart and Diagrams. Crown 8vo. 7s. 6d.

Other Worlds than Ours;
The Plurality of Worlds Studied under the Light of Recent Scientific Researches. By R. A. PROCTOR, B.A. With 14 Illustrations. Cr. 8vo. 10s. 6d.

The Universe of Stars;
Presenting Researches into and New Views respecting the Constitution of the Heavens. By R. A. PROCTOR, B.A. Second Edition, with 22 Charts (4 Coloured) and 22 Diagrams. 8vo. price 10s. 6d.

The Transits of Venus;
A Popular Account of Past and Coming Transits. By R. A. PROCTOR, B.A. 20 Plates (12 Coloured) and 27 Woodcuts. Crown 8vo. 8s. 6d.

Saturn and its System.
By R. A. PROCTOR, B.A. 8vo. with 14 Plates, 14s.

The Moon, and the Condition and Configurations of its Surface.
By E. NEISON, F.R.A.S. With 26 Maps & 5 Plates. Medium 8vo. 31s. 6d.

A New Star Atlas, for the
Library, the School, and the Observatory, in 12 Circular Maps (with 2 Index Plates). By R. A. PROCTOR, B.A. Crown 8vo. 5s.

Larger Star Atlas, for the
Library, in Twelve Circular Maps, with Introduction and 2 Index Plates. By R. A. PROCTOR, B.A. Folio, 15s. or Maps only, 12s. 6d.

A Treatise on the Cycloid,
and on all forms of Cycloidal Curves, and on the use of Cycloidal Curves in dealing with the Motions of Planets, Comets, &c. and of Matter projected from the Sun. By R. A. PROCTOR, B.A. With 161 Diagrams. Crown 8vo. 10s. 6d.

Dove's Law of Storms,
considered in connexion with the Ordinary Movements of the Atmosphere. Translated by R. H. SCOTT, M.A. 8vo. 10s. 6d.

Air and Rain; the Beginnings of a Chemical Climatology.
By R. A. SMITH, F.R.S. 8vo. 24s.

Schellen's Spectrum Analysis,
in its Application to Terrestrial Substances and the Physical Constitution of the Heavenly Bodies. Translated by JANE and C. LASSELL, with Notes by W. HUGGINS, LL.D. F.R.S. 8vo. Plates and Woodcuts, 28s.

NATURAL HISTORY and PHYSICAL SCIENCE.

Professor Helmholtz'
Popular Lectures on Scientific Subjects. Translated by E. ATKINSON, F.C.S. With numerous Wood Engravings. 8vo. 12s. 6d.

Professor Helmholtz on
the Sensations of Tone, as a Physiological Basis for the Theory of Music. Translated by A. J. ELLIS, F.R.S. 8vo. 36s.

Ganot's Natural Philosophy
for General Readers and Young Persons; a Course of Physics divested of Mathematical Formulæ and expressed in the language of daily life. Translated by E. ATKINSON, F.C.S. Third Edition. Plates and Woodcuts. Crown 8vo. 7s. 6d.

Ganot's Elementary
Treatise on Physics, Experimental and Applied, for the use of Colleges and Schools. Translated and edited by E. ATKINSON, F.C.S. Eighth Edition. Plates and Woodcuts. Post 8vo. 15s.

Arnott's Elements of Physics
or Natural Philosophy. Seventh Edition, edited by A. BAIN, LL.D. and A. S. TAYLOR, M.D. F.R.S. Crown 8vo. Woodcuts, 12s. 6d.

The Correlation of Physical Forces.
By the Hon. Sir W. R. GROVE, F.R.S. &c. Sixth Edition, revised and augmented. 8vo. 15s.

Weinhold's Introduction
to Experimental Physics; including Directions for Constructing Physical Apparatus and for Making Experiments. Translated by B. LOEWY, F.R.A.S. With a Preface by G. C. FOSTER, F.R.S. 8vo. Plates & Woodcuts 31s. 6d.

A Treatise on Magnetism,
General and Terrestrial. By H. LLOYD, D.D. D.C.L. 8vo. 10s. 6d.

Elementary Treatise on
the Wave-Theory of Light. By H. LLOYD, D.D. D.C.L. 8vo. 10s. 6d.

Fragments of Science.
By JOHN TYNDALL, F.R.S. Sixth Edition, revised and augmented. 2 vols. crown 8vo. 16s.

Heat a Mode of Motion.
By JOHN TYNDALL, F.R.S. Fifth Edition in preparation.

Sound.
By JOHN TYNDALL, F.R.S. Third Edition, including Recent Researches on Fog-Signalling. Crown 8vo. price 10s. 6d.

Researches on Diamagnetism and Magne-Crystallic Action;
including Diamagnetic Polarity. By JOHN TYNDALL, F.R.S. New Edition in preparation.

Contributions to Molecular Physics in the domain of Radiant Heat.
By JOHN TYNDALL, F.R.S. Plates and Woodcuts. 8vo. 16s.

Six Lectures on Light,
delivered in America in 1872 and 1873. By JOHN TYNDALL, F.R.S. Second Edition. Portrait, Plate, and Diagrams. Crown 8vo. 7s. 6d.

Lessons in Electricity at
the Royal Institution, 1875-6. By JOHN TYNDALL, F.R.S. With 58 Woodcuts. Crown 8vo. 2s. 6d.

Notes of a Course of
Seven Lectures on Electrical Phenomena and Theories, delivered at the Royal Institution. By JOHN TYNDALL, F.R.S. Crown 8vo. 1s. sewed, or 1s. 6d. cloth.

Notes of a Course of Nine
Lectures on Light, delivered at the Royal Institution. By JOHN TYNDALL, F.R.S. Crown 8vo. 1s. sewed, or 1s. 6d. cloth.

Principles of Animal Mechanics.
By the Rev. S. HAUGHTON F.R.S. Second Edition. 8vo. 21s.

Text-Books of Science,
Mechanical and Physical, adapted for the use of Artisans and of Students in Public and Science Schools. Small 8vo. with Woodcuts, &c.

Abney's Photography, 3s. 6d.

Anderson's (Sir John) Strength of Materials, 3s. 6d.

Armstrong's Organic Chemistry, 3s. 6d.

Barry's Railway Appliances, 3s. 6d.

Bloxam's Metals, 3s. 6d.

Goodeve's Mechanics, 3s. 6d.

———— Mechanism, 3s. 6d.

Gore's Electro-Metallurgy, 6s.

Griffin's Algebra & Trigonometry, 3/6.

Jenkin's Electricity & Magnetism, 3/6.

Maxwell's Theory of Heat, 3s. 6d.

Merrifield's Technical Arithmetic, 3s. 6d.

Miller's Inorganic Chemistry, 3s. 6d.

Preece & Sivewright's Telegraphy, 3/6.

Rutley's Study of Rocks, 4s. 6d.

Shelley's Workshop Appliances, 3s 6d.

Thomé's Structural and Physiological Botany, 6s.

Thorpe's Quantitative Analysis, 4s. 6d.

Thorpe & Muir's Qualitative Analysis, price 3s. 6d.

Tilden's Systematic Chemistry, 3s. 6d.

Unwin's Machine Design, 3s. 6d.

Watson's Plane & Solid Geometry, 3/6.

Light Science for Leisure
Hours; Familiar Essays on Scientific Subjects, Natural Phenomena, &c. By R. A. Proctor, B.A. 2 vols. crown 8vo. 7s. 6d. each.

An Introduction to the
Systematic Zoology and Morphology of Vertebrate Animals. By A. Macalister, M.D. Professor of Comparative Anatomy and Zoology, University of Dublin. With 28 Diagrams. 8vo. 10s. 6d.

The Comparative Anatomy and Physiology of the Vertebrate Animals. By Richard Owen, F.R.S. With 1,472 Woodcuts. 3 vols. 8vo. £3. 13s. 6d.

Homes without Hands;
a Description of the Habitations of Animals, classed according to their Principle of Construction. By the Rev. J. G. Wood, M.A. With about 140 Vignettes on Wood. 8vo. 14s.

Wood's Strange Dwellings; a Description of the Habitations of Animals, abridged from 'Homes without Hands.' With Frontispiece and 60 Woodcuts. Crown 8vo. 7s. 6d.

Wood's Insects at Home;
a Popular Account of British Insects, their Structure, Habits, and Transformations. With 700 Woodcuts. 8vo. 14s.

Wood's Insects Abroad;
a Popular Account of Foreign Insects, their Structure, Habits, and Transformations. With 700 Woodcuts. 8vo. 14s.

Wood's Out of Doors; a
Selection of Original Articles on Practical Natural History. With 6 Illustrations. Crown 8vo. 7s. 6d.

Wood's Bible Animals; a
description of every Living Creature mentioned in the Scriptures, from the Ape to the Coral. With 112 Vignettes. 8vo. 14s.

The Sea and its Living
Wonders. By Dr. G. Hartwig. 8vo. with numerous Illustrations, price 10s. 6d.

Hartwig's Tropical
World. With about 200 Illustrations. 8vo. 10s. 6d.

Hartwig's Polar World;
a Description of Man and Nature in the Arctic and Antarctic Regions of the Globe. Chromoxylographs, Maps, and Woodcuts. 8vo. 10s. 6d.

Hartwig's Subterranean
World. With Maps and Woodcuts. 8vo. 10s. 6d.

Hartwig's Aerial World;
a Popular Account of the Phenomena and Life of the Atmosphere. Map, Chromoxylographs, Woodcuts. 8vo. price 10s. 6d.

Kirby and Spence's Introduction to Entomology, or Elements of the Natural History of Insects. Crown 8vo. 5s.

A Familiar History of Birds. By E. STANLEY, D.D. Fcp. 8vo. with Woodcuts, 3s. 6d.

Rocks Classified and Described. By BERNHARD VON COTTA. An English Translation, by P. H. LAWRENCE (with English, German, and French Synonymes), revised by the Author. Post 8vo. 14s.

The Geology of England and Wales; a Concise Account of the Lithological Characters, Leading Fossils, and Economic Products of the Rocks. By H. B. WOODWARD, F.G.S. Crown 8vo. Map & Woodcuts, 14s.

Keller's Lake Dwellings of Switzerland, and other Parts of Europe. Translated by JOHN E. LEE, F.S.A. F.G.S. New Edition, enlarged, with 206 Illustrations. 2 vols. royal 8vo. 42s.

The Primæval World of Switzerland. By Professor OSWALD HEER, of the University of Zurich. Edited by JAMES HEYWOOD, M.A. F.R.S. With Map, 19 Plates, & 372 Woodcuts. 2 vols. 8vo. 16s.

The Puzzle of Life and How it Has Been Put Together; a Short History of Praehistoric Vegetable and Animal Life on the Earth. By A. NICOLS, F.R.G S. With 12 Illustrations. Crown 8vo. 3s. 6d.

The Origin of Civilisation, and the Primitive Condition of Man; Mental and Social Condition of Savages. By Sir J. LUBBOCK, Bart. M.P. F.R.S. 8vo. Woodcuts, 18s.

A Dictionary of Science, Literature, and Art. Re-edited by the late W. T. BRANDE (the Author) and the Rev. Sir G.W. COX, Bart., M.A. 3 vols. medium 8vo. 63s.

The History of Modern Music, a Course of Lectures delivered at the Royal Institution. By JOHN HULLAH, LL.D. 8vo. 8s. 6d.

The Transition Period of Musical History, from the Beginning of the 17th to the Middle of the 18th Century. A Second Series of Lectures. By the same Author. 8vo. 10s. 6d.

Loudon's Encyclopædia of Plants; comprising the Specific Character, Description, Culture, History, &c. of all the Plants found in Great Britain. With upwards of 12,000 Woodcuts. 8vo. 42s.

De Caisne & Le Maout's System of Descriptive and Analytical Botany. Translated by Mrs. HOOKER; edited and arranged according to the English Botanical System, by J. D. HOOKER, M.D. With 5,500 Woodcuts. Imperial 8vo. 31s. 6d.

The Treasury of Botany, or Popular Dictionary of the Vegetable Kingdom; with which is incorporated a Glossary of Botanical Terms. Edited by J. LINDLEY, F.R.S., and T.MOORE, F.L.S. With 274 Woodcuts and 20 Steel Plates. Two Parts, fcp. 8vo. 12s.

Rivers's Orchard-House; or, the Cultivation of Fruit Trees under Glass. Sixteenth Edition, re-edited by T. F. RIVERS. Crown 8vo. with 25 Woodcuts, price 5s.

The Rose Amateur's Guide. By THOMAS RIVERS. Latest Edition. Fcp. 8vo. 4s. 6d.

Town and Window Gardening, including the Structure, Habits and Uses of Plants; a Course of Sixteen Lectures given out of School-Hours to Pupil Teachers and Children attending the Leeds Board Schools. By Mrs. BUCKTON, Member of the Leeds School Board. With 127 Woodcuts. Crown 8vo. 2s.

CHEMISTRY and PHYSIOLOGY.

Miller's Elements of Chemistry, Theoretical and Practical. Re-edited, with Additions, by H. MACLEOD, F.C.S. 3 vols. 8vo.
PART I. CHEMICAL PHYSICS. 16s.
PART II. INORGANIC CHEMISTRY, 24s.
PART III. ORGANIC CHEMISTRY, New Edition in the press.

Animal Chemistry, or the Relations of Chemistry to Physiology and Pathology: a Manual for Medical Men and Scientific Chemists. By CHARLES T. KINGZETT, F.C.S. 8vo. price 18s.

Health in the House: Twenty-five Lectures on Elementary Physiology in its Application to the Daily Wants of Man and Animals. By Mrs. BUCKTON. Crown 8vo. Woodcuts, 2s.

A Dictionary of Chemistry and the Allied Branches of other Sciences. By HENRY WATTS, F.C.S. assisted by eminent Scientific and Practical Chemists. 7 vols. medium 8vo. £10. 16s. 6d.

Third Supplement, completing the Record of Chemical Discovery to the year 1877. PART I. 8vo. 36s. PART II. completion, in the press.

Select Methods in Chemical Analysis, chiefly Inorganic. By WM. CROOKES, F.R.S. With 22 Woodcuts. Crown 8vo. 12s. 6d.

The History, Products, and Processes of the Alkali Trade, including the most recent Improvements. By CHARLES T. KINGZETT, F.C.S. With 32 Woodcuts. 8vo. 12s.

The FINE ARTS and ILLUSTRATED EDITIONS.

In Fairyland; Pictures from the Elf-World. By RICHARD DOYLE. With a Poem by W. ALLINGHAM. With 16 coloured Plates, containing 36 Designs. Folio, 15s.

Lord Macaulay's Lays of Ancient Rome. With Ninety Illustrations on Wood from Drawings by G. SCHARF. Fcp. 4to. 21s.

Miniature Edition of Macaulay's Lays of Ancient Rome, with Scharf's 90 Illustrations reduced in Lithography. Imp. 16mo. 10s. 6d.

Moore's Lalla Rookh. TENNIEL's Edition, with 68 Woodcut Illustrations. Fcp. 4to. 21s.

Moore's Irish Melodies, MACLISE's Edition, with 161 Steel Plates. Super-royal 8vo. 21s.

Lectures on Harmony, delivered at the Royal Institution. By G. A. MACFARREN. 8vo. 12s.

Sacred and Legendary Art. By Mrs. JAMESON. 6 vols. square crown 8vo. price £5. 15s. 6d.

Jameson's Legends of the Saints and Martyrs. With 19 Etchings and 187 Woodcuts. 2 vols. 31s. 6d.

Jameson's Legends of the Monastic Orders. With 11 Etchings and 88 Woodcuts. 1 vol. 21s.

Jameson's Legends of the Madonna. With 27 Etchings and 165 Woodcuts. 1 vol. 21s.

Jameson's History of the Saviour, His Types and Precursors. Completed by Lady EASTLAKE. With 13 Etchings and 281 Woodcuts. 2 vols. 42s.

The Three Cathedrals dedicated to St. Paul in London. By W. LONGMAN, F.S.A. With numerous Illustrations. Square crown 8vo. 21s.

The USEFUL ARTS, MANUFACTURES, &c.

The Art of Scientific Discovery.
By G. GORE, LL.D. F.R.S. Author of 'The Art of Electro-Metallurgy.' Crown 8vo. 15s.

The Amateur Mechanics' Practical Handbook;
describing the different Tools required in the Workshop. By A. H. G. HOBSON. With 33 Woodcuts. Crown 8vo. 2s. 6d.

The Engineer's Valuing Assistant.
By H. D. HOSKOLD, Civil and Mining Engineer, 16 years Mining Engineer to the Dean Forest Iron Company. 8vo. 31s. 6d.

Industrial Chemistry; a
Manual for Manufacturers and for Colleges or Technical Schools; a Translation (by Dr. T. H. BARRY) of Stohmann and Engler's German Edition of PAYEN's 'Précis de Chimie Industrielle;' with Chapters on the Chemistry of the Metals, &c. by B. H. PAUL, Ph.D. With 698 Woodcuts. Medium 8vo. 42s.

Gwilt's Encyclopædia of
Architecture, with above 1,600 Woodcuts. Revised and extended by W. PAPWORTH. 8vo. 52s. 6d.

Lathes and Turning, Sim-
ple, Mechanical, and Ornamental. By W. H. NORTHCOTT. Second Edition, with 338 Illustrations. 8vo. 18s.

The Theory of Strains in
Girders and similar Structures, with Observations on the application of Theory to Practice, and Tables of the Strength and other Properties of Materials. By B. B. STONEY, M.A. M. Inst. C.E. Royal 8vo. with 5 Plates and 123 Woodcuts, 36s.

A Treatise on Mills and
Millwork. By the late Sir W. FAIRBAIRN, Bart. C.E. Fourth Edition, with 18 Plates and 333 Woodcuts. 1 vol. 8vo. 25s.

Useful Information for
Engineers. By the late Sir W. FAIRBAIRN, Bart. C.E. With many Plates and Woodcuts. 3 vols. crown 8vo. 31s. 6d.

The Application of Cast
and Wrought Iron to Building Purposes. By the late Sir W. FAIRBAIRN, Bart. C.E. With 6 Plates and 118 Woodcuts. 8vo. 16s.

Hints on Household
Taste in Furniture, Upholstery, and other Details. By C. L. EASTLAKE. Fourth Edition, with 100 Illustrations. Square crown 8vo. 14s.

Handbook of Practical
Telegraphy. By R. S. CULLEY, Memb. Inst. C.E. Seventh Edition. Plates & Woodcuts. 8vo. price 16s.

A Treatise on the Steam
Engine, in its various applications to Mines, Mills, Steam Navigation, Railways and Agriculture. By J. BOURNE, C.E. With Portrait, 37 Plates, and 546 Woodcuts. 4to. 42s.

Recent Improvements in
the Steam Engine. By J. BOURNE, C.E. Fcp. 8vo. Woodcuts, 6s.

Catechism of the Steam
Engine, in its various Applications. By JOHN BOURNE, C.E. Fcp. 8vo. Woodcuts, 6s.

Handbook of the Steam
Engine, a Key to the Author's Catechism of the Steam Engine. By J. BOURNE, C.E. Fcp. 8vo. Woodcuts, 9s.

Examples of Steam and
Gas Engines of the most recent Approved Types as employed in Mines, Factories, Steam Navigation, Railways and Agriculture, practically described. By JOHN BOURNE, C.E. With 54 Plates and 356 Woodcuts. 4to. 70s.

Encyclopædia of Civil
Engineering, Historical, Theoretical, and Practical. By E. CRESY, C.E. With above 3,000 Woodcuts. 8vo. 42s.

Ure's Dictionary of Arts,
Manufactures, and Mines. Seventh Edition, re-written and enlarged by R. HUNT, F.R.S. assisted by numerous contributors. With 2,604 Woodcuts. 4 vols. medium 8vo. £7. 7s.

Practical Treatise on Metallurgy.
Adapted from the last German Edition of Professor KERL'S Metallurgy by W. CROOKES, F.R.S. &c. and E. RÖHRIG, Ph.D.   3 vols. 8vo. with 625 Woodcuts. £4. 19s.

Anthracen; its Constitution,
Properties, Manufacture, and Derivatives, including Artificial Alizarin, Anthrapurpurin, &c. with their Applications in Dyeing and Printing. By G. AUERBACH. Translated by W. CROOKES, F.R.S   8vo. 12s.

On Artificial Manures,
their Chemical Selection and Scientific Application to Agriculture ; a Series of Lectures given at the Experimental Farm at Vincennes in 1867 and 1874-75. By M. GEORGES VILLE. Translated and edited by W. CROOKES, F.R.S. With 31 Plates. 8vo. 21s.

Practical Handbook of Dyeing and Calico-Printing.
By W. CROOKES, F.R.S. &c. With numerous Illustrations and specimens of Dyed Textile Fabrics. 8vo. 42s.

Mitchell's Manual of Practical Assaying.
Fourth Edition, revised, with the Recent Discoveries incorporated, by W. CROOKES, F.R.S. Crown 8vo. Woodcuts, 31s. 6d.

Loudon's Encyclopædia of Gardening ;
the Theory and Practice of Horticulture, Floriculture, Arboriculture & Landscape Gardening. With 1,000 Woodcuts. 8vo. 21s.

Loudon's Encyclopædia of Agriculture ;
the Laying-out, Improvement, and Management of Landed Property ; the Cultivation and Economy of the Productions of Agriculture. With 1,100 Woodcuts. 8vo. 21s.

RELIGIOUS and MORAL WORKS.

Four Lectures on some
Epochs of Early Church History. By the Very Rev. C. MERIVALE, D.D. Dean of Ely. Crown 8vo. 5s.

A History of the Church
of England ; Pre-Reformation Period. By the Rev. T. P. BOULTBEE, LL.D. late Fellow of St. John's College, Cambridge. 8vo. 15s.

Sketch of the History of
the Church of England to the Revolution of 1688. By T. V. SHORT, D.D. Crown 8vo. 7s. 6d.

The English Church in
the Eighteenth Century. By CHARLES J. ABBEY, late Fellow of University College, Oxford; and JOHN H. OVERTON, late Scholar of Lincoln College, Oxford. 2 vols. 8vo. 36s.

The Human Life of Christ
revealing the Order of the Universe, being the Hulsean Lectures for 1877 ; with an APPENDIX. By G. S. DREW, M.A. Vicar of Holy Trinity, Lambeth, 8vo. 8s.

An Exposition of the 39
Articles, Historical and Doctrinal. By E. H. BROWNE, D.D. Bishop of Winchester. Eleventh Edition. 8vo. 16s.

A Commentary on the
39 Articles, forming an Introduction to the Theology of the Church of England. By the Rev. T. P. BOULTBEE, LL.D. New Edition. Crown 8vo. 6s.

Historical Lectures on
the Life of Our Lord Jesus Christ. By C. J. ELLICOTT, D.D. 8vo. 12s.

Sermons preached mostly
in the Chapel of Rugby School by the late T. ARNOLD, D.D. Collective Edition, revised by the Author's Daughter, Mrs. W. E. FORSTER. 6 vols. crown 8vo. 30s. or separately, 5s. each.

The Eclipse of Faith ; or
a Visit to a Religious Sceptic. By HENRY ROGERS. Fcp. 8vo. 5s.

Defence of the Eclipse of
Faith. By H. ROGERS. Fcp. 8vo. 3s. 6d.

Nature, the Utility of
Religion and Theism. Three Essays by JOHN STUART MILL. 8vo. 10s. 6d.

A Critical and Grammatical Commentary on St. Paul's
Epistles. By C. J. ELLICOTT, D.D. 8vo. Galatians, 8s. 6d. Ephesians, 8s. 6d. Pastoral Epistles, 10s. 6d. Philippians, Colossians, & Philemon, 10s. 6d. Thessalonians, 7s. 6d.

Conybeare & Howson's Life and Epistles of St. Paul.
Three Editions, copiously illustrated.

Library Edition, with all the Original Illustrations, Maps, Landscapes on Steel, Woodcuts, &c. 2 vols. 4to. 42s.

Intermediate Edition, with a Selection of Maps, Plates, and Woodcuts. 2 vols. square crown 8vo. 21s.

Student's Edition, revised and condensed, with 46 Illustrations and Maps. 1 vol. crown 8vo. 9s.

The Jewish Messiah;
Critical History of the Messianic Idea among the Jews, from the Rise of the Maccabees to the Closing of the Talmud. By JAMES DRUMMOND, B.A. 8vo. 15s.

The Prophets and Prophecy in Israel;
an Historical and Critical Inquiry. By Prof. A. KUENEN, Translated from the Dutch by the Rev. A. MILROY, M.A. with an Introduction by J. MUIR, D.C.L. 8vo. 21s.

Mythology among the Hebrews and its Historical Development.
By IGNAZ GOLDZIHER, Ph.D. Translated by RUSSELL MARTINEAU, M.A. 8vo. 16s.

Bible Studies. By M. M.
KALISCH, Ph.D. PART I. *The Prophecies of Balaam.* 8vo. 10s. 6d. PART II. *The Book of Jonah.* 8vo. 10s. 6d.

Historical and Critical Commentary on the Old Testament;
with a New Translation. By M. M. KALISCH, Ph.D. Vol. I. Genesis, 8vo. 18s. or adapted for the General Reader, 12s. Vol. II. Exodus, 15s. or adapted for the General Reader, 12s. Vol. III. Leviticus, Part I. 15s. or adapted for the General Reader, 8s. Vol. IV. Leviticus, Part II. 15s. or adapted for the General Reader, 8s.

Ewald's History of Israel.
Translated from the German by J. E. CARPENTER, M.A. with Preface by R. MARTINEAU, M.A. 5 vols. 8vo. 63s.

Ewald's Antiquities of Israel.
Translated from the German by H. S. SOLLY, M.A. 8vo. 12s. 6d.

The Types of Genesis,
briefly considered as revealing the Development of Human Nature. By A. JUKES. Crown 8vo. 7s. 6d.

The Second Death and the Restitution of all Things;
with some Preliminary Remarks on the Nature and Inspiration of Holy Scripture. By A. JUKES. Crown 8vo. 3s. 6d.

Commentaries, by the Rev.
W. A. O'CONOR, B.A. Rector of St. Simon and St. Jude, Manchester.

Epistle to the Romans, crown 8vo. 3s. 6d. Epistle to the Hebrews, 4s. 6d. St. John's Gospel, 10s. 6d.

Supernatural Religion;
an Inquiry into the Reality of Divine Revelation. Complete Edition, thoroughly revised, with New Preface and Conclusions. 3 vols. 8vo. 36s.

Lectures on the Origin and Growth of Religion, as illustrated by the Religions of India;
being the Hibbert Lectures for 1878, delivered at the Chapter House, Westminster Abbey, in 1878, by F. MAX MÜLLER, M.A. Second Edition. 8vo. price 10s. 6d.

Introduction to the Science of Religion, Four Lectures delivered at the Royal Institution; with Two Essays on False Analogies and the Philosophy of Mythology. By MAX MÜLLER, M.A. Crown 8vo. price 10s. 6d.

The Four Gospels in Greek, with Greek-English Lexicon.
By JOHN T. WHITE, D.D. Oxon. Square 32mo. 5s.

Passing Thoughts on Religion. By ELIZABETH M. SEWELL.
Fcp. 8vo. 3s. 6d.

Thoughts for the Age.
by ELIZABETH M. SEWELL. New Edition. Fcp. 8vo. 3s. 6d.

Preparation for the Holy
Communion; the Devotions chiefly from the works of Jeremy Taylor. By ELIZABETH M. SEWELL. 32mo. 3s.

Bishop Jeremy Taylor's
Entire Works; with Life by Bishop Heber. Revised and corrected by the Rev. C. P. EDEN. 10 vols. £5. 5s.

Hymns of Praise and
Prayer. Corrected and edited by Rev. JOHN MARTINEAU, LL.D. Crown 8vo. 4s. 6d. 32mo. 1s. 6d.

Spiritual Songs for the
Sundays and Holidays throughout the Year. By J. S. B. MONSELL, LL.D. Fcp. 8vo. 5s. 18mo. 2s.

Christ the Consoler; a
Book of Comfort for the Sick. By ELLICE HOPKINS. With a Preface by the Bishop of Carlisle. Second Edition. Fcp. 8vo. 2s. 6d.

Lyra Germanica; Hymns
translated from the German by Miss C. WINKWORTH. Fcp. 8vo. 5s.

The Temporal Mission
of the Holy Ghost; or, Reason and Revelation. By HENRY EDWARD MANNING, D.D. Crown 8vo. 8s. 6d.

Hours of Thought on
Sacred Things; a Volume of Sermons. By JAMES MARTINEAU, D.D. LL.D. Crown 8vo. Price 7s. 6d.

Endeavours after the
Christian Life; Discourses. By JAMES MARTINEAU, D.D. LL.D. Fifth Edition. Crown 8vo. 7s. 6d.

The Pentateuch & Book
of Joshua Critically Examined. By J. W. COLENSO, D.D. Bishop of Natal. Crown 8vo. 6s.

Lectures on the Penta-
teuch and the Moabite Stone; with Appendices. By J. W. COLENSO, D.D. Bishop of Natal. 8vo. 12s.

TRAVELS, VOYAGES, &c.

A Voyage in the 'Sun-
beam,' our Home on the Ocean for Eleven Months. By Mrs. BRASSEY. Cheaper Edition, with Map and 65 Wood Engravings. Crown 8vo. 7s. 6d.

A Freak of Freedom;
or, the Republic of San Marino. By J. THEODORE BENT, Honorary Citizen of the same. With a Map and 15 Woodcuts. Crown 8vo. 7s. 6d.

One Thousand Miles up
the Nile; a Journey through Egypt and Nubia to the Second Cataract. By AMELIA B. EDWARDS. With Plans, Maps & Illustrations. Imperial 8vo. 42s.

The Indian Alps, and How
we Crossed them; Two Years' Residence in the Eastern Himalayas, and Two Months' Tour into the Interior. By a LADY PIONEER. With Illustrations. Imperial 8vo. 42s.

Discoveries at Ephesus,
Including the Site and Remains of the Great Temple of Diana. By J. T. WOOD, F.S.A. With 27 Lithographic Plates and 42 Wood Engravings. Medium 8vo. 63s.

Memorials of the Dis-
covery and Early Settlement of the Bermudas or Somers Islands, from 1615 to 1685. By Major-General Sir J. H. LEFROY, R.A. With Maps, &c. 2 vols. Imp. 8vo. 60s.

Eight Years in Ceylon.
By Sir SAMUEL W. BAKER, M.A. Crown 8vo. Woodcuts, 7s. 6d.

The Rifle and the Hound
in Ceylon. By Sir SAMUEL W. BAKER, M.A. Crown 8vo. Woodcuts, 7s. 6d.

C

Guide to the Pyrenees,
for the use of Mountaineers.   By CHARLES PACKE.   Crown 8vo. 7s. 6d.

The Alpine Club Map of
Switzerland, with parts of the Neighbouring Countries, on the scale of Four Miles to an Inch.   Edited by R. C. NICHOLS, F.R.G.S.   4 Sheets in Portfolio, 42s. coloured, or 34s. uncoloured.

The Alpine Guide.   By
JOHN BALL, M.R.I.A.   Post 8vo. with Maps and other Illustrations.

The Eastern Alps, 10s. 6d.

Central Alps, including all
the Oberland District, 7s. 6d.

Western Alps, including
Mont Blanc, Monte Rosa, Zermatt, &c. Price 6s. 6d.

On Alpine Travelling and
the Geology of the Alps.   Price 1s. Either of the 3 Volumes or Parts of the 'Alpine Guide' may be had with this Introduction prefixed, 1s. extra.

The Fenland Past and
Present.   By S. H. MILLER, F.R.A.S. F.M.S.; and S. B. J. SKERTCHLEY, F.G.S. of H.M. Geological Survey. With numerous Illustrations and Maps. Royal 8vo. 31s. 6d.   Large Paper, fcp. folio, 50s. half-morocco.

WORKS of FICTION.

Novels and Tales.   By the
Right Hon. the EARL of BEACONSFIELD, K.G.   Cabinet Editions, complete in Ten Volumes, crown 8vo. 6s. each.

Lothair, 6s.	Venetia, 6s.
Coningsby, 6s.	Alroy, Ixion, &c. 6s.
Sybil, 6s.	Young Duke &c. 6s.
Tancred, 6s.	Vivian Grey, 6s.

Henrietta Temple, 6s.

Contarini Fleming, &c. 6s.

Tales from Euripides;
Iphigenia, Alcestis, Hecuba, Helen, Medea.   By VINCENT K. COOPER, M.A. late Scholar of Brasenose College, Oxford.   Fcp. 8vo. 3s. 6d.

Whispers from Fairyland.   By the Right Hon. E. H. KNATCHBULL-HUGESSEN, M.P.   With 9 Illustrations.   Crown 8vo. 3s. 6d.

Higgledy-Piggledy;   or,
Stories for Everybody and Everybody's Children.   By the Right Hon. E. H. KNATCHBULL-HUGESSEN, M.P. With 9 Illustrations.   Cr. 8vo. 3s. 6d.

Stories and Tales.   By
ELIZABETH M. SEWELL.   Cabinet Edition, in Ten Volumes, each containing a complete Tale or Story :—

Amy Herbert, 2s. 6d.   Gertrude, 2s. 6d. The Earl's Daughter, 2s. 6d.   The Experience of Life, 2s. 6d.   Cleve Hall, 2s. 6d.   Ivors, 2s. 6d.   Katharine Ashton, 2s. 6d.   Margaret Percival, 3s. 6d.   Laneton Parsonage, 3s. 6d. Ursula, 3s. 6d.

The Modern Novelist's
Library.   Each work complete in itself, price 2s. boards, or 2s. 6d. cloth.

By Lord BEACONSFIELD.

Lothair.
Coningsby.
Sybil.
Tancred.
Venetia.
Henrietta Temple.
Contarini Fleming.
Alroy, Ixion, &c.
The Young Duke, &c.
Vivian Grey.

THE MODERN NOVELIST'S LIBRARY—*continued.*

By ANTHONY TROLLOPE.
Barchester Towers.
The Warden.

By Major WHYTE-MELVILLE.
Digby Grand.
General Bounce.
Kate Coventry.
The Gladiators.
Good for Nothing.
Holmby House.
The Interpreter.
The Queen's Maries.

By the Author of 'The Rose Garden.'
Unawares.

By the Author of 'Mlle. Mori.'
The Atelier du Lys.
Mademoiselle Mori.

By Various Writers.
Atherstone Priory.
The Burgomaster's Family.
Elsa and her Vulture.
The Six Sisters of the Valleys.

The Novels and Tales of the Right Honourable the Earl of Beaconsfield, K.G. Complete in Ten Volumes, crown 8vo. cloth extra, gilt edges, price 30s.

POETRY and THE DRAMA.

Lays of Ancient Rome; with Ivry and the Armada. By LORD MACAULAY. 16mo. 3s. 6d.

Horatii Opera. Library Edition, with English Notes, Marginal References & various Readings. Edited by Rev. J. E. YONGE, M.A. 8vo. 21s.

Poems by Jean Ingelow. 2 vols. fcp. 8vo. 10s.
FIRST SERIES, containing 'Divided,' 'The Star's Monument,' &c. Fcp. 8vo. 5s.
SECOND SERIES, 'A Story of Doom,' 'Gladys and her Island,' &c. 5s.

Poems by Jean Ingelow. First Series, with nearly 100 Woodcut Illustrations. Fcp. 4to. 21s.

Brian Boru, a Tragedy. By J. T. B. Crown 8vo. 6s.

Festus, a Poem. By PHILIP JAMES BAILEY. 10th Edition, enlarged & revised. Crown 8vo. 12s. 6d.

The Iliad of Homer, Homometrically translated by C. B. CAYLEY, Translator of Dante's Comedy, &c. 8vo. 12s. 6d.

The Æneid of Virgil. Translated into English Verse. By J. CONINGTON, M.A. Crown 8vo. 9s.

Bowdler's Family Shakspeare. Genuine Edition; in 1 vol. medium 8vo. large type, with 36 Woodcuts, 14s. or in 6 vols. fcp. 8vo. 21s.

Southey's Poetical Works, with the Author's last Corrections and Additions. Medium 8vo. with Portrait, 14s.

RURAL SPORTS, HORSE and CATTLE MANAGEMENT, &c.

Annals of the Road; or, Notes on Mail and Stage-Coaching in Great Britain. By Captain MALET. With 3 Woodcuts and 10 Coloured Illustrations. Medium 8vo. 21s.

Down the Road; or, Reminiscences of a Gentleman Coachman. By C. T. S. BIRCH REYNARDSON. Second Edition, with 12 Coloured Illustrations. Medium 8vo. 21s.

Blaine's Encyclopædia of
Rural Sports; Complete Accounts, Historical, Practical, and Descriptive, of Hunting, Shooting, Fishing, Racing, &c. With 600 Woodcuts. 8vo. 21s.

A Book on Angling ; or,
Treatise on the Art of Fishing in every branch ; including full Illustrated Lists of Salmon Flies. By FRANCIS FRANCIS. Post 8vo. Portrait and Plates, 15s.

Wilcocks's Sea-Fisher-
man : comprising the Chief Methods of Hook and Line Fishing, a glance at Nets, and remarks on Boats and Boating. Post 8vo. Woodcuts, 12s. 6d.

The Fly-Fisher's Ento-
mology. By ALFRED RONALDS. With 20 Coloured Plates. 8vo. 14s.

Horses and Riding. By
GEORGE NEVILE, M.A. With 31 Illustrations. Crown 8vo. 6s.

Horses and Stables. By
Colonel F. FITZWYGRAM, XV. the King's Hussars. With 24 Plates of Illustrations. 8vo. 10s. 6d.

Youatt on the Horse.
Revised and enlarged by W. WATSON, M.R.C.V.S. 8vo. Woodcuts, 12s. 6d.

Youatt's Work on the
Dog. Revised and enlarged. 8vo. Woodcuts, 6s.

The Dog in Health and
Disease. By STONEHENGE. With 78 Wood Engravings. Square crown 8vo. 7s. 6d.

The Greyhound. By
STONEHENGE. Revised Edition, with 25 Portraits of Greyhounds, &c. Square crown 8vo. 15s.

Stables and Stable Fit-
tings. By W. MILES. Imp. 8vo. with 13 Plates, 15s.

The Horse's Foot, and
How to keep it Sound. By W. MILES. Imp. 8vo. Woodcuts, 12s. 6d.

A Plain Treatise on
Horse-shoeing. By W. MILES. Post 8vo. Woodcuts, 2s. 6d.

Remarks on Horses'
Teeth, addressed to Purchasers. By W. MILES. Post 8vo. 1s. 6d.

The Ox, his Diseases and
their Treatment ; with an Essay on Parturition in the Cow. By J. R. DOBSON, M.R.C.V.S. Crown 8vo. Illustrations, 7s. 6d.

WORKS of UTILITY and GENERAL INFORMATION.

Maunder's Treasury of
Knowledge and Library of Reference ; comprising an English Dictionary and Grammar, Universal Gazetteer, Classical Dictionary, Chronology, Law Dictionary, Synopsis of the Peerage, Useful Tables, &c. Fcp. 8vo. 6s.

Maunder's Biographical
Treasury. Latest Edition, reconstructed and partly re-written, with above 1,600 additional Memoirs, by W. L. R. CATES. Fcp. 8vo. 6s.

Maunder's Treasury of
Natural History ; or, Popular Dictionary of Zoology. Revised and corrected Edition. Fcp. 8vo. with 900 Woodcuts, 6s.

Maunder's Scientific and
Literary Treasury ; a Popular Encyclopædia of Science, Literature, and Art. Latest Edition, partly re-written, with above 1,000 New Articles, by J. Y. JOHNSON. Fcp. 8vo. 6s.

Maunder's Treasury of
Geography, Physical, Historical, Descriptive, and Political. Edited by W. HUGHES, F.R.G.S. With 7 Maps and 16 Plates. Fcp. 8vo. 6s.

Maunder's Historical
Treasury ; Introductory Outlines of Universal History, and Separate Histories of all Nations. Revised by the Rev. Sir G. W. COX, Bart. M.A. Fcp. 8vo. 6s.

The Treasury of Botany,

or Popular Dictionary of the Vegetable Kingdom; with which is incorporated a Glossary of Botanical Terms. Edited by J. LINDLEY, F.R.S. and T. MOORE, F.L.S. With 274 Woodcuts and 20 Steel Plates. Two Parts, fcp. 8vo. 12s.

The Treasury of Bible

Knowledge; being a Dictionary of the Books, Persons, Places, Events, and other Matters of which mention is made in Holy Scripture. By the Rev. J. AYRE, M.A. Maps, Plates & Woodcuts. Fcp. 8vo. 6s.

A Practical Treatise on

Brewing; with Formulæ for Public Brewers & Iustructions for Private Families. By W. BLACK. 8vo. 10s. 6d.

The Theory of the Mo-

dern Scientific Game of Whist. By W. POLE, F.R.S. Tenth Edition. Fcp. 8vo. 2s. 6d.

The Correct Card; or,

How to Play at Whist; a Whist Catechism. By Captain A. CAMPBELL-WALKER, F.R.G.S. New Edition. Fcp. 8vo. 2s. 6d.

The Cabinet Lawyer; a

Popular Digest of the Laws of England, Civil, Criminal, and Constitutional. Twenty-Fifth Edition, corrected and extended. Fcp. 8vo. 9s.

Chess Openings. By F.W.

LONGMAN, Balliol College, Oxford. Second Edition. Fcp. 8vo. 2s. 6d.

Pewtner's Compre-

hensive Specifier; a Guide to the Practical Specification of every kind of Building-Artificer's Work. Edited by W. YOUNG. Crown 8vo. 6s.

The English Manual of

Banking. By ARTHUR CRUMP. Second Edition, revised and enlarged. 8vo. 15s.

Modern Cookery for Pri-

vate Families, reduced to a System of Easy Practice in a Series of carefully-tested Receipts. By ELIZA ACTON. With 8 Plates and 150 Woodcuts. Fcp. 8vo. 6s.

Food and Home Cookery.

A Course of Instruction in Practical Cookery and Cleaning, for Children in Elementary Schools, as followed in the Schools of the Leeds School Board. By Mrs. BUCKTON, Member of the Leeds School Board. With 11 Woodcuts. Crown 8vo. 2s.

Hints to Mothers on the

Management of their Health during the Period of Pregnancy and in the Lying-in Room. By THOMAS BULL, M.D. Fcp. 8vo, 2s. 6d.

The Maternal Manage-

ment of Children in Health and Disease. By THOMAS BULL, M.D. Fcp. 8vo. 2s. 6d.

The Farm Valuer. By

JOHN SCOTT, Land Valuer. Crown 8vo. price 5s.

Economics for Beginners

By H. D. MACLEOD, M.A. Small crown 8vo. 2s. 6d.

The Elements of Bank-

ing. By H. D. MACLEOD, M.A. Fourth Edition. Crown 8vo. 5s.

The Theory and Practice

of Banking. By H. D. MACLEOD, M.A. 2 vols. 8vo. 26s.

The Resources of Mod-

ern Countries; Essays towards an Estimate of the Economic Position of Nations and British Trade Prospects. By ALEX. WILSON. 2 vols. 8vo. 24s.

Willich's Popular Tables.

for ascertaining, according to the Carlisle Table of Mortality, the value of Lifehold, Leasehold, and Church Property, Renewal Fines, Reversions, &c. Also Interest, Legacy, Succession Duty, and various other useful tables. Eighth Edition. Post 8vo. 10s.

The Patentee's Manual;

a Treatise on the Law and Practice of Letters Patent, for the use of Patentees and Inventors. By J. JOHNSON, Barrister-at-Law; and J. H. JOHNSON, Assoc. Inst. C.E. Solicitor and Patent Agent, Lincoln's Inn Fields and Glasgow. Fourth Edition, enlarged. 8vo. 10s. 6d.

INDEX.

Spottiswoode & Co., Printers, New-street Square, London.

www.ingramcontent.com/pod-product-compliance
Lightning Source LLC
Chambersburg PA
CBHW031049110726
47900CB00003B/865